The ValueReporting™ Revolution

The ValueReporting™ Revolution

Moving Beyond the
Earnings Game

Robert G. Eccles
Robert H. Herz
E. Mary Keegan
David M.H. Phillips

JOHN WILEY & SONS, INC.

New York • Chichester • Weinheim • Brisbane • Singapore • Toronto

Library of Congress Cataloging-in-Publication Data:

The ValueReporting revolution : moving beyond the earnings game / by Robert Eccles . . . [et al.].
    p. cm.
  Includes index.
  ISBN 0-471-39879-9 (alk. paper)
  1. Corporation reports. 2. Financial statements. I. Title: Value
reporting revolution. II. Eccles, Robert G.
HG4028.B2 V35 2001
658.15'12—dc21   00-068493

Printed in the United States of America.

10 9 8 7 6 5 4 3 2 1

Contents

Preface

This book sends a wake-up call—to executives, securities analysts, market regulators, investors, and, not least of all, to accountants: The world of external corporate reporting is ripe for a revolution. And all have a vital interest in making it happen.

When I joined the accounting profession 20 years ago, stock ownership in my country, the United States, was largely limited to a small fraction of upper-income households. At that time, those with the resources to do so typically made investment decisions after scrutinizing a company's quarterly and annual corporate reports, consulting with a broker, and perhaps trotting off to the local library to do a bit of research on their own. Once they acquired stock in a company, they usually held it for years—even decades. In most other developed countries, all but the most affluent had about as much exposure to equity investing as they did to quantum physics.

Things have changed. For better *and* for worse, the common man and woman have evolved into *Homo investus*. In the United States, more than half of the adult population now owns stock, directly or indirectly through pension and mutual funds. In the United Kingdom, the number is 25 percent, and in Europe it's more than 12 percent and growing rapidly.

In many developed countries, stock market capitalization—the market value of all listed companies—now rivals or exceeds the size of the domestic economy. Initial public offerings (IPOs) and market gyrations are the stuff of everyday conversations. Electronic chat rooms ply us with investment advice. Stock alert pagers keep us constantly in touch. And after-hours trading keeps us buying and selling into the night.

It's not just investor behavior that has changed; the ways in which businesses compete and create value have changed, too. These days, many companies measure their worth in "clicks" rather than "bricks," while others possess assets—like an outstanding work force, a commanding market share, or instant brand recognition—that provide value far in excess of their tangible assets. Certainly, the market recognizes these "soft" assets and, to widely varying degrees of accuracy, factors them into projections of cash flow and then prices shares accordingly.

Technology—most spectacularly evidenced by the Internet—has changed the investment world, too. Today, information travels unconstrained by time and distance. With a click of a mouse, investors can have immediate delivery of a mind-boggling array of investment data and advice. All too often, it's the sort that's worth exactly what they pay for it—next to nothing.

But the kinds of information that companies regularly report, and that firms like mine audit and assure, simply do not serve today's investors well. While technologies are emerging to support assured, data-rich, online, real-time corporate reporting, it's fair to state that the accounting profession has yet to deliver on the promise of the Information Age.

Likewise, despite great strides in the development of internal performance measurement systems, the kinds of information that business executives report to the market—and the means by which they do so—have changed hardly at all in the past 100 years.

Let's face it: When it comes to corporate reporting, our mental models have not kept pace with change. Certainly, traditional financial statements, designed to the requirements of an industrialized age, have lagged far behind the evolution of our knowledge-and-network economy. They do not speak to the interests of stakeholders beyond the finite circle of a company's shareholders. An historical reporting perspective alone seems totally inappropriate to a world living on Internet time.

Nevertheless, once standards, regulations, and mental models are set, they become very hard to alter. The fear of harming our respective national reporting systems—which up to this point have worked pretty well—has held many of us back from trying something new.

Nature abhors a vacuum, in this case an information vacuum. To fill it, in have stepped analysts and advisors of every stripe. Good, bad, or indifferent, most don't understand how to test and validate their opinions, and they seldom expect to be held accountable for their judgments. The worst of them go so far as to try to manipulate markets.

While I don't believe in a divine right to existence for accounting firms, I do believe that firms like mine are distinguished by their responsibility to further the public's vital interest in having someone ensure that objective and relevant corporate information is made available. If the information needs of investors aren't being served, it's time to set things right. As a start, I think all can agree that too little of the information that really matters finds its way to the marketplace.

Clearly, we need a more expansive, flexible approach to corporate reporting and auditing. One that acknowledges that the world has grown more complex and demanding. One that recognizes that in today's world, aggregative, reductive methods alone do not impart a solid understanding of value, opportunity, and risk.

A new approach must be forged through creative discussion and intense debate among all parties involved, worldwide. Doing that will require leadership. I contend that no organization is better qualified to lead on these matters than mine.

So, consider this book an opening shot across the bow. Not everyone will agree with the views expressed herein. Indeed, some may feel discomfort or even anger at what they read here. This book will certainly raise tough questions for members of the accounting profession and for my own firm. But if it succeeds in stirring further thought and action, it will have served a good purpose.

To the authors—Bob Eccles, Bob Herz, Mary Keegan, and David Phillips—I offer my personal appreciation for their unwavering enthusiasm for spreading the gospel of quality, relevancy, and transparency and for fanning the flames of the ValueReporting Revolution. Also to them I extend my gratitude for going beyond what's merely known and getting all the way to what really matters. I hope you will profit from their ideas as much as I have.

J. Frank Brown
Global Leader, Assurance and Business Advisory Services
PricewaterhouseCoopers

Foreword

This book was Joel Kurtzman's idea. He suggested to both Harold Kahn, a former U.S. partner at PricewaterhouseCoopers, and Bob Eccles, an advisor to the firm and former professor at the Harvard Business School, that it was time to pull all of the research that had been done on ValueReporting into a book. Because they wanted this book to have a broader focus than just the United States, they called into the project David Phillips, a U.K. partner who was instrumental in designing the first ValueReporting model.

Things changed when Harold Kahn accepted an offer to become chief financial officer (CFO) at Scudder Kemper Investments, where he is now in a position to practice what we've been preaching. Bob Herz then joined the team. As the chief technical partner in the United States, he lives these issues every day. This turned out to be a fortuitous and valuable addition. It then made eminent sense to include Mary Keegan, head of the Global Corporate Reporting Group, whose office is right next door to David's, but who spends much of her life traveling.

In Mary and Bob we have the firm's top two technical partners, whose knowledge of accounting standards and regulations spans the world. Although the early part of this book focuses on the U.S. market as a representative example, we wanted to ensure that it also had global relevance and appeal.

Harold has remained an involved supporter of ValueReporting, and we value his advice and friendship. We would also like to recognize some fellow revolutionaries who were with us in the very early days of the revolution, but who have been called away to fight other wars: Ian Coleman who had the good idea for the global survey and has served as a constant source of intellectual support; Dan Keegan, retired but not forgotten; Len Lindegren, a believer from the beginning; Glen Peters, a man of many ideas and boundless energy; Heather Richards, now raising two children; and Philip Wright, who led us so well in the beginning.

Writing a book of this scope in the time period we did—six months—

would have been impossible without a tremendous amount of help from many extremely talented people. To start, we'd like to thank our core ValueReporting team in the United States, Matt Wissell and Kuntal McElroy. Matt's dedication, many good ideas, and numerous contributions were critical to completing this book. Kuntal's excellent quantitative analyses, especially in Chapter 7, and rigorous attention to quality control were invaluable assets. Both Matt's and Kuntal's continuous assistance, critical comments, and mastery of the Internet were crucial to finishing this book on time, and their voices are heard in these pages.

We benefited enormously throughout the book-writing process from the insights of Richard Baird, Dick Dubois, Jonathan Hayward, Joel Kurtzman, Ellen Masterson, and Mike Willis, all partners at PricewaterhouseCoopers. Rich is one of those "action" guys who sees how to turn vision into reality, and we look forward to working with him to do just that. Dick has responsibility for formulating PricewaterhouseCoopers' "Next Generation Assurance" model and provided invaluable insights from the perspective of one for whom this is real life. Jonathan is one of those "big ideas" guys whose insights into the profession and where it's going are still ahead of what we've been able to describe here.

In addition to making this project happen in the first place, Joel made a number of important interventions along the way. He has a knack for suggesting structural changes that always work out right, despite their initially radical appearance. Ellen, with her experience as a CFO, made our thinking clearer by showing how much harder it is actually to make this happen than it is to write a book about what needs to happen. Mike has been our technological conscience. Without him, an entire dimension of this book would not exist, and it would have been incomplete. (He's also very interested in leases.)

Bill Dauphinais has earned our gratitude for his unswerving support and for encouraging us to say what we felt, even though the message might make some people, both inside and outside the firm, uncomfortable. As you'll see, this turned out to be the case.

In retrospect, it is also clear that we took a big step forward when we began doing industry surveys. John Fletcher suggested surveying the banking industry, and Rusty Nelligan offered to do the same for insurance. Thanks to the support of Rocco Maggiotto, Rick Richardson, and Jeremy Scott, both happened. Both before and after the survey, Rudi Bless (banking) and Ian Dilks (insurance) provided input that improved the final product.

For the development of Chapter 1, we are especially grateful for two important contributions. The first is from two executives at Swiss Re, John

Fitzpatrick (CFO) and Walter Kielholz (CEO), and the Pricewaterhouse-Coopers partner on this account, Rusty Nelligan. From all three we learned much about what it takes to bring ValueReporting into the real world, as well as what its benefits can be. Their insights are reflected in our discussion of Swiss Re in Chapter 1 and others.

We'd also like to thank Robert Bittlestone of Metapraxis for his conversations over many years about performance measurement and what needs to be done to have good numbers—beyond the traditional financial ones—that can be reported to the market. From him we also obtained one of the most complete "business models" we've seen. It, too, is discussed in Chapter 1. We'd also like to thank Leon Olsen of PricewaterhouseCoopers in Denmark for a very thoughtful e-mail that forced us to be clearer and crisper in the terms and concepts discussed in the first chapter.

Chapters 2 and 3 presented some technical challenges. Here we benefited from the careful reviews and critiques of Maurizo Lualdi, a former colleague at PricewaterhouseCoopers and now a sell-side analyst at Credit Suisse First Boston. (Just for the record, we'd like you to know that some of our best friends are sell-side analysts.) Scott Newquist, of Advisory Capital Partners, formerly a managing director at Morgan Stanley and the head of investment banking at Kidder Peabody, was a tough but fair critic of both the theory and the conclusions of these chapters. This shows that we can also work with investment bankers, as Bob Eccles and Scott launched Advisory Capital Partners together. Let us also go on record that Scott provided some useful insights into Chapter 14 as well. You'll know better what this means after you've read the chapter.

We managed to do Chapters 4 and 5 largely on our own, although we relied extensively on the research of a number of extremely capable academics. One who deserves special recognition is Baruch Lev, a professor at New York University, for his well-reasoned and carefully researched arguments about the importance of intangible assets. We'd like to thank Marc Gerstein of *Market Guide* for some last-minute, but very insightful, analysis on quarterly earnings announcements by Internet companies.

Chapter 6 also presented some unique challenges to the first author since he is not a trained accountant but a bit of a closet one. Here we'd like to thank Jim Harrington, a member of Bob Herz's group, for his patient tutorials of the other Bob. Jim's understanding of the history of the accounting profession in the United States, the complexities of its current situation, and what needs to be done to improve it made this chapter much better.

For Chapter 7, we depended on a parallel data collection process, even as we wrote the other chapters, to gather up the extremely revealing data on company reporting practices and market perceptions in the high-tech industry. Our thanks must begin with Paul Weaver, who sponsored this project in the first place, and to George Rough for his help in the design of the survey instrument. We could never have collected such rich data without the help of Terry Proveaux of The Center for Investor Relations Education, as well as that of Jim Stapleton. Jan Akers had the good idea of adding venture capitalists to this survey, and these results are discussed elsewhere (www.valuereporting.com).

Chapter 8 was another in which specific content expertise became very important. For insights and a rather substantial section on risk in banking firms, we'd like to thank Kirsten Doody and Elaine Lin, as well as Bob Moritz both for his ideas and for making Kirsten and Elaine available for this project. John Bromfield, Mike Haubenstock, Brian Kinman, Juan Pujadas, and Bob Sullivan also provided good ideas, and each knows enough to write an entire book on the subject of risk. We've learned more from them than this chapter even begins to show. Bob Bhave, another member of Bob Herz's group, also provided some cogent summaries of complex subjects. Our representations of them would have been impossible without his help.

Wanting to show that we can practice modern management techniques as well as write about them, we essentially outsourced Chapter 9 to Jennifer Woodward in the London office of PricewaterhouseCoopers. Jennifer went above and far beyond the call of duty here. In very short order she wrote the chapter, relying on her deep knowledge of sustainability and her ability to integrate the message of this book with the vision of Shell. She would, however, have been unable to do this without the assistance of Tom Delfgaauw of Shell, who kindly shared his view of the Shell story in conversations with Jennifer and to whom we would like to extend our sincere thanks. We can think of no better evidence of Shell's commitment to transparency than their active participation in this book, resulting in a chapter that has candor uncommon in the reporting world today. The chapter was written with the support of Malcolm Bailey and David Wright. Others who contributed to our understanding of sustainability include Jorgen Cramon and Helle Bank Jorgensen, both PricewaterhouseCoopers' partners in Denmark.

We wrote Chapter 10 all by ourselves! But even here, we relied extensively on surveys conducted for PricewaterhouseCoopers by Market & Opinion Research International (MORI), and so ably supervised by Roger Stubbs, Allan Hyde, and Robert Carlisle. MORI also collected the banking and insurance data used throughout the book.

For much of the content of Chapter 11, we also depended on the contributions of others. Janice Lingwood, of the London-based core Value-Reporting team, spearheaded collecting many interesting examples of new practices in external reporting, which are discussed more fully in the Price-waterhouseCoopers *ValueReporting Forecast 2001*. Mark O'Sullivan and Caroline Carden ably assisted her. Paddy Boyce, Denise Gleeson, and Annette Watson also contributed to this effort and to other important related ones. Thanks also to Carsten Lonfeldt of Coloplast for his insights into the measurement of intellectual capital, which go deeper than we were able to explore here. Mike Willis and Eric Cohen provided insights for this chapter about the Internet and technology in general that greatly strengthened the discussion.

Chapter 12 is a complex subject in its own right and well worth its own book. Here we owe a debt of gratitude to Catherine Bromilow and Richard Steinberg, who have actually written that book, for many conversations and a tremendous amount of insightful feedback. Without them, this chapter would have been much longer and much less clear. Margaret Blair of The Brookings Institution also helped ensure the accuracy and relevance of this chapter.

The foundation of Chapter 13 was laid in a meeting of the Pricewater-houseCoopers Future of Assurance team on August 15, 2000, just outside London. We challenged the team with a question: "Taking off the kid gloves and worrying more about being honest than being nice, what key message should this book deliver to the accounting profession?" Here we will eschew the false modesty of authors who sometimes "thank" someone but then "take full responsibility" for what the other said. The team members at this meeting own the message of this chapter just as much as we do—they're as much on the hook as we are—so we want to expose them publicly. Attention! The following individuals please stand: Dick Dubois and Barry Winograd, co-heads of this group; and Philip Ashton, Richard Baird, Jeremy Booker, Jonathan Hayward, Ellen Masterson, Karl Pfalzgraf, and Mike Willis.

For the highly explosive Chapter 14, Denis Salamone, we owe you big time for your support and realize full well the challenge this presents to you and Barry Winograd. No one's commitment to the ValueReporting Revolution could be greater. We also benefited from conversations with John Kattar of The Boston Company Asset Management and Ted Truscott of Scudder Kemper. Thanks also to Alison Thomas for the introduction to John and for her insights as well, even before she joined the ValueReporting team in London. And, once again in a very long list, thanks to Harold Kahn for the introduction to Ted and for the many conversations we've had with him on this subject.

Mike Willis and his colleague Eric Cohen made another major contribution in Chapter 15. As the big guns on technology, they made sure we got this section right. And, as they can attest, it took more than a few tries.

A number of people joined us at the end of the project. Although their time was brief, their contributions were large. So much must be done to make sure that every "i" is dotted and every "t" crossed in a high-stakes book like this one. Elizabeth Lotito was the lawyer who made sure everything was buttoned down from a permissions, copyright, and risk management perspective. (This is real life for us, after all.) But she went beyond that important role and made some very useful, substantive suggestions as well.

Trent Boggess and Mike Campbell chased down many facts, as did Andy Cantos early on before moving on to dot-com land. Melissa Luo came on board on a temporary basis to help out in a number of ways, but soon decided to join the revolution on a permanent basis. Sally Evans and Pam Morski of Advisory Capital Partners made a number of contributions throughout the process, not the least of which was tolerating the first author's bouts of ill-humor and bad temper.

Sheck Cho, our editor at John Wiley & Sons, gave us the freedom to write while making sure that the final product was right. His colleagues, Peter Knapp and Colleen Scollans, deserve credit for the title of the book, which, in turn, significantly sharpened its message.

But the best we've saved for last: Max Russell. Max, we couldn't have done it without you. So let us practice a little transparency ourselves in front of the whole wide world. Rather than having people guess how three accountants and a former professor could write a book on such a complicated and even arcane subject as this, we'll just come clean and say it could never have happened without you. We marvel at how you took our labored prose and turned it into something—self-serving though this may sound—that we think of as a work of art. So thank you, thank you, thank you, Max. And thank you, Joel, for bringing Max into the project and for your suggestion on Thomas Paine.

And thank you Roger Lipsey for your exquisite ear for the English language, for your wise counsel at key points along the way, and for the finishing touch you and Max put on this book. Ending well is always infinitely harder than getting started, and thanks to you we think we did both.

Looking back, we would like to thank the leadership of PricewaterhouseCoopers for their unwavering support for ValueReporting and for this book during a time that has been tumultuous, both for the accounting profession and for the firm. Looking forward, we would like to thank Frank

Brown, the new global leader of the firm's Assurance and Business Advisory Services. He has already demonstrated the courage to support a revolution that will no doubt prove contentious, and he is taking concrete actions to make sure the revolution happens. Books can rabble-rouse, but in the end revolutions require deeds as well as words. Frank, indeed, is a man who gets things done.

On a personal note, Bob Eccles would like to thank his wife, Anne, and their four children, Charlotte, Philippa, Isabelle, and Gordon. He was an absentee husband and father, often physically and always mentally, while this book was being written. His disclosure to them is that he knows this and that he owes them big time. He intends to make up for it in the respite between the submission of this book and its publication.

Bob Herz would like to thank his wife, Louise, and his children, Michael and Nicole, for their patience and understanding. They put up with many late nights and weekends over the past year while he read, edited, and reread the many different versions this book went through. They have also been a constant source of support and encouragement throughout his professional career.

Mary Keegan's support and encouragement come from her many friends and colleagues around the world. To them, and to her family, her thanks are due.

Bob and Mary would also like to thank the dedicated and highly skilled professionals in their groups. They work tirelessly, day in and day out, to help PricewaterhouseCoopers' engagement teams and clients deal with the myriad tough accounting and auditing issues in today's increasingly complicated reporting environment. Their efforts make Bob, Mary, and PricewaterhouseCoopers look good.

For David Phillips, thanks go to his wife, Caroline, and his three children, Lucinda, Charlotte, and Thomas, and to the many equine members of the family who covered for him on weekends.

Robert G. Eccles
Robert H. Herz
E. Mary Keegan
David M.H. Phillips

October 11, 2000

Part One

Preparing for the Revolution

I wish that every human life might be pure transparent freedom.
Simone de Beauvoir, *The Blood of Others*

Prologue

A Manifesto for
the Second Revolution

*Perhaps the sentiments contained in the following pages, are not yet
sufficiently fashionable to procure them general favor; a long habit of not
thinking a thing wrong, gives it a superficial appearance of being right,
and raises at first a formidable outcry in defence of custom. But tumult soon
subsides. Time makes more converts than reason.*

Thomas Paine, *Common Sense*
February 14, 1776

The corporate reporting model has failed those whom it intends and ought
to serve best. Neither the companies that report, nor the investors who listen, fare well. That must change.

The last major innovation in more than a century of corporate reporting in the United States was, ironically and tellingly, a regulatory one. Following the stock market crash of 1929, the Securities and Exchange
Commission (SEC) required all publicly traded companies to publish annual financial statements, audited by independent accounting firms, based
on a set of accounting standards that the profession had initially established itself.

Since then, the model has been improved in many important ways. It
has also become vastly more complex. Numerous and seemingly endless incremental clarifications and additions have altered and often improved the
basic *content of the information* that managers report and *how they report it*. Still
the model has not even begun to keep pace with the extraordinary changes
in how executives manage their companies—in strategy, organization, technology, and human resources.

This book provides more than ample evidence of this. Not that it's a secret. In 1997 and 1998, PricewaterhouseCoopers surveyed hundreds of insti-

tutional investors and sell-side analysts in 14 countries. Only 19 percent of
the investors polled and 27 percent of the analysts found financial reports
very useful in communicating the true value of companies.

The preparers of these reports—the companies themselves—agree.
Only 38 percent of executives in the United States felt their reports were
very useful. Even more dramatically, in a similar survey of the high-tech
industry in the United States and Canada, only 7 percent of investors, 16
percent of analysts, and 13 percent of company executives found reported financial information very useful in determining the true value of
a company.

On top of this, managers, analysts, and shareholders feel themselves
trapped in a short-term earnings game that none of them really likes, but
all see no choice but to play. This results in a capital market too focused
on the short term and lacking the information it needs to properly establish value. Great arguments rage over whether companies are valued
too high or too low. The heat they generate is reflected in extraordinary
stock price volatility, both for individual companies and for the market as
a whole.

The time has come to change the game. Because it's not really a game
in the end. It has deadly serious consequences. For how capital gets allocated across companies. For how value is created in society. For the return
individuals get on the hard-earned capital they risk when they invest. For
how companies account for the needs of all stakeholders.

The magnitude of the needed change is monumental. And change
must happen quickly. It will require a revolution. This book is a call to arms
to make the revolution happen.

YOU SAY YOU WANT A REVOLUTION

In 1991, an article called "The Performance Measurement Manifesto" appeared in the *Harvard Business Review*. It described a revolution already in
progress, one that would result in a "shift from treating financial figures as
the foundation for performance measurement to treating them as one
among a broad set of measures."[1] The article said that making this shift required answering three questions:

1. What are the most important measures of performance?
2. How do these measures relate to each other?
3. What measures truly predict long-term financial success of the business?

It is now only a matter of time before this revolution in performance measurement is won. The emergence of the New Economy and the transformation of the Old have made managers and investors alike vastly more aware of the limitations they struggle under when they use financial measures alone to make investment decisions—limits on managers' decisions within the company and on investors' decisions among companies.

Thanks to the growing popularity of the balanced scorecard concept, most large companies and many smaller ones have made at least some progress in implementing a new philosophy of performance measurement based on integrating leading indicator nonfinancial measures with financial ones.[2] And the ever-increasing power of information technology makes it possible for companies to generate a much broader range of performance measures and to analyze the relationships among them.

Performance Measurement → Performance Reporting

With victory in the performance measurement revolution clearly in sight, the time has come for a new revolution—in performance reporting. Until the new revolution is also won, the full promise of the first will go unrealized.

Information on a broader range of performance measures has as much importance and relevance to analysts and investors as it has to managers. Until managers begin reporting performance on all the measures they use internally, they will continue to be the pawns in The Earnings Game—forced to slightly beat quarterly earnings expectations and carefully managing them prior to their announcement.

This second revolution has a name: ValueReporting. This is its manifesto: a call to managers to adopt a philosophy of complete transparency— to report information to the market on *all* the measures they use internally to manage. And that encompasses performance dimensions that other stakeholders regard as important as well, including social and environmental responsibility.

No One Ever Said It Would Be Easy

Revolutions are always exciting, but they always have their casualties too. In the performance measurement revolution, all these casualties were hidden inside company lines. The market felt the revolution's impact only by the effect it had on reported financial results.

Now, the stakes have been raised much higher. In the ValueReporting Revolution, there will be varying degrees of consequences, good and bad, all around, not only for companies, but also for the accounting profession, sell-side analysts, and even the regulators.

For companies, the opportunities far outweigh the consequences. Companies that join the revolution early and take meaningful, productive steps toward better disclosure can gain enormous competitive advantages. They can, but will they?

Victory will be theirs only if they truly prove that they have identified all of their key performance measures—both financial and nonfinancial, that they know how each relates to others, that they've measured and reported on them, and most important, that they've actually created real value. If they fail on these fronts, companies will feel the consequences—and they won't be good ones.

They will avoid the worst only if they conscientiously and completely revolutionize themselves. If they allow their competitors to capture the lead, they only add to their suffering. In the ValueReporting Revolution, indecision and hesitation are leading indicators of disaster.

Sharing the Risk

Companies aren't alone in their exposure to the risk inherent in this revolution. Accounting firms and so-called sell-side analysts, who typically work at investment banks and write research reports for investors, stand at risk too. The former risk losing relevance as the market focuses less and less on traditional and regulated financial information, and more on the nonfinancial sort. Others abound who can step forward to provide such information and attest to it as well. In fact, they already do.

The sell-side analysts risk losing the trust of the investors they supposedly serve. They will face questions about the objectivity of the research they provide. Here, too, others have already begun to seize the day. This new breed can provide individual and institutional investors with more and different types of analysis, drawing information from companies and numerous other sources, that will enable investors to make more well-informed decisions. The Internet gives the new breed easier and faster tools for both getting and analyzing information. Such a democratizing force will help the revolution successfully run its course.

A revolution sweeps everyone up in its wake, the willing and the not so willing, supporters and detractors alike. This includes regulators. They too must change or end up regulating a deserted outpost far removed from the landscape the revolution has taken by storm.

THE REVOLUTION *WILL* HAPPEN

Like the revolution in performance measurement, the revolution in performance reporting must happen. The forces behind it are powerful ones—the energies and enthusiasms of free enterprise, new technologies on the verge of release, and, at least in the United States, the yet-to-be-seen full impact of one of the most controversial rulings ever made by the SEC since its inception, Regulation Fair Disclosure (FD). These three forces combined will provide the motivation, the ammunition, and the discipline required for the revolution's success. They cannot be ignored.

It is *inevitable* that a key contribution to solving a problem deeply embedded in the capital markets will come from the product markets. The market hungers for more—and more useful—information, delivered more quickly than ever. It *will* be satisfied. Entrepreneurs working inside garages and inside corporate behemoths will seize this opportunity to satisfy the market's hunger for information and will profit from doing so.

These profits will turn into value. The smartest will recognize the double benefit they gain by signing on early to the revolution and disclosing more themselves. Their double benefit will accrue directly in full market value for their companies, and indirectly as they blaze the disclosure trail for others. Those who follow will become the trailblazers' best customers for information and analysis, allowing the trailblazers to reap greater rewards: even more profits and more value for their shareholders.

It is *felicitous* when a new technology emerges that a revolution can press immediately into service. Those who recognize how new technologies can create a clear advantage on the battlefield—as did cannons over sabers—often win revolutions. The new technology for the ValueReporting Revolution has an appropriately arcane name, XBRL. For now we'll leave it at that, except to say that with XBRL virtually anyone can take information from a company's website and directly download it to software on any device, including the Internet, for quick and easy analysis in any number of ways.

Companies that do not arm themselves with XBRL, and rely instead on the increasingly outmoded arsenal of corporate reporting media and practices, will compare to those who eschewed the telephone in favor of carrier pigeons. Providers of capital want to align with companies that look to the future, not those that cling to the past.

It is *timely* that a new U.S. regulation has come forward to focus directly on a core component of corporate disclosure. Regulations, most often, are lobbed at contemporary problems, and usually only when the magnitude of the problem demands attention. The problem targeted by Regulation FD—approved by the SEC on August 10, 2000—concerns unequal access to company information. Sell-side analysts and the very largest institutional investors have long had the advantage of earlier insight into company performance to the distinct disadvantage of the growing legions of individual investors. From this day forth companies must disclose all material information to everyone simultaneously.

Not surprisingly, individual investors overwhelmingly favored Regulation FD. They should likewise overwhelmingly favor the ValueReporting Revolution, for its purpose dovetails precisely. It aims to make sure that all investors, great and small, and all other concerned stakeholders as well, receive the relevant performance information they need. But to get it, they must demand it. If one and all wait for another to raise the revolutionary flag, it will not fly. The more quickly and aggressively investors demand their full information rights, the sooner the revolution will be won.

BATTLE PLAN

This book intends to fan the flames that have already started to burn throughout the corporate reporting terrain. The first chapter shows that most companies are working to secure a strong position from which they can participate in the revolution. Chapters 2 through 5 survey the grounds on which the revolution will play out: the capital markets and the reporting practices that should be overthrown. Chapter 6 traces a failed earlier attempt to launch the revolution and identifies some inertial forces that must be overcome.

Chapters 7 through 9 lay out how companies must change their ways of reporting information to shareholders and other stakeholders, and how they think about and report on risk. These chapters foreshadow battles that must be fought and won for the revolution to succeed.

Chapter 10 describes the spoils of victory. Chapter 11 offers some early reports from the front where a few brave hearts have already entered into battle. The next three chapters put boards of directors, accounting firms, and sell-side analysts on notice about what they can do to become part of the solution, not part of the problem. The final chapter argues that the revolution is inevitable, and that the choice is a simple one: Join today, or you can bid farewell to tomorrow.

You can enlist today at www.valuereporting.com

In the following pages I offer nothing more than simple facts, plain arguments, and common sense; and have no other preliminaries to settle with the reader, than that he will divest himself of prejudice and prepossession, and suffer his reason and his feelings to determine for themselves; that he will put on, or rather that he will not put off, the true character of a man, and generously enlarge his views beyond the present day.

Thomas Paine, *Common Sense*
February 14, 1776

1

Common Sense

Only a brave person is willing to honestly admit, and fearlessly face, what a sincere and logical mind discovers.

Rodan of Alexandria

The ValueReporting Manifesto has sounded the call to action. Those brave and visionary enough to join the revolution today must take heed: Do not simply start reporting volumes of more detailed information to investors. This revolution requires planning and preparation.

If you've decided to join, or at least find the prospect intriguing, there are four commonsense steps to hastening the rise of the ValueReporting Revolution:

Step 1:   Construct a business model that shows the cause-and-effect relationships among key value drivers; then identify the most meaningful measures for them.

Step 2:   Develop new measurement methodologies if they don't already exist.

Step 3:   Validate the business model and the measures through testing and use.

Step 4:   Compare management's view with the market's view on what measures are important.

Describing these steps is easy; it is done in this chapter. Taking them is hard. Before managers even try to walk this talk, they should heed the revolutionary's response to two of the most commonly held, yet misguided, management beliefs.

11

○ **Misguided management belief 1**
I possess an excellent intuitive sense of my business. I don't need some hotshot business model to tell me what I already know.

The revolutionary's response
Stop kidding yourself. Would you rely solely on your intuition to manage your financial performance? I think not!

Quiet reflection on the dialogue
Although ValueReporting revolutionaries certainly must be adaptable and may justifiably rely on intuition for quick tactical decisions, they always fare better when their intuitive decisions are informed by rigor, discipline, and a clear plan of attack.

○ **Misguided management belief 2**
I already know the type of information investors need and want. They should take what I give them and like it.

The revolutionary's response
What makes you think you know so much about what investors want and need? You've never bothered to ask them!

Quiet reflection on the dialogue
More than any other group of managers, chief executive officers (CEOs), chief financial officers (CFOs), and heads of investor relations believe number two. Extending their logic to other constituencies, companies wouldn't survey employees or customers for their views either. Yet they do. What can possibly justify ignoring investors and sell-side analysts? ValueReporting revolutionaries thrive on external intelligence. They regularly dispatch reconnaissance teams just to make sure they keep an eye trained on the constantly shifting battle.

GET READY TO GET STARTED

In 1991, the already-cited *Harvard Business Review* article called for a broader set of measures for performance measurement and management.[1] Exactly one year later, Robert Kaplan and David Norton published a paper, also in the *Harvard Business Review,* in which they coined the term *balanced scorecard.*[2] It's now on the tip of every executive tongue in the corporate world. Rightfully so. It was an idea whose time had come, as further evidenced by an article that L.S. Maisel published that same year using the same term.[3]

Since then, there has been a maelstrom of books, articles, and conferences whirling around the balanced scorecard.[4] Most major accounting and consulting firms have a balanced scorecard practice, by whatever name, and boutique consulting firms have been founded solely to provide consulting and software to help companies implement balanced scorecard systems. A proliferation of calls for nonfinancial measures and a focus on intangible assets has resulted.

Although many companies have adopted balanced scorecards for a variety of reasons, rarely, if ever, do they cite as a reason the explicit intention to improve external reporting. Kaplan and Norton, for example, depict the balanced scorecard as the foundation of a strategic management system that involves the following:

- Clarifying and translating the vision and strategy
- Communicating and linking
- Planning and target setting
- Strategic feedback and learning[5]

Based on extensive experience in implementing balanced scorecards for many companies, Olve, Roy, and Wetter have concluded that companies do so for two major reasons.[6] The first, which descends from an executive level, is to improve strategic focus and control. The second, which rises up in the organization, is to improve operational control. In both cases, these authors emphasize the importance of information technology and using the information it produces to improve the company's knowledge management.

Clearly the balanced scorecard focuses on *value creation*, as depicted in Exhibit 1.1. Olve, Roy, and Wetter have one short chapter on external reporting. Although they note some circumstances when reporting balanced scorecard information proves useful, they do not make a strong argument for it. Similarly, Kaplan and Norton virtually ignore the subject of external reporting. Nevertheless, Exhibit 1.1 makes clear that the balanced scorecard is a useful tool that culminates in *value realization*. In between lies *value preservation* through risk management and tax planning.

Among the many reasons given for the utility of a balanced scorecard is that financial measures are lagging indicators, a concept often explained using the metaphor of steering a car by looking into the rearview mirror.

Exhibit 1.1

The Value Continuum

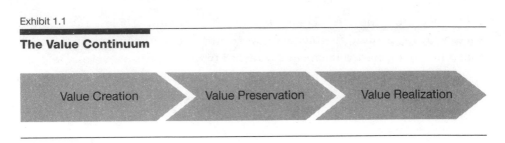

In fact, nearly every measure can serve as both a leading and a lagging indicator of one or more other measures. A leading indicator is a value driver that logically occurs before another. Its value in the current period correlates with the value of the other measure in a future period. The converse is true for a lagging indicator.

To understand an overall *business model* made up of a company's value drivers, you have to understand their relationships to each other and the appropriate measures for each. It's essential for successfully implementing a balanced scorecard, by whatever name you may call it.

A Business Model Example

Exhibit 1.2 is an example of the product of an exercise, usually done in workshops or brainstorming sessions, to identify value drivers and their relationships. Metapraxis, the software and consulting company that developed this diagram for a fast-moving consumer goods company, calls it a "Business Driver Analysis."

Robert Bittlestone, founder and CEO of Metapraxis, notes that the Business Driver Analysis is simply a framework for the consistent presentation and interpretation of cause-and-effect relationships; it is not in itself a statement about what these cause-and-effect relationships should be in any particular case. He also notes that because "each of us has some kind of mental model of the business anyway, sharing these models by making them explicit and discussing them is a step forward in improving management dialogue."

Every company, based on its industry and its strategy, will have to work out for itself the appropriate Business Driver Analysis for each of its major business units. Obviously, it would look very different, particularly on the left side of the model, for a high-tech company or a pharmaceuticals firm.

As Bittlestone observes, developing such diagrams forces management to take a rigorous and disciplined view of the business model it implicitly uses in allocating internal resources. By doing so, different business unit

Exhibit 1.2

A Business Driver Analysis
Linking Consumer Behaviour to Shareholder Value

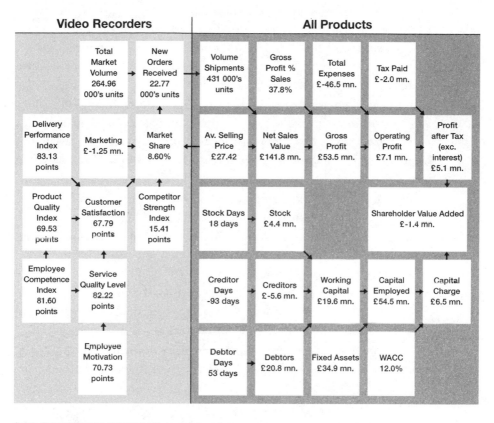

Source: Robert Bittlestone, Metapraxis Ltd., www.metapraxis.com

managers in a company can see just how similar or different their respective business models are and then reconcile them into a common view. After all, how can a management team whose members operate from very different business models ever expect to reach consistent and high-quality decisions? Every management team should go through some form of this exercise to make sure that everyone is singing off the same business page.

Insights from the Business Model

Exhibit 1.2 illustrates the key characteristics of any such exercise done properly:

- Because earnings per se are not the best bottom line measure for determining stock price, deduct from earnings a charge for capital employed.
- Financial measures can serve as both leading and lagging indicators. Gross profit, for example, is a leading indicator of operating profit (gross profits are first earned and then operating expenses are deducted) and a lagging indicator of net sales volume (gross profits are earned only after a sale has been made).
- Nonfinancial measures can serve as both leading and lagging indicators. Customer satisfaction, a leading indicator of market share (which goes up as customer satisfaction improves) is also a lagging indicator of product quality (better products result in more satisfied customers).
- Both tangible (e.g., fixed assets) and intangible (e.g., employee competency) assets are important.
- Measures are generated using information from both inside (e.g., volume of shipments and employee motivation) and outside (e.g., customer satisfaction and market share) the company.
- Measures of combined performance across all products tend to be mostly financial, while information on specific products (e.g., video recorders) tends to be mostly nonfinancial.
- Nonfinancial measures tend to be leading indicators of financial measures, sometimes involving a number of cause-and-effect relationships.
- The measures at the beginning of the chain of cause-and-effect relationships tend to be mostly nonfinancial (e.g., delivery performance index and product quality index) and/or relate to intangible assets (e.g., employee motivation and employee competency index).
- The values on some measures derive from performance on a large number of other measures (e.g., market share is a function of marketing expenses, customer satisfaction, competitor strength index, new orders received, and average selling price).
- Many nonfinancial measures are important; few of them are reported.

What's Good for the Goose

This last characteristic, seen in the context of Exhibit 1.2, underscores the importance of reporting performance on the nonfinancial measures. Indi-

vidually and collectively, they are leading indicators of the financial performance that ultimately results in value to shareholders. For example, an improvement in product quality will work its way through customer
satisfaction, market share, and eventually to profits after taxes. An investor
who knows that product quality will improve can anticipate, with at least
some degree of precision and confidence, that the improvement will have a
positive impact on profits. This results in a higher value for the company
compared to another company with higher profits but poorer or declining
product quality.

Investors who use a company's current earnings and its earnings track
record to predict future earnings believe that this set of relationships has
more strength than the relationships between current nonfinancial measures
and future earnings. If the relationship between past/current and future
earnings had strong statistical significance and resulted in few surprises,
those investors would assume accurately. They rarely do. For evidence, simply
consider the enormous negative effect that even a small earnings surprise
can have on a company's stock price. The market simply assumes that one
quarter of bad earnings indicates a sustained period of lower future earnings, and therefore deducts the present value of this from the company's
stock price. Yet it often—but not always—quickly climbs back.

Current earnings are certainly an important leading indicator of future earnings, but so are measures like delivery performance, service quality, and customer satisfaction. If the market had information on these other
leading indicators, it could put current earnings—especially when they
come in above or below expectations, the whisper number, or even the über-
whisper number—into the proper perspective. (Chapter 4 talks more about
the mysterious and mischievous whisper numbers and their siblings and off-
spring.) Sometimes a drop in current earnings *does* signal a long-term problem. Sometimes it's just an artifact of the company's bookkeeping system
and management's admirable unwillingness to play The Earnings Game
(also deconstructed in Chapter 4).

The Business Driver Analysis in Exhibit 1.2 does not indicate the time
lags involved or the strength of these relationships. Determining both is difficult, but it can be done. A study by McKinsey & Company, for example,
found that many e-commerce companies spend more to acquire a new customer—an average of $250 in advertising and marketing costs—than they
will likely make in profit. Bearing in mind that only 5 percent of the visitors
to a site buy something, a typical customer spends $24.50 in the first quarter
and another $52.50 in every quarter after that, assuming a repeat purchase.
Unfortunately, two-thirds never make a repeat purchase.[7]

Customer retention, therefore, is the key. The McKinsey study further shows that improving customer retention by 10 percent would add 9.5 percent in shareholder value. Similar calculations were made for 10 percent improvements in two measures of *attraction*, three measures of *conversion*, and four measures of *retention*. By way of contrast, a 10 percent improvement in visitor acquisition costs added only 0.7 percent in shareholder value.

Exhibit 1.2 also does not indicate cyclical cause-and-effect relationships, such as the effect of service quality on employee motivation, although such relationships often exist as well. Performance measures can interact in complex ways, resulting in relationships that are not simple linear ones, or one-to-one relationships for those of us who studied only literature or history.

For example, in a study of individual customers at a telecommunications company, Ittner and Larcker found nonlinear relationships between customer satisfaction in the current year and retention rates and changes in revenue in the next.[8] At a certain level of customer satisfaction, there was no further improvement in the other two performance measures. The relationship between customer satisfaction in the current year and revenues in the next year, however, was linear.

This can all get rather complicated and, like everything else in life, it can reach the point of diminishing returns. Management must decide just how much effort it wants to put into quantifying the relationships precisely. How much depends on its likely value and the availability of the data. It may also be easier to do than it first appears. Bittlestone suggests that "once you get familiar with the qualitative aspects of Business Driver Diagrams, the quantitative aspects can follow, and by then you won't find them half as scary as you think you do now."

"KEY" MEANS "FEW"

Just as the Business Driver Analysis in Exhibit 1.2 breaks shareholder value-added down into its constituent financial parts, it can depict any single box in terms of the underlying drivers that determine any particular variable. This can happen at a high level of detail. Bittlestone offers an example of the determinants of the single variable "product demand" based on a sophisticated and empirically tested model of brand equity and consumer loyalty developed by Rory Morgan (see Exhibit 1.3).[9]

Morgan identifies 36 determinants of product demand alone. Not every one of these should necessarily be measured for internal decision-making purposes, nor should they all necessarily be reported externally.

Exhibit 1.3

The Research International Equity Engine and Loyalty Driver Models, Expressed as a Business Driver Analysis

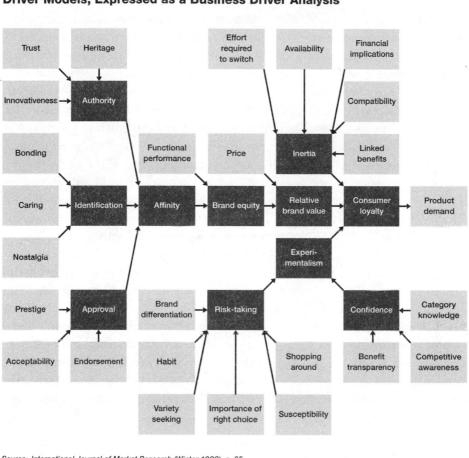

Source: *International Journal of Market Research* (Winter 1999), p. 65

This exhibit does, however, vividly illustrate that once a company gets serious about measures other than financial, its list can grow very long indeed.

Management, of course, doesn't set out with the objective of making the list as long as possible. Even the best managers can pay attention to and manage only a limited number of key performance indicators. Besides, how many indicators can really be key? The objective is to identify those measures that really do matter, that encapsulate a lot of relevant information in the same way as earnings and cash flow when they are measured properly. Oh yes, and the objective also includes reporting them to the market as well.

Miller and O'Leary identified a very good example of a truly key nonfinancial value driver, *die yield*, in their field study of Intel's reporting practices.[10] They reported, "Die yield, a measure that expresses in percentage terms the amount of good die produced from a wafer of silicon, was mentioned repeatedly by senior corporate executives as one of the more important indicators of manufacturing performance across different generations of microprocessors."[11] Comparing die yields across different generations of microprocessors and looking at the rate of improvement gave Intel executives information on the health of the technology as well as insights into the quality of process control and the design of manufacturing systems and methods as well.

Comparing die yields with those of competitors—difficult to do because the information was hard to get—was considered a valuable way of assessing comparative competitive advantage. Miller and O'Leary said one Intel director of manufacturing concluded that die yield "is a very powerful measure" that "has many phenomena coming together" and so "is an aggregate indicator that gets quite a lot of visibility."

This is all well and good, but if die yield really has that much importance, Intel should consider reporting on it to the market. Although the company does publish a bit of data on this measure occasionally, indicating how each generation of chip does better over time and better than the one before on this measure, it offers less information than analysts need to make meaningful comparisons (see www.chipanalyst.com). If all semiconductor companies measured and reported on die yield, Intel and its analysts and investors could perform this very important comparative analysis themselves.

LEARNING HOW TO COUNT

The deepest underlying causes in Exhibit 1.3 all relate to intangible assets that would most likely be measured in nonfinancial terms: trust, innovativeness, bonding, caring, nostalgia, prestige, and acceptability. It is by no means clear that all of these variables can be measured or, if they can be, that the measure has validity, reliability, relevance, and predictive value. All are essential to define:

- *Validity.* Whether the measure corresponds to the phenomenon of interest.
- *Reliability.* Whether the measurement process is free from bias and produces numbers within an acceptable margin of error.

- ○ *Relevance.* The usefulness of the measure in helping managers make decisions.
- ○ *Predictive value.* Whether the measure truly is a leading indicator of other measures as represented in a cause-and-effect diagram.

Methodologies for the measures reported in financial statements have validity and reliability if they are produced according to a well-defined set of accounting rules. Whether they have relevance and predictive value poses more of a problem, which helps explain why so much interest has emerged over the past decade in identifying measures that, in fact, do have predictive value. This is what business models are all about. And this is what investors want to know as well. Their focus is all about what their return will be in the future.

So Many Measures

The first reporting revolution notwithstanding, companies have available to them many other performance measures that have been produced for years. Here, too, great variation exists in their validity, reliability, relevance, and predictive value. Manufacturing, logistics, and distribution functions generate an avalanche of data based on measures of productivity, quality, and timeliness. Sales and marketing also produce a large number of performance measures on such things as intensity of the sales calling program, proposal success rate, and advertising effectiveness.

Measures of human resources include the percentage of employees who received their performance appraisals, employee turnover, employee training hours, and employee satisfaction, among many others. Useful product development measures include the success rate of new product introductions, the growth rate of new products, and time-to-market. Measures of the research and development (R&D) function include number of patents received, number of papers published in refereed journals, and percentage of employees with a doctorate.

Usually, one can find a number of ways to measure a nonfinancial value driver. The same holds true for many financial measures. The challenge lies in choosing the methodology that provides the most valid, reliable, and relevant measure with meaningful predictive value.

So Many Ways of Getting Them

Constructing a balanced scorecard taps many different sources of information for use in developing measurement methodologies. These sources include the following:

- ○ *Measures that already exist.* If they do, then it's simply a matter of integrating them with other measures. Typically, the finance function, which obviously has most of the financial measures (but not all—shadow systems still exist!), plays a modest role, at best, in generating the nonfinancial measures that reside in other functional departments. Pulling them together requires an act of organizational coordination that must sometimes break down political barriers.

- ○ *Measures that don't exist but that can be created by aggregating existing data.* A representative example is "customer profitability." To quantify that measure might require aggregating sales data across business units with manufacturing cost data from a centralized unit.

- ○ *Measures that don't exist and that require a new methodology, but for which the organization can generate the data.* An example is sales calling effort where the sales force must start filing reports on sales calls.

- ○ *Measures that don't exist, that require a new methodology, and also require data or other types of input from an outside organization.* This often happens because another organization can gather more easily the necessary information, or more valid and reliable information than the company can. Third-party database companies can often gather and analyze information that the company's internal information systems cannot. Common examples include market share, market growth, customer satisfaction, and market share by customer (often called *share-of-wallet*).

TRUST BUT VERIFY

Developing a balanced scorecard based on an underlying business model with new measurement methodologies, as necessary, compares in many ways to formulating a hypothesis. Management posits a set of cause-and-effect relationships among the variables that they manage to create value for shareholders. Whether these relationships really do exist, their level of strength, and the time lags between variables form an empirical question that can be tested with data.

By collecting information over a period of time, management can determine whether the hypothesized relationships actually exist. If they do, management gets confirmation that it has an appropriate business model. It can then use the data to make the model more sophisticated by specifying the strength of the cause-and-effect relationship—for example, a 5 percent improvement in customer retention leads to a 1 percent increase in market share, which results in a 10 percent increase in earnings.

Of course, not all relationships are simple linear ones. In some cases, improvement on a certain measure may lead to diminishing or negative returns on another (e.g., gaining market share by capturing unprofitable customers will cut into earnings). Alternatively, each incremental improvement on one measure may have a larger impact on another measure than the one before (e.g., as employee turnover goes down, employee productivity goes up at an increasing rate because of a multiplier effect from a more skilled work force). Finally, it may even be possible to specify the time lags involved (e.g., improvements in earnings occur six months after improvements in market share, which occur nine months after improvements in customer retention).

THE SOFTER SIDE

Very few companies have reached the level of sophistication just described. Most haven't had their balanced scorecards in place long enough, and most simply don't have enough data collected over a sufficient period of time to perform the necessary analysis. This is particularly true when a large number of the measures require new methodologies. In this situation, managers must collect data over time before they can test their business model hypothesis.

Testing the hypothesis is easier when the company has a large number of identical or similar units—for example, a franchise chain or retail operation with many stores. Sears offers one of the best examples available in the public domain of developing and testing a business model. Exhibit 1.4 shows the business model Sears developed as part of the largely successful effort to turn around this floundering retail giant.[12]

Yet another *Harvard Business Review* article details this effort, describing how the Sears Phoenix Team took on the job of designing "a corporate transformation and renewal among 300,000 employees at more than 2,000 locations" and began "to think in terms of a business model that would link employees, customers, and investors into a single logical entity."[13]

The Phoenix Team looked for leading indicators, "a set of nonfinancial measures that would be every bit as rigorous and auditable as financial ones."[14] They eventually came up with the model shown in Exhibit 1.4, which indicates that a 5-unit increase in employee attitude leads to a 1.3-unit increase in customer impression, which then leads to a 0.5 percent increase in revenue growth.

Exhibit 1.4

Sears' Revised Model

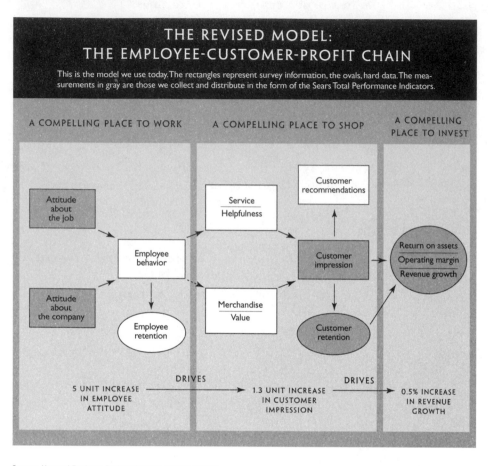

THE REVISED MODEL:
THE EMPLOYEE-CUSTOMER-PROFIT CHAIN

This is the model we use today. The rectangles represent survey information, the ovals, hard data. The measurements in gray are those we collect and distribute in the form of the Sears Total Performance Indicators.

A COMPELLING PLACE TO WORK   A COMPELLING PLACE TO SHOP   A COMPELLING PLACE TO INVEST

Attitude about the job

Employee behavior

Attitude about the company

Employee retention

Service Helpfulness

Customer recommendations

Merchandise Value

Customer impression

Customer retention

Return on assets
Operating margin
Revenue growth

DRIVES   DRIVES

5 UNIT INCREASE IN EMPLOYEE ATTITUDE → 1.3 UNIT INCREASE IN CUSTOMER IMPRESSION → 0.5% INCREASE IN REVENUE GROWTH

Source: *Harvard Business Review* (January–February 1998)

The Phoenix Team did not easily arrive at this precise and elegant business model. It went through a period of trial and error. In developing the model itself, for example, they could not prove that the expected effect of personal growth and development and empowered teams had a statistically significant relationship with customer data. Another example relates to the measures the team used. Measures of customer retention, for example, did not exist and needed to be developed.

Sears, however, had enough confidence in its "revised model" that compensation has been linked to it. The company bases executive incentives one-third on employee measures, one-third on customer measures, and one-third on investor measures. Sears recognizes that despite knowing "vastly more than we once did," it will have to continually evolve its model because "it tells us less than we would like to know—and less, probably, than we need to know."[15]

Such modesty reflects wisdom. Few companies today have the precise insights about what creates value for shareholders that Sears has developed. Once a company gains such insights, however, managers know a lot about very important things that create value in their companies. They simply then have to consider reporting them to shareholders.

Things Don't Always Work Out That Way

Data, of course, don't always confirm hypotheses, so managers may find that their numbers don't support the relationships they assumed existed among measures. This can happen for two reasons.

First, they are simply using the wrong business model. Certain measures just don't have predictive value because there is no cause-and-effect relationship. In this case, management has gained a very valuable insight and should rethink the business model. That's the bad news. The good news comes from the advantage of having already collected a lot of performance information that can be used to test alternative models. This is a very tangible example of organizational learning.

Second, managers may not be able to empirically verify the business model because certain measures are not valid. They do not properly capture the underlying phenomena that management wants to understand. In this situation, there actually is a cause-and-effect relationship, but measurement problems have obscured it.

For example, customer penetration and market share may actually be related, but the relationship is not evident when the company measures customer penetration in terms of the number of products customers purchased. Had management measured customer penetration in terms of the number of products its customers purchased from the company and didn't purchase from any other supplier, the relationship might indeed have been proven.

Use Your Judgment

Determining whether the lack of a strong empirical relationship reflects a problem with the model or with the measurement may prove difficult. In such cases, management must exercise its best judgment. Developing rigorous business models with the proper measures doesn't supplant judgment; it informs judgment. Rigorous thinking doesn't substitute for intuition and risk taking; it makes both of them better.

Managers must also exercise judgment in determining whether a model has become inappropriate or irrelevant. Just because a set of cause-and-effect relationships exists doesn't mean that they always will. The competitive dynamics of industries change.

Going for market share may be appropriate in the early stages of an industry; many Internet firms have employed such a strategy. At a certain point, however, management may need to shift the emphasis to innovation and new product development to ensure that it can continue to offer high-margin products to the existing customer base. Maintaining this customer base and serving its needs as completely as possible may prove far more profitable than spending more money to gain market share by adding customers at the margin.

If managers continue to apply the same business model—however well defined and empirically demonstrated—in an uncritical manner, that business model can actually become a mental straitjacket. Waiting to change it until the empirical relationships no longer exist is waiting too long. By then, the company will have lost its competitive advantage to another company that may have only the rudiments of a business model. A primitive but correct model beats a sophisticated one that is wrong. Managers should constantly question their business model, or they may find it's too late to change.

If management explains its business model to analysts and investors, it can also benefit from their feedback about whether the model is the right one. This assumes, of course, that management will listen. The greater transparency called for in ValueReporting works both ways. Tell the market more; listen to it better. Chapter 10 says a lot about how to do this and why.

CAN WE AGREE?

Once managers have developed the business model and verified its measures, they not only have a substantial amount of very useful performance information, they can consider reporting it to investors. Will investors pay any attention? Do they *really* care about anything other than next quarter's earnings?

In their study of Intel mentioned earlier, Miller and O'Leary found that both technical and financial analysts shared management's view that a measure called "die yield" was extremely important. One analyst remarked that it was becoming even more so because of price competition. In this instance, management and the market held a similar view of the importance of a key nonfinancial measure.

Intel is not an exception. This book offers substantial evidence that the market does care about a lot of measures other than the traditional financial ones. Chapter 7 makes this especially clear in reporting on the results of our high-tech industry survey. It also shows that managers do a relatively poor job of providing information to analysts and investors. Companies, however, do a much better job of providing information on the bottom line and a few other key financial measures, but on little else that really matters.

Answer the Question

Does this mean that *not a single* company does a good job of satisfying the information needs of its investors? Each company has to answer this question for itself as objectively and nondefensively as possible. To arrive at the complete answer, a company actually has to answer five other questions first:

1. Are the measures that are important to management also important to the market?
2. Does management know all the measures the market considers important?
3. Do internal systems provide reliable information on each important measure?
4. Does management think it does a good job of reporting information on these measures?
5. How satisfied is the market with the information it gets?

The answers to these questions will tell management whether the market agrees that the company's business model(s) can explain how value is created. If the company does business in distinctly different sectors, it may need to create a number of different models.

Business Models versus Financial Models

Here, we want to explicitly distinguish between a *business model,* which includes all relevant financial and nonfinancial measures (Exhibit 1.2), and a *financial model,* which focuses solely on the financial portion of the business model. Most analysts and investors use only financial models because they

can construct them more easily and get the required information from public sources or from the company directly. The nonfinancial information they
use is essentially captured in the assumptions made in projections (e.g.,
growth rates) and risk (e.g., discount rates). Few analysts or investors attempt
to construct a model even vaguely resembling the one shown in Exhibit 1.2.

The ValueReporting Capital Markets Survey

One of the most effective ways to determine the extent to which management and the market agree on a business model is through a research instrument called the ValueReporting Capital Markets Survey. At the core of
this instrument is a list of performance measures that management regards
as important or potentially important. The obvious starting point for constructing such a list is internal balanced scorecards and management information reports. For completeness, a few analysts and investors should review
this list of measures. The survey can also include other questions that address such factors as:

- The usefulness of the company's financial reports and website
- The nature of the company's disclosure policies
- The effectiveness of individual and group meetings
- The perceptions investors have of sell-side analysts
- The benefits of better disclosure

Once constructed, the questionnaire is then completed by senior
management team members and some leading analysts and investors.
Supplementing the quantitative results with insights gained from in-
depth interviews with selected analysts and investors adds more meaning
to the findings.

Companies may also want to include the board of directors as a separately surveyed group. Both senior management and the members themselves pay too little attention to determining the board's information
needs. The survey offers a good way of remedying that. Chapter 12 addresses in greater detail the role the board plays in the ValueReporting
Revolution.

The survey produces objective and quantitative data on the capital
market's satisfaction with the information it gets. Companies rarely seek to
learn this in such a complete and rigorous fashion. Ironically, they often
conduct surveys to determine customer and employee satisfaction. Why
shouldn't they solicit shareholder feedback as well?

By looking at differences within groups, management can see how much of a consensus exists. This is especially interesting and important for ascertaining whether all of a group's members really agree on a common business model. Of course, these data alone are not conclusive. Considered in isolation, for example, the data reveal only whether the members of the management team attach the same level of importance to the measures listed on the survey; they reveal very little about the deeper cause-and-effect relationships between measures. Determining that requires further discussion, which can be structured around the survey results.

Nevertheless, such a survey yields some immediate benefit by identifying a potential lack of clarity about strategy and the management team's lack of a commonly shared business model. Understanding how the market looks at you reveals a lot about how you look at yourself.

FORGET THE MYTH OF SWISS NEUTRALITY

Swiss Re, one of the world's leading reinsurers headquartered in Switzerland, got a head start on the ValueReporting Revolution when it agreed to allow PricewaterhouseCoopers to conduct a ValueReporting Capital Markets Survey in late 1998. In fact, an internal initiative had already been launched, which then was combined with the PricewaterhouseCoopers project. At that time the company had a fairly new CEO, Walter Kielholz, on board for less than two years, and a new CFO, John Fitzpatrick, appointed just that year. Both had a great deal of interest in continuing to increase the company's transparency, an effort that had begun in the early 1990s and was further "pressed forward" in 1994 under the former CEO, Lukas Muhlemann, when he took over this classically secretive Swiss financial institution.

Under Kielholz, the company developed balanced scorecards for internal purposes and began reporting in U.S. Generally Accepted Accounting Principles (GAAP) as an additional framework for internal reporting. This effort was aimed at instilling better internal financial discipline, providing more useful information to investors, and supporting the option of a potential future listing in the United States, if and when necessary and desirable.

In collaboration with the Swiss Re people involved in the already initiated project and Swiss Re's investor relations function, we developed a questionnaire that listed 56 performance measures divided into the five groups: financial performance, capital management, customers/markets, organization/processes, and human resources. Surveys were completed by 13 Swiss Re senior executives, 29 sell-side analysts, and 42 institutional investors, most of them sampled from the top 109 shareholders, who owned 58 percent of the company's registered shares.

The results of the survey generated an abundance of useful insights:

- Swiss Re executives regarded all five groups of measures as equally important.
- Executives rated nonfinancial measures more important than analysts and investors did.
- Executives perceived that the company did not very actively report information on the "human resources" and the "customers/markets" measures.
- Executives felt that internal systems for consistently measuring "customers/markets" worldwide needed substantial improvement.
- Analysts and investors were most dissatisfied with the information they received on "capital management."
- All respondent groups agreed on the major benefits of better disclosure: increased credibility of management, increased share price, increased number of long-term investors, and reduced cost of capital.

The survey findings identified three important financial measures on which, management admitted, Swiss Re provided very little information to the market, even though they recognized the market had an interest in them: economic profit, risk-adjusted capital, and embedded value. Kielholz and Fitzpatrick decided that embedded value, essentially the present value of life insurance contract portfolios, which will produce accounting earnings for many years, was the financial measure that would be of most use to the market. A 1999 global survey of major life insurance companies, which is discussed later in this book, confirmed the importance of embedded value more generally. Swiss Re decided to defer expanded disclosures concerning economic profit and risk-adjusted capital, mainly because there is no generally accepted method in use in the marketplace today for calculating such measures, even though Swiss Re calculates them extensively for its own internal management use.

Swiss Re realized that before it could start reporting information on embedded value, it needed a more stable and globally consistent measure than it currently used for internal purposes only. As Fitzpatrick noted: "Public disclosures must pass an exacting standard. The measure must reflect only changes in real economic value, not changes in accounting systems that sometimes occur around the world. Management can evaluate and accept such non-economic changes in value, but the public markets cannot."[16]

By February 2000, the company was comfortable enough with the measures it had of embedded value that it publicly committed to report the 1999 embedded value numbers in February 2001, to be followed by the 2000 figures a few months after that. Such disclosure currently falls well outside the realm of typical reporting reviewed by independent accountants. The growing importance of such information, however, has led to increased scrutiny from many quarters. Kielholz remained adamant the company must ensure that such information is subject to suitable control, review, and audit-type procedures. He also noted the importance of this in light of its use in compensation programs.

Kielholz recognized that once Swiss Re began publicly reporting information on embedded value or other additional measures, there was no going back. He commented, "Once it's out there, you can't get rid of it." Rather than seeing this as a burden, both he and Fitzpatrick saw clear benefit in doing so. They felt that publishing embedded value-oriented and other key targets and results would drive changes in behavior among employees and investors. First, internal managers would pay more attention to the company's important value drivers as this was published externally. Second, investors, relieved of the burden of guessing at the embedded value, could instead focus their time and attention on estimating the value of the franchise that generates the growth in embedded value.

Voluntarily providing information on embedded value was only one element in Swiss Re's much broader program of improved disclosure. In August 2000, both top executives reviewed with us a program that Kielholz described as going "way beyond reported earnings" and said it was a program they planned to implement over the next 18 months.

The program included new types of information, new ways of delivering it, and much more active communication with analysts and investors by Kielholz, Fitzpatrick, and other senior company executives. In discussing the program, both executives expressed their strong belief that it was the right thing to do even though they did not expect to see any impact of the increased disclosure reflected explicitly in their stock price in the short term. Fitzpatrick noted that "increased ValueReporting is a long journey" and that both performance and how clearly the company reported it would ultimately determine Swiss Re's stock price.

The company had clearly moved in the right direction. Since taking over as CEO, Kielholz had seen Swiss Re's stock price rise from SF1429 at the end of 1996 to SF3581 at the end of 1998. Reflecting the volatility of the reinsurance industry and the volatility in the markets as a whole (discussed in the next chapter) Swiss Re's stock price then fell to below SF2800 by May 9, 2000, the day before it announced its earnings for 1999. By the end of August 2000, however, the stock was trading back in the range of SF3500, reaching a high of SF3808 in mid-November 2000. Exhibit 1.5 shows the rise in Swiss Re's stock price, culminating in two "strong buy" recommendations from major investment banks, which pushed both the stock price and volume higher.

During this same period, the company had increased its level of transparency in a variety of ways, including the publication of some impressive figures on cost management and a performance matrix of targets on a number of dimensions. This transparency in content was matched by a labor-intensive and transparent process that involved Kielholz, Fitzpatrick, and a number of other top Swiss Re executives. During the month of May they met with a total of 162 investors and analysts, as Exhibit 1.6 shows, to talk about their performance and their plans, and to answer any questions raised.

Also during this time period external circumstances had been favor-

Exhibit 1.5

Swiss Re Share Price Movement, Year 2000

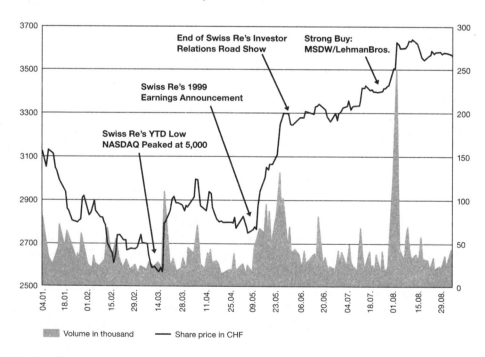

Source: Swiss Re

Exhibit 1.6

Swiss Re Investor Relations Schedule, May 2000

Date	Place	Type	Number of Investors[a]	Swiss Re Participants
10 May	Zurich	Analysts' meeting Presentation	Attendance: 38 Sell side 6 Buy side 17 institutions (Call-in)	Swiss Re Executive Management
12 May	Geneva	Presentation	25 Institutions 6 Institutions (at luncheon)	CEO
16/17 May	London	2 Presentations 8 One-on-ones	20 Institutions 9 Institutions	CEO, CFO, Investor Relations
18/19 May	New York/Boston	9 One-on-ones	10 Institutions	CEO, Corporate Finance
22 May	New York	5 One-on-ones	6 Institutions	CEO, Corporate Finance
22 May	Frankfurt	1 Presentation 2 One-on-ones	6 Institutions 2 Institutions	CFO, Investor Relations
23 May	Stockholm/ Amsterdam	2 Presentations 2 One-on-ones	17 Institutions 2 Institutions	CFO, Investor Relations
24 May	Milan	5 One-on-ones	6 Institutions	Europe Division Head, Corporate Finance
25 May	Paris	2 Presentations 1 One-on-one	14 Institutions 1 Institution	Europe Division Head, Corporate Finance
Totals		9 Presentations 32 One-on-ones	17 U.S. Investors 38 U.K. Investors 107 Cont. Europe Investors **162 Total in 10 days**	

[a] Institutions

Source: Swiss Re

able. For example, the market had expectations that the U.S. Federal Reserve had stopped raising interest rates for the time being, a clear boon to the stocks of financial companies. There were also clear signs that the nonlife insurance industry would raise prices. Kielholz and Fitzpatrick both believed that the combination of a better external environment, better performance, and better reporting had led to a higher stock price. And although neither pretended to know how much weight should be attributed to each of these factors, both were convinced that better reporting was helping the company get the full benefit of better performance and a better external business environment.

Part Two

A Survey of the Battlefield

The facts will eventually test all our theories, and they form, after all, the only impartial jury to which we can appeal.

Jean Louis Rodolphe Agassiz, *Geological Sketches*

Where Has All the Value Gone?

Reality is things as they are.
Wallace Stevens, *The Necessary Angel*

The market is in the dark—or at least dim—when it comes to establishing stock prices. It simply doesn't have or can't get the kind of information it needs to value companies properly or accurately. The results? Extreme volatility. Arguments about the relative valuations of Old Economy and New Economy companies. And an unhealthy concentration of value in a small number of companies of both types—typically those for which a great deal of information is available. Heed the consequence: a less than optimal allocation of capital in terms of the trade-off of risk and return.

These conditions foreshadow revolution. Whenever great fractures occur in an established order, pressures come to bear for great change. Wide swings in sentiment, an unequal distribution of wealth and power, and questions about who contributes to the common good, all mean that the status quo cannot go unchallenged.

This does not mean that the current regime is completely without moral justification. After all, the market does use a lot of information when it prices a company's shares. But a decreasing proportion of that information, especially what a company reports, relates clearly to intrinsic value—what a company is "really" worth. Instead, when it comes to setting market prices, chat room rumors and gossip, earnings surprises, external events, and market sentiment now outweigh in importance the kind of performance information companies currently provide.

Momentum investors accept this as a fact of life. In fact, it *is* life for them. As long as they can stay ahead of the curve on rumors, gossip, surprises, external events, and overall market sentiment, they will make money. Many others regard this as no different than playing the lottery.

Investors who follow a different investment strategy—value or growth or whatever—look for information that enables them to make their own calls about whether, over the long term, a company's stock is overvalued or undervalued. These investors need quality information not easily available today because the traditional financial measures covered by accounting regulations contribute less and less to their understanding of a stock's real value. The result is big questions about values in the market and what determines them.

VOLATILITY IN VALUES

The headlines during the first half of 2000 impart a vivid sense of how much volatility exists in the U.S. markets today: "Roller-Coaster Markets,"[1] "Stocks Fall Off a Cliff—and Climb Back,"[2] "Mercurial Markets,"[3] "A White-Knuckle Ride,"[4] "A Test of Nerves,"[5] "After Market's Wild Quarter, the Future Is Just a Guess,"[6] and "The Diary of a Mad Quarter."[7] Vivid, yes, but mere words fall short of the gut-churning reality experienced on the market floors.

April 4, 2000

The most dramatic day in that remarkable time period. At 1:18 P.M. the NASDAQ Composite Index was down 574.57 points, almost 14 percent, on a total trading volume of 2.79 billion shares—significantly exceeding the previous record of 2.19 billion set just one month earlier. Three minutes later, at 1:21 P.M., investors across all exchanges saw a cumulative paper loss of about $1.19 trillion in market value. Little more than one hour later, the NASDAQ index had recovered 451.84 points and closed the day down only 74.79, slightly less than 2 percent.[8] A real head-scratcher.

In economic theory, a company's stock price is the net present value of future cash flows. Could the future prospects of so many NASDAQ companies really have changed so dramatically in a single day? Had the market reacted to a piece of news in the morning, like an announcement of a new technology that would make the Internet irrelevant, and then learned in the afternoon that the rumor was false? Did every NASDAQ company on this one-day roller coaster fall prey to an unforeseen set of whipsaw forces, first for the worse and then for the better? Did investors pull out their spreadsheets and calculate declining future cash flows in the morning, only to calculate them back up right after lunch?

Of course not. Such a high degree of volatility had little or nothing to do with information about the listed companies' fundamentals. Something else—like momentum investing, buying on margin, low-cost online trading, and chat room speculations—had sparked it. Would providing a broader range of quality information about true underlying performance make these forces of volatility go away? Probably not, but it would mitigate them.

Two Exciting Years

Those who think that the volatility of April 4, 2000, was an aberration and that no firm conclusions about its causes can be drawn would rightfully suggest taking a look at the NASDAQ's performance over a longer period of time. Indulge them; take a look at Exhibit 2.1. In the course of less than two years, the NASDAQ went from 2,000 to 5,000, down to almost 3,000, and back to 4,000 less than one month after that. Just to put that level of volatility into real-time perspective, consider that both the high and low levels occurred during the two months we were working on this chapter.

The NASDAQ Composite Index, with its concentration of New Economy high-tech stocks, has earned the dubious distinction as America's most volatile index. But it certainly doesn't hold the patent on turbulence. The

Exhibit 2.1

Value Milestones of the NASDAQ Composite Index and Yahoo!

NASDAQ Milestone	Date Reached	Yahoo!'s Stock Price[a]
100	2/05/71	Pre Yahoo!
1000	7/17/95	Pre Yahoo!
2000	7/16/98	187
3000	11/03/99	181
4000	12/29/99	404
4500	2/17/00	163
5000	3/10/00	178
5000	3/24/00	194
4500	3/30/00	170
4500	4/03/00	160
3500	5/11/00	125
3042[b]	5/24/00	123
4000	6/20/00	148

[a] At close of trading day
[b] NASDAQ low, year 2000 through July 31, 2000

traditionally staid Dow Jones Industrial Average and S&P 500 have had their own shares of extreme volatility—often in the opposite direction of the NASDAQ—as investor sentiment swung back and forth between the growth stocks of the New Economy and the value stocks of the Old Economy. The largest one-day swings from high to low on both the Dow Jones Industrial[9] and NASDAQ[10] Composite indices occurred on the same day— April 4, 2000.

Yahoo! Too!

While the volatility of the major U.S. stock exchanges has been high, that of individual stocks has been even higher. Exhibit 2.1 also shows Yahoo!'s stock price as one of the key NASDAQ milestones. Between July 1998 and December 1999, the company had a very good year and a half. Its stock more than doubled from 187 to 404, creating value of approximately $118 billion for its shareholders. It then had a very bad two and a half months when the stock price fell to 163 on February 17, 2000, losing approximately $131 billion in shareholder value.[11] On May 24, 2000, when NASDAQ hit its low point year-to-date, Yahoo! closed at 123.

No doubt some of this stock price volatility resulted from the difficulty the market has in coming to terms with the Internet phenomenon and one of its most prominent members' prospects. Bouts of optimism and pessimism are only natural in such circumstances. The causes of these bouts, of course, can differ for the market as a whole and for individual companies. Exhibit 2.1 provides evidence of that. For example, during Yahoo!'s bad two and a half months, the NASDAQ as a whole actually went from 4,000 to 4,500.

The fact that Yahoo! only went public in April 1996 and has a limited operating history serves to compound this problem. Yet, on that exciting day of April 4, Yahoo!'s stock fell from a high of $171 to about $133 and then recovered to about $167 at the end of the day, suggesting that more than rational analysis based on performance information goes into explaining Yahoo!'s stock price volatility.

The Beta Test

Not unexpectedly, New Economy companies encounter higher volatility than their Old Economy counterparts. A traditional measure of a company's stock price volatility is its beta. Stocks with betas of less than 1.0 are less volatile than the market as a whole; the reverse is true for stocks with betas of greater than 1.0. General Motors, for example, has a beta of 0.99. Cisco

Systems, however, has a beta of 1.45, which is relatively high. Yahoo!'s was 3.45 in mid-July 2000.

The average beta for the 25 New York Stock Exchange companies with the largest market caps is 1.11. Their NASDAQ counterparts have an average beta of 1.46. Some large-cap high-tech companies have even higher ones. In mid-2000, Amazon.com's was 2.63. Arguably, the younger and smaller high-tech stocks, for which a reliable beta cannot even be calculated, will likely experience even greater volatility than their more established, large-cap counterparts.

One of the reasons for this greater volatility is that the traditional financial measures of earnings and cash flow are much less meaningful for high-tech companies. Furthermore, as discussed in Chapter 3, no consensus has emerged on how to value companies that have negative earnings and cash flow. As a result, other bits of information become extremely important. Unfortunately, the market has a hard time distinguishing between reliable and unreliable information in the short term, causing an extraordinary amount of volatility.

Volatility and Transparency

It would be naïve to assert that even total transparency regarding all the performance measures used to manage the company would eliminate volatility. It won't. Volatility caused by forces that are information independent will continue. These forces will and should affect stock prices. The question is how to find the right balance between value-relevant internal information and value-relevant external information.

Just as more information can reduce the perceived risk of an investment, it can also reduce uncertainty about a company's future prospects, and this can lessen volatility to some extent. For companies to gain the benefit of greater market confidence, however, they need to provide information that the market believes is important in creating value.

Doing so represents a major challenge for most companies. Much of the information the market wants is nonfinancial, and a consensus has yet to emerge on how best to measure and report such information. It also demands a major change in how and what companies report. Change rarely comes easily. Sometimes it requires a revolution.

RELATIVE VALUES

On March 27, 2000, Cisco Systems, the New Economy paragon, became the most valuable company in the world, achieving a market capitalization of

$555.44 billion after only 10 years as a publicly traded company. On that same day, General Motors, a 91-year stalwart of the Old Economy, had a market cap of about $88.19 billion. (See box below.)

A month earlier, analyst Paul Weinstein of Credit Suisse First Boston had forecast that Cisco Systems would become the world's first company worth $1 trillion.[12] That this New Economy supplier of hardware and services for the Internet had displaced Microsoft as the world's most valuable company—and achieved a market value more than five times greater than General Motors—seems all the more remarkable because it took little more than a decade to accomplish.

Fast forward to May 2, 2000. Four-year-old Amazon.com—which went public in July 1997—with its cumulative life losses of $1.19 billion, had a market cap of $19.6 billion. That's about 25 percent of the $78 billion market cap of Procter & Gamble on that same day, a company that has been in

---

Go Figure

By all that traditional accounting holds dear and true, it just doesn't add up. But on March 27, 2000, the New Economy's Cisco Systems had a market cap of $555.44 billion, more than five times greater than that of the Old Economy's General Motors, which had a total market cap of about $88.19 billion.

General Motors' lower value, about 16 percent of Cisco's, came despite the fact that the automobile manufacturer had higher earnings in 1999. In roughly the same period, GM earned $5.59 billion (net income ending June 2000), while Cisco earned $2.56 billion for the trailing 12 months (net income ending April 2000). Yet the price/earnings multiple on GM's earnings of 6.54 was far below Cisco's P/E ratio of 194.23.[a]

Furthermore, General Motors had assets of $274.73 billion[b] on its balance sheet compared to Cisco's $21.39 billion.[c] So 10 times as many assets in an accounting sense generated one-fifth as much value, a truly breathtaking difference.

GM's book value per share of $33.33 equates to a price/book ratio of 2.55, while Cisco's book value/share of $2.40 equates to a price/book ratio of 33.35.[d] It can be inferred that most of the differential in price/book ratios is due to the difference in intangibles not required to be valued and disclosed by current GAAP standards.

---

a. Yahoo! Finance, http://finance.yahoo.com
b. General Motors Corporation 1999 Annual Report.
c. Cisco Systems 1/29/2000 10-Q.
d. Yahoo! Finance, http://yahoo.marketguide.com

business since 1837 and has had an uninterrupted record of paying dividends since its incorporation in 1890. The dividends per share have increased every year since 1955. Even more impressive, the company has shown a profit every year except 1921, because of an inventory write down, and fiscal year 1992–1993, because of a restructuring charge.

But these New Economy valuations can go the other way as well. By June 30, 2000, Amazon.com's market cap had dropped to approximately $13 billion whereas Procter & Gamble's held steady at about $75 billion. Other examples abound of young, recently gone public Internet companies with no earnings to speak of whose market value exceeds that of established companies that have been generating earnings for decades.

Although admittedly dramatic, the comparisons between Cisco Systems and General Motors and between Amazon.com and Procter & Gamble vividly illustrate a debate that started when New Economy companies began to achieve market values that vastly exceeded Old Economy ones. These are strong companies that have been around for many more years, have solid earnings track records, and have lots of hard assets on their balance sheets. Were the New Economy companies being overvalued? Were the Old Economy companies being undervalued? Were both true?

As the pendulum swung in the direction of New Economy companies, their supporters said the market was rewarding those companies for their central role in helping to bring this New Economy into being. They also said the market recognized the declining competitive advantage, or even competitive disadvantage, of brick-and-mortar companies that were poorly positioned for this new world and were adjusting to it at a lethargic pace. These venerable old companies had lower valuations for good reason: They were worth less.

Then, as the pendulum swung in the other direction, critics of high valuations for New Economy companies said that a speculative bubble was finally about to burst. Investors were in a "flight to quality." Bottom-line earnings performance still mattered. And twenty-somethings with no business experience were about to get their comeuppance. These critics also noted that the line between new and old had blurred as New Economy companies used their high stock prices to acquire hard assets, and Old Economy companies used their positive cash flows to build Internet capabilities.

As with volatility, this debate arises from the inevitable uncertainty that accompanies the kind of transformation going on in the business landscape today. It also has its roots in old methodologies for measuring performance and determining value, which haven't kept up with the transformation. This is as true for the New Economy start-ups as for the Old Economy stalwarts.

Debating the Numbers

Can a bit of quantitative analysis inform this rather heated debate? The answer turns out to be rather ambiguous, suggesting that we don't have all the right numbers to do the analysis. Since earnings and earnings growth are among the most common measures for evaluating stock prices, we'll start there. When both the price/earnings (P/E) ratio and expected earnings growth are high by historical standards, it suggests that either values are unreasonable or that earnings no longer have the relevance they once had. We will deal with unreasonableness in Chapter 3 and irrelevance in Chapter 4.

For now, refer back to Exhibit 2.1 to see just how quickly the tech-heavy NASDAQ, on which many of the most notable of the New Economy companies are listed, has generated tremendous value. The NASDAQ Composite Index soared from 2,000 to 5,000 in less than two years, a two-and-a-half-fold increase. In the prior three-year period, it had doubled from 1,000 to 2,000. Yet NASDAQ stocks had taken the previous 24 years to inch from 100 to 1,000. This suggests that the New Economy's emergence in full force is quite a recent phenomenon. It's not surprising that so much debate swirls about valuations and how to determine them, or that so much volatility exists.

The tremendous gains in New Economy stocks made the respectable gains in Old Economy stocks pale by comparison. Remembering that the long-term growth in equity values hovers around 11 percent, compare that to the 84.3 percent gain in the NASDAQ Composite in 1999 alone, the Dow Jones's 25.2 percent gain, and the 19.6 percent gain in the S&P 500. Between January 1, 1995, and January 1, 2000, the NASDAQ gained more than 450 percent, the Dow Jones gained nearly 200 percent, and the S&P 500 gained 217 percent.

Higher earnings growth in the high-tech sector accounts at least in part for why the New Economy stocks performed so well. *The Financial Post* quoted Bruce Steinberg, chief economist at Merrill Lynch & Co. in New York, as saying, "The U.S. tech sector is displaying much faster sales and earnings growth than the overall economy." He also said he expected technology earnings to increase by 30 percent during 2000 compared to 10 percent for nontech companies.[13]

This offers good evidence to support high high-tech valuations. In the 1980s, the earnings of high-tech companies grew at 3 percent per year compared to 9 percent for the rest of the market. By the 1990s, high-tech company earnings were growing twice as fast as the market as a whole.[14]

The expectation that such high earnings growth can continue contributes to high P/E ratios, further boosting the value of a stock. In July 2000, the 100 biggest stocks on the NASDAQ traded at a multiple of about

90 compared to about 20 for the Dow Jones stocks. One dollar of earnings for these 100 NASDAQ companies had four and one-half times the worth of the same dollar on the Dow Jones.

As recently as 1995, the P/E ratios of both Old and New Economy companies were about the same as for the Dow Jones Industrial Average stocks today, right around 20.[15] By the end of 1999, the 432 nontech stocks in the S&P 500 were priced at an average of 22 times next 12-month earnings, less than half that of the other 68 technology stocks, which had an average P/E ratio of 47.[16]

Show Me the Money

Such unprecedented P/E multiples for high-tech companies, even assuming that expected earnings growth will continue and that the multiple is justified, seem all the more remarkable given the decline in investors' expectations for dividends. The average dividend yield—annual dividend per share divided by the current stock price per share—in the 1980s was 4.2 percent. By 1999, it had gone down to 1.14 percent.[17] Investors, rather than expecting cash dividends on stocks they intended to hold for some time, now look primarily for capital gains on stock price appreciation. This increases their risk. Rather than getting some cash in their pocket at the end of every quarter, they rely almost completely on selling the stock for more than they bought it for, in volatile markets to boot.

Not surprisingly, this lack of dividends holds especially true for high-tech stocks. Many of these companies have a policy of paying no dividends at all, figuring the money is better spent on investing in new technologies and acquisitions to grow revenues and to defend and strengthen their competitive positions. None of the companies in the ISDEX (Internet stock index) paid any dividends at all in either 1998 or 1999.

Cash later, not now, will be the *de facto* investment strategy of anybody who buys stock in such companies, except, of course, for momentum investors who believe they can successfully anticipate and act quickly to take advantage of market movements in the short term. Those "exceptional" investors aside, most others need a longer-term view of intrinsic value—one that looks beyond short-term volatility—and sufficient information to decide whether a stock is worth what they'll have to pay for it.

CONCENTRATION OF VALUE

Extreme volatility and a lively debate about the relative valuations of Old and New Economy companies provide two good reasons to question the accuracy with which today's markets set stock prices. A third, albeit more subtle reason, is the high degree of concentration in market value.

Just as concentration in market share can be measured in product markets, it can be measured in capital markets as well. And value in the capital markets is extremely concentrated. A very small percentage of companies accounts for a large proportion of total market value. At the end of 1999, for example, 5 percent of the companies listed on the NASDAQ, which is heavily weighted with high-tech, accounted for 75 percent of the total market value of all the companies listed. The top 10 companies alone accounted for about 56 percent of market value.[18] As Exhibit 2.2 shows, this concentration in value is a worldwide phenomenon with high concentrations in markets as far-flung as Toronto, São Paulo, Deutsche Börse, Paris, Hong Kong, and Switzerland.

Exhibit 2.2

Concentration in Value in Selected Markets Worldwide

Exchange	Percentage of Total Market Value in Top 5% of Companies	Percentage of Total Market Value in Top 10 Companies
NASDAQ	75	56
NYSE	67	23
Toronto	73	41
Buenos Aires	63	76
Sao Paulo	64	44
Amsterdam	72	92
Deutsche Börse	80	54
Italy	61	55
London	80	38
Madrid	76	60
Paris	81	42
Switzerland	79	75
Australia	77	46
Hong Kong	84	68
Korea	80	59
Taiwan	54	37
Tokyo	69	30

Source: International Federation of Stock Exchanges

Even though concentration is high, the possibility exists that it can actually increase. E.S. Browning, in a November 8, 1999, article in *The Wall Street Journal*, "Handful of U.S. Stocks Drive NASDAQ Index Gains," points out that the 40 percent gain in that index over the previous month could be credited to three stocks: Microsoft, Cisco Systems, and Intel. Add MCI WorldCom and Sun Microsystems and you have a full 50 percent of the total gain. When the growth in value becomes concentrated in a small number of companies, the total concentration in the market will increase over time. The rich get richer; the poor have lots of company.

For those rich lucky few, it's a self-fulfilling prophecy. Their increasing stock prices attract more analysts and investors, which in turn boosts stock prices even higher. More analysts following a company means that more information is being generated about it. When this information is positive, as it often is, more investors are attracted as well. As value increases, index investors must increase their positions to keep the proper weightings, further propelling the stock upward.

Retail investors can have the same effect as they attempt to get on the bandwagon. They talk about the stock to their friends. The media pays more and more attention to the company. Attention and valuation reinforce each other in an ugly but intended circle, although the circle is easily broken, as Chapter 4 will describe.

Impact of P/E Ratios on Concentration

Concentration in value correlates highly with differences in P/E ratios. In February 2000, the top 20 percent of the S&P 500 had a median P/E ratio of 70.8, nearly five times (4.8) that of the other 80 percent's median P/E of 14.7. This ratio of ratios of 4.8 compares to the historical average of 2.2, which has remained consistent for the past 30 years through market peaks and plunges with only a few exceptions like the early 1970s.[19]

The concentration of value in firms with extremely high P/E ratios also holds true for the market as a whole today. The most expensive 10 percent of stocks in the Wilshire 5000 Index, which includes nearly all (7,200) U.S. publicly traded companies, accounts for approximately 75 percent of the total value on that index. That small number of companies had a P/E ratio of 41.2 in January 2000 compared to 22.6 for the remaining 90 percent.[20] Obviously, many small- and mid-cap companies have been left out of the greatest bull market in U.S. history.

If the historical averages for P/E ratios still hold true, today's market places far too much value in a small number of firms by according them extremely high P/E ratios. According to the February 24, 2000, issue of *The Wall Street Journal*, a Sanford C. Bernstein research report concludes that: "The current era exceeds any in our database in both concentration and valuation, making the risk of this setting unprecedented."[21]

Thus, questions about concentration and valuation are closely related. High valuations driven by high P/E ratios lead to an especially high concentration of value in a small number of companies. The managers in the dominant ones are satisfied with the market's valuation of their shares. Most managers in the rest of the companies think the market undervalues them.

Are Market Values Fair Values?

In a survey of CFOs and heads of investor relations in 200 large U.S. companies, conducted by Market & Opinion Research International (MORI) for PricewaterhouseCoopers, 61 percent of the respondents felt that their companies' stocks were undervalued. Another 31 percent felt that their stocks were properly valued, and only 5 percent felt that the stocks were overvalued. Despite the fact that the Dow Jones had risen 5.4 percent and the NASDAQ 28.2 percent between December 3, 1998, and January 29, 1999, many executives thought their companies' shares were undervalued—even in a raging bull market.

This same phenomenon exists in the high-tech industry—and even more dramatically. A PricewaterhouseCoopers survey of high-tech companies in the United States and Canada found that most of those companies' executives also thought their shares were undervalued. Only 18 percent thought their share prices were about right. Another 45 percent thought their shares were slightly undervalued, with 30 percent of the opinion that theirs were strongly undervalued. Just 1 percent thought their shares were slightly overvalued and no one thought they were strongly overvalued. (Believe it or not, 5 percent had no opinion.) Mind you, these data were collected during a major market correction—mid-2000. But, at the time of the survey, many people maintained that a still larger correction was yet to happen.

WHO'S RIGHT?

Managers, who often have stock options and are only human, generally tend to place their company's worth higher than the market does. (What parents don't think their children are exceptional?) Perhaps they are right, and the market *does* in fact undervalue their company's shares. After all, these managers have information about their company that the market doesn't. Only with such information could the market make a reasonable determination of stock value.

Managers also have a detailed understanding of their company's current performance and know their future plans for creating value. If the market had equal access to this information and reached a different conclusion, managers' perceptions that shares are undervalued could be explained away as delusional self-interest. After all, sometimes the market does get it right. It doesn't value a company's shares very highly because very little value is being created.

But the market can get it wrong as well, and it often does so because it lacks the right kind of information. That lack leads to uncertainty and results in more conservative projections of revenues, earnings, and cash flows. Uncertainty can also increase the perception of risk, which results in a higher discount rate being applied to profit projections because of the higher cost of capital. The outcome is a lower stock price than might be justified if more and different information were available.

Of course, uncertainty and lack of information sometimes contribute to higher market values. Remember the market's torrid, but quickly cooled, love affair with the dot-coms?

WHOSE JOB IS IT ANYWAY?

Some of the responsibility for the lack of information about a company lies with the sell-side analysts and their employers, the investment banking firms. They're the ones that took so many high-tech companies public with promises of extensive and frequent research analyst coverage. Then once the initial public offering (IPO) was completed, the banks and their promises slipped away overnight. In our high-tech survey referenced earlier, two-thirds of the companies reported that five or fewer analysts followed them; only 6 percent reported being followed by more than 20 analysts.

But no one is forcing these companies to rely exclusively on sell-side analysts to report performance information to investors. The companies can take on the responsibility themselves. Those that abrogate this responsibility do so at their own peril. High-tech company executives themselves admit they don't aggressively provide information on key performance measures like market growth, speed to market with new products, and revenues from new products. Yet, both the executives and the investors in our survey considered all of these measures as very important. This is discussed in more detail in Chapter 7.

In extreme cases, a lack of information about a company can cause an investor to avoid investing in its stock at all. A recent survey conducted for *Investor Relations Magazine* by Rivel Research Group provides the evidence. Of 1,700 investment professionals surveyed (sell-side analysts, buy-side analysts, portfolio managers, etc.), 78 percent said they did not recommend or invest in a stock because of inadequate information.[22]

Such behavior on the part of investors and the analysts who want to guide them reduces the liquidity of a company's shares and increases the bid/ask spread. The stock becomes an even riskier investment relative to expected returns, which further reduces the interest of potential investors. Thus, the virtuous circle turns vicious, and a large number of small and middle market companies, without the good fortune of being high-tech, have felt its bite.

The implications are clear. Executives who feel that their company's shares are being undervalued should seriously consider if it's because of a lack of information. If they don't think that's the case, those executives simply must accept that the market is completely irrational and patiently wait and hope that it will regain its senses soon.

3

Analyze This

Facts do not cease to exist because they are ignored.
Aldous Huxley, *Proper Studies*

It's a classic dilemma: Should you invest in the stock market now, or is it the time to get out? It all depends. It's difficult enough to decide even if you believe that the existing rules for valuing companies still apply. If you believe the old rules should be swept away by the revolution, the decision becomes even more difficult.

Should you invest now? If you believe the market has peaked, you're unlikely to move more money into equities. However, if you think the market will continue to go up, investing in stocks makes sense. Then it's just a question of how active you want to be, buying and holding an index fund at one extreme or day-trading a small number of stocks at the other.

Stay in or get out? The answer also depends on your view of current valuation techniques and the information that goes into them. Those who rely on traditional financial metrics have good reason to suggest that the market has peaked, and further gains like the market experienced in the decade roughly preceding the turn of the century are unlikely.

Consider that between January 1990 and June 2000 the Dow Jones Industrial Average went up 395 percent, the Standard & Poor's (S&P) 500 went up 430 percent, and the NASDAQ Composite Index increased 880 percent. Despite extreme volatility, as noted in Chapter 2, the general trend has been extremely positive.

The bulls in the marketplace point out that the traditional metrics, which the bears use to argue their perspective, are so flawed they can no longer serve as guides—however useful they may have been in the past. The bulls say that P/E ratios are a poor predictor of future returns, that traditional metrics fail to recognize investors' changing perceptions of risk, and that current measurement methodologies are inadequate. They argue that with new metrics (particularly nonfinancial ones), new measurement methodologies (especially of intangible assets), and a "real options" perspective, today's stock prices are not as outlandish as the doomsayers insist. Instead, they maintain, today's prices fairly accurately reflect true or intrinsic value.[1]

"Not true!" the bears respond. They regard the new approaches to measurement and valuation as gimmicks invented to justify unjustifiably high stock prices and to con investors into continuing to pour money into the market. All will end in tears, they insist, when the market returns to sensible levels and when traditional measures prove as valid for New Economy stocks as they have for those of the Old Economy.

The truth probably lies somewhere in between. That may sound like a cop-out, but our purpose here isn't to take a position on the level of current valuations. We're not your broker after all. Rather, we're focusing on the most appropriate way to determine value and the information the market needs to do that. On that front, we find the evidence clear that the usefulness of traditional financial measures such as earnings and P/E ratios has declined, and new measures for recognizing the value of intangible assets and evaluating performance on nonfinancial dimensions have increased in importance.

IT'S A MATTER OF TIME

Even if the market rises and then falls for a while, history suggests it will rise again and keep doing so in the future. Bailing out when the market troughs, therefore, would seem misguided unless your risk/return profile has shifted downward for some reason. Otherwise, it's best to hang in there, as Jeremy J. Siegel of the Wharton Business School at the University of Pennsylvania recommends in his book *Stocks for the Long Run*:

> For most of us, trying to beat the market leads to disastrous results. We take far too many risks, our transaction costs are too high, and we often find ourselves giving into the emotions of the moment—pessimism when the market is down and optimism when the market is high. Our actions lead to substantially lower returns than can be obtained by just staying in the market.[2]

Siegel speaks with some authority. Andrew Smithers, who founded a firm that advises fund managers on asset allocation strategies, and Stephen Wright, a lecturer at Cambridge University, call Siegel "the most convincing advocate of the buy-and-hold-strategy" in his "brilliantly argued and superbly documented book."[3] What makes Siegel's recommendation even more interesting is that he frequently and seriously questions the current prices of certain stocks—especially, and not surprisingly, those of some Internet companies.

MIND YOUR Ps AND Es

What if Siegel's "for the long run" turns out to be "the *very* long run"? Consider that on June 30, 2000, the P/E ratio for the New York Stock Exchange Composite stocks was 28.4, about twice the historical average of 14.5. Many attribute this enormous difference to investors gambling that the market will continue to go up rather than to the market's underlying fundamentals.

In his highly praised book, *Irrational Exuberance*, Robert Shiller, a well-respected economist at Yale University, noted, "The present stock market displays the classic features of a *speculative bubble*: a situation in which temporarily high prices are sustained largely by investors' enthusiasm rather than by consistent estimation of real value."[4]

Enthusiasm indeed! During the first six months of 2000, investors poured more than $212.45 billion into stock mutual funds, double the amount for the same time period one year earlier.[5] Many, of course, don't expect to stay in the market for 10, 20, or 30 years. They are momentum traders who want to ride the rocket as long as it keeps going up and bail out before it starts going down—or at least goes down too far!

Such a strategy requires exquisite timing. Volatility suggests that success with this investment strategy will be a matter of luck more than anything else. Shiller puts it this way: "Even though the market could possibly maintain or even substantially increase its price level, the outlook for the stock market into the next ten or twenty years is likely to be rather poor—and perhaps even dangerous."[6]

And Mind Your *Q*s as Well

Despite their laudatory remarks about Professor Siegel's book, Smithers and Wright share Shiller's rather grim view of the market's longer-term prospects. They base their argument on the value of q, the ratio of the value of the stock market to total corporate net worth (assets minus liabilities). They cite data showing that when the q ratio exceeds 1.0, the market almost always declines, sometimes precipitously, since stock values exceed the replacement cost of their assets.

As of May 2000, the q ratios for both the Dow Jones Industrial Average and the S&P 500 were about 2.8, their highest levels in the past 100 years.[7] If Smithers and Wright are correct, the Dow Jones quite possibly could fall quickly 50 to 60 percent from its mid-year 2000 number of nearly 10,600 to somewhere slightly less than 5,300—its level as recently as January 1996.[8]

The two authors conclude that even though stocks "are not too unpredictable over the longer term" and that "the buy-and-hold strategy is sound most of the time," now is not that time. Because stocks can occasionally become "grossly overpriced," the smart investor will recognize this and "sell when the market becomes wildly overpriced, as at present."[9] The truly rational investor will do so even though it is very difficult to predict whether the market really has peaked. "The risks you are running if you hold stocks in such circumstances," they caution, "are simply too great."[10]

Although Smithers and Wright believe that q can serve as a powerful and useful guide to making investment decisions, they note two reasons why few actually use it. First, they say, "q is virtually useless as a guide to the short-term market movements that stockbrokers are asked to forecast."[11] Second, "q can show that markets are overpriced for prolonged periods of time" and thus "can seriously damage the incomes of stockbrokers, since investors don't buy shares if they think they will lose money."[12] This again raises the issue of time frames and the role of analysts, a subject we will address in more detail in succeeding chapters.

P/Es AREN'T ALL THEY'RE CRACKED UP TO BE

Some of the more sophisticated bulls and bears can agree on at least one thing: Comparing current to historical P/E ratios is too simplistic and a rather primitive way of trying to judge when a market has reached its peak. Smithers and Wright point out that although the market's P/E ratio looked high in 1932, and was actually rising, those who failed to invest missed "the bargain of the century."[13] This happened because the P/E ratio is an imperfect indicator of future returns due to the volatility of earnings and the fact that stock prices may be a leading indicator of earnings rather than vice versa. An unusually high P/E doesn't necessarily mean that future returns won't be favorable.[14]

Risk: Past and Present

Michael Edesess, the chief economist at Lockwood Advisors, offers another caution about drawing conclusions based on current P/E levels. He argues that current levels aren't too high. Rather, past levels were too low because perceptions of risk were higher. "In the past," Edesess says, "the information investors needed to assess the value of an investment was far less readily available than it is today."[15] This caused investors to become overly conservative. After looking at the predictive power of P/E ratios on future earnings growth, Edesess concludes, "Had investors known what we now know, and had they been less skittish about the unknown, the market then would probably have looked much as it does now."[16]

In their controversial book, *Dow 36,000,* James K. Glassman and Kevin A. Hassett of the American Enterprise Institute note that as a result of better information and more experience, the risk premium—the percentage return above a zero-risk investment that investors demand for owning stocks—has been going down. They argue that the natural conclusion—a Dow Jones Industrial Average of about 36,000, or about four times current levels—is quite reasonable. For them, "The single most important fact about stocks at the dawn of the twenty-first century: They are cheap."[17]

In their opinion, for true long-term investors, owning stocks involves no more risk than owning government treasuries. Sure, stocks are more volatile, but that shouldn't matter to long-term investors. The historical evidence on average stock returns is so compelling that it suggests a risk premium of zero. And because earnings and dividends rise each year, a 1 percent earnings return conservatively matches the cash return on bonds. This means a P/E of 100!

If Glassman and Hassett are right, and needless to say many experts don't think so, current expectations about what are reasonable P/E ratios will require substantial modification. It's also true if they're only half right. The key point is that stock prices and their multiples are heavily influenced by investors' expectations about the relationship between risk and return. Chapter 8 discusses in more detail how the information investors receive about risk can affect their expectations.

Getting a Grip on an Intangible World

Contemporary P/E ratios come under even more fire. Critics argue that they are unrealistically high because the "E" part is unrealistically low. Many intangible assets—an issue raised in the previous chapter—such as expenditures for R&D, information technology, marketing, branding, and customer loyalty programs, are treated as expenses by today's accounting standards. That these expenses continue to increase because of competitive pressures and the cost of innovation only makes the problem worse.

Expensing what in reality are investments results in large costs in the period in which they are incurred. The fundamental problem is a mismatch between costs, such as restructuring charges and R&D investments that are taken in a current period, and the future revenues that these costs make possible. Earnings are lower than they would have been had these expenses been capitalized and amortized over the period during which they contribute to generating revenues. According to Baruch Lev and Paul Zarowin, two notable accounting professors at New York University who have extensively studied this problem, the result is "a disconnect between financial information and market values."[18]

Research supports the contention that the market treats certain expenses as intangible assets important to creating value. In one study of Internet companies, for example, John R.M. Hand of the Kenan-Flagler Business School at the University of North Carolina found that measures other than earnings, including marketing expenses and R&D expenditures, are highly related to market values.[19] Others have found similar results. In their study of Internet companies, Elizabeth Demers and Baruch Lev found that "product development (R&D) and advertising expenses (customer acquisition costs) appear to be capitalized as assets by investors in their assessment of Internet company value."[20] Similarly, in yet another study of Internet companies, Trueman, Wong, and Zhang found that gross profits before sales and marketing and R&D expenses are positively and significantly associated with stock prices.[21]

Rating the Ratios

At the end of 1982, the S&P 500 had a market value to book value ratio of 1.3. By the end of 1998, this number had increased by a factor of 5 to 6.5,[22] underscoring the growing importance of intangible assets relative to hard assets, which are captured on the balance sheet. We estimate that for the largest 24 Internet companies in terms of market cap, this ratio is 21.8. Critics of the q ratio point out that because these intangible assets do not appear on a company's balance sheet, they are not taken into account. If they were, q ratios would look more reasonable.

In addition to making the analysis of current and historical ratios less reliable, accounting practices that understate both earnings and assets weaken the relationship between earnings and stockholder returns. Lev, one of the most outspoken critics of current accounting practices, and Zarowin have shown a definite deterioration over the past 20 years in the association between earnings and stock returns.[23] Neither current earnings nor current P/E ratios, therefore, are very good indicators of future stock prices. They find the same is true for cash flow, even though its advocates argue that it serves as a truer measure and is less subject to manipulation. This, they maintain, demonstrates that *both* measures have limited usefulness in predicting shareholder returns.

TAKING ACCOUNT OF INTANGIBLE ASSETS

One obvious solution to the measurement distortions caused by expensing items that are really assets is to capitalize them. Lev and Zarowin are vocal advocates of this approach, as is Steve Wallman, a former commissioner of the Securities and Exchange Commission.[24]

For many, this is a controversial suggestion and raises many concerns. First, they're concerned that the true value of intangible assets in producing future revenues is hard to ascertain in terms of amount and timing. They worry that the value of intangible assets may prove very ephemeral, as intangibles are most commonly associated with knowledge-intensive markets in which new technologies emerge constantly, and new competitors can easily enter the fray.

Finally, they suspect that capitalizing such costs will enable managers to make earnings look better than they are by spreading them out. Or worse yet, managers will manipulate earnings because they often exercise discretion over whether the cost of an intangible is an expense or an asset. Intangible assets aside, the quality of earnings is an important issue that will be covered in more detail in the next two chapters.

Are these concerns well founded? In their study of software companies (the one exception is within U.S. GAAP, where R&D expenses can be capitalized), Aboody and Lev found a positive association between the amount of annually capitalized software expenses and stock prices, and also between the total software asset value and stock prices. They also found no evidence that this practice hurt the quality of reported earnings. They concluded that the practice produces value-relevant information more useful to investors than when software costs are expensed in the period in which they are incurred.[25]

The Knowledge Capital Scoreboard®

Although Lev would like to see the accounting rules regarding intangible assets changed, he's not sitting around waiting for that to happen. To address the growing disparity between the hard assets recorded on a company's balance sheet and the soft (or intangible or knowledge) assets that are not—but that are reflected in a company's market value—Lev has developed the Knowledge Capital Scoreboard in collaboration with Marc

Bothwell, a portfolio manager at BEA-Credit Suisse Asset Management. The Knowledge Capital Scoreboard, on which Lev has a patent pending, is, in his words, "a tool for measuring the economic consequences of investment in knowledge assets."[26]

Here is a simplified explanation of Lev's methodology. From the normalized earnings, which reflect three years of historical data plus three years of forecasted earnings based on I/B/E/S International consensus estimates, deduct earnings derived from tangible and financial assets. This gives you knowledge capital earnings (KCE). Then, divide KCE by a knowledge capital discount rate of 10.5 percent (based on the average after-tax rate of return for three knowledge-intensive industries: software, biotechnology, and pharmaceuticals), and you arrive at a figure for knowledge capital. This methodology can also yield new financial metrics, such as knowledge capital margin (KCE/sales) and knowledge capital operating margin (KCE/operating income).

The "Second Annual Knowledge Capital Scoreboard," published in the February 2000 *CFO Magazine*,[27] presented measures for a range of industries and for some specific companies. The report also offered evidence that knowledge earnings and knowledge earnings growth correlate more highly with market returns than do the more traditional measures of earnings (and earnings growth) and operating cash flow (and operating cash-flow growth).

When you add the intangible asset of knowledge capital to the hard assets included in book value and obtain the measure of "comprehensive value," outlandish ratios start to look more reasonable. For example, the market value to book value ratio for the hard asset–intensive forestry and paper industry is 2.56. In contrast, this ratio for America Online (AOL) is 194.4.[28] When AOL's knowledge capital of $45.4 billion is added to its book capital of $597.9 million, the market value to book value ratio becomes 2.5. But when the forestry and paper industry's relatively small knowledge capital is added to book value, the market value to book value ratio decreases to only 2.14. On a market value of $116.2 billion on September 30, 1999, AOL's market value/book value ratio was a whopping 194.4!

Price/Growth-Flow Ratio

Another way to deal with perceived accounting distortions regarding R&D investments is the price/growth-flow (P/GF) ratio proposed by Michael Murphy.[29] The denominator in this ratio is after-tax earnings plus R&D expenses. Murphy views adding in R&D expenses as important because they do not show up as depreciation from a capital account. Instead, they represent tomorrow's return on investment. Because Murphy is concerned with advising investors on how to pick high-tech stocks, this approach, which is simpler than Lev's, deals with only one category of expenses, R&D.

BEHOLD THE NEW METRICS!

Properly measuring the value of intangible assets is an important problem to solve, but there are others. One that has received considerable interest is how to value New Economy stocks, particularly for companies in the Internet and biotechnology sectors that don't have any earnings and don't appear as if they will for some time.

Consider the 24 largest Internet companies traded on the ISDEX by market cap. Collectively, they had a net income of $42 million and had a combined market cap of $1,045 billion! In the past, the venture capital community took care of the problem of valuing companies with no earnings. They waited until a company showed earnings before they took it public. This enabled the market to use its traditional techniques, however useful they really are, to determine the company's value.

But with companies now going public at much earlier stages, and long before they turn a profit, the public equity markets must address the problem as well. How big has the problem become? Twenty percent of the NASDAQ's total value is made up of 506 companies that have gone public since January 1, 1999. Of those, 75 percent have no earnings at all.[30]

Search for Other Ratios

In the absence of regularly reported earnings, the markets search for other measures. Echoing the elegant simplicity of the P/E ratio, the price to revenue or sales ratio has emerged as a common method for valuing New Economy companies. A particular company's price/sales ratio, when compared to those of similar companies, helps the market determine if the company's stock is expensive or cheap, similar to the way the market uses P/E comparisons.

The price/sales ratio has also come into play with some of the more well-established New Economy companies like Cisco Systems, which has a strong record of revenue and earnings growth. As Susan Pulliam commented in *The Wall Street Journal*, "Revenue, once used as a benchmark for measuring only companies with no earnings, now turns up in analysts' reports as a way to size up Cisco's stock price."[31] Because Cisco's P/E ratio is so large compared to the average company, some think that the price/sales ratio is a more meaningful figure. Even then, the figures can astonish.

Whereas Cisco traded at six times next year's revenues in the early 1990s, in the first quarter of 2000 it traded at about 25 times future revenues. As a consequence, the benchmarks on another ratio, the so-called "peg ratio"—the P/E ratio divided by the growth rate—have had to change.

Historically, a stock was considered fully valued when the P/E ratio matched the growth rate, thus yielding a peg ratio of 1.0. Now that P/E ratios have become so high, they far exceed even very high growth rates. Witness Cisco's peg ratio on next year's earnings, which was 4.5 in April 2000.[32] This means that the multiple contribution of growth rate to the P/E ratio has gone up substantially for a number of companies.

Given how outlandish some of these variations in financial ratios appear, it's not surprising that nonfinancial measures are being used to determine value. One somewhat exotic example is the "average value per unique user," a measure particularly relevant to Internet companies. It is calculated by dividing total market capitalization by the number of unique users. Similarly, an "average value per pageview," "per marketing dollar spent," or "per hours of use" ratio can be calculated.

New Metrics Stir Controversy

Given the short history of using these new and sometimes exotic valuation metrics, they not surprisingly have stirred up a controversy as great as the one surrounding the valuations themselves. As Alan Webber put it in *Fast Company*, some see these new metrics as a kind of "New Math for a New Economy."[33] Others regard them as gimmicks for justifying outlandish valuations in order to continue to draw in gullible investors. Roger McNamee, general partner at Integral Capital Partners, for one, observed, "None of this makes sense, but no one wants the party to end. People know it's a mania, and they still want to be there."[34]

Those concerned about new metrics like the price/sales ratio argue that the sell-side analysts have their logic exactly backward. Instead of advising investors on a company's worth, these analysts rationalize what investors are willing to pay, even though the investors may be betting on momentum and not worrying about fundamental value. But as Susan Pulliam pointedly asked, "With the focus on what investors are willing to pay rather than what they should pay, is the tail wagging the dog?"[35]

Critics of the new metrics like to use the word *mania*. One of the most vocal, Edward Kerschner, a PaineWebber investment strategist, noted that new metrics have been used before to justify other manias, such as the conglomerate and leveraged buyout (LBO) crazes. He pungently commented, "New metrics are not new—just foolish," and concluded, "As was the case with prior manias, the complete demise of the new metrics era may well take a few years. But, the initial corrective stage will likely be quite damaging just the same."[36]

The new metrics' skeptics point out that eventually every company, even the sexy Internet ones, has to make money. In a quick April 1999 analysis of AOL, Wharton Business School professor Jeremy Siegel speculated that if AOL's P/E declines from 700 on trailing 12 months earnings (or 450 on expected 1999 earnings) to a still very respectable 30 times earnings once it reaches maturity, it will have to deliver net profits of $6.7 billion in order to maintain a $200 billion market value. He also noted that in 1998, General Electric (GE) was the only American company that achieved this level of profitability. At a 10 percent profit margin, AOL would have to achieve annual sales of $67 billion, a level seen in only seven U.S. companies in 1998 (General Motors, Ford, Wal-Mart, Exxon, GE, IBM, and Citigroup), whose average margin was only 5.7 percent.[37]

Time for a Reality Check

In 1999, AOL's revenues were $4.78 billion with net income of $762 million. To reach the revenues and earnings levels Siegel calculated, AOL would have to grow revenues at a 70 percent compounded growth rate and earnings at 54 percent. Ignoring AOL's merger with TimeWarner, such a revenue growth figure does seem possible since AOL's revenue growth for the past five years has averaged 129.4 percent. It's impossible to calculate an earnings growth rate for that period; AOL became profitable only in 1998. Yet an earnings growth rate only two-thirds of the revenue growth rate also seems fairly reasonable.

IN DEFENSE OF NEW METRICS

If the new metrics were nothing but an attempt to rationalize stock prices that can't be justified by traditional financial metrics, one would not expect to see any relationship between new metrics and stock prices. In irrational markets, investors have no interest in how and how much value is being created. They're interested only in stocks that will continue to go up, because others will buy them. This has nothing to do with performance along any dimension, financial or nonfinancial.

New Metrics in the New Economy

Some recent studies of Internet companies—in which new metrics are most prevalent and most controversial—have, however, suggested that the new metrics are indeed related to stock prices. This implies that they are value relevant in that the market distinguishes between companies that do well on certain performance dimensions and those that do not.

Perhaps the most interesting of these recent studies is one by Elizabeth Demers and Baruch Lev that includes data through the first quarter of 2000, when the Internet sector took a brutal beating.[38] They note, "In the absence of positive profits or other traditional financial valuation variables, and given the increasing skepticism of investors about the prospects of Internet companies, the search for the fundamental value drivers of these companies is of considerable importance to investors and managers."[39] The key nonfinancial value drivers Demers and Lev examined include reach, the number of unique individuals who visit a site; stickiness, how well a site retains an individual who visits; and customer loyalty, the extent to which visitors return.

They found that measures of these value drivers, along with certain financial measures, such as cash burn rate, explained a significant proportion of cross-sectional variation in market-to-book ratios. Similarly, Trueman, Wong, and Zhang found that the nonfinancial measures of unique visitors and pageviews provide additional explanatory power for stock prices, especially for e-tailers like Amazon.com.[40] They hypothesize that determining pageviews for e-tailers is useful in predicting future revenues "as it reflects potential future demand for the company's products and, at least indirectly, affects the rates the firm can charge for advertising on its web site(s)."[41]

New Metrics in the Old Economy

As discussed in Chapter 1, the importance of nonfinancial value drivers is not restricted to Internet companies. Two Wharton Business School professors, David F. Larcker and Christopher D. Ittner, studied the relationship between various customer measures and financial measures in such industries as durable manufacturing, nondurable manufacturing, retail, telecommunications, and financial services.[42] They found that customer satisfaction levels are indeed leading indicators of future financial performance measures such as revenues, revenue growth, profit margins, and return on sales.

Need for New Metrics

So where does that leave us? Admittedly, the use of new metrics is a fairly new experience. We're only beginning to understand which ones are most important in any given industry. No doubt new metrics can and will be misused. But the need for them is clear. The old financial metrics no longer lead to clear conclusions about value, even for those who still place more importance on the old than on the new. According to Susan Pulliam, Ed Kerschner of PaineWebber—one of the most vocal critics of the new metrics—thinks Cisco is actually cheap at a multiple of 150 to 175 times earnings on a growth rate of 28 percent.[43]

In May 2000, Cisco's highest P/E was 148.2, at the bottom of the range Kerschner considers reasonable. On September 20, 2000, the P/E ratio was 172.2—still within Kerschner's range. Yet Jeremy Siegel, who shares Kerschner's concerns about the current mania for Internet companies, believes that Cisco is overpriced. He thinks that smaller Internet companies are more likely than a large company like Cisco to have the growth rates necessary to justify high price/revenue ratios.[44] These are the companies that arouse Kerschner's greatest suspicion. He perceives that these new "New" companies offer growth in revenues but not in value. Where does that leave everyone else when two vocal critics of New Economy valuations can't even agree on the valuation of one of its most prominent members? In search of new metrics, that's where.

LET'S GET REAL

No discussion of new metrics for valuing companies would be complete without at least a mention of the somewhat arcane topic of real options. This concept applies financial option theory to real investments (such as for brands, R&D, and manufacturing plants) and is relevant to both New and Old Economy companies. Although not widely practiced in valuing companies currently, real-options values could generate even more controversy than the new metrics, both financial and nonfinancial, now under debate.

If or when these real options evolve from a mostly conceptual perspective—the data requirements are high and the mathematics are extremely complicated—to actual use in practice, debates like the one between Kerschner and Siegel over Cisco's valuation might be resolved. Perhaps Cisco's tremendous value lies in the real options it has.

One vocal advocate of real options is Michael Mauboussin, a research analyst at Credit Suisse First Boston. He suggests that, "stocks of companies that participate in highly uncertain markets are best viewed as a combination of the discounted cash flow value of the current, known businesses plus a portfolio of real options."[45] These real options create value because they capture a company's ability to take advantage of unforeseen opportunities. Mauboussin poses and then answers his own question about real options, "Is it valuing the unimaginable? Yes. Is the unimaginable valuable? Yes."[46]

Mauboussin identifies seven common types of options, which he places into three categories[47]:

1. Invest/Grow Options
   - *Scale up* to add capacity to take advantage of future opportunities
   - *Switch up* to switch products, processes, or plants as demand changes
   - *Scope up* to leverage an investment made in one industry to another industry
2. Disinvest/Shrink Options
   - *Scale down* to shrink capacity in midstream according to new information
   - *Switch down* to shift to more cost-effective and flexible assets according to new information
   - *Scope down* to shrink or abandon operations in a related industry if necessary
3. Defer/Learn
   - The opportunity to invest, but not doing so until conditions warrant

Amazon.com at the Real Options Table

Mauboussin calls Amazon.com an "options smorgasbord" and cites four ways that real options have enabled the company to create value.

First, Amazon.com has exploited *scope-up options* by leveraging its position in key markets to launch similar businesses. Second, it has exploited *scale-up options* by adding distribution capabilities to support higher sales volumes from existing businesses and new ventures. Third, *learning options* have come from making acquisitions that may provide the platform to create value in the future. And fourth, Amazon.com has taken an *equity stake* in some promising new companies that are best valued using options methods. Exhibit 3.1 schematically demonstrates how Amazon.com has increased its market value through real options.

Exhibit 3.1

Amazon.com
Building Value through Options

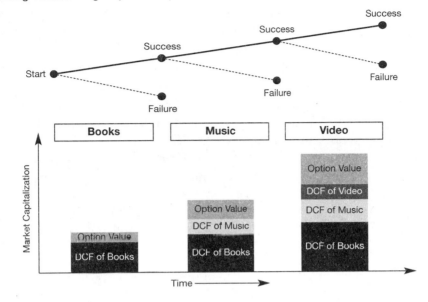

Source: *Frontiers of Finance*, Vol. 10, June 23, 1999, p. 20, Credit Suisse First Boston, New York

Real Options for the Old Economy

Old Economy companies can exploit real options as well. Consider Enron. According to the June 7, 1999, issue of *Business Week*, "Enron President and Chief Operating Officer Jeffrey K. Skilling credits real-options thinking with helping Enron transform itself from a domestic natural-gas pipeline company in the United States into a global wheeler-dealer that trades commodities including gas, electricity, water and, most recently, telecom bandwidth."[48]

One example of such real options thinking was the company's decision to build gas-fired plants to generate its own electricity. Although these plants produce electrical power at a cost 50 to 70 percent higher than the most efficient facilities, the article notes that they give Enron an "option" on electricity. Because gas can be used to generate power, Enron can take advantage of electricity's recently demonstrated extreme price volatility, which has created price levels 175 percent higher than historical averages in recent years.

According to *Business Week*, although neither industry analysts nor Enron's annual report refer directly to the company's real-options strategy, Enron has consistently outperformed other prominent players in the industry with a consistently higher P/E ratio since early 1999. Enron is using real options, and the market knows it. Enron's P/E ratio of around 50 in July 2000 was two to four times greater than those of major competitors.

Real-options value may seem a bit like smoke and mirrors, but it's based on rigorous thinking and sophisticated mathematical calculations. Like any methodology, it has limitations related to both assumptions and the quality of the underlying data. And because it requires large databases for estimating probabilities, it proves very difficult to use.

Perhaps over time some of these technical difficulties will be solved and real options will become a more common analytical tool. Many believe it will, and a number of academics and commercial enterprises have been working toward that end.

Now Here's a Concept

In the meantime, simply using a real-options perspective may be a way of putting some discipline and rigorous thinking against the often extraordinary prices of so-called concept stocks. Examples include General Magic, which had a stunning price/sales ratio of 1,761 in February 2000, and Sunrise Technologies International with an even more remarkable price/sales ratio of 2,781. "Oh brave new world that hath such concept stocks in it!,"[49] waxed Robert McGough in *The Wall Street Journal*.

Those skeptical about concept stocks—often with good reason— point out that in the past they have generally preceded significant downturns. But even these skeptics sometimes find themselves getting at least some exposure to concept stocks in order to participate in their rise. Failure to do so can hurt the performance of their overall portfolio, whether or not they can find economic justification for the prices they pay.

Real-options thinking offers one way to separate chaff from wheat— the concept stocks that are ephemeral from those that reflect a truly new business model with long-term viability. It attempts to take a disciplined view of the value inherent in those companies that operate in highly uncertain environments and have real options, which will enable them to recognize and take advantage of opportunities to innovate.

After all, it wasn't so long ago that Microsoft was just such a concept stock. And what about Cisco Systems, Dell Computer, Qualcomm, and MCI WorldCom? All have vastly exceeded early expectations because of innovations that took them well beyond their original businesses. They created new products, new services, and new markets. They had real options, and they used them well.

Such successes notwithstanding, the stakes here are high. As of June 30, 2000, the average P/E for the NASDAQ was 181.[50] Classic valuation techniques cannot distinguish among the few that deserve such stratospheric ratios and the many that do not. Without new techniques like real-options analysis, choosing among such stocks equates to simply rolling the dice. But not choosing can mean missing out on some very real value creation, as value investors painfully learned over the 1990s.

4

The Earnings Game

Laugh where we must, be candid where we can.
Alexander Pope, *An Essay on Man*

Here's a play that surely deserves a page in The Earnings Game record book. On April 5, 2000, Yahoo! announced a first-quarter profit of $0.10 per share,[1] exceeding by more than 11 percent the $0.09 per share consensus estimate forecasted by 29 professional Wall Street analysts.[2]

One month earlier, a Multex.com report had noted that this $0.09 per share would exceed the prior year's quarterly earnings by 125 percent[3] and went on to say, "The investment community's confidence in the earnings forecast is very high." The report also noted that because there was a "much lower deviation in the consensus estimate" for the company than for the market as a whole that "any significant variation of actual results from expectations could have a very adverse effect on the price of company shares."

So the market rejoiced that Yahoo! had soundly beaten the consensus estimate. Not!

When the NASDAQ closed that April 5, Yahoo!'s stock price had fallen to $165.5625. It fell even further in after-hours trading. A week later, Yahoo! stock closed down nearly 18 percent, while the NASDAQ Composite was down only 9.5 percent. Only one week after its highly favorable earnings announcement, Yahoo! had lost $16 billion in market value—more than the total market cap of Nike ($12.2 billion) or Federal Express ($11.9 billion).

Tim Koogle, Yahoo!'s CEO, took it all in stride. "The stock market sometimes is nutty," he said. "But the market we really care about is the one we derive revenues from."[4] Koogle knows whereof he speaks. The stock market can be downright nutty, and now more than ever. In fact, it can turn positively irrational. When rationality breaks down, revolutions break out.

WHAT'S REALLY GOING DOWN HERE?

Was Yahoo!'s plunge the result of some bad news not reflected in the earnings result? To the contrary, all the news about Yahoo! boded well. The company's revenue, which many consider one of the key value drivers for an Internet company, had more than doubled from the previous quarter, significantly exceeding analysts' expectations.

The number of registered users (customers who had signed up for Yahoo!'s services) had risen from 100 million to 125 million in the previous quarter. And more good news: Yahoo!'s advertising revenues from banners, sponsorships, and other marketing sources had grown as well. *The Wall Street Journal* of April 6 published the glad tidings: "The performance of the Internet bellwether [Yahoo!] was rock-steady in comparison with the stock market's volatility of the past few days."[5]

So what's the problem? Psssst! It appears that the company's $0.10 earnings per share had fallen below the unofficial "whisper" earnings estimate of $0.12 per share. Therefore, because reported earnings did not exceed what the market expected the actual above-expectation results to be, Yahoo!'s stock price fell precipitously.

Confused? You're not alone. The capital markets, especially in the United States, embody a fundamental contradiction that negatively affects investment decisions both within companies and in the market.

What's the contradiction? While research shows that reported earnings are decreasingly important in explaining value over the long term, the market's focus on reported earnings has become as obsessive as it has become increasingly short term. Thus, the short-term stakes for companies, sell-side analysts, and investors have risen regarding reported quarterly earnings. They've risen especially high in terms of how reported earnings compare to both the official expectations and to the unofficial understanding that those expectations will be exceeded.

Thus begins The Earnings Game. It's a game no one really enjoys playing, and it's played by a set of rules that nobody really likes—with the possible exception of sell-side analysts who make a living estimating and second-guessing earnings estimates, among other things.

THE GAME AS PLAYED IN THEORY

In the pristine world of economic theory, three relatively simple rules govern how The Earnings Game should be played. The rules are perfectly consistent with existing regulations that require a company only to file a proxy statement, its annual 10-K report, and quarterly 10-Q reports in the United States, and to hold an annual shareholders' meeting.

- *Rule 1: Companies should report their earnings the way they are.* Managers should do the best job possible: run the company, make trade-offs between the short and long term, and simply report whatever the quarterly earnings turn out to be with no attempt to smooth them out or manage the market's expectations.
- *Rule 2: Analysts should interpret earnings, not speculate on what they may be.* Analysts should exert minimal effort in guessing what earnings will be and focus more closely on interpreting—within the context of other information about the company, its industry, and the macro economy—what the reported figures mean for a company's future prospects.
- *Rule 3. Investors should act on what the analysts tell them.* Investors should read what the analysts say and recommend, and then decide whether to sell the stock (or lighten their position) or buy it (or strengthen their position).

In theory, these three rules should work. Assuming, of course, that:

- Reported current earnings is a "real" number that provides a great deal of information about likely future earnings.
- Reported earnings provides extremely useful guidance to the market in setting stock prices.
- As current earnings change, stock prices do as well because such short-term changes are good indicators of future changes.
- No one questions the quality of reported earnings because no one else has tried to make them higher or lower than they "really would be."[6]

Good in theory, but does anyone really play by these rules anymore? Consider what happens in the real world.

THE GAME AS PLAYED ON THE STREET

A recent National Investor Relations Institute survey found that only about one in ten companies abstain from helping analysts prepare their earnings estimates forecasts.[7] The remaining 90 percent actively play a version of The

---

The Seven Rules of The Earnings Game

Rule 1: Deliver a track record of consistent earnings growth.

Rule 2: Manage earnings expectations carefully.

Rule 3: Slightly beat earnings expectations.

Rule 4: Make business decisions to meet or beat expectations.

Rule 5: Hammer stocks that fail to meet expectations.

Rule 6: Listen carefully for the whisper number.

Rule 7: Hammer stocks that fail to meet the whisper number.

Earnings Game much more complex than the pristine version described earlier.

This more complex version, not surprisingly, has more rules—seven in fact (see sidebar). But both games and their sets of rules share something in common: They focus on one number—earnings—as the key to determining value. As long as such a singular focus endures—whether the number is earnings, cash flow, EVA® (Economic Value Added®), or something else— playing the game by any set of rules, whatever they be, will never lead to an optimally functioning capital market.

How well do these rules work in practice? Do they support sound corporate decision making? Do they supply the market with reliable valuation information? Do they contribute to value creation for companies and their shareholders? Consider the facts and decide for yourself.

Rule 1: Deliver a Track Record of Consistent Earnings Growth

Accepted doctrine now says that any well-run company will have planning and control systems that reduce uncertainty. These systems set quantitative targets, track progress in meeting these targets, make in-course corrections as necessary, and reward (or punish) managers for meeting (or not meeting) objectives.

Managers by nature seek to reduce uncertainty because the market ultimately judges their performance and consequently dictates their rewards. A consistent trend of reporting growth in quarterly earnings is the key. By doing so, management sends a strong signal to the market that the company will continue to perform as well or better in the future. The outcome should be a strong stock price and a great deal of credibility for management.

Most executives accept this as an article of faith, and many examples support that they do. But even when managers achieve the difficult objec-

tive of reporting continuous growth in quarterly earnings, they have no
guarantee that the market will always react in the desired way. Important a
number as it may be, earnings is not the only thing that captures the market's attention.

Consider the case of Emerson Electric Co. Through April 1999, Emerson had logged an amazing record of 165 quarters of uninterrupted net-
income growth.[8] For many years, the market had rewarded the company
with higher stock prices and an increasing P/E multiple. In 1994, Emerson's
P/E was 14.8; by 1997, it had risen to 23.1.[9]

Since then, the multiple has not risen above that ceiling and by mid-
2000 stood at roughly 21. Why, then, did Emerson's multiple not improve
over those last three years even though the company continued its uninterrupted string of quarterly earnings growth? As discussed in Chapter 3, one
of the components in the P/E ratio is the company's growth rate. In Emerson's case, as Carl Quintanilla reported in *The Wall Street Journal*, investors
are concerned that with its emphasis on cost cutting, the company is not doing all the things it should, like making acquisitions, to grow revenues and
ensure the company's long-term performance.

Rule 2: Manage Earnings Expectations Carefully

Sell-side analysts, using more-or-less sophisticated financial models, spend a
great deal of time estimating a company's next quarterly earnings. They
compare their estimates to the company's past performance (previous quarter and same quarter from last year) and to the estimates for other similar
companies, and then opine on whether the stock represents a buying or a
selling opportunity. The sheer amount of effort that goes into this seems all
the more striking as quarterly figures aren't audited and are often restated.

Come Dance with Me

Because estimates garner so much publicity, they give company managers an
excellent opportunity to influence the market's perception of what these
earnings should be. Managers usually do this through careful conversations
with analysts in what one financial columnist called "a well-choreographed
waltz."[10]

Arthur Levitt, chairman of the Securities and Exchange Commission,
offers a less poetic description. He candidly declares that "analysts seek
constant guidance from companies to frame those expectations"[11] and has
more bluntly referred to the practice as a "web of dysfunctional relationships."[12]

Companies participate in the practice freely, even enthusiastically. A 1998 National Investor Relations Institute survey of 227 companies found that 77 percent of respondents informed analysts if their earnings estimates were out of line, 71 percent told analysts whether they felt comfortable with the estimates, and 46 percent offered guidance on future trends.[13]

Large market cap companies (over $1.5 billion) gave more guidance than small market cap companies (under $500 million). Medium market cap companies ($500 million to $1.5 billion) came in somewhere between. More generally, 86 percent of all companies in the survey reviewed and commented on drafts of analysts' reports, and nearly four out of five actually reviewed and commented on analysts' projections or models before they were published.[14]

Lend a Helping Hand

Why do companies provide all this help? Because analysts explicitly ask for it. A July 1999 *CFO Magazine* survey of *Fortune* 500 CFOs showed that the majority believed that analysts aren't bashful in asking for guidance in estimating corporate earnings. On a scale of one to five—subtle to brazen— 62 percent of the CFOs gave a ranking of four or five on the question of "How explicit are analysts in asking for your assessment of consensus estimates?"[15] Time will tell if the new SEC fair disclosure regulation will limit such practices.

Recent academic research, supported by survey data, confirms the common perception that companies actively manage analysts' earnings expectations. Burgstahler and Eames used the Zacks Investment Research database to study actual and forecast earnings per share for the years 1986 to 1996.[16] They found that "distributions of annual earnings surprises include a smaller than expected number of negative earnings surprises and a larger than expected number of 'no' and 'small' positive earnings surprises, consistent with the conjecture that managers take conscious actions to avoid negative earnings surprises."[17]

Companies and the analysts alike benefit from fewer negative surprises, at least in the short term. Analysts look smart because they came up with the "right" number for actual earnings. It's like taking a quiz, knowing that the results will be made public and that your peers all have access to the teacher's answer sheet. Brave, indeed, are the analysts who disagree in either direction with a company's guidance and risk looking dumber than their peers.

The company is happy as well. It prevented the analysts from being overly optimistic, only to be disappointed when the actual results came out;

or from being overly pessimistic, which would raise doubts about how well the company is doing, simply disappointing investors sooner.

Managing Expectations with No Earnings At All

This rule of managing expectations now extends to companies that have no earnings at all, as is the case with many Internet stocks. Here, the variation on Rule 2 addresses managing expectations about revenues or losses.

According to Marc Gerstein, director of investment research at *Market Guide* and author of the Technology Corner column at www.marketguide.com, "While it's still OK to lose money, even a lot of money, it's not OK to post a per-share deficit that's deeper than the consensus Wall Street expectation."[18] Gerstein kindly provided a quick analysis based on data in the wake of the big Internet sector correction in the first half of 2000 that nicely makes this point. He examined the 713 money-losing Internet companies (out of a total of 840) for the 13-week period ending September 28, 2000.

During this period the share prices of these companies *declined* an average of 26.94 percent. The 272 Internet companies that posted a loss smaller than expected saw their price decline slightly less, only 24.38 percent. This difference was more dramatic for the 108 companies whose losses were less than expected by more than 20 percent; their share prices decreased by only 13.65 percent. However, the 32 companies that did worse than expected by more than 20 percent (i.e., their losses were even greater than expected by more than 20 percent), saw their share prices decline by nearly 40 percent (39.32).

Brought to You by HBO

Consider the case of HBO and Company (HBOC) and its management of earnings expectations. HBOC followed Rule 2 and kept The Street informed of its prospects and earnings expectations without appearing to be overly aggressive or overly conservative. For more than 28 consecutive quarters leading up to its merger with McKesson Corporation, HBOC met or slightly exceeded consensus earnings estimates.[19]

In early 1998, analysts listed HBOC's stock as a "buy" or "accumulate" recommendation.[20] Dow Jones Online News service reported, "HBO has been viewed as something of a bellwether for the health-care information sector . . . and has met or exceeded analysts' earnings estimates every quarter since 1991."[21] Financial analyst Steve Shook, of Interstate Johnson Lane, commented in March 1998, "HBO & Co. is one of a handful of firms that dominate the industry, and they are well positioned to take advantage of future growth." Shook also noted that HBOC's stock "doubled in value over the last year."[22]

Rule 3: Slightly Beat Earnings Expectations

The public disclosures for HBOC contained every type of cautionary language, risk alert, and caveat concerning HBOC's prospective results of operations and current financial conditions. Yet, quarter after quarter, HBOC met or exceeded predicted earnings as results of operations. The pattern of earnings warnings and risk followed by earnings "blowouts" continued from 1991 until HBOC's merger agreement with McKesson Corporation in 1998.

Along the way, HBOC's stock price, adjusted for stock splits, rose steadily in value from $18.63 per share in January 1996 to $70.50 per share in June 1998. At the date of the merger with McKesson Corporation, HBOC's stock price had more than tripled and stood at $59.13 per share on October 16, 1998.

Pleasant surprises quarter after quarter helped nudge HBOC's market value higher and higher. Of course, HBOC isn't the only company that likes to give the market a pleasant earnings surprise along with an upward nudge to its stock price at the same time. In third quarter 1999, well over one-fourth of S&P 500 companies exactly matched consensus estimate expectations; only about 12 percent fell below. The remaining companies, about 60 percent, exceeded consensus expectations, most of them by a small amount.[23]

For the Russell 2000, an index made up of mid-cap companies that receive less analyst coverage and generally have less sophisticated investor relations departments, only one out of ten companies met expectations exactly. But only 14 percent fell below. Thirty percent beat expectations by a small amount (less than 10 percent) and the rest did so to varying degrees more.[24]

Companies and analysts must have learned how to work together better to manage expectations. Kinney, Burgstahler, and Martin studied 22,000 annual composite forecasts and actual reported earnings between 1992 and 1997.[25] They found a 29 percent decrease in the number of firms with negative surprises and a 41 percent increase in the number of firms with no earnings surprises. Positive surprises increased by 14 percent.

They concluded that there has been either an "increased management of earnings" or "more accurate forecasting by analysts." Similarly, the April 20, 2000, edition of *The Wall Street Journal* published an analysis showing that at mid-year 1992, about half of all firms had earnings equal to or above expectations, and the other half failed to meet expectations. In contrast, by the end of 1999, fully 70 percent of companies equaled or met expectations, and only 30 percent did not.[26] According to the article, the change occurred because "companies have become ever more skilled at the game of managing analysts' expectations" and because business "is going great guns."[27]

If companies and analysts weren't working together to develop earnings estimates that meet or slightly beat expectations, one would expect a rough bell curve distribution of actual earnings compared to reported earnings. The number of positive surprises would just about equal the number of negatives, and few would lie at either extreme. To the contrary, these data show that positive surprises roughly outweigh negative surprises four to one, and the positive skew is much greater.

Rule 4: Make Business Decisions to Meet or Beat Expectations

The great virtue of setting objectives and measuring against them is that people will work extremely hard to see that targets are met, particularly if doing it affects their compensation. From a positive point of view, they will work harder, take risks, and find creative ways to accomplish their goals.

From a negative point of view, they may make decisions that deliver short-term results and sacrifice the longer-term benefit. Classic examples include delaying maintenance on plant and equipment or cutting prices to generate sales before the period closes. Coupled with perfectly legitimate accounting "judgment calls," such decisions are designed to cast the most favorable light possible on the numbers. In some cases, exercising so much discretion pushes the allowable limits. When it exceeds the limits, it becomes accounting fraud. Any way you slice it, it's earnings management, a subject of great interest to companies, investors, regulators, and academics alike.

Use Your Discretion

Both sell-side analysts and institutional investors believe that companies have ample opportunity to practice their earnings management craft. In the PricewaterhouseCoopers global survey of institutional investors mentioned earlier, 62 percent agreed that companies have "a great deal of discretion" in determining their reported earnings in any given period. Only 18 percent didn't think so; the rest had no firm opinion.

These results varied little across the entire sample. And although many perceive U.S. GAAP as the most rigorous accounting methodology and the one with the most rules, the percentage of U.S. investors who thought companies have such discretion was actually higher than the average at 76 percent. The sell-side analysts expressed similar opinions. Across all countries surveyed, an average of 65 percent agreed that companies have discretion in the earnings they report. Very similar results among analysts and investors were found in the high-tech survey; 77 percent of analysts and 78 percent of investors agreed.

Work with Me Here
Burgstahler and Eames's research, cited earlier, supports the belief that companies exercise discretion in managing reported earnings. They found that companies manage expectations downward so that the estimates are equal to reported earnings, and they also manage earnings "upward to meet analysts' forecasts," particularly to avoid negative earnings surprises.[28]

Curiously, even though the market knows that companies manage earnings, it appears to have little effect on the market's satisfaction with the earnings information that companies report. Seventy-nine percent of investors and 82 percent of analysts in our global survey indicated they receive adequate information on earnings. Similarly, in our high-tech industry survey, 70 percent of investors and 90 percent of analysts also said they receive adequate information on earnings.

In the United States, the percentages are significantly higher than in other countries, suggesting that although the market knows earnings are being managed, it's satisfied as long as these managed earnings meet or beat expectations. Burgstahler and Eames's research substantiates this, showing clearly that earnings management involves collaboration between companies and analysts. Analysts take guidance from companies to develop their forecasts. Companies act aggressively to ensure that forecasts are met.

Perhaps somewhat disingenuously, executives of the companies surveyed think they have less discretionary power to manage earnings than the market thinks they do. Only 9 percent of the CFOs in the U.S. survey strongly agreed that companies have a great deal of discretion in determining the level of reported earnings in any given period. Another 27 percent tended to agree. But 39 percent tended to disagree, and 10 percent strongly disagreed. In the high-tech survey, only 2 percent strongly agreed and 21 percent tended to agree; 40 percent tended to disagree, and 15 percent strongly disagreed.

Taken at face value, this would mean that the practice of earnings management is limited to influencing the forecasts—something managers readily admit they do. Other research suggests that, in at least some circumstances, managers can and do use accounting degrees of freedom to affect their reported earnings. Ron Kasznik in his statistical study reported in the April 1, 1999, *Journal of Accounting Research*, concluded that "managers use positive discretionary accruals to manage reported earnings upward when earnings would otherwise fall below management's earnings forecasts."[29]

He also found that the greater the degree of discretion available to managers, the more they tend to exercise it to narrow the gap between forecasts and actual reported earnings. "I also found that managers of firms having more flexibility reduce their forecast errors more than do managers of firms with less flexibility," he noted.[30]

Not So Fast

Few doubt that most companies manage earnings. What should be done about it appears less clear-cut. In a comprehensive review of the academic literature on this subject, Healy and Wahlen note that although academic studies provide solid evidence that earnings management occurs, most of the research is "of only limited value to standard setters and regulators" since the studies provide "little evidence on questions of interest . . . such as whether earnings management is commonplace or relatively infrequent, which accruals are managed, and effects on resource allocation decisions."[31] They conclude that it is difficult to determine whether "current standards are largely effective in facilitating communication with investors, or whether they encourage widespread earnings management."[32]

In the United States, attempts have been made to constrain the ability of companies to manage earnings by relying on "materiality loopholes" through SEC Staff Accounting Bulletin No. 99—Materiality, issued August 12, 1999. Until that date, materiality was largely based on accepted rules of thumb, a percentage threshold number, essentially giving managers latitude to exercise a fair amount of discretion in determining their reported earnings.[33]

The new bulletin sets additional criteria and explicitly says that simply falling below the threshold doesn't guarantee that materiality guidelines have been followed. For example, it would be a violation of the new rule if "the misstatement masks a change in earnings or other trends" or if "the misstatement hides a failure to meet analysts' consensus expectations for the enterprise."

In essence, the ruling attempts to ensure that managers meet the spirit and not just the letter of the law. Somewhat ironically, it is doing so by adding more letters to the "law." We believe that this will simply perpetuate the play as long as The Earnings Game itself remains in place. For the spirit to change, The Earnings Game will have to become The Value Game.

How to Make the Market Very Nervous—Break the Rules

Most companies play according to Rule 4. The few who break the rule make the market very nervous, although regulators would no doubt applaud those brave enough to live in the world of unmanaged earnings.

An article in *The Wall Street Journal Europe* about Cleveland-based automobile insurer Progressive Corporation—a company that doesn't manage earnings—underscores the rarity of this behavior: "Here's an exercise bound to give some CEOs a panic attack: Imagine what would happen if you didn't 'manage,' or smooth out, your quarterly earnings."[34]

And what happens if the company breaks Rule 2 (manage expectations) and Rule 4 at the same time? The article addresses that as well: "Imagine you didn't give analysts any 'guidance' on your un-doctored earnings. Who in their right mind would blow off Wall Street that way?"

For one thing, the uncertainty created by the lack of earnings guidance makes the analysts' job much more difficult. And that really upsets them. One was described as having trouble sleeping because guessing Progressive's earnings was "like taking a final exam."

One consequence of Progressive's refusal to play by Rule 4 has been short-term volatility in its stock price. Progressive's stock went up 20 points on October 16, 1998, beating analysts' consensus earnings estimates by $0.44 per share, and then dropped 30 points three months later when earnings came in at $0.49 per share below expectations.[35] The company's stock has also been volatile over the long term. Progressive's beta is 1.4 compared to Allstate's of 0.89.

Such volatility hasn't hurt Progressive's returns to shareholders, however. The company has outperformed the S&P 500 consistently for years. Through April 1999, Progressive's 15-year return was 4,438 percent compared to 735 percent for the S&P 500.

How does Progressive get away with this? *The Wall Street Journal Europe* article notes that Peter Lewis, the largest shareholder, with 13 percent of the stock, runs the company. Similarly, Berkshire Hathaway and Loews, where the CEO is a major shareholder, makes a virtue of not providing earnings guidance to The Street. Lewis feels that managing earnings "is not honest" and actually hurts management's ability to run the company properly, noting that "the accounting stuff that's required to smooth things out causes management to mislead itself."

Who's Fooling Whom?

Managers mislead themselves when they forget the discretion they exercised to produce the reported results in the first place. They may forget that the

good results they show represent little more than an artful use of the accounting rules or the decisions they've made to accelerate revenues and delay costs—robbing from the future to satisfy present needs. When such
behavior occurs for only a quarter or two, and things eventually get put
right, delayed decisions get made—such as investments that create value
over the long term—and the numbers return to a closer depiction of economic reality.

But what happens if each succeeding quarter requires a bigger and
bigger stretch to meet the numbers? Management finds itself on a slip-
pery slope that at some point crosses the line of accounting and managerial discretion and becomes outright fraud. Remember the highly
publicized HBOC case, in which most recently the Justice Department announced grand jury indictments against HBOC's former top executives,
Albert Bergonzi and Jay Gilbertson, and the SEC announced civil charges
against these same individuals for violations of the anti-fraud provisions of the Securities Act of 1933 and the Securities Exchange Act of
1934. In the words of the SEC's San Francisco district office administra-
tor, Helane L. Morrison, "This is one of the largest financial reporting
frauds ever, both in terms of the scope of scheme and the impact on in-
nocent investors."[36]

As it turned out, and the SEC complaint revealed, HBOC's carefully or-
chestrated management of earnings was a tissue of lies. The SEC's complaint states that Bergonzi and Gilbertson "were the architects of this
fraudulent scheme to 'cook the books.' While carrying out this scheme, defendants unjustly enriched themselves with lucrative bonuses tied to the
company's financial performance, as well as sales of HBO & Company stock
at prices inflated by their fraud."[37]

The inflation referred to was accomplished by an ongoing and perva-
sive program of earnings management designed to achieve ever increasing,
and, apparently, predictable earnings in line with market and analysts' expectations. However, when HBOC revenues and earnings faltered, senior
management crossed the line into the dark side of accounting irregularities
and impermissible earnings management in order to continue to meet financial market expectations.

In April 1999, when McKesson HBOC announced that it was launch-
ing an internal investigation into accounting irregularities related to HBOC
software sales, the company's stock price plummeted from approximately
$65 to approximately $34. This decline translated into a market value loss of
more than $9 billion.[38]

Rule 5: Hammer Stocks That Fail to Meet Expectations

No one doubts the temptation companies face to do everything necessary to meet the market's expectations about earnings—as fashioned by the sell-side analysts. Failure to do so, especially when the surprise is negative, can have dramatic consequences.

Procter & Gamble, the 163-year-old Old Economy stalwart, now knows how stringently Rule 5 applies. On March 7, 2000, the company announced that expected quarterly earnings would fall 10 to 11 percent lower than the previous year, rather than rise 7 percent higher as previously expected.[39] As investors dumped the company's stock, P&G lost nearly one-third of its total market capitalization—worth $76.4 billion—in a single day.

All the more remarkable, the company's stock had already declined some 20 percent from its 12-month high in January after P&G announced its acquisition of two pharmaceutical companies, Warner Lambert and American Home Products. And all this occurred despite the fact that throughout the 1990s P&G had generally outperformed the market and had shown less volatility than the average stock.

Surprise, Surprise
Numerous academic studies have confirmed the market's negative reaction to a negative earnings surprise. Kinney, Burgstahler, and Martin call the relationship between earnings surprises (or unexpected earnings) and stock returns "perhaps the most extensively studied empirical relation in accounting research."[40]

Recently, the three researchers completed a study on the effects of small earnings surprises. They found that positive surprises are associated with positive returns, and negative surprises are associated with negative returns. In some cases, small surprises are associated with large returns.

They also found that in a number of cases the relationship is the opposite of what one would expect. For their total sample, they found that "the explanatory power of earnings surprise for all of our tests is very low." They conclude, "Security returns clearly incorporate a large set of information beyond earnings surprise, because earnings surprise information explains only a small fraction of the overall variations in returns."[41]

If the relationship between earnings surprises and returns is so weak, and sometimes in the opposite direction, why do managers worry so much about managing and meeting earnings expectations? For one, managers can't be certain that the statistical average applies to their own circumstances. Even Kinney, Burgstahler, and Martin noted that a small surprise could produce a large effect. And this was for annual earnings data, which no doubt are more stable because by the time they're released the market has already incorporated three quarters of actual earnings. Had the researchers used quarterly data, the results might have been different. The same can be said for Kasznik's study, as he also used annual data.

In any case, managers face significant pressures to live in the short term, where small deviations from earnings expectations can have a large impact on their company's stock price, at least in the short term. This can prove especially troublesome when the company attempts an acquisition or a merger and then subsequent declines in stock price put the deal at risk or at least on less favorable terms. Declines in stock price can also affect the stock option value in an executive's compensation package. In the extreme case, declines in a stock price can lead to the dismissal of the CEO after a fairly short period of time.

Overreaction or Justified Response?

Is the market totally irrational when it reacts so strongly to short-term surprises? To some extent it does overreact. A study by Swaminathan and Lee provides evidence to that effect. They say their results "paint a picture of a stock market in which prices constantly undershoot and overshoot intrinsic value in response to public and private information" and "that it may take a long time for the market to correct the pricing errors."[42] But the market has some justification for its response, especially when the surprise is negative. Shouldn't any CFO worth his or her salt be able to come up with a few pennies to meet expectations?

Failure to come up with a few cents from some rainy day fund suggests that the surprise to the market was also a surprise to management. An especially troubling circumstance, it may indicate a lack of control over a business that has deeper problems than management realizes or is willing to admit. The market then becomes concerned that the current negative surprise may signal a series of bad quarters. The first piece of bad news becomes the harbinger of a spate of bad tidings. The piper must be paid for all the past fancy footwork that created reported earnings slightly above expectations for several sequential quarters.

Managers, of course, know all about these consequences and attempt to avoid them by sending early signals to the market that consensus earnings estimates are higher than the actual earnings will be. This can prompt the market to react more quickly, but managers hold out hope for a more muted response because they had the good grace not to surprise and embarrass the analysts. So, in addition to offering guidance on expected earnings, management can also find itself preannouncing the announcements of the actual earnings, the amount of which has been carefully determined by managing expectations and creatively meeting them.

A *CFO Magazine* survey of *Fortune* 500 CFOs found that 72 percent admitted to issuing pre-announcements or guidance on earnings.[43] A National Investor Relations Institute survey identified similar behavior when a company's earnings results promised to fall far below consensus forecasts.[44] Only one in ten companies said they would do nothing. Most (70 percent) said they would issue a press release and then contact analysts individually. The remaining practiced various forms of selective disclosure—contacting individual analysts, arranging conference calls, and giving new estimates in conversations as they come up—to signal that actual results wouldn't meet expectations. Presumably, this will cease with the passage of the SEC's fair disclosure regulation.

If nothing else, it all adds up to a lot of management time, energy, and creativity spent in a completely unproductive pursuit because the rules of The Earnings Game require it. And it's big-ticket management time, energy, and creativity that are being squandered.

The *CFO Magazine* survey found that three out of five CFOs spend more than 10 percent of their time dealing with analysts and two out of five give analysts more than 20 percent of their time.[45] The Seven Rules of The Earnings Game may have made this necessary for preserving value, but the time spent with analysts is most definitely time not spent managing the business and creating value.

Rule 6: Listen Carefully for the Whisper Number

Sell-side analysts can demonstrate as much creativity and skill as managers do when playing The Earnings Game. They know the rules just as well, and particularly how managers make sure they meet or beat earnings expectations. At the most basic level, analysts hope managers succeed, because they know they will earn the admiration of the investors who bought a stock that went up on a positive earnings surprise.

At some point, however, this management/analyst collaboration turns self-defeating. If everyone in the market knows the consensus estimate—the one the companies have helped develop and fully expect to meet or beat by a few pennies—they also know that the quarterly earnings report will offer little or no valuable information unless it's negative.

The game then turns to figuring out by how much the company's actual earnings will exceed the consensus estimate. Those clever enough to get the right answer will also know when the results are reported whether to buy, stay put, or sell. It all revolves around getting an inside edge on other professionals, most of whom have equally mastered The Earnings Game.

Enter the "whisper numbers," the "real" earnings forecasts that the sell-side analysts are providing favored institutional clients, or so the market believes. Typically, whisper numbers are higher than official forecasts. This has certainly been true during a bull market, and it remains to be seen whether whisper numbers will become lower than consensus estimates when the bull turns into a bear. Investors, who know that whisper numbers will be much higher than the consensus estimate and buy the stock before the whisper becomes a roar, can expect to earn a trading profit once official earnings are announced.

Whisper numbers haven't been around all that long. A widely cited study by academic researchers Bagnoli, Beneish, and Watts cites a 1994 source as the earliest reference to the term.[46] Awareness of whisper numbers has grown steadily over the past few years with the growth of Internet stocks, which through 1999 consistently beat earnings estimates—at least among those that had earnings. For many, rumors that whisper numbers even existed reinforced their belief that investment banks favor institutional over individual investors.

Consider this definition given by Tom Byrne of StreetIQ.com, an Internet-based investor information service that provides company financial information, whisper numbers, and industry news:

> First, let me define the term. Whisper numbers are unofficial and unpublished earnings per share forecasts that circulate among professional traders on Wall Street, securities analysts and big investors, and they are specifically meant for the favored and very wealthy clients of top brokerage firms. Even the definition is appalling.[47]

Byrne goes on to accuse analysts of intentionally publishing forecasts lower than what they think the company will actually achieve in an attempt "to provide another value-added service to their wealthy clients." StreetIQ.com positions itself as "empowering the individual investor" and protecting "the little guy" as it provides at no charge the kind of information that I/B/E/S, a vendor of analysts' estimates, sells for $15,000 per year in its "Earnings Surprise Indicator."

In a final rhetorical flourish, Byrne decries the existence of whisper numbers and says that they send a clear message to retail investors: "The little guy doesn't count for squat, and if he loses money because of a whisper number whipsawing a stock, then let 'em eat mudcakes."[48]

The Web Learns to Whisper, Too

As one might expect in the Internet Age, some see such unfairness as an opportunity. Within just the past few years, a number of websites emerged to supply whisper numbers to investors regardless of wealth or rank. It's also a prime example of a market solution—not a regulatory one—to the problems inherent in The Earnings Game.

In addition to StreetIQ.com, there's EarningsWhispers.com, Whisper-Number.com, TheWhisperNumbers.com, and JustWhispers.com, all of which provide whisper numbers. First Call, the grandfather of earnings estimates, has also gotten into the game with so-called "hisper numbers," which use a company's historical performance (hence the "h") over the past four quarters to adjust analysts' consensus estimates. Although not known for sure, First Call may have developed its whisper number, at least in part, because of a study by Bloomberg that showed that EarningsWhispers.com's earnings estimates were twice as accurate as First Call's.[49]

Where Do Whispers Come From?

The companies that produce publicly available whisper numbers use a variety of information sources and reasonably sophisticated methodologies—demonstrating yet again how the Internet can level the playing field and make vast amounts of valuation information available to all investors. Investors themselves serve as one valuable information source. The Internet, with its feedback mechanisms, acts as a simultaneous information collection/information dissemination tool. As information flows to the market, and the market digests it, more information is collected reflecting the new intelligence.

Here's how WhisperNumber.com—the self-proclaimed "first company on the Internet (or anywhere for that matter) to actually provide whisper numbers to the individual investor, analyst and media"—generates its whisper numbers. First, it polls and collects data from those who access its website. According to the site, proprietary software also searches "through hundreds of thousands of data sources on a daily basis, with a constant scan from our full-time data miners, full-time news reporters, operations manager, specialized programmers, and two directors."[50] On its website, the company claims a 74 percent accuracy rate in predicting stock movement.

EarningsWhispers.com takes a different approach: "Our first source for a whisper number," according to the company's website, "is a contact associated with a company"—an officer, employee, or an accountant working within the firm.[51] Notice how the Internet facilitates the anonymous collection of data from inside sources, the obvious problems regarding accuracy and legality notwithstanding.

If EarningsWhispers.com can't find an inside information source, it seeks information from a vendor or a corporate customer of the company it's scrutinizing. They query brokers and investors who might have some whisper numbers. They also look at e-mail messages sent voluntarily by people who believe they have useful information.

Because EarningsWhispers.com believes that some of these messages have value, it says it has "recently put in place a method of verifying or authenticating anyone who submits whisper numbers through our online forms." Their "last resort" is to search message boards. All of the collected information goes into calculating a whisper number, which they then compare to analysts' estimates, particularly those that have been most accurate in the past, and to the company's past performance in beating expectations. In some cases, an adjustment is made to the whisper number.

Such a methodology reveals a kind of "meta-earnings expectation." Rather than simply going with guidance from the company or the consensus estimate, the whisper number attempts to take that into account plus a lot of other information and the historical track record of both analysts and the company in order to correct for any inherent biases. It attempts to scrub a process that has benefited companies, sell-side analysts, and institutional investors to the disadvantage of individual investors. In doing so, it also tries to level the playing field by removing any advantage large institutions and wealthy clients may have because of their access to superior information sooner.

Whispers Can Be Managed, Too
Not surprisingly, whisper numbers have their own set of problems emblematic of the openness and democratization of the Internet. Just as the Internet makes collecting and disseminating lots of valuable information easier, it can just as easily do the same with misinformation. Availability does not guarantee accuracy.

An article called "Pssst. Want to Manipulate a Whisper Number?" by Jack Reerink recounts several examples of how some investigative journalists from Reuters, tipped off by a suspicious individual investor, experimented with manipulating the whisper numbers on WhisperNumber.com's website. In one instance, they succeeded in upping an earnings whisper for a small high-tech company from a loss of 8 cents per share to break even for the quarter. They did it by simply inserting their own estimates into the website, which is how data are collected to produce the whisper estimate, and they did it in less than two minutes.[52]

The reporters then notified WhisperNumber.com about the experiment. The company's founders, Paul Hauck and John Scherr, conceded that investors can, in fact, manipulate the website's data. But they also noted that the site is still a good predictor of stock movement, claiming a 60 to 70 percent accuracy rate. They may well be right since this is better than the percentage of official consensus forecasts that accurately predict reported earnings.

The fact remains that what the journalists did was to usefully demonstrate that whispers themselves fall far short of being purely unbiased. Some see this as just another part of the game, and indeed, small investors may prefer a game they can manipulate to one inherently rigged against them.

Rule 7: Hammer Stocks That Fail to Meet the Whisper Number

Do whisper numbers actually help investors make money? Should investors sell stocks in companies that fail to meet the whisper number?

WhisperNumber.com offers evidence that this is indeed the case, and investors should sell when earnings fail to meet the whisper number. Based on data from second quarter 1999, their whisper numbers accurately predicted stock price movement 74 percent of the time over a five-day period and 64 percent of the time over a 24-hour period.[53]

Want more evidence that whisper numbers are more important to market prices than consensus estimates? Nearly 70 percent of companies that met the consensus estimate but failed to live up to whispered expectations saw their stock prices drop over a five-day period, and more than 56 percent saw it drop over a 24-hour period.

The Bagnoli, Beneish, and Watts study, possibly the first to examine how well whisper numbers predict actual quarterly earnings, offers further evidence that whisper numbers provide more important information than consensus estimates. Using whisper numbers and analysts' estimates for a sample of 127 mostly high-tech firms, their study concluded that:

- Whisper numbers are more accurate than First Call estimates.
- Whisper numbers tend to overestimate earnings, whereas First Call estimates tend to underestimate them.
- Whisper numbers are a "better proxy for the market's expectations of earnings than are First Call forecasts."

○ Significant economic profits can be earned by trading on the difference between the whisper number and the First Call forecast.[54]

DO WHISPERS HELP YOU WIN THE EARNINGS GAME?

They do not, and for several good reasons. First, as whisper numbers become more widely available, their utility diminishes. When whisper numbers, with their presumably better information, were available to only a few people, market prices did not incorporate the information in setting a stock's price. Consequently, those who had the information also had a trading advantage over those who did not. Once whispers become shouts, this game-within-a-game is over.

Now the latest talk centers on what might be called the "metawhisper number." Henry Blodget, an Internet analyst at Merrill Lynch, wrote in a report in early October 1999 that Yahoo!'s earnings of $0.14 per share "exceeded the consensus of $0.09 and whispers of $0.11 to $0.12" and "even beat the double-secret, über-whisper of $0.13."[55] Perhaps that's why Yahoo!'s stock fell two quarters later when it failed to meet the whisper number. After all, any company that can top a double-secret, über-whisper should be able to beat its mere whisper number. All that this does, of course, is add a layer of complexity to the game that perhaps suggests a Rule 8—Listen for the über-whisper.

And that leads to the second reason the whisper number doesn't solve The Earnings Game problem. It has simply replaced the consensus estimate as the focus of attention, creating the need for the über-whisper on top of it. This double-secret number eventually becomes as secret as the "double-secret probation" that Faber College's Dean Wormer imposed on the Delta Tau Chi fraternity in the movie *Animal House*. In fact, The Earnings Game sounds exactly like something the fraternity brothers would invent just to play at their next toga party.

This leads to the third reason why whisper numbers aren't the solution. Once whisper numbers become the market's focus of attention, they create the expectations that companies must manage and beat. It's like going from brown belt to black belt.

Finally, whisper numbers don't alleviate The Earnings Game problems because they focus only on the very short term. Note that WhisperNumber.com touts the utility of its numbers in time periods of five days and 24 hours. All that whisper numbers really do is reinforce a short-term orientation and increase the amount of time and energy now being spent just prior to the earnings announcements.

Rather than reducing the importance of the game, whisper numbers simply raise the stakes. They contribute no useful information about a company's long-term prospects. John Markese, president of the American Association of Individual Investors, adds his own emphasis: "Whisper numbers encourage short-term or frequent trading, and that in and of itself isn't a sound investing strategy."[56]

WILL FAIR DISCLOSURE SILENCE THE WHISPERS?

On August 10, 2000, the U.S. Securities and Exchange Commission approved the so-called Regulation FD, its new rule regarding fair disclosure. With its new regulation, the SEC aims to ensure that companies provide all material information to everyone at the same time. In theory, no longer will analysts and large institutional investors get insights about expected earnings or changes in expected earnings before the market does as a whole. Chapters 14 and 15 discuss Regulation FD's implications in much greater detail.

The question in the context of this chapter is: "Will Regulation FD finally silence the whisper numbers?" Clearly, a company that whispered information about earnings to a favored analyst that the analyst could then whisper to favored clients, would violate the rule. But Regulation FD will probably do very little to change The Earnings Game and might, ironically enough, just make playing it more fun and raise the value of whispers even more.

With fewer inside tips, analysts will have to rely more heavily on their own research—not a bad thing in itself—and the deviation in their earnings estimates will most likely increase. This will make the consensus estimate a more uncertain number and a whisper about what the real number will be even more useful.

As we have seen, whisper numbers have now become institutionalized on websites, and nothing in Regulation FD will make them go away. Note also that Regulation FD applies only to high-level executives. Lower-level employees with access to relevant company information can whisper away without violating anything. So fair disclosure might just result in whisper numbers faring fairly well!

However, over time, Regulation FD could have a very salutary effect on corporate reporting and disclosure. Less able to privately tell their stories to selected analysts and investors, company executives and investor relations personnel may conclude that the best alternative is to provide relevant and timely information to the market as a whole. Any bets?

5

The False Prophet of Earnings

Sincerity and truth are the basis for every virtue.
Confucius

Revolutions often arise from conflicts between ideologies. In the Value-Reporting Revolution, the entrenched ideologues follow a prophet, albeit a false one, called reported earnings. As it turns out, earnings, the very premise of The Earnings Game, have become much less important than other measures in properly valuing a company. Once investors come fully to this realization, they will reject the false prophet and seek the truth.

Reported earnings, in essence, simply serve as a measure of past performance. They tell shareholders and the investment community how well a company performed financially over a specified, and relatively short, period of time. But now, reported earnings have become the end game itself. And companies work very hard to make sure the number comes out a certain way. They're not using earnings to manage the business; they're using earnings to manage the market.

A ROAD PAVED WITH BEST INTENTIONS

To be totally fair, the original design of the current financial reporting model was created with the best of intentions. Its practices, however, have mutated over the past 70 years into a problem of their own.

Current U.S. reporting practices had their origins in the Securities Act of 1933 (the 1933 Act) and the Securities Exchange Act of 1934 (the 1934 Act). These acts came in response to the Crash of 1929 and the Great Depression that followed.

In fact, as Volume 1 of the *Accountants' Handbook* points out, "It was widely believed that inferior accounting and reporting practices had contributed to the stock market decline and depression that began in 1929."[1]

The acts, therefore, were intended to correct two primary problems: the lack of uniform reporting methods and the absence of a third party to verify that the proper methods had been used to produce the reported numbers.

The 1934 Act established the Securities and Exchange Commission to standardize and regulate how publicly traded companies report on their financial performance to shareholders. Almost immediately, the SEC turned to the accounting profession to establish a set of uniform principles for external financial reporting. It then gave the profession the mandate to affirm that companies had indeed followed accepted accounting principles in their reports. The *Accountants' Handbook* calls this mandate "a legally defined social obligation: to assist in creating and sustaining investor confidence in the public capital markets."[2]

The CPAs, however, were less than thrilled to accept the obligation. Throughout the 1930s the accounting profession resisted the SEC's mandate. It pointed out the difficulty of producing uniform accounting principles because of "the limitations of audits and the subjectivity of financial reports,"[3] especially because there were so many different types of users of financial reports.

The profession also felt deep concern about its legal liability and its relationships with its clients. "The legal environment certainly colored the profession's responses, but the close allegiance between most practitioners and their managerial clients also made an adversarial relationship unattractive."[4]

Eventually, the accounting profession accepted the responsibility to audit the financial statements that companies must file every year. Today, the Big Five firms—(in order of size[5]) PricewaterhouseCoopers, Deloitte & Touche, KPMG, Ernst & Young, and Arthur Andersen—do most of this auditing work for large domestic and multinational corporations. And they do it under a set of rules established by the American Institute of Certified Public Accounts (AICPA) and accounting principles enunciated by the Financial Accounting Standards Board (FASB).

Reaping What Was Sown

Although regulation and the profession have changed significantly since 1934, the seeds of today's Earnings Game madness were sown in those early days. In 1929, the New York Stock Exchange asked the American Institute of Accountants (now the American Institute of Certified Public Accountants) to collaborate on the reforms that culminated in the 1934 Act.

The Special Committee on Co-operation with Stock Exchanges was formed with George O. May, one of the most influential accountants of his day, as chairman. J.M.B. Hoxsey, chairman of the New York Stock Exchange at the time, had a particular interest in the disclosure of income data and reducing the extent to which companies used reserves to smooth income.

The Special Committee, however, resisted moving in this direction out of a concern that investors would fail to understand "the subjective nature of accounting income determination" and would instead take this income measure as a "fact" that could be multiplied "by 10 or 20 to determine the current value of a firm."[6] The practices of sell-side analysts today certainly justify May's early concern.

Continuing Controversy

There have been, and continue to be, important questions and considerable controversy about the calculation of net income. For example, should the calculation of net income be based on an historical cost model or on current costs? Should net income provide a "current operating" measure of performance or an "all-inclusive" one? To what extent should net income or "earnings" exclude noncash charges such as depreciation of fixed assets and amortization of goodwill and intangibles? Such questions underlie much of the debate over the current major accounting issues, such as how to account for business combinations or employee stock options, and whether to account for financial assets and liabilities at fair value.

It's no wonder, then, that a variety of alternative earnings measures have sprung up in recent years: earnings before unusual items; earnings before goodwill (EBG); earnings before interest, taxes, depreciation, and amortization (EBITDA). Core earnings. Sustainable earnings. One well-known New Economy company recently went so far as to report "earnings before marketing expenses," presumably on the theory that marketing expenses represent an investment in the future and, therefore, should not be included in evaluating the company's current performance. From here it's only one small step to EBEWDWTDFE—earnings before expenses we don't want to deduct from earnings.

WILL THE REAL EARNINGS NUMBER PLEASE STAND UP?

While the FASB and comparable standard-setting bodies in other parts of the world have begun to focus on reporting on performance, the prospects for quick fixes from them appear dim. The current state of affairs continues. Companies in their press releases and analysts in their reports remain largely free—

and increasingly appear committed—to rearrange the officially reported GAAP numbers to present the right or best picture of current earnings.

First Call Corporation, a research company that tracks analysts' estimates of corporate earnings, has announced that it will begin publishing two different sets of estimates of earnings per share (EPS) for 20 Internet companies.[7] The first set is based on regular earnings, including goodwill charges. The second set, called "cash EPS," reports earnings before merger-related costs for goodwill, the premium paid for acquired assets. This is often very high in Internet acquisitions, as their market prices are high relative to their book values. In most cases, cash EPS will exceed regular EPS.

As further evidence of how complicated this issue has become, First Call has drawn the line on letting companies omit the losses of their Internet businesses. But how does this play out?

Laura Johannes, writing in *The Wall Street Journal*, provided one example. Staples, the office supply chain, had persuaded analysts not to include losses in its Staples.com division in their forecasts.[8] First Call, in turn, threatened to drop the complying analysts' forecasts from the major survey it sends to numerous institutional investors.

The article notes that "While First Call has become more indulgent in recent years about letting companies and analysts slice earnings the way they see fit, First Call research director Chuck Hill says that excluding Internet losses is beyond the pale."[9] The article quotes Staples CEO Thomas Stemberg as saying that the issue is "more complicated" than First Call believes, and that Staples breaks out these figures separately anyway. Staples just doesn't think that its Internet losses should be added to non-Internet profits.

Is the market really so easily deceived? After all, doing the arithmetic isn't that hard. If the market is in fact deceived, there's something wrong with it. If it isn't, the argument is specious. In either case, this example merely illustrates how utterly dysfunctional focusing on one number—bottom-line earnings however defined—has become. Others agree. In fact, the market itself acknowledges that things have careened out of control, especially when the focus remains so very short-term.

LIFE IN THE SHORT TERM

Quarterly reporting in the United States was originally intended to give investors a sense of how things were going, a kind of interim progress report to supplement the "final grades" companies give themselves every 12

months. Now, it has become an end in itself, so much so that the importance
of the 12-month figures has greatly diminished.

One outgrowth of quarterly earnings reports seems to be that the market, and consequently companies, has become too short-term oriented. A
survey of 200 U.S. companies conducted by PricewaterhouseCoopers tested
this broad belief. Fifty-eight percent of the respondents strongly agreed that
the financial community tends to focus on short-term earnings; another 35
percent tended to agree. Only 6 percent tended to disagree, and virtually
nobody strongly disagreed.

We obtained similar results in our survey of high-tech companies. Even
though these companies live in a much shorter time frame than companies
in general, the market's short term is too short even for them. Here, 36 percent strongly agreed that the market has become too short-term oriented,
47 percent tended to agree, 13 percent tended to disagree, and only 1 percent strongly disagreed. These data simply confirm general perceptions in
the corporate community.

Of more interest is the fact that the market itself—sell-side analysts and
institutional investors—shares this view. The survey collected data on the
same question among sell-side analysts and institutional investors in 14
countries in North America, Europe, and Asia.[10] For the entire sample, 62
percent of analysts and 63 percent of investors felt that the market focused
too intensely on short-term earnings. These views were most strongly held in
the United States, consistent with the greater emphasis on quarterly earnings in the United States compared to other countries.

And within the United States, analysts and investors in the fast-paced,
high-tech industry see the market as even more short-term oriented. Eighty-eight per cent of analysts and 81 percent of investors in our survey held that
opinion. On the one hand this is surprising, given how quickly things happen for them. At Internet speed, one year can seem like an eternity. On the
other hand, these analysts and investors recognize that in their industry investments made today will not produce a positive return until many years
into the future.

BEWARE THE CONSEQUENCE

But does it matter? One could argue that quarterly reporting is simply good
capital market discipline. It keeps the management team sharp because they
know they will be called to account every three months. This, in turn,
should lead to diligent attention to investing only in projects that will create
value for shareholders.

The countervailing view, of course, is that the short-term focus will cause managers to sacrifice long-term value creation opportunities to satisfy short-term pressures. This could be especially true when managers have stock options, the value of which is determined by prices set by short-term earnings.

Here too the U.S. company survey documents that managers believe that the short-term focus of the market is not a good thing. Fifty-six percent of the respondents who believed that the market is too short-term oriented thought that this generally discouraged companies from investing in long-term value creation projects. This number was 61 percent in the high-tech survey. Interestingly, only 39 percent in the U.S. company survey felt this applied to their own companies. And an even lower 19 percent in the high-tech survey felt this way.

The market shared this view. In the global survey, 61 percent of U.S. analysts (56 percent for the entire 14-country sample) and 77 percent of U.S. investors (57 percent for the entire sample) also felt that short-term pressures interfered with longer-term value creation. In the high-tech survey, 49 percent of analysts and 55 percent of investors agreed as well.[11] All the parties who comprise the capital market—from users of capital (companies) to providers of capital (investors) to those who make recommendations on capital allocation (sell-side analysts)—believe that the activity they engage in is too short term oriented and that it causes problems for long-term value creation.

While there's no conclusive proof that a market less focused on short-term earnings would create more value for shareholders, one way to test the hypothesis is to look at returns in those countries where quarterly earnings are not released. The problem with this is that a lot of other variables can affect returns, including the competitive strength of a country's economy, the size and liquidity of its capital market, its trade policies, and so forth.

Furthermore, there are companies and industries, particularly in the Internet sector, where the market clearly hasn't focused on earnings because none exist. But if the people who play the quarterly Earnings Game all believe that the game is dysfunctional, it probably is.

WHAT A TANGLED WEB

The complex rules of The Earnings Game and the extent to which the rules are bent and broken offer further evidence of just how dysfunctional the game has become. A great deal of energy is spent on a complicated set of activities that contributes very little to creating value for shareholders over the long term.

Although Healy and Wahlen's comprehensive review article on the earnings management literature noted that reported earnings "have been widely found to be value-relevant,"[12] other academic research, such as that of Lev and Zarowin cited in Chapter 3, shows that the relevance of this earnings information has been declining over the past 20 years.[13]

Earnings versus Cash Flow

Things become even more complicated when the issue of the relative importance of earnings versus cash flow comes into the valuation debate. Healy and Wahlen assert that earnings "are better predictors of future cash flow performance than are current cash flows."[14] Lev and Zarowin, on the other hand, say, "Cash flows are often claimed to be more informative than earnings because they are less amenable to subjective assumptions and managerial manipulation than accrual earnings."[15] Although their analysis shows that the association between cash and stock returns isn't appreciably greater than the one between earnings and stock returns, many market participants feel otherwise.

The Wall Street Journal reports that stock analysts at such firms as J.P. Morgan, Goldman Sachs, and Credit Suisse First Boston are "ditching reported earnings in favor of cash flow in making stock valuations."[16] That they are doing so even though "no accounting rules exist governing the proper calculation of cash flow" and "U.S. accounting regulators don't plan to issue rules covering cash-flow calculations" provides evidence that the perceived utility of earnings results is declining.[17]

The same can be said for the growing popularity of Economic Value Added® or EVA®, a measure of profitability developed by Stern Stewart, which incorporates a charge for capital. Advocates of EVA point out that companies can report positive earnings even as they destroy shareholder value because accounting earnings don't reflect the cost of capital.

In his book expounding the principles of EVA, G. Bennett Stewart refers to "an overwhelming body of established academic research" that shows that "accounting measures of performance" such as earnings, earnings per share, earnings growth, and return on equity "are only coincidentally related to stock prices and are not the primary movers and shakers."[18] Stewart rails against "the myth of earnings" and the "earnings totem," which, in conjunction with "a hopelessly obsolete financial management system," conspire to interfere with creating value for shareholders.

Stewart bases his solution on a simple idea: valuation, decision making, and compensation should all be tied to EVA, defined as "operating profits less the cost of all the capital employed to produce those earnings."[19] Although the implementation of this simple idea can be quite complicated, involving more than 160 potential adjustments to GAAP earnings, a growing number of companies use it to improve their capital allocation process, typically by tying incentives to this adjusted bottom line figure. Some companies—Coca-Cola, Siemens, Bank of Montreal, Alcan Aluminium, and Tate & Lyle, to name a few—also report EVA figures. And analysts are working up this measure for themselves independently.

Sophisticated investors, and particularly those with a long-term investment strategy, know full well the limitations of using earnings figures to determine longer-term returns. But earnings announcements can have an effect on stock prices in the short term, and that affects momentum investors trying to ride stocks up only to get off before the price goes down. They care very much about how earnings affect stock prices in the short term.

So do the managers whose stock options are affected by short-term stock prices and the companies that want to use their stock to make acquisitions. The result is an enormous, complicated apparatus of accounting rules, auditing, regulatory bodies, company finance departments, sell-side analysts, retail and institutional investors, investor relations consulting firms, and websites for anticipating, producing, and reacting to earnings releases.

Such activity deserves to be called a game. Its players—companies, analysts, and investors—all vie for a highly prized goal. Companies want to have earnings announcements bolster their stock price. Analysts want to anticipate the numbers so they can advise their investment clients and build personal credibility. Investors, particularly those with short-term strategies, want to make money by selling the stocks of companies that will have disappointing earnings (or selling short if they want to be more aggressive) and buying the stocks of companies that will have strong earnings.

BROKE OR FIXABLE?

As noted in Chapter 4, Healy and Wahlen have said that it is difficult to determine whether current standards are part of the solution or part of the problem. As with all good academics, they see great opportunities for future research.

Arthur Levitt, chairman of the Securities and Exchange Commission, doesn't want to wait for the results of that research. He believes the current standards are good; they simply need stricter enforcement. For him, the

standards are the solution to the problem of earnings management, not the
cause. In a tough speech at New York University in 1998, he launched a vig-
orous, rhetorical campaign against the "too little-challenged custom" of
earnings management.[20]

> Increasingly, I have become concerned that the motivation to meet
> Wall Street earnings expectations may be overriding common sense
> business practices. Too many corporate managers, auditors, and an-
> alysts are participants in a game of nods and winks. In the zeal to sat-
> isfy consensus earnings estimates and project a smooth earnings
> path, wishful thinking may be winning the day over faithful repre-
> sentation.[21]

Some well-known and vocal supporters have jumped on Levitt's
rhetorical bandwagon. Warren Buffett, who ranks notably among them,
urges his shareholders to support Levitt in getting "corporate America to
deliver a straight story to its owners," calling it a "Herculean job" because
"many CEOs think this kind of manipulation is not only okay, but actually
their duty."[22]

In his critique, Buffett focuses on restructuring charges and merger accounting. He cites as one of the major reasons for these "accounting
shenanigans" or "un-admirable accounting stratagems" management's desire to have as fully priced a stock as possible to facilitate merger and acquisition deals. He also maintains that managers receive at least implicit
support from their accounting firms. He chides managers who engage in
such practices because "everybody else does," saying, "Once such an everybody's-doing-it attitude takes hold, ethical misgivings vanish."

Levitt details a more complete list of dubious earnings management
practices—citing five common examples of "accounting hocus-pocus,"
which he says are the main culprits for providing misleading information to
investors and analysts. In essence they are:

1. *"Big bath" charges.* When companies pad restructuring charges in
    order to boost future reported earnings.
2. *Creative acquisition accounting.* A variety of techniques for protecting
    future earnings. Among the most controversial: the classification of
    "in-process" research and development (R&D), which can all be
    written off as a one-time charge with no impact on future earnings.
3. *Miscellaneous "cookie jar reserves."* Overestimating future liabilities
    for sales returns, loan losses, or warranty costs to create a rainy

day fund that can be dipped into as needed to meet earnings expectations.

4. *Materiality.* The intentional recording of errors in one's favor that fall below a defined percentage ceiling of what constitutes "material."

5. *Revenue recognition.* When a company overly aggressively defines when a sale occurs in order to get revenues and profits into the current period.

HE REALLY MEANS IT

Levitt is waging more than a rhetorical campaign. He has outlined a nine-point action plan that calls for greater regulatory scrutiny, tighter enforcement of standards by auditing firms, more training and supervision of audit firms' staffs, creation of more standards as necessary, and properly constituted and functioning audit committees.

The business press picked up on his speech with enthusiasm. *Fortune* published an article, "Lies, Damned Lies and Managed Earnings," that led off: "The crackdown is here. The nation's top earnings cop has put corporate America on notice: Quit cooking the books. Cross the line, you may do time."[23] *Business Week* chimed in with "Earnings Hocus-Pocus: How Companies Come Up with the Numbers They Want."[24]

Levitt's campaign seemed to have had at least some short-term effect. In-process R&D write-offs in acquisitions declined 66 percent, and other merger-related write-offs declined by half even though the total value of merger and acquisition activity declined only 10 percent. The number of asset write-downs shrunk by 28 percent.

To be sure, Levitt's approach to solving the earnings management problem has its vocal critics. The biggest complaint was that Levitt failed to direct any concrete actions toward those whom many others perceive as the biggest culprits—the sell-side analysts. Stephen Barr in *CFO Magazine* comments, "His proposed remedies suggest he is mistaking the symptoms for the disease."[25]

Former Secretary of Commerce Barbara Franklin said, "Levitt won't solve anything by attacking only one side of the problem. There's only so much management and board members can do."[26] Indeed, all Levitt says to or about sell-side analysts—The Street—is his exhortation to "look beyond the latest quarter" and to "punish those who rely on deception, rather than the practice of openness and transparency."[27] He seems to think that this will only happen if everyone embraces "nothing less than a cultural change" without saying anything about how to make this cultural change come about. More regulations are not the best way to solve this problem and certainly not regulations that ignore one side in The Earnings Game.

CHANGE THE RULES

What then is the solution to The Earnings Game? It's not simply stricter regulation on how earnings are measured and reported, as Levitt suggests, although reducing abuses is certainly a good thing. The SEC should speak out more aggressively on the role that sell-side analysts play in perpetuating a game with dramatic and often negative short-term consequences and little long-term significance.

Although the SEC has no regulatory authority over the securities firms themselves in this area—somewhat ironic given the Commission's name and purpose—its chairman and commissioners could certainly use their bully pulpit to speak out on this issue. Chairman Levitt certainly hasn't shied away from doing so on other issues. Past SEC commissioners, notably Steve Wallman, have done so as well.

Our solution? Eliminate The Earnings Game altogether. To do this, two things must happen. First, make quarterly earnings releases a nonevent by providing earnings and other financial information on a monthly, weekly, or even daily basis—whatever period makes sense. Although expensive in terms of systems development, it is probably a good investment compared to putting a company's stock at the mercy of self-serving earnings estimators who distort prices in the short term.

The subject of so-called continuous business reporting has been around for a long time and has received support from such notables as Steve Wallman. If the market receives relevant, accurate information on a near-continuous basis, clarity about the current quarter's earnings will gradually emerge over the quarter, save for a few accounting adjustments. Because current market prices will already reflect this information, the quarterly earnings release will simply document what the market already knows. Analysts' estimates, preannouncements, whisper numbers, and meta-whisper numbers will all go away.

Second, dramatically reduce the attention paid to earnings or cash flow or any single bottom-line measure for short periods of time. Such information is critical to momentum investors and day traders, but much less relevant to value and growth investors who try to figure out which companies will create value over at least the next several years.

These longer-term investors need access to information on nonfinancial performance and intangible assets, the basis for how value will be created. Of course, value must eventually be turned into earnings and cash flow. But when investors have access to all—and that means all—relevant information, bottom-line measures will resume their original purpose: to tell investors how well the company has done rather than predict how well it may do in the future.

6

Inside the Exciting World
of Accounting Standards

And how his audit stands, who knows save heav'n.
Shakespeare, *Hamlet*

Given the madness of The Earnings Game, and given that its very object has lost much of its relevance, why haven't the revolutionary forces already supplanted a regime that has survived for far too long?

Shouldn't executives enthusiastically support any initiative that seeks to change the game? Shouldn't they, in fact, work actively to change the game themselves? Couldn't they just say, "We're not going to play anymore," and start offering the market the information on nonfinancial measures and intangible assets it wants and needs?

Certainly no one requires companies to provide such information, but no one says they can't. Managers who think their companies' stocks are undervalued, and most do, should be especially motivated to do this. And they should provide earnings information as regularly as possible to mitigate the event nature of quarterly earnings announcements as well.

Likewise, investors—unless, of course, they're momentum investors—should support any initiative that diminishes the potency of The Earnings Game. Large institutional investors, who typically take the longer-term view, should use their considerable influence to promote such change. And they could if they started demanding additional and more insightful performance information instead of standing on the sidelines as mere spectators at The Earnings Game.

Finally, shouldn't those responsible for ensuring that the market gets the information it needs push hard to change the rules of the increasingly dysfunctional Earnings Game? The Securities and Exchange Commission and its counterparts in other countries should call for a revamping of a financial reporting model based largely on principles established in a by-gone era.

Regulators should also press for more responsible behavior on the part of sell-side analysts by encouraging them and investors alike to focus on much more than near-term, projected earnings. Standard setters world-wide should work with industry consortia to develop new standards for re-porting of intangible assets and nonfinancial value drivers, as discussed in Chapter 13.

So how should these new standards emerge? Perhaps we can take a les-son from the late nineteenth and early twentieth centuries, when managers began to recognize the need to report information about their companies to their investors. Working with accounting firms, they developed standards for financial reporting. Only later did the accounting profession formalize these practices into standards. Even later, the regulators decided that they should "own the standards." The entire process took decades.

In the New Economy, we don't have decades to spare. The process could be exactly the same, but the time frame must be shorter, because the need is so great—as the previous four chapters have demonstrated—and because the progress to date has been minimal, as this chapter will show.

Despite the plodding progress by the accounting profession and reg-ulators, the forces of the New Economy increasingly draw the market's in-terest and attention toward a range of performance measures not covered by existing accounting standards. The brutal reality is that relatively little has been done to systematically address the need or process for providing the information the market wants. Instead, the inexorable activities of regulators and accounting standard setters, particularly those in the United States, continue to generate more and more rules that further complicate a financial reporting model that many view as increasingly less relevant. Equally unfortunate, there are also strong, firmly constructed barriers to speeding up the process of developing a new reporting and disclosure model.

WHO FEELS THE NEED FOR SPEED?

Most corporate executives instinctively oppose reporting on new dimen-sions of performance. They feel that the costs of greater disclosure outweigh the benefits, particularly if they have to disclose first. We challenge this view, just as we challenge the view that regulators can solve the market's informa-tion needs.

We do, however, sympathize with management's view that when external financial reporting is highly regulated, and the market is focused on short-term earnings, the benefits of experimentation must be carefully weighed against its costs and risk. Although they don't like The Earnings Game, managers don't want to start a new game until all the players agree to a new set of rules. Better the devil that you know than the devil that you don't.

Institutional investors, God bless them, certainly want more information. But they want it all to themselves in hope of gaining a proprietary advantage. Thus, they seek to get this information in private meetings with companies. Company executives then face the dilemma of providing such information to these large and important investors without violating SEC rules against selective disclosure. This has become even more complicated now that the SEC has adopted new standards for fair disclosure, the so-called Regulation FD discussed in more detail in Chapter 14.

Sell-side analysts, of course, have no interest in changing the game at all, given the central part they play in it. Their importance, and no doubt their salaries, would certainly shrink if investors could get the information they need directly from companies, and if quarterly earnings announcements became largely irrelevant. Sell-side analysts enjoy the fortunate situation of getting information provided by companies and using it to make the investment recommendations that generate trading commissions for their firms.

These analysts occupy a happy space. They bear no legal liability for getting an information advantage; that is borne only by executives and their companies who provide information to them through selective disclosure practices. Although extensive regulations apply to securities firms (e.g., "Chinese Walls" to separate research and investment banking), questions arise about the extent to which these regulations are actually enforced.

For many years, an uneven regulatory playing field artificially gave analysts an advantaged position compared to all but the very largest investors. Even before passage of Regulation FD, however, market forces had begun to erode this advantage. Large institutional investors now rely less and less on the sell-side analysts' recommendations. The Internet helps level the playing field even more by making more information (much of it coming from sources other than the company itself) and more powerful analytical tools available to *all* investors.

Regardless of the communications medium they use, managers have the choice of providing only the information required by regulation and letting external market forces supply the rest, or taking a more proactive approach to providing information themselves whether or not reporting regulations require it. It is in everyone's best interest when managers fully understand the information needs of shareholders and other stakeholders and take direct responsibility for providing the information themselves.

Manage It or Not, Change Will Come

Clearly, all the players can take some measure of responsibility for erecting institutional barriers to changing the very nature of corporate disclosure in terms of both content and process. Given the inevitability of such change, however, companies should follow the example of their predecessors, lead the process, and stay one step ahead of the regulators. After all, the market sees the need for the change and will force it to happen, with or without regulatory solutions.

This has already begun. On August 16, 2000, three Internet site traffic auditors (ABC Interactive, BPA International, and Engage I/Pro) declared their plans to launch a new collaborative site called Audit Central. This site will eventually contain detailed data from some 600 online Internet traffic audits. All of the clients involved have agreed to allow Audit Central to make their information publicly available. For the first time ever, investors will have a single source for comparing companies' performance along measures like "pageviews" and "average number of pages viewed per visit."[1] Chapter 13 examines Audit Central in more detail.

MR. JENKINS'S GOOD INTENTIONS

The market solution offered by Audit Central stands in marked contrast to a well-meaning but ultimately unsuccessful attempt to take a more "regulatory" approach to the problem. Nearly 10 years ago, well before the phrase "New Economy" became a standard part of business parlance, the American Institute of Certified Public Accountants (AICPA) formed the Special Committee on Financial Reporting chaired by Edmund L. Jenkins, a senior partner at Arthur Andersen. Now known as the Jenkins Committee, it was formed out of concern over the relevance and reliability of financial reporting and disclosure policies.

In its final report, *Improving Business Reporting—A Customer Focus*, delivered in December 1994,[2] the committee concluded that current reporting practices were inadequate. The rapid change brought about by increased competition and new technologies had resulted in new ways of: (1) organizing and managing, (2) developing products, (3) managing risk, and (4) creating alliances with other organizations. Corporate reporting, however, had not kept pace.

Taking its cue from companies' increasing customer focus, the Jenkins Committee argued that companies should apply the same thinking to "customers" or users of their external reporting—the providers of equity and debt capital and the sell-side analysts who advise them. (Although the "sell side" and the "buy side" differ significantly, the Jenkins Committee did not distinguish between them.)

The committee's report noted that companies "are developing new performance measures often designed to focus on activities that provide long-term value and competitive advantage, including non-financial measures such as product development lead time and financial measures such as economic value." It then posed the rhetorical question: "Can effective business reporting exclude new performance measures on which management is focusing to manage the business?"[3]

Acting on the obvious answer, "No," the report recommended some far-reaching changes in what companies disclose to the market:

- More forward-looking information including management's plans, opportunities, risks, and measurement uncertainties
- More focus on factors that create longer-term value, including nonfinancial measures that indicate how key business processes are performing
- More congruency between the information executives use to manage the company and what they provide to the market

In an appendix, this report presented a "comprehensive model of business reporting" and detailed how it differs from current reporting by U.S. public companies. The model incorporated five new major information components for business reporting:

1. *Financial and nonfinancial data.* The high-level operating data and performance measures management uses to run the business but is currently not required to report. It also includes more detailed business segment data, both financial and nonfinancial.
2. *Management's analysis of financial and nonfinancial data.* The management analysis of trends and changes in financial data contained in current financial statements is extended to nonfinancial data and reported in more detail by business segment.
3. *Forward-looking information.* Information about opportunities and risks, including those from key trends; management's plans and

identification of critical success factors; and comparison of actual performance to previously disclosed opportunities, risks, and plans. This is in marked contrast to almost all currently reported retrospective information and comparisons. The discussion of opportunities and risks is also moved out of the general "Management Discussion & Analysis" and highlighted in a separate section. The subject of risk is important and we devote Chapter 8 to it.

4. *Information about management and shareholders.* Includes identification of directors, senior management, their compensation, shareholders, transactions, and relationships among related parties. No major differences between current practice and the model were identified here.

5. *Background about the company.* Includes broad objectives and strategies, scope and description of business and properties, and impact of industry structure on the company. Although companies are not currently required to report the first and last elements, many already do.

Support from Mr. Wallman

While the Jenkins Committee circulated its report for comments, Steven M.H. Wallman, an SEC commissioner at the time, began actively promoting ideas consistent with the committee's recommendations in a series of speeches and articles. Like the committee, he saw the need for major changes in today's accounting and reporting systems and practices. One major shortcoming he identified is the complete lack of recognition for soft assets such as intellectual property, trademarks, brand names, copyrights, and human capital.[4]

Indeed, while at the SEC, Wallman convened a high-level symposium on the reporting of intangible assets in the fall of 1996. In addition to the content of today's reports, Wallman also expressed concern about their timeliness, especially in light of how short product development and product life cycles have become and how "various new financial instruments have allowed companies to change their entire direction and risk profile literally overnight."[5]

Most Didn't Care

Despite the Jenkins Committee's very substantial report (including a 1,600-page database of research on the information needs of users) and Wallman's tacit support, the response to the committee's recommendations was underwhelming. Company managers voiced a number of objections including the cost of providing additional information, the legal risk in doing so (particularly the forward-looking information, which the Committee recognized was a problem), and the possibility that competitors would use such information to gain competitive advantage.

Some executives wondered whether users really wanted this information, whether they would know what to do with it if they got it, and whether companies would get the purported advantages, such as a lower cost of capital—something heavily emphasized in the Jenkins Committee's report.

Implicit in all of these concerns is the opposition to even more reporting regulations. These same executives implied that a market approach was better, arguing that companies already provide a lot of additional information and would continue if there were real advantages in doing so. They perceived more onerous reporting requirements as unnecessary. Cynics suggested that the report was simply a way to generate additional work for the audit firms. The user community, for its own part, failed to come out vocally in support of the Committee's recommendations.

As a result of the response—and lack thereof—to the report, Dennis Beresford, then chairman of the FASB, said, "My feeling is that most of our constituents aren't interested in wholesale changes to our current financial reporting system."[6] He also did not think that the preference for the status quo would change anytime soon: "My prediction is that the FASB is going to be quite cautious about expanding its role beyond traditional financial statement matters."[7] Nevertheless, he, like many other critics of the report, agreed that over time companies would, in fact, provide more information to the market. "If history has any lesson in this matter," he said, "it is that as time goes by, finance executives will almost certainly find themselves preparing ever more information."[8]

In its summary of a symposium on improving business reporting, *The CPA Journal* quoted Dan Goldwasser, a member of the American Bar Association's Committee on Law and Accounting, as saying, "I have never met an analyst who would not welcome more information. I have never met a corporate controller who was ready to provide that additional information."[9]

Maybe he hasn't met them all. Chapters 9 and 11 take a closer look at how greater corporate transparency is playing out in the real world.

SEEMINGLY ENDLESS SAGA

Despite the flak over the Jenkins Committee's recommendations, others launched similar corporate disclosure initiatives. For example, in October 2000, The Brookings Institution's Task Force on Understanding Intangible

Sources of Value released a report titled "Unseen Wealth," detailing its findings and recommendations regarding the measurement and reporting of intangible sources of value. And the FASB put together a Business Reporting Research Project to look at current best practices in the reporting of nonfinancial measures. It published its first report, *Electronic Distribution of Business Reporting Information* (www.rutgers.edu/Accounting/raw/fasb), on January 31, 2000. A second publication will deal with redundancies between SEC and FASB reporting requirements as a way to "eliminate overlap and duplication."

More recently still, probably because of the high market values of Internet start-ups and the extreme volatility of the market in late 1999 and early 2000, SEC chairman Arthur Levitt asked Jeffrey E. Garten, dean of the Yale School of Management, to form a high-level panel to address the question: "What is value in the new economy and whether the investment community and financial markets have adequate information to assess the value of companies?" Perhaps this will provide the regulatory impetus and direction needed to focus development efforts on a new reporting and disclosure model.

Interest in rethinking the current model of corporate reporting is not confined to the United States. In the United Kingdom, the government has created a Company Law Review commission which, among other things, is investigating how companies should change the way they communicate with the market. One reason for this is that "current accounting and reporting fails to provide adequate transparency and qualitative and forward looking information which is of vital importance in assessing performance and potential for shareholders, investors, creditors and others."[10] The Canadian Institute of Chartered Accountants sponsored a project "to examine the issues and opportunities for reporting nonfinancial performance measures to boards of directors," both in terms of what should be done and what was already being done.[11] In Europe, the Organization for Economic Co-operation and Development (OECD) (www.oecd.org) sponsored a symposium in Amsterdam in mid-1999 on measuring and reporting intellectual capital in light of "the growing importance of intangible assets in enterprises, of which human capital constitutes a major element."[12]

What can be said of all these well-intentioned efforts? All hat and no cattle. And what is the lesson here? It's simple. Regulators, professional standard setters, and academics simply cannot *initiate* new reporting practices for new measures without support from the business community. The executives who run the companies that need the capital have responsibility for providing to investors the information they need. The success of the

ValueReporting Revolution depends on these executives' taking the initiative. Once they do, others can lend their support. But until executives take the lead, nothing much—or nothing much good—will happen.

There are encouraging signs, however, like the Intangibles Research Project at the Stern School of Business at New York University spearheaded by Professor Baruch Lev. Lev has organized a group of interested corporate executives, academics, members of the accounting profession, consultants, and representatives of various government agencies and think tanks to promote relevant research on this topic. The group will also act as a clearinghouse for the research and will hold a major conference every year to promote information and idea exchange.

THE GAAP ENGINE GRINDS ON

The chairman and the chief accountant of the SEC often proclaim that the United States has the best financial reporting system in the world. If quality is measured by the sheer number of pronouncements, rules, and regulations and by their level of detail and complexity, then America certainly leads the rest of the world. The U.S. Generally Accepted Accounting Principles represents a vast array of official pronouncements made over the past 40 years by various bodies, including the FASB and its predecessors, the Accounting Principles Board (APB) and the Committee on Accounting Procedure (CAP), the FASB Emerging Issues Task Force (EITF), and the Accounting Standards Executive Committee (AcSEC) of the AICPA.

These pronouncements appear in various forms: FASB statements, interpretations, technical bulletins and implementation guides, EITF consensuses, AcSEC Statements of Position, and industry accounting and audit guides, just to name the principal ones. The FASB alone has issued more than 130 FASB statements, 44 FASB interpretations, more than 400 EITF consensuses, 7 concepts statements, more than 50 technical bulletins, and a number of special implementation guides containing hundreds of questions and answers. If this weren't sufficient, for public companies there is also another whole set of rules and regulations that interpret and supplement the GAAP rules. Those interested will find them in the SEC's core rules, such as Regulations S-X and S-K, as well as in more than 100 specific Staff Accounting Bulletins, almost 50 Financial Reporting Releases, and hundreds of Accounting Series Releases.

Had enough yet? In order to stay fully current with GAAP, it is not sufficient to know and understand just the official pronouncements; the SEC staff regularly deems it appropriate and important to proclaim their latest views on particular reporting and disclosure matters through speeches and comments at EITF and other professional meetings, which, although not official, effectively carry the same weight for anyone trying to comply with all the rules.

All this effort ends up as an extraordinarily detailed and complicated set of rules about what companies can and cannot do in their external financial reporting. These rules have become so complex that a rapidly decreasing number of CFOs and professional accountants can fully comprehend all the rules and how to apply them. As a telling illustration of that, PricewaterhouseCoopers, the largest Big Five accounting firm, has more than 100 U.S. technical experts who specialize in one or more areas of technical accounting and SEC rules.

Round and Round We Go

Because the regulations are very precise and detailed, they have become self-perpetuating, which promises that their overall framework will continue to increase in complexity. Every new regulation specifying how a company should account for a certain transaction presents an opportunity for a creative investment banker to find a way around it. This, in turn, creates the need for a new regulation to tighten the new loophole or the need for new structures and new rules. The pages multiply. Rules beget rules that beget more rules. Change and refinement are constant, while real improvement is difficult, if not impossible, to find.

A Little Lesson in Leases

Take, for example, lease accounting. FAS 13, "Accounting for Leases," the original FASB pronouncement, was issued in November 1976. An important issue here is whether the lease is a simple operating lease, like a rental agreement, or a capital lease. In the latter case, lessors must show the value of the lease on their balance sheets. One of the criteria for determining if a lease is a capital lease is that the present value of the minimum lease payment is at least 90 percent of the fair market value of the property. To get around this criterion, an entire industry of lease-structuring specialists has emerged to create lease arrangements in which, among other things, the minimum payments amount to no more than 89.9 percent of fair market value.

The FASB and the SEC staff typically respond to such clever attempts to circumvent their pronouncements by issuing many more. A recent chapter by James Adler in the *Accountants' Handbook* reports that since the FASB originally issued FAS 13, it has released 10 related FASB statements, 6 FASB interpretations, 11 FASB technical bulletins, and 24 EITF issues papers!

As Adler notes, "These numerous pronouncements are an indication of the complexity and controversy surrounding the accounting for leases."[13] But writing ever more rules appears highly unlikely to resolve the issue, because the fundamental criteria for determining whether a lease is an operating or capital one inevitably depend on estimates, such as the economic life of an asset, that are subject to management judgment. Similarly, two recent FASB pronouncements, "Accounting for Transfers of and Servicing of Financial Assets and Extinguishments of Liabilities" (FAS 125) and "Accounting for Derivatives and Hedging Activities" (FAS 133), have already spawned voluminous and detailed additional follow-on rules, interpretations, and guidance.

NOT ALL FOR NAUGHT

Please don't construe this little lesson in leases as a blanket condemnation of U.S. standard setting. The FASB's many pronouncements have included some very useful contributions to improving financial reporting. One example, FAS 106, "Employers' Accounting for Postretirement Benefits Other than Pensions," provides investors with very relevant information on a company's postretirement benefits obligations. It helped focus companies' attention on these costs and how to manage them better.

Another example, FAS 131, "Disclosure about Segments of an Enterprise and Related Information," responded to requests from analysts and investors for a better sense of the pieces comprising the whole, not just annually but quarterly as well. The slow but steady movement toward reporting more financial instruments at fair value and for greater disclosure on how companies use financial instruments and the implications for market and credit risk offer still more examples.

WHEREFORE ART THOU, STANDARD SETTERS?

The sheer volume and complexity of the current model for financial reporting resembles the archaic design of an aging factory that continuously gets patched, rebuilt, renovated, and altered by work-arounds just to keep up with new product production requirements. It's bad enough that the importance of financial measures reported long after the fact constantly decreases. Even worse, the apparent compulsion to continuously expand and expound on the rules suggests that most users don't even understand what the numbers really mean. As a result, they focus on only a few simple measures like earnings and revenues.

Consequently, the FASB finds itself in the middle of a battle between companies and the SEC, each with opposing ideologies. Because companies feel pressure from the market to deliver a consistent record of smooth earnings growth, their managers usually oppose rules that would increase volatility in reported earnings. They believe, based on substantial experience, that this will also increase the volatility of their stock prices. The SEC, on the other hand, believes that volatility is a natural condition of the economy and the market and should therefore be reflected in reported earnings. Thus, the SEC pushes for reporting rules that reflect this volatility by having earnings reflect events as they occur.

Many of the most recent debates over controversial issues reflect this tension between companies and the SEC—for example, the FASB's proposal to eliminate pooling accounting for merger and acquisition transactions, to fair value employee stock options, or to expand the use of market values for financial instruments.

Earnings—Yet Again

Companies respond by coming up with new definitions of earnings, as discussed in Chapter 5. These definitions typically exclude certain charges, such as goodwill or book losses on the value of securities still held, that aim to make earnings appear more favorable and stable than they would be otherwise.

This has heightened the need for the FASB and other standard setters around the world to address the issue of reporting financial performance in a way that reduces the excessive emphasis on one bottom-line earnings number. The intention is to develop measures that have more predictive value for future earnings and cash flows than do current earnings.

Thus, the G4 + 1—the formal accounting standard setters of Australia, Canada, the United Kingdom, and the United States—together with the International Accounting Standards Committee (IASC) has proposed reformatting the income statement by operating, financing, and investing activities. If, however, the FASB's experience with business combinations is any guide, any official pronouncement on such a fundamental issue as the reporting of financial performance may be slow in coming.

Confounding Combinations

The current rules on business combinations found in APB Opinion No. 16, "Business Combinations," were issued in 1970. While calls to revise and update APB 16 have been heard for many years, the FASB officially began working on changing it only in the last four years. This has spawned highly controversial proposals to eliminate pooling of interests accounting and to generally shorten the amortization period for goodwill. Important sectors of the business community have reacted predictably, arguing that such proposals could have a negative effect on mergers and acquisitions (M&A) as well as on overall capital formation by unnecessarily depressing postacquisition earnings.

If the market could truly focus on value, this accounting convention wouldn't make any difference because goodwill charges would be seen easily before they were deducted from earnings. Indeed, the growing focus on cash earnings offers evidence that the market is already singling out goodwill charges when it looks at earnings. If a deal really does create value for shareholders, the market should recognize it whether or not goodwill charges dilute earnings. In fact, most M&A deals don't create value. But that's a consequence of strategy, implementation, and culture—not accounting conventions.

Even as the debate over purchase and pooling continues, the rules remain vague on a wide variety of other business relationships, such as joint ventures, alliances, and partnerships. Three common methods exist for accounting for the range of formal relationships between companies: historical cost, equity, and consolidation.

Typically, historical cost is used when one entity owns less than 20 percent of another and does not have significant influence. No profits are shown until cash dividends are earned. Equity accounting is used when one entity owns between 20 and 50 percent of another and has significant influence but does not have control. Here, it earns its proportion of the profits and shows them in its income statement. The third method, consolidation, is used when one entity owns more than 50 percent, which implies that it has control. Profits and losses, therefore, must be consolidated into the entity's income statement—unless it can show that it does not have effective control.

The New Economy has added another distinct facet to this issue: the proliferation of other types of relationships among organizations that lie somewhere in between pure market transactions among completely independent entities and internal transfers within integrated firms. These so-called soft contracting relationships typically result in a network of relationships, sometimes called a virtual organization, between a company and its various joint venture, alliance, and other partners, which may be collaborators and competitors at the same time. These relationships are becoming increasingly important, and so is reporting on their results.

For example, just in terms of alliances, the percentage of revenues that the 1,000 largest U.S. companies earn from them grew from less than 2 percent in 1980 to 21 percent in 1997.[14] One reason for this is that the firms that are actively involved in alliances do better—they have a return on equity 40 percent higher than the average *Fortune* 500 company.[15] As a result, more than 60 percent of chief executives in the United States now approve of alliances compared to only 20 percent five years ago.[16] And alliances occur across all industries and in all countries.

Even more interesting is the fact that many of these allies are also adversaries. Perhaps that's one reason that less than half of them ask their partners for evaluations; they don't want to give valuable information to their competitors. But for alliances to work, their overall performance must be measured and reported, a likely frequent occurrence in the future. This increase in transparency between alliance partners will be a powerful force for increased transparency in general, the topic of Chapter 11.

Fine-Tuning at the FASB

In a world where even the definition of what the relevant entity is for which results should be reported is debated, the current accounting rules reflect a view that the boundaries of the firm are well defined. So while the FASB has spent 18 years considering changes in the rules relating to consolidation and equity method accounting, the world itself has changed. FASB considerations on combinations have barely delved into the new types of arrangements noted above.

There is also a certain irony to the controversy being stirred up by some of these recommendations since many high-tech executives fear that they will hit New Economy companies particularly hard, especially those regarding purchase versus pooling, stock options, and a host of issues surrounding revenue recognition. The irony is that the current chairman of the FASB, who must have the resolve to push these new regulations through, is none other than Edmund L. Jenkins himself.

WOULDN'T IT BE NICE?

What if you could wave a magic wand and create an absolute consensus about all current and pending FASB pronouncements? Analysts and investors would agree that the FASB and SEC have responded to all their concerns about reporting, and companies would happily provide the desired information in the manner required.

Even in this magical world, one big problem would still exist: Every country has its own set of rules about external disclosure in terms of accounting standards and practices, regulatory and enforcement mechanisms, and principles of corporate governance. When each country had its own largely self-contained capital market, this problem didn't exist. This is no longer the case—a consequence of the globalization of business. Multinational companies that operate in many different countries' product markets must report their results in those countries using local accounting conventions. These results can be different than they would be using the company's home-country accounting conventions. But both the results and the methodologies for deriving them are usually different. This undermines the credibility of both sets of numbers. "Without uniform accounting principles, the credibility of accounting is at risk."[17]

One consequence of the lack of a set of global uniform standards is that market forces are seeking to fill this void. Sell-side analysts often produce reports that attempt to reconcile the financial statements of global competitors located in different countries and reporting under different accounting standards.

Morgan Stanley Dean Witter, for example, publishes "Apples to Apples" reports that compare major international companies in selected industries. Investors who want to select the best companies in a sector, regardless of its location, find this useful. So do companies that want to compare their performance to that of their global sector competitors. As international consolidation continues to produce global-scale players within industries, the need for apples-to-apples comparisons of the companies in those sectors becomes increasingly important.

Another pressure for common accounting standards comes from the consolidation of stock exchanges in different countries. By tradition, each country's stock exchange has had a country-based regulator that requires country-based accounting standards for companies that list on the exchange. But when exchanges consolidate across countries, two tough questions must be answered: Who should regulate the exchange? And which accounting standards should be used?

Technology also increases the need for common accounting standards. Today, investors can go to the Internet and glean detailed financial information on companies all over the world. They can also feed this information into software packages and analyze it in many different ways. Unfortunately, this doesn't result in a truly comparative analysis, because the software doesn't make the necessary adjustments across different accounting standards. This, of course, limits the utility of such analytical packages.

The coming of Extensible Business Reporting Language (XBRL), discussed in more detail in Chapter 15, will further increase the pressure for a set of common global accounting standards. For now, just note that XBRL vastly increases the ease and speed with which users can download financial information directly from the Internet into analytical programs. The lack of any meaningful comparability of company performance across national borders will only exacerbate the frustration that investors and analysts feel when they can't take full advantage of the technological resources available to them.

Here is a bold solution to the lack of a common accounting language, one we might even trademark: TRUST GAAP (Totally Resolved United STates GAAP). In this imaginary future, once all FASB issues have been resolved, every country would use TRUST GAAP's well-defined and detailed accounting conventions. Why not? After all, the U.S. capital market is by far the largest in the world—in 1998, it accounted for 49 percent of the entire world's total market capitalization.

The problem here is that if U.S. GAAP challenges the understanding of U.S. executives, those in other countries will find it nearly impossible to use unless they want to make it their lifes' work. This hardly makes U.S. GAAP, or even TRUST GAAP, an exportable product. A set of international accounting standards (IAS) that companies all over the world can use offers a much better solution.

THE CURRENT STATE OF PLAY

Achieving global standards will not be easy. Fields Wicker-Miurin, a consultant with A.T. Kearney, summarized the challenge in the May 15, 2000, edition of *The Wall Street Journal*: "Accounting is probably the toughest nut to crack because it goes to national company law, and national company law is about as intimate and personal a national characteristic as you can get."[18] The issue may be less in the writing of the standards than in their implementation. National pride, different approaches to capital market regulation, and the lack of a recognized controlling legal authority have created major stumbling blocks to making the idea a reality.

Like most good ideas, the concept of global accounting and reporting standards is hardly new. In fact, the idea dates back to at least 1904, when the first international accounting conference took place in St. Louis, Missouri.[19] Then, in 1973, a group of visionaries from the accounting profession created the International Accounting Standards Committee (IASC) with valuable input from financial executives, analysts, academics, and others.

For the first 15 years of its existence, the IASC focused on developing standards that essentially codified the accounting practices used in various parts of the world. Thus, its standards often allowed for multiple treatments of a matter. Beginning in the early 1990s, however, the focus of the IASC's efforts has shifted toward narrowing the range of acceptable alternatives in its existing standards. This effort became known as the "Improvements Project."

The next step forward came with an agreement between the IASC and the International Organization of Securities Commissioners (IOSCO) to cooperate in developing global standards. This would serve as the basis for IOSCO to endorse the use of the International Accounting Standards for cross-border stock exchange listings. The initiative also involved creating a standards interpretative function, the Standing Interpretations Committee, similar to the U.S. EITF. As a member of IOSCO, the U.S. SEC continues to take a leading role in driving forward the IASC's process of change.

Taking Stock

The IASC standards achieved credibility slowly but surely in the 1990s. Companies from many developed and developing economies have started to report their results through IAS or to reconcile their country-GAAP results to IAS. This has helped to introduce a certain amount of comparability across regulatory borders, although major differences still remain. Many countries' stock exchanges now accept listings from foreign companies that report according to IAS. The United States and Canada are notable exceptions.

In the United States, the SEC continues to require that any foreign company desiring to list on a U.S. exchange must either use U.S. GAAP reporting rules or provide detailed schedules reconciling net income and shareholders' equity (as reported under IAS or other countries' principles) to what would have been reported under U.S. GAAP. The SEC justifies this insistence with its assertion that the U.S. approach provides more accurate information and better protection to investors because of its much more complete and detailed set of rules that limits the degree of discretion and judgment management can exercise in the numbers it reports.

The sheer size of the U.S. capital market[20] and the imprimatur conferred upon a company listed on the New York Stock Exchange (NYSE) or National Association of Securities Dealers Automated Quotation system (NASDAQ) are strong incentives for foreign companies to list in the United States.[21] This despite the great expense—$10 million or more for a large company—of converting to and maintaining U.S. GAAP numbers.

At the same time, the greater flexibility of non-U.S. exchanges has prompted an even greater number of foreign listings on those exchanges. At the end of 1999, there were 394 foreign companies listed on the New York Stock Exchange, 13 percent of the total of 3,025.[22] In contrast, in September 2000, the London Stock Exchange's main market had 502 foreign listings, 21 percent of its total of 2,403.[23]

This disparity has caused the NYSE and the NASDAQ to begin aggressively lobbying the SEC to permit foreign companies to list on those exchanges using IAS. The SEC has exhibited caution in doing so. It has signaled a belief that International Accounting Standards require insufficient rigor in the preparation and reporting of financial results, but it is also concerned about companies on U.S. exchanges reporting by two different sets of rules. But if foreign-domiciled companies that are listed on U.S. exchanges were allowed to report under IAS, U.S. companies would probably lobby hard for the right to do so as well.

Turning the Corner

The year 2000 may prove to have been pivotal in the saga of global accounting standards. Agreement was reached to restructure the IASC and position it as the global accounting standard setter. This restructuring, which will take effect in early 2001, will involve creating a new IASC Board, comprised largely of independent full-time members, supported by a larger staff and with funding raised by a senior group of IASC trustees. Both the SEC and the FASB have voiced strong support for this.

Across the Atlantic, the 15 governments of the European Union announced an intention to harmonize listed company financial reporting by 2005—using IAS as the common standard. The G7 governments (Canada, France, Germany, Italy, Japan, United Kingdom, and United States) have also named IAS as one of the 12 core standards in the Financial Stability Forum project to strengthen financial systems.

The question remains whether the SEC will allow foreign companies to use IAS in U.S. filings without reconciliation to U.S. GAAP. Current views are that full acceptance of the International Accounting Standards in U.S. markets will require a continuing effort to close the significant gap between it and U.S. GAAP. Many believe this will happen. Companies and investors alike strongly desire a common reporting framework.

The big uncertainty is just how long putting one in place will take. We would hope that to avoid widening this gap, the SEC and FASB would refrain whenever possible from creating new, even more complex U.S. rules.

Instead, they should focus their efforts in support of the IASC and a common international framework for accounting and reporting standards.

WHERE TO NOW?

In the meantime, market solutions that do not involve companies or accounting firms, such as those developed by sell-side analysts, will emerge to at least partially meet the need. There is much to be said for this. But the fact remains that such market-driven solutions, as well as the proliferating data put out by companies themselves and others over the Internet, are selective and vary in their reliability. Much more satisfactory would be financial statements and other information on key performance measures and business value drivers based on a set of standards and attested to by competent, independent auditors.

We believe that these can be developed through a modified market solution model that involves collaboration among companies, users, and accounting firms. Initially, this should be done through broad principles and experimentation. Eventually, if enough agreement can be reached on measurement definitions and methodologies, this experimentation will evolve into more formal standards with regulatory blessing. We fervently hope, however, that any new set of rules will never reach the arcane complexity of current U.S. accounting regulations.

Part Three

Battles That Must Be Won

Justice is the constant and perpetual wish to render to every one his due.
Justinian I, *Institutes, I*

7

Out, Out Damned Gap!

All men by nature desire knowledge.
Aristotle, *Metaphysics*

A global set of accounting standards would be an enormous step forward. It would set the foundation for a common language among all ValueReporting revolutionaries. If they could communicate more clearly with each other, they could certainly accomplish their mission more effectively.

Yet this useful *first* step would be only that—the beginning of a long and arduous journey to victory. The numbers found in financial statements represent, in a way, the mileposts along the road that tell what's already been passed. Investors need other information—like the road signs that say "Detour Ahead" or "Resume Normal Speed"—to make sound decisions about which way to go.

Companies should make sure those road signs are erected by identifying all the other information investors need—as Swiss Re has done—and then endeavor to make it as descriptive and readily available to investors as possible. This will signal their commitment to the revolution and will challenge others to follow their lead.

WHAT INFORMATION?

Over a four-year span, PricewaterhouseCoopers conducted a series of surveys to identify just what other information investors want and need. These surveys represent a starting point for developing measurement methodologies to provide that information in a valid and reliable way.

The first survey replicated a previous study of U.S. companies, analysts, and investors done by Eccles and Mavrinac in 1993 to identify the types of information, both financial and nonfinancial, that are most important in making investment decisions.[1] PricewaterhouseCoopers, however, went global, surveying institutional investors and sell-side analysts not only in the

United States, but in 13 European and Asian countries as well.[2] In that global study, respondents clearly and overwhelmingly agreed on nine measures (out of a total list of 21) they consider particularly important in making sound investment decisions:[3]

1. Earnings
2. Cash flow
3. Costs
4. Capital expenditures
5. R&D investment amounts
6. Segment performance
7. Statements of strategic goals
8. New product development
9. Market share

Note that this list includes both financial and nonfinancial measures. Some are more relevant to past and near-future performance; others are more relevant to longer-term prospects. The survey also asked about the quality of information the respondents received in each category. Not surprisingly, both investors and analysts generally report higher levels of satisfaction with the quality of information they get on the financial measures than on the nonfinancial ones. The world may not know ValueReporting by its name, but the need for it is global.

Surveys like this one become especially useful when they concentrate on a particular industry. Such surveys can evaluate a customized set of performance measures in terms of their industry-specific importance to companies and the market, the quality of information, the systems companies use to produce the information, how good a job managers think they're doing in reporting information, and the market's level of satisfaction with the quality and quantity of information it receives.

PricewaterhouseCoopers has already conducted industry-focused surveys in banking, insurance, and high-tech. Surveys for pharmaceuticals, consumer goods, retailing, oil and gas, electric utilities, telecommunications, and entertainment and media are in process.

In this chapter, we pay particular attention to the results of the high-tech survey. Given the debate over valuations and the concerns about volatility, this industry serves as a prime example of why the world wants and needs value-based reporting.

For survey purposes, the high-tech industry included companies in computers and peripherals, networking and communications, semiconductors and related equipment, software, and Internet and e-commerce companies. Of the companies surveyed, 85 percent were listed on the NASDAQ and 12 percent on the New York Stock Exchange. At the time of the survey, 55 percent of them expected earnings growth of 21 percent or more over the next three years.

The companies surveyed spanned a wide range of revenues and market caps. Many were quite small. More than half had revenues of less than $100 million, and more than 40 percent had a market cap of less than $250 million. The survey also included a good sampling of sell-side analysts, institutional investors, and venture capital firms to determine their information needs and how well they were being met.[4] For details on this survey, including subsector analyses and a separate venture capital analysis, go to www.valuereporting.com

WHAT'S *REALLY* IMPORTANT?

The high-tech survey asked CFOs, heads of investor relations, and other executives, such as CEOs or presidents, to evaluate 37 different performance measures that are particularly relevant to high-tech companies.[5] That list, of course, wasn't exhaustive, and the relative importance of a particular measure varied by a company's role (e.g., software versus Internet and e-commerce) in the high-tech sector. For our purposes here, the aggregate data will suffice. Exhibit 7.1 shows how the managers in the companies surveyed rate the relative importance, from high to low, of the various measures.

Of the 10 "high-importance" measures, only three are financial. Only one, earnings, is subject to strict regulatory standards regarding its definition and reporting. Definitions for gross margins and cash flow vary from company to company, and although both are commonly reported, companies are not required to do so. Fairly recently, however, a growing number of companies have started to report various "free cash flow" measures.

Three of the remaining seven "high-importance" measures—strategic direction, quality/experience of the management team, and speed to market (first to market)—come from internal company data. The first two of the three are hard to reduce to a single number, and the third, which measures time, is not always easy to quantify precisely. The other four high-importance measures—competitive landscape, market size, market growth, and market share—all require data not typically captured by internal information systems.

portance of Performance Measures for Companies[a]

High Importance	Medium Importance	Low Importance
• Strategic direction • Cash flow • Market growth • Gross margins • Quality/experience of management team • Market size • Competitive landscape • Earnings • Speed to market (first to market) • Market share	• Revenues from new products • Intellectual capital • Sales and marketing costs • New product success rate • Employee retention rates • R&D expenditures • Product development cycle • Distribution channels • Cash burn rate • Brand equity/visibility • Revenue per employee • Customer turnover rates • Capital expenditures • Segment performance	• Employee acquisition costs • Brand development costs • Customer acquisition costs • Licensing revenues • Order fulfillment rate • Utilization of manufacturing capacity • Reject rates • Traffic growth • Royalty revenue • Warranty costs • Inventory write-downs • Traffic patterns • Bartering agreements

[a] Respondents were asked to evaluate measures on a five-point scale with 1=very valuable and 5=not at all valuable. Measures of high importance had scores between 1.00 and 1.99, measures of medium importance had scores between 2.00 and 2.99, and measures of low importance had scores of 3.00 or higher. The least important score had a numerical value of 4.21 and all the rest were between 3.00 and 3.99.

What's Kind of Important?

Most of the 14 "medium-importance" measures fall into one of three categories:

1. *Customers:* sales and marketing costs, distribution channels, brand equity/visibility, and customer turnover rates
2. *Employees:* intellectual capital, employee retention rates, and revenue per employee

3. *Innovation:* revenues from new products, new product success rate, R&D expenditures, and product development cycle

Of these 14, seven are financial. For a number of them, basic financial systems cannot generate the needed measure. Financial numbers need to be combined with nonfinancial numbers to produce the needed information. For example, "revenues from new products" requires a definition of "new product," a set of rules for determining what is and what's not a new product, and systems that capture revenue at the product level.

The remaining seven measures are nonfinancial and, in most cases, somewhat difficult to quantify. This is particularly true for brand equity/visibility and intellectual capital, which are generally referred to as intangible assets and often used, in the high-tech sector especially, to explain vast differences between market value and book value. But how reliable can that explanation be if the measures doing the explaining are unreliable themselves?

What's Really Not That Important?

Most of the 13 "low-importance" measures are either financial or operating statistics, and all are relatively easy to measure given the sophisticated financial and manufacturing control systems most companies use.[6] The reverse is true of most of the high-importance measures. Apparently, what's easy to measure isn't important, and what's important isn't easily measured.

It is also interesting to note that revenue-based measures dominate in the medium-importance category, whereas cost-based measures dominate in the low-importance category. Given the importance of revenue growth, often much more important than earnings growth (in determining the value of a high-tech company), this is not surprising.

But What Does the Market Think?

Guess what? Sell-side analysts and investors actually concur with company managers on which measures have real importance in valuing a company's stock. Exhibit 7.2 shows a striking agreement: the "Top Ten" lists for all three groups are identical, although the order of importance varies somewhat within each.

The magnitude of the differences doesn't justify drawing any strong conclusions, but there are some interesting things to note:

- "Earnings" tops the list for investors and lands near the bottom for managers, with analysts ranking the measure somewhere in between.

Exhibit 7.2

Top Ten Hit Parade of Performance Measures[a]

Companies	Analysts	Investors
1. Strategic direction	1. Market growth	1. Earnings
2. Cash flow	2. Strategic direction	2. Cash flow
3. Market growth	3. Competitive landscape	3. Quality/experience of management team
4. Gross margins	4. Quality/experience of management team	4. Competitive landscape
5. Quality/experience of management team	5. Earnings	5. Market growth
6. Market size	6. Market size	6. Strategic direction
7. Competitive landscape	7. Gross margins	7. Gross margins
8. Earnings	8. Market share	8. Market share
9. Speed to market (first to market)	9. Cash flow	9. Speed to market (first to market)
10. Market share	10. Speed to market (first to market)	10. Market size

[a] The measures above are those that appeared in the "high-importance" list for all three groups and are listed in an ascending rank order.

- Analysts add an eleventh measure, revenues from new products, to their complete list of high-importance measures.
- Investors have the longest list of high-importance measures. In addition to those shown in their Top Ten list, investors also rank as highly important the measures of revenues from new products, new product success rate, brand/equity visibility, distribution channels, segment performance, and utilization of manufacturing capacity.

Again, these differences aren't always large, and the smaller size of the investor sample cautions against drawing any firm conclusions. One thing can be said with unequivocal certainty, however: Investors are very interested in earnings, and they are very interested in many other things as well.

How's It Going?

While it is not surprising that managers and the market agree on the measures that are important in creating and communicating value, it's nice to have some empirical confirmation. That's the good news. Exhibit 7.3, however, starts to tell the other side of the story in three parts.

Exhibit 7.3

The Top Ten Story Continues
Perceptions about Other Aspects of the Top Ten Measures

Measure	Quality of Internal Systems	How Actively Reported by Companies	How Adequate Information Is to Analysts	How Adequate Information Is to Investors
Earnings	High	High	High	Medium
Gross margins	High	High	High	Medium
Cash flow	High	High	Medium	Medium
Strategic direction	Medium	High	Medium	Medium
Quality/experience of management team	Medium	Medium	Medium	Medium
Speed to market (first to market)	Low	Medium	Medium	Medium
Market size	Low	Medium	Medium	Medium
Market growth	Low	Medium	Medium	Medium
Market share	Low	Medium	Medium	Medium
Competitive landscape	Low	Medium	Medium	Medium

First, managers rate their internal measurement systems as high quality only for the financial measures. They rate them as medium for two measures, "strategic direction" and "quality/experience of the management team," and as low for the remaining five—all the measures that require data external to the firm.[7]

Second, and despite their self-identified quality problems with internal systems, managers see themselves as fairly active when it comes to providing information to the market.[8] This is especially true for the three financial measures and "strategic direction."

Third, there is a close relationship between how actively managers say they try to provide information to the market on a measure and how satisfied the market is with the information it gets from them[9] with two important exceptions:

1. Managers believe they do a better job of providing information on "strategic direction" and "cash flow" than the market thinks they do.

2. Analysts register more satisfaction than investors with the information they get on "earnings" and "gross margins."

The second exception is discussed in more detail later in this chapter, and Chapter 14 puts the issue in a broader policy context.

The Gaps Are Gaping

The analysis of Exhibit 7.3 suggests that high-tech company managers make a reasonable effort to provide information to the market, despite some information quality problems, and that the market is reasonably satisfied with the information it gets. This conclusion is based on the absolute level of the responses. When the data are analyzed in terms of relative importance of the measures' levels, however, the story takes a different turn.

Exhibit 7.4 explains the general approach taken to this deeper analysis. Note that managers often "value" their companies higher than the market does. This is certainly the case in the high-tech survey. Thirty percent of high-tech managers believe their companies' shares are undervalued a lot, 45 percent believe they are undervalued somewhat, 18 percent feel their company is properly valued, and only 1 percent feel the market overvalues their company somewhat. Not a single one of the respondents feels the market overvalues their company by a lot.

Exhibit 7.4 identifies five communication gaps:

Exhibit 7.4

Sources of the Value Gap

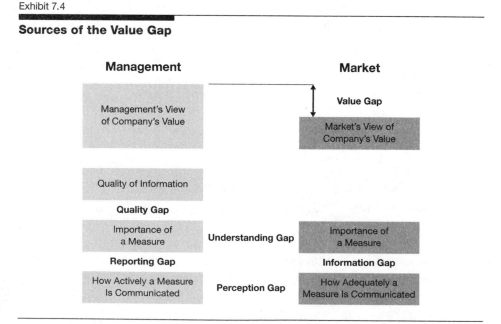

1. *Information Gap.* The difference between the importance analysts and investors attach to a measure and how satisfied they are that their information needs on that measure are being met by companies' managers.
2. *Reporting Gap.* The difference between the importance managers attach to a measure and how actively they work to report on it.
3. *Quality Gap.* The difference between the importance managers attach to a measure and the reliability of the information their internal systems provide on it.
4. *Understanding Gap.* The difference between the importance managers attach to a measure and the importance analysts and investors attach to it.
5. *Perception Gap.* The difference between how actively managers think they work to report on a measure and how analysts and investors perceive the adequacy of the information they get on it.

Some of these gaps are very large, as subsequent examples will show. This is especially true for the first three of the five gaps, and they are the most important. The conclusion is obvious. The market disagrees with most managers' valuations of their companies, at least in part because it lacks enough information to make a proper determination. And managers, to a substantial extent, simply don't provide the information the market needs.

Of course, managers offer up many reasons for not providing more information, some more legitimate than others. Chapter 10 goes into much more detail about that. For now, let's simply say that managers can't have it both ways. They can either keep their cards close to the vest and accept the price the market sets using limited information, or they can open their kimonos and let the market set prices based on the same information the company has. Managers who don't report information that the market considers important, and then whine that their stock prices are too low, will find little solace in this book.

GAP 1: THE INFORMATION GAP

When the market lacks the information it considers important, it will more likely err on the side of caution and value a company's stock lower than the managers will, because managers have access to more performance information and future strategies and plans. Chapter 10 discusses how information affects valuations in more detail.

Lack of information, of course, can also contribute to excessive optimism in the market if the company has more problems than the market realizes. That can't last forever. Usually sooner rather than later the "truth be
known," and the stock crashes. In one of those interesting little twists of fate,
a single piece of bad news, which thanks to the Internet spreads like wild-
fire, can "burn" a stock for a long time. But one piece of good news usually
can't lift it out of the depths for any sustained period.

Some might argue that the market already gets most of the information it needs to properly price a company's stock. But does it really? Exhibit
7.5 shows that it does not. Note the significant Information Gap for both analysts and investors on a number of performance measures.

Recall that the Information Gap is the difference between the importance analysts and investors attach to a measure and how satisfied they are that
their information needs on that measure are being met by managers. Because
the Information Gap takes into account the relative importance of a measure,
it offers a more meaningful way to assess if the market's information needs are
being met compared to simply looking at the market's absolute level of satisfaction. Moderate market satisfaction on a very important measure is more of
a problem than moderate satisfaction on an unimportant measure.

Exhibit 7.5 offers some insight into the Information Gap for both analysts and investors. The exhibit offers a lot of information, so read the note
before diving into the findings. Exhibit 7.5 shows that seven of the analysts'
Top Ten measures (as well as the measure "revenues from new products")
have significant Information Gaps. Five of those gaps are very large. Investors perceive Information Gaps on 14 of the 15 measures they consider
highly important. Nine of these gaps are very large.

For the 11 measures that analysts rate as highly important, they express
satisfaction with the adequacy of information they get on only three. It's
even worse for investors. They express satisfaction with the adequacy of information on only one of the 16 measures they rank as highly important.
This isn't a gap, it's the Grand Canyon.

But there's more. It is no big surprise that the only measures in the analysts' Top Ten that have no Information Gaps are the financial ones. Even
more revealing, the investors perceive large gaps in earnings and cash flow,
the most basic financial measures and the top two on their list. This, in combination with investor Information Gaps on 26 of the full list of 37 measures,
means that the overall Information Gap for investors is larger than for the
analysts who had only 18 total gaps out of all the measures. Even worse, investors perceive very large Information Gaps on 15 of the measures; analysts
perceive only seven.

Exhibit 7.5

The Information Gap for Analysts and Investors[a]

Size of Gap	Analysts	Investors
Very Large	• Market growth* • Revenues from new products^ • Competitive landscape* • Market share* • Market size* • Intellectual capital • Customer turnover rates	• New product success rate^ • Market growth* • Order fulfillment rate • Employee retention rates • Customer turnover rates • Product development cycle time • Competitive landscape* • Intellectual capital • Distribution channels^ • Customer acquisition costs • Brand equity/visibility^ • Segment performance^ • Utilization of manufacturing capacity^ • Speed to market* • Strategic direction*
Large	• Employee retention rates • New product success rate^ • Segment performance^ • Customer acquisition costs • Speed to market* • Product development cycle time • Strategic direction* • Distribution channels^ • Quality/experience of management team* • Brand equity/visibility^ • Brand development costs	• Cash flow* • Brand development costs • Employee acquisition costs • Quality/experience of management team* • Earnings* • Market share* • Inventory write-downs • Revenues from new products^ • Market size* • Traffic growth • Traffic patterns

[a] Measures are in rank order by the size of the Information Gap. A "very large" Information Gap exists when the absolute value of the difference between the importance of the measure and the adequacy of information provided on it is 1.00 or greater. A "large" Information Gap occurs when the absolute value of the difference is between .50 and .99. In this table, the symbol ^ indicates that analysts or investors consider the measure very important, but company managers do not. An asterisk means a measure made the Top Ten list.

The conclusion is inescapable: The people who make the ultimate investment decisions think they're missing out on a lot of important information. Sell-side analysts, who have better access to companies than most investors do, still want a lot of information they don't get. Chapter 14 has more to say on the implications of sell-side analysts' access compared to investors'—and what managers should do about it.

GAP 2: THE REPORTING GAP

Gap 1, the Information Gap, exists for a good reason. The market doesn't have information on the measures it considers highly important because managers don't provide it. This is the Reporting Gap, the difference between the importance managers attach to a measure and how actively they work to report on it, as shown in Exhibit 7.6.

This exhibit delivers two pieces of good news:

1. There are no very large Reporting Gaps for any of the Top Ten measures.
2. Managers believe they work hard to communicate information on strategic direction, earnings, gross margins, cash flow, and sales and marketing costs.

This means that the companies do report information on their strategy and its bottom-line consequences. What's missing is information on all

Exhibit 7.6

The Reporting Gap[a]

Very Large	Large
• Employee retention rates	• Speed to market (first to market)*
• Customer turnover rates	• Brand development costs
• Product development cycle time	• Reject rates
• Employee acquisition costs	• Market growth*
• Intellectual capital	• New product success rate^
• Customer acquisition costs	• Brand equity/visibility^
	• Revenues from new products
	• Order fulfillment rate
	• Market share*
	• Revenue per employee
	• Market size*
	• Distribution channels^
	• Quality/experience of the management team*
	• Competitive landscape*

[a] Measures are in rank order by the size of their Reporting Gaps. A "very large" Reporting Gap exists when the absolute value of the difference between the importance of the measure and how actively managers work to report on it is 1.00 or greater. A "large" Reporting Gap occurs when the absolute value of the difference is between .50 and .99. In this table, the symbol ^ indicates that analysts or investors consider the measure highly important, but company managers do not. An asterisk means a measure made the Top Ten list.

those value drivers in between, such as market potential, market position, people, customers, innovation, and brands, which turn strategy into financial performance.

The rest of Exhibit 7.6 is strictly bad news. Of the six measures with very large Reporting Gaps, managers, analysts, and investors concur that four of them are important: employee retention rates, customer turnover rates, product development cycle time, and intellectual capital. Both the analysts and the investors consider "customer acquisition costs" important, and investors rank "employee acquisition costs" important as well. Somewhat ironically, although nearly all companies would say they "treasure" their people and "appreciate" their customers, they offer very little information about either group to the market.

Exhibit 7.6 also shows that six of the Top Ten measures have large Reporting Gaps. Another five measures that managers regard as important and analysts and investors regard as either highly important or important have "large" gaps—new product success rate, brand/equity visibility, revenues from new products, revenue per employee, and distribution channels. "Brand development costs" and "order fulfillment rate" round out the list of measures that have large gaps and that analysts, investors, or both rank as important.

Actually, there is one more tidbit of good news in Exhibit 7.6. The large Reporting Gap for "reject rates" shouldn't cause anyone much worry because none of the three groups care about it very much anyway.

Taking Sherlock Holmes's "the dog that didn't bark" lead, we can deduce another fact from the 20 measures listed in Exhibit 7.6, or rather the 17 measures not listed. On these 17 measures, managers provide information to the market in proportion to the importance they accord it, and about half are seen as relatively unimportant. Managers do rank the other half as important, at least for their own decision-making purposes.

The message here is clear as well. It's not because the market isn't listening to the information it's getting: There's simply nothing to listen to.

GAP 3: THE QUALITY GAP

To some extent, there's nothing to listen to for a good reason. Some information lacks sufficient reliability for it to be communicated to the market. When making internal decisions, managers can take a bit more latitude with lower-quality information. They have a good sense of its relative reliability because they know the virtues and faults of the systems that produce it. Managers can also assess the validity and reliability of information within a broader context than the market can.

A company that provides the market with information it knows to be unreliable plays a risky and dangerous game. Analysts and investors, who are less able to assess information reliability, may draw conclusions that aren't truly justified. Or they may place more importance on a piece of information than they would if it they could assess it in a broader overall context.

Even worse, questionably reliable information sometimes leads to revisions in measures that have been previously reported to the market. When managers have to revise numbers they've already reported, they can lose enormous amounts of credibility. The effect on the company's stock price can be equally devastating. Managers show wisdom when they ensure the high quality of information before they report it to the market.

Information importance and reliability are the two basic components of the Quality Gap—the difference between the importance managers attach to a measure and the reliability of the information their internal systems provide on it. As a reporter on the Quality Gap, Exhibit 7.7 tells only bad news.

Every single measure that has a "very large" Quality Gap appears on the Top Ten Hit Parade of Performance Measures. The four measures that have a "large" Quality Gap are all considered "important" by managers and as "important" or "highly important" by analysts and investors.

The Quality Gap clearly tells companies what they should do. They must make significant improvements in the measurement methodologies for the measures that create value for shareholders.

Exhibit 7.7

The Quality Gap[a]

Very Large	Large
• Market growth* • Market size* • Competitive landscape* • Strategic direction* • Speed to market (first to market)* • Market share* • Quality/experience of management team*	• Brand equity/visibility^ • Intellectual capital • New product success rate^ • Product development cycle time

[a] Measures are in rank order by the size of the Quality Gap. A "very large" Quality Gap exists when the absolute value of the difference between the importance of the measure and the ability of internal systems to provide reliable information on it is 1.00 or greater. A "large" Quality Gap occurs when the absolute value of the difference is between .50 and .99. In this table, the symbol ^ indicates that analysts or investors consider the measure highly important but company managers do not. An asterisk means a measure made the Top Ten list.

Until companies can close the Quality Gaps, large Reporting Gaps will—and should—appear, and they in turn create large Information Gaps with all the associated problems. Exhibit 7.8 shows a clear relationship between Quality Gaps and Reporting Gaps. Note that all of the Top Ten measures (except strategic direction) that have very large Quality Gaps (see Exhibit 7.7) also have large Reporting Gaps. The four measures that have large Quality Gaps also have either very large or large Reporting Gaps, as Exhibit 7.8 shows. If management's efforts to report information on a measure are disproportionate to the quality of information reported, are they good faith efforts or just bad judgment?

What does Exhibit 7.8 say about the measures that have significant Reporting Gaps but no meaningful Quality Gaps? The question becomes particularly intriguing for those measures that managers rank as important:

- Employee retention rates
- Employee acquisition costs
- Customer turnover rates
- Customer acquisition costs
- Revenue from new products
- Revenue per employee

Exhibit 7.8

Quality and Reporting Gaps[a]

	Very Large Quality Gap	Large Quality Gap
Very Large Reporting Gap		• Product development cycle time • Intellectual capital
Large Reporting Gap	• Market growth* • Market size* • Competitive landscape* • Speed to market (first to market)* • Market share* • Quality/experience of management team*	• Brand equity/visibility^ • New product success rate^

[a] An asterisk means a measure made the Top Ten list. In this table, the symbol ^ indicates that the analysts or the investors consider the measure highly important, but company managers do not.

○ Distribution channels

Developing measures on the value drivers is relatively straightforward. Companies don't report on them because they believe they have reason not to. For example, if companies have concerns about how competitors will use the information or they think the market doesn't care about the information, they will not report it.

GAP 4: THE UNDERSTANDING GAP

The high-tech survey doesn't offer insight into what managers think the market thinks is important. It does, however, point out significant differences between the measures that managers consider important and the measures analysts and investors do. This is the Understanding Gap shown in Exhibit 7.9.

Unlike the tables on the Information, Reporting, and Quality Gaps, Exhibit 7.9 delivers mostly good news. Again, adopting the "dog that didn't bark" analytical method, there are no measures managers regard as important that analysts and investors do not. What managers consider important to creating value for shareholders is the same as what analysts focus on in making their recommendations and investors focus on in making their investment decisions. This strongly suggests that managers and markets are not using different business models and cannot explain their different views on values. Rather, these different views are grounded in the Information Gaps resulting from Reporting Gaps that are largely driven by Quality Gaps.

That analysts and investors consider a number of measures more important than managers do mitigates this conclusion to some extent. Perhaps some of the differences in perceptions about value result from managers' not paying attention to some things that the market does.

Mitigating the mitigation is the fact that only one measure in Exhibit 7.9, "distribution channels," is considered highly important, and this just for investors. Overall, there is only a small Understanding Gap, which shows there is a broadly shared agreement on the relative importance of the different measures.

GAP 5: THE PERCEPTION GAP

The last gap—the Perception Gap—reflects more subtle differences than the other four. The Perception Gap is the difference between how actively managers think they work to report on a measure and how analysts and investors perceive the adequacy of the information they get. If managers think

Exhibit 7.9

The Understanding Gap
Measures More Important to the Market than to Companies[a]

	Analysts	**Investors**
Very Large	• Royalty revenue^	• Utilization of manufacturing capacity^^ • Royalty revenue^ • Inventory write-downs^ • Traffic growth^ • Traffic patterns^ • Segment performance^^ • Licensing revenue^
Large	• Segment performance^ • Licensing revenue^ • Bartering agreements • Traffic patterns • Traffic growth	• Order fulfillment rate^ • Customer acquisition costs^ • Brand equity/visibility^^ • Bartering agreements • Warranty costs • Distribution channels^^ • Capital expenditures^

[a] A "very large" Understanding Gap occurs when the absolute value of the difference between the importance managers attach to a measure and the importance analysts and investors attach to it is 1.00 or greater. A "large" Understanding Gap occurs when the absolute value of the difference is between .50 and .99. There were no examples in which a measure had significantly more importance to managers than to analysts or investors. ^^ indicates that the measure is ranked "high in importance" to analysts or investors and ^ indicates that the measure is ranked "medium in importance" to analysts or investors.

they work noticeably harder at reporting on a measure than the market does, a positive Perception Gap occurs. A negative Perception Gap indicates the opposite.

The Perception Gap shows how realistically managers perceive the quality of their communications with the market. A large Information Gap and a large Reporting Gap on the same measure says the market doesn't get the information it wants, but at least managers know they don't provide it, for whatever reasons. A positive Perception Gap exists when managers actually think they are doing a better job providing information than the market thinks they are. A negative Perception Gap means that managers do a good job of providing information to the market but don't even know it!

Exhibit 7.10, with a few notable exceptions, delivers some good, albeit ironic, news. Nearly all of the Perception Gaps are negative. On 14 measures for analysts and on 11 measures for investors, the market is actually more satisfied with the information it gets than one would expect from the effort that managers make to provide it. But only one of these measures, "utilization of manufacturing capacity," ranks as a "highly important" measure and just for investors. Such negative gaps, no doubt, have less to do with managers actively providing information on these measures, or the level of satisfaction analysts and investors have regarding the information they receive.

Exhibit 7.10

The Perception Gap[a]

	Analysts	Investors
Positive gap: Managers don't report as well as they think they do.		• Earnings* • Gross margins* • Strategic direction*
Negative gap: Managers report better than they think they do.	• Royalty revenue^ • Traffic growth • Revenue per employee^ • Inventory write-downs • Employee acquisition costs • Bartering agreements • Licensing revenues^ • Warranty costs • Traffic patterns • Utilization of manufacturing capacity • Reject rates • Brand development costs^ • Customer acquisition costs^ • Employee retention rates^	• Royalty revenue^ • Licensing revenue^ • Bartering agreements • Traffic growth^ • Reject rates • Utilization of manufacturing capacity^^ • Warranty costs • Employee acquisition costs^ • Customer acquisition costs^ • Revenue per employee^ • Traffic patterns^

[a] A positive Perception Gap exists when managers rate "how actively they report information on a measure" higher than analysts or investors rate the "adequacy of the information they get" on a measure. A negative Perception Gap exists when the managers' rating on a measure is lower than the analysts' or investors' rating. Measures listed in this table are for absolute differences of .50 or greater. The symbol ^^ indicates the measure's importance rating as "high." The symbol ^ indicates the measure's importance rating is "medium." An asterisk means the measure made the Top Ten list.

It's simply that a low level of satisfaction is exceeded only by an even lower level of effort.

As amusing as the negative Perception Gaps may be, the three positive Perception Gaps for investors on measures that made the Top Ten list—earnings, gross margins, and strategic direction—cause more concern and have greater consequences. These gaps indicate that managers think they do a better job of reporting on key measures to investors than they really do. It's just one more piece of evidence that communication between managers and investors needs a lot of improvement. And remember that earnings, which has the largest positive Perception Gap of all, also ranks number one on the list of highly important measures for investors. That's a Perception Gap that is really agape.

CLOSING THE GAPS

The five gaps described in this chapter are not unique to the high-tech industry. Nor are they unique to newer and smaller companies, including most of the Internet companies surveyed. Our analysis revealed nearly identical patterns when we analyzed the data by revenue or market cap. A similar survey of major banks and insurance companies in the United States, Europe, Canada, and Australia yielded very similar findings. There's every reason to expect that surveys of other industries will do the same.

Such surveys show convincingly that no amount of fine-tuning of today's U.S. GAAP will close these important gaps. A set of global accounting standards won't close them either. Of course, regulators won't rush immediately to establish standards in the area of nonfinancial measures, where the gaps of every ilk are the greatest. No one expects them to, either. Their demonstrated concern about the issue, however, would offer welcome recognition that major changes should be made in what information is provided to the market and how.

The best way to start closing these gaps, and to reap the benefits of doing so, is for managers to recognize that the gaps exist. Chapter 1 described how Swiss Re did just that. When managers fail to report information, a large Information Gap opens, particularly if analysts and investors think the measure is important. When a Quality Gap leads to a Reporting Gap, companies should start developing better internal measurement systems. Even with all the recent enthusiasm over balanced scorecards, much work remains to be done in developing measurement methodologies for some very important value drivers.

Managers must ask themselves whether the benefits of not reporting information to the market are really worth the price they pay for not doing so. And the price they pay is often in shareholder value. Chapter 10 discusses the benefits of better disclosure in much greater depth.

But before moving to that, we'd like to point out another major gap in external disclosure. It's the gap in the reporting of risk that managers are taking to create value for shareholders and how they manage these risks, both on the upside and on the downside. Chapter 8 addresses this risky business in considerable detail.

8

Risky Business

We cannot help putting an end to our doubt in one way or another, because we would rather be mistaken than believe nothing.
Jean-Jacques Rousseau, *The Creed of the Savoyard Priest*

Even if companies reported all the relevant financial and nonfinancial mea sures that show how they create value and how much they create, investors would still need more information. They would also want to know the risks the company is taking to create this value. As with the ValueReporting Revolution itself, creating value requires taking risks, and the greater the risk, the greater the potential to create value—but also the greater the potential to destroy value. Investors got a pointed reminder of that lesson during the spring and summer of 2000 when the Internet sector in the U.S. markets had a near-total meltdown.

Investors know that creating value requires taking risk. But they would like to have a better sense of the risk and its potential upside as well as the downside and how it would be managed. Current reporting regulations focus on either a narrow set of risks, primarily the market and credit risk of financial instruments, or on special circumstances, like a securities offering where a broader set of risk factors must be disclosed in the offering memorandum.

The Securities and Exchange Commission requires companies to discuss risk factors in their annual 10K filings, but gives little guidance about how to do it. Just as regulations cover only a small portion of value-relevant performance information, they also cover only a small portion of what the market really needs to know about risk. This leads to significant differences in how much risk information different companies report and how they report it.

In most cases, investors have great difficulty getting a complete and integrated view of a company's risk/opportunity profile. That will change only when companies take the necessary steps to reduce their existing—and usually significant—Risk Information Gaps. As with all of the Communication

143

Gaps discussed in the previous chapter, the Risk Information Gap lies at the end of a domino effect. A large Quality Gap in risk management and measurement information can create a large Reporting Gap, which in turn can create a large Information Gap—in this case a Risk Information Gap.

Just listing a lot of risks in the company's Form S1 or Form S3, the SEC filings for security offerings, or the 10K, won't close the gap. Many investors can figure out these risks on their own. To close this Risk Information Gap, managers should be more forthcoming not only about the risks they take, but also about how they manage them. The market wants to know both, and few companies today discuss risk in such an integrated way.

Once investors have such integrated information, they can decide for themselves if a company's risk and value offering fits their individual investment risk profile. Risk seekers like companies that offer a big upside, even though the downside might look substantial. They have a special fondness for companies that take "smart" risks and know how to manage the downside as well. Investors reward these companies with a cost of capital lower than their other high-risk peers. Because investors have better information, they face less uncertainty. Consequently, they demand a lower risk-taking premium.

Risk-averse investors, of course, are attracted to companies that minimize the downside. But even they need to know the opportunities the company has forgone in the process of reducing its risks.

THE NEED FOR BETTER RISK REPORTING

In the world of regulated corporate reporting, companies have nothing that even approaches a comprehensive framework for giving the market a complete sense of their overall risk profile or its major components. Several recent academic studies, however, underscore the need for just such a framework.

A laboratory simulation of the oil industry done by Dietrich, Kachelmeier, Kleinmuntz, and Linsmeier suggests that better risk reporting can create value.[1] First, they found that "Explicit disclosures lead to more efficient market reactions, even when the same information can be inferred from the financial statements."[2] Second, "One-sided disclosure of upside opportunity produces an upward bias in market prices, but only for firms that experienced a decrease in expected oil reserves."[3]

In other words, when reported oil reserves turn out to be less than expected, the market doesn't take the negative information into full account. The reverse, however, was not true when companies reported only downside risk. The most efficient markets occurred with "a two-sided disclosure of upside opportunity *and* downside risk," which mitigated "the bias induced by the upside disclosure alone."[4]

The researchers offered two suggestions to standard setters:

1. "Financial reporting standards that make information easier to process will facilitate investors' decision making, thereby enhancing the efficiency of the capital markets."
2. "Standards mandating disclosure of both upside opportunities and downside risks could limit management's ability to manipulate market prices through voluntary presentation of upside opportunities alone."

Of course, managers might be tempted to take advantage of market inefficiencies by reporting only the upside opportunity. The board of directors should see that they don't. Chapter 12 talks more about the board's role in external reporting in more detail.

Another academic study, this one by Baruch Lev and Paul Zarowin on how the market values R&D expenditures, offers more proof that companies should practice better disclosure about risks that involve both a significant upside and a significant downside.[5] They found that the market places more value on R&D expenditures that: (1) pay off sooner rather than later and (2) have more certain outcomes. Both reduce risk. They also reported, "The fundamentals we examine explain only a small fraction (5 percent–10 percent) of the variation" and suggest that one of the reasons is "the paucity of disclosure" by firms regarding their R&D activities.

Another group of researchers, Deng, Lev, and Narin, note that the information companies report on R&D is inadequate for investment analysis because it is "generally scant and not timely." Companies also don't include "information on the extent of *basic research*" as separate from the *total research* budget, which includes applied research and product development.[6] Yet using data from another source, CHI Research, the authors demonstrated a clear relationship between current R&D activity and future performance in the capital markets. This provides just one more example of how the market can get the information it wants even when companies don't provide it themselves, a subject addressed in more detail in the next chapter.

DIMENSIONS OF RISK

Imagine the tremendous progress in risk reporting that companies could make if they simply tried to supply enough information to answer the three following questions, which correspond to a three-dimensional concept of risk—namely opportunity, hazard, and uncertainty.[7] The three questions companies should answer are:

1. What do you do to create value?
2. What can happen to destroy value?
3. What degree of confidence do you have in the estimated distribution of outcomes?

The first question addresses the *opportunity* dimension of risk and recognizes that risk taking has positive implications and is necessary for creating value. For example, adding manufacturing capacity, spending money on advertising, introducing a new product, or forming a joint venture in another country all aim at increasing value by growing revenues and profits. In annual reports, CEOs usually discuss such actions in the letter to shareholders and the management discussion and analysis (MD&A) section. Executives also discuss them in public speeches to analysts and investors and in interviews with the press. Company websites report on them in various ways.

Not surprisingly, when companies discuss the opportunity dimension of risk, they almost exclusively stick to the upside, the good things that can happen when they take risks. In fact, they hardly ever use the word *risk* at all, preferring instead to use words like opportunity, entrepreneurial, new initiatives, innovation, and adapting to change—all to describe the exciting things the company is doing to create shareholder value. This is all well and good, but every upside has a corresponding downside. A completely meaningful description of the opportunity dimension of risk would also illuminate the downside, including explanations of what management is doing to maximize the positive and minimize the probability and extent of any adverse outcomes.

Companies *do* use the word *risk* when they address its *hazard* dimension. When they do, they usually talk about the bad things that can happen either inside or outside the company. One study found that 80 percent of managers actually think of risks only as negative outcomes.[8] Internal "negative outcomes" could include theft, fraud, accidents, ethics violations, and actions that lead to lawsuits. External risks might relate to weather disasters, power failures, introduction of new and superior technologies, failure of another party to meet its obligations to the company, and changes in market prices.

When companies identify these risks in their annual reports and 10Ks, they generally offer some explanation of how they manage them with hedging positions, insurance, and internal control systems. Remember how virtually every U.S. company commented about Y2K in their 1998 annual reports, assuring one and all that they had everything under control? Fortunately, they were right.

The third question companies should answer about risk addresses the *uncertainty* dimension—the degree of confidence management has in its expectations about various outcomes. The greater the degree of uncertainty, the greater the degree of risk. Many banks, for example, calculate a Value-at-Risk (VaR) number for measuring market risk—the impact of changes in market prices on the value of their portfolios. VaR is the maximum amount of money that a bank believes, with a certain degree of confidence, it could lose in a single day. When a bank says that at a 95 percent confidence level it could lose no more than $10 million in any single day, it means that 95 percent of the time this will be true. A similar exposure at a 90 percent confidence level is riskier—twice as often the loss could exceed $10 million.

Although there are some fairly precise ways to measure uncertainty for market risk, those companies that use them are rare exceptions. In most instances, companies simply can't calculate the value of a maximum upside and downside at a certain confidence level in a statistically meaningful way. Management has no choice but to go with its own intuition about the likelihood that any of the possible outcomes may materialize.

CISCO SYSTEMS: A LOT OF RISK, A LOT OF VALUE

Cisco Systems, the Internet wunderkind, takes a great deal of risk to create value for its shareholders. Chapter 3 pointed out just how much value Cisco has created. It also noted that Cisco's beta, one measure of risk, runs fairly high at 1.31.[9] Not surprisingly, the company listed 21 risk factors in its 10Q filing for the first quarter of 2000, as shown in Exhibit 8.1. Twelve of these risks are shown in Exhibit 8.2 as a simplified set of relationships that helps explain how taking risks creates value—a lot of it, in Cisco's case—for shareholders.

Exhibit 8.2 essentially creates a "business model" for Cisco of cause-and-effect relationships, a concept discussed in Chapter 1. It simply takes 12 of the 21 risk factors that Cisco has identified and looks at their upside—or opportunity dimension—and puts them together in a cause-and-effect diagram, relying substantially on comments gleaned from Cisco's 1999 annual report.

Exhibit 8.1

Cisco Systems Reports on Risk
Cisco Systems listed these 21 risk factors in its first quarter 2000 10Q filing[a]

1. Growth rate	10. Competitive risk factors	12. (Regulation of) The Internet
2. (Decline in) Gross margins	a. Price	13. Availability of products
	b. Performance	
3. Acquisitions	c. Ability to provide end-to-end solutions and support	14. Natural disasters
4. Industry consolidations		15. Fluctuations of quarterly data
5. Dependence on new product development	d. Conformity to standards	16. Organizational changes
6. Entering new or developing markets	e. Ability to add value-added features like security and reliability	17. Service provider sales
		18. Stock price volatility
7. International operations risk		19. Foreign exchange rate risk
	f. Market presence	
8. Strategic alliances	11. Employees	20. Y2K
9. Portfolio investments		21. Infringement risk

[a] These risk factors appear in a different order in Cisco's filings.

For example, Cisco's strong competitive position, bolstered by its aggressive acquisition strategy, creates enormous shareholder value. So do Cisco's high growth rate and gross margins. Going step by step through this simplified model would be a valuable exercise for understanding how one company's risk factors can also be viewed in the brighter light of opportunity.

We certainly don't claim that this is the right, much less a complete, business model for Cisco. It is not based on any input from the company's management other than what could be obtained from public sources. We present it here merely to point out the possibilities of looking at both the upside and downside dimensions of risk in an integrated way. The business model concept is just one way of doing this.

As Cisco vividly illustrates, risk factors have both an upside and a downside. The company recognizes that many of the things it does so successfully to create value could just as easily become vulnerabilities if not managed properly, as management quite openly acknowledges in its 10K and 10Q disclosures.

Exhibit 8.2

Risk and Value at Cisco Systems

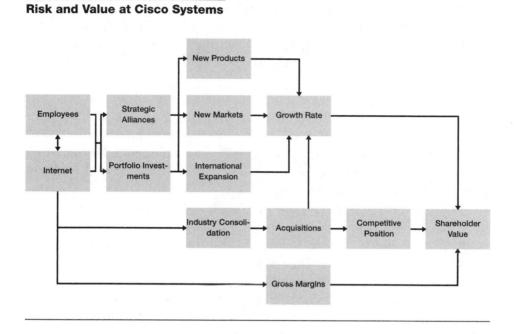

Nonetheless, Cisco reports information about the upside of risk quite apart from its discussion about the downside aspects. And that raises a burning question, at least in the context of this chapter. Would both Cisco and its shareholders benefit even more if the company reported risk information in a totally integrated way that included the upside potential of risk, the downside element, and the degree of uncertainty for both?

IS IT SAFE TO PLAY WITH YOUR TOYS ONLINE?

Barely older than some of its end-users and younger than most, two-year-old eToys went public in May 1999 at $20 a share. On its first day of trading, the company's stock zoomed to $76.56 per share.

By June, analysts at the leading brokerage firms had gone gaga over eToys, saying things like "buy aggressive," "market performer," and "buy." One analyst whose investment bank was a lead underwriter for eToys' initial public offering (IPO) gave the company the rating "market outperformer."

On October 11, 1999, eToys stock reached its all-time high of $86 per share with a market cap of over $10 billion. By comparison, its bricks-and-mortar competitor Toys 'R' Us had a market cap barely more than one-third that amount.[10]

Then everything went kaboom! On April 17, 2000, one share of eToys stock could be had for only $4.75—less than the price of a starter set of Pokémon® cards. By month end, the bricks-and-mortar incumbent, Toys 'R' Us, had a market cap more than three times higher than that of eToys. The highflier of Internet start-ups had, as one journalist put it, "crashed to Earth over the last five months."[11]

By the summer of 2000, the jury was still way more than out on eToys' prospects. Some felt that the company's $100 million war chest, a result of its convertible preferred stock offering, combined with rock-bottom prices in the Internet retailing sector, had opened up a great opportunity for eToys to build its customer base, grow revenues, reduce costs, and cool down competition by making acquisitions.

Others suggested that a pure Internet-based toy-retailing model obviously would not work, and that eToys should partner with a company that could provide the bricks-and-mortar capabilities it lacked. In early 2000, Chet Dembeck, writing in *E-Commerce Times*, had put forth Toys 'R' Us as a possible partner, odd as that might seem by his own admission, or, even better, Amazon.com.[12] Six months later, neither suggestion was even a possibility, at least in the short term. Toys 'R' Us and Amazon.com spoiled the wedding party by announcing their plans to join forces.

Those who had invested in eToys, but missed out on the IPO or failed to get out early enough, paid dearly. They certainly couldn't say they weren't warned. In the Registration Statement for its IPO, eToys had disclosed no less than 34 risk factors (see Exhibit 8.3). They fell into three general categories:

1. Risks unique to or especially high in start-up companies that do an IPO
2. Risks unique to or especially high in an Internet company
3. Risks inherent in any retailing venture

While we used our best judgment in categorizing these risks, we probably erred on the side of caution by classifying a risk into one of the first two categories if it would likely be a low risk for an established bricks-and-mortar retail firm. The company disclosed additional risks in subsequent 10Q and 10K filings—but the list in Exhibit 8.3 makes the point quite dramatically.

History, albeit a short one, has proven management right in advising potential eToys investors to exercise caution. If anything, management underestimated the risks considering the large number it added in subsequent filings with an explicit note that they were not contained in the S1.

Exhibit 8.3

Thirty-Three Risk Factors Identified by eToys in Public Filings[a]

Start-up IPO Risks	Internet Risks	Retailing Risks
• We have a limited operating history	• We have capacity constraint and system development risks	• Our market is highly seasonal
• We have a history of losses and we anticipate future losses and negative cash flow	• We are exposed to risks associated with online commerce security and credit card fraud	• Consumer trends change and we face significant inventory risk
• We face risks associated with our accounting and financial reporting systems	• Our common stock price may be volatile	• We rely on key toy vendors and key distributors
• Our future operating results are unpredictable	• We depend on the Internet and the development of the Internet infrastructure	• We need to manage growth in operations
• We need to manage growth in operations	• Rapid technological change may adversely affect us	• Our markets are highly competitive
• We will need additional capital	• Protection of domain name is uncertain	• We may enter new business categories
• We have discretion as to use of proceeds	• We may become subject to burdensome government regulation	• We face fulfillment operations risks
• Control by officers and directors	• We may be liable for Internet content	• Intellectual property claims against us can be costly and result in the loss of significant rights
• Anti-takeover provisions	• We may be subject to sales and other taxes	• Protection of our trademarks and proprietary rights is uncertain
• Shares eligible for future sale		• We depend on key personnel
• We do not intend to pay dividends		• We face Year 2000 risks of system failures
		• There are risks associated with potential acquisitions

[a] Risk factors in this list were identified by eToys in its Registration Statement for its IPO, May 19, 1999.

Whose Is Bigger?

But how risky is eToys' competitor, the nearly 20-year-old Toys 'R' Us? Apparently less risky than eToys, considering that Toys 'R' Us has a beta of only .73. And in its 1999 10K filing, Toys 'R' Us lists only five risk factors:

1. Interest rate risk
2. Foreign exchange rate risk
3. Year 2000 risks
4. Inability to process transactions
5. Increased sales returns of products containing hardware or software components

But is Toys 'R' Us really as much of a lower-risk investment as these comparative lists suggest? Not really. After all, any retail company has at least 13 of the risks listed in Exhibit 8.3. Nine more of these risks apply to any Internet retailing company, including Toysrus.com, which launched just before eToys went public.

Some might argue, with justification, that the combined effect of being a start-up/IPO company and an Internet retailer compounds risk. Yet others could say that a new company with a clean slate on which to write its business model would be more likely to succeed than an existing bricks-and-mortar company trying to break into the Internet. Experience to date suggests that neither model is a formula for guaranteed long-term success. Both companies have had their shares of difficulty. In terms of risk, however, an investor who read the SEC filings by both companies would have found it difficult to make meaningful comparisons.

GOING PUBLIC

New companies just going public have a very keen awareness of risk—just look at the ever-increasing size of the risk sections in IPO prospectuses for proof. Although no one keeps statistics on how many pages companies use to describe risk factors in their IPO filings, Terzah Ewing writing in *The Wall Street Journal* says, "Anecdotal evidence from Wall Street underwriters and seasoned investors suggests that the average has ballooned to somewhere around 10 to 12 pages from what used to be a handful."[13] Some risk sections go on for 20 pages or more. As Ewing points out, this makes the lawyers happy because it's a "have your cake and eat it too situation." The company gets a high stock price because of the exciting opportunities it portrays and at the same time minimizes the threat of lawsuits because of its fulsome disclosures.

Just as start-up companies may be hyper-risk-aware, well-established companies may underestimate risk, in terms of both opportunity and hazard. This is especially true in the New Economy where the Internet creates both types of risks for established companies. If they successfully adapt, as Cisco keeps urging them to do, they can uncover vast opportunities. If they don't adapt, enormous hazards loom. For investors trying to learn which companies have adapted or could, current disclosures about risk offer little help. They generally reflect only management's perceptions of risk, perhaps tweaked by a concern about getting sued.

Not only do companies have no integrated framework for reporting upside and downside risk, even very similar companies vary tremendously in the downside risks they disclose. Most of the guidelines for reporting of risk are still fairly broad and much of the information does not require auditing. Investors, therefore, must depend heavily on managers to provide adequate risk information in a meaningful way.

TALK TO ME ABOUT RISK

The relatively few existing requirements about risk disclosure are scattered throughout numerous pronouncements by different regulators. Exhibit 8.4, Current U.S. GAAP and SEC Risk Disclosure Requirements, summarizes these pronouncements. Most focus on the downside—what can go wrong, its potential financial impact, and management's attempts to try to prevent the downside from happening. These requirements fall into the following categories:

- Market risk
- Credit risk
- Operational risk
- Accounting risk

The disclosures about *market risk* and *credit risk* focus largely on derivatives and other financial instruments. Managers must report the amount of risk in quantitative terms, along with the assumptions and methodologies they use to arrive at these estimates. They must also report how they are managing risk in terms of management objectives and policies. In addition, they must disclose the fair value of all financial instruments, when it's practical to do so, and the methodologies and assumptions they

Exhibit 8.4

Current U.S. GAAP and SEC Risk Disclosure Requirements
An Overview of What Companies Must Disclose

Market Risk	Credit Risk	Operational Risk	Accounting Risk
1. Quantitative information about the market risk associated with derivatives and other financial instruments including: • Interest rates • Foreign exchange rates • Commodity prices • Equity prices They can select one of the following three methods for presenting the information: • Tabular presentation • Sensitivity analysis • Value at Risk (VaR) method 2. Assumptions and limitations relating to these quantitative disclosures 3. Quantitative information about gains and losses recognized in earnings when those gains and losses represent the amount of ineffectiveness for fair value and cash-flow hedges 4. Qualitative (i.e., descriptive) disclosures about: • The company's primary market-risk exposures stemming from derivatives and other financial instruments • How the company is managing those exposures 5. Risk-management objectives and policies for the major types of risks it is hedging with derivatives and other instruments 6. The fair values of all the financial instruments for which it is practicable to estimate fair value and the methods and significant assumptions that the company used in the estimation process	1. All the significant concentrations of credit risk arising from all financial instruments, regardless of whether the credit risk arises from an individual counterparty or a group of counterparties. 2. The disclosures should: • Indicate what the maximum amount of loss would be in a worst-case scenario • Outline the company's policy related to obtaining collateral • Explain other methods the company uses to manage credit risk	1. Information regarding liquidity, capital resources, and results of operations by identifying capital needs, commitments, trends, uncertainties, material changes, and effects of inflation 2. A narrative description of the principal products and services: • Sources and availability of raw materials • Duration and effect of patents, licenses, franchises, etc. • Seasonal nature of the business • Whether the company depends on a single customer or a few customers • Backlog orders • Competitive conditions • Amount spent on research and development activities • Effects of environmental regulations on the company's capital expenditures, earnings, and competitive position 3. Certain concentrations if they make the company vulnerable to the risk of a severe impact in the near term. For example, the volume of business done with a particular customer, supplier, or lender 4. Its accounting policy regarding the accrual of environmental remediation obligations when environmental matters materially affect its financial position or results of operation 5. An explanation if the auditor concludes that there is substantial doubt about the company's ability to continue as a going concern for a reasonable period of time	1. An explanation that the company's preparation in conformity with GAAP requires the use of management's estimates 2. If certain significant estimates could change in the near term, the nature of the uncertainty and, if possible, an estimate of the potential loss or range of loss 3. The nature of loss contingencies and an estimate of the possible loss or range of loss. If the company is unable to estimate loss, it should state as much in the financial statements

used to arrive at these values. Some of these disclosures are audited, most are not.

Operational risk must be discussed in both the MD&A portion of the annual report and the 10K filing. This broad, catch-all category includes all other types of risk such as capital needs, the effects of inflation, concentration of revenues (by customers, products, geographies, etc.), and competitive conditions and environmental remediation obligations. These disclosures are largely qualitative in nature, and most are not audited.

The final category, *accounting risk*, concerns the use of estimates in preparing financial statements. The required disclosures are intended to inform readers about significant undertakings that may underlie key estimates used in preparing the company's financial statements. This would include disclosures related to significant estimates contained in the financial statements and how the resolution of major unknowns might affect the company's results and financial condition over the next year. These disclosures are also largely qualitative.

RISK MANAGEMENT AND RISK REPORTING

The financial services industry has in place the most highly developed systems for managing risk. Just as the *raison d'être* for eToys and Toys 'R' Us is selling toys, the core business of financial institutions is managing risk for their clients and, by extension, for themselves. This makes the financial services industry the natural place to turn for guidance on how to communicate most effectively about risk to the market.

Financial institutions have many different types of risk exposures, but in quantifying and disclosing risk, they focus primarily on two, and to an increasing degree on three, of the four risk categories discussed earlier:

1. *Market risk:* the uncertainty of future earnings because of changes in the value of financial instruments caused by movements in market parameters
2. *Credit risk:* the risk of loss that arises when an obligor fails to meet the terms of a financial contract or otherwise fails to perform as agreed
3. *Operational risk:* a wide-ranging risk category relating to human error, management failure, or deficiencies in operating systems

As risk management methods have evolved, so too has risk disclosure, although not to the same level of sophistication. In other words, while the

Quality Gap in internal risk management systems has narrowed significantly, the Reporting Gap remains high, resulting in a large Information Gap. (See Chapter 7 if you have gaps in your recollection of the various Gaps' definitions.) For financial institutions, this is true for both the amount and type of their risk exposures, as well as their risk management practices for managing their exposures.

Walter Kielholz, CEO of Swiss Re, a company that's in the business of helping manage risk for companies that manage risk for others (Swiss Re likes to call itself "the investment bank of the insurance industry"), noted that "Risk disclosures can be negative unless you can also disclose how you are managing this risk." This from a CEO predisposed to the highest level of transparency possible.

John Fitzpatrick, Swiss Re's CFO, echoed Kielholz's sentiment: "We would like to disclose the most significant risks that could affect the company." The company, however, still struggles with how much to disclose for three primary reasons: (1) there's no generally accepted method in the industry on how risk should be disclosed, (2) disclosures are extremely complicated and based on a number of assumptions and sophisticated actuarial methodologies, and (3) there is risk inherent in greater risk disclosure. As Kielholz commented, "If we disclose more about risk, but competitors do not follow our lead, will investors be able to make any relative judgments, and as a consequence will we derive any benefit?"

This insight helps explain the large Information Gaps for both the amount of risk and how it's managed. The PricewaterhouseCoopers multicountry survey of major banks and insurance companies offers more evidence. For example, the survey identified a very large Information Gap for both investors and analysts on market risk exposure. The same was true for investors on risk management practices where the gap for analysts was large.[14] (See www.valuereporting.com for copies of the reports by industry.)

The survey also found Reporting Gaps for both measures, although for market risk exposure the gap was smaller than for risk management practices while the Information Gap was larger. This reinforces how much importance the market places on knowing as much as possible about a financial institution's market risk exposure. The fact that market risk exposure had no meaningful Quality Gap says that managers feel they have this problem under control. They just don't tell the market as much as they themselves know about it. The market knows that managers know and wants to know as well.

Market Risk

Of the three broad types of risks, financial institutions have made the most progress in both managing and disclosing market risk. The concept of market risk has been around for as long as simple trading contracts have been used. The techniques for quantifying, monitoring, and reporting it, however, have changed dramatically, driven as much by phenomenal improvements in technology and processing power as by necessity.

Until fairly recently, market risk was simply measured by outright exposure—for example, the total value of the financial instrument. When derivatives, financial instruments whose value is derived from an underlying asset, came into being, more sophisticated risk measures were introduced based on the derivative's price sensitivity to factors such as interest rates and price volatility. These measures are indispensable tools for traders and managers. But because they do not allow for the aggregation of the risks—representing them as a single number—within, for example, a bond portfolio, they don't permit comparing the risks among different portfolios. Nor can these measures be summed to create an aggregate single number for all the risks of a firm's holdings.

One commonly used solution to this problem is a measure called Value at Risk (VaR), which has grown in popularity over the past decade or so. VaR statistically estimates the maximum loss that could occur in a portfolio over a certain time period to a specified confidence interval under normal market conditions. This is generally from a market risk perspective only (i.e., the portion of the firm's value that could be diminished as a result of changes in external circumstances).

For example, in 1999, J.P. Morgan calculated its average market risk DEaR (Daily Earnings at Risk), which is J.P. Morgan's terminology for VaR, as $29 million at a 95 percent one-sided confidence level. This means that, statistically, J.P. Morgan did not expect to lose on average more than $29 million in the course of one day for 95 out of 100 days. Most of the time, therefore, the value at risk for the bank's entire portfolio in any single day was only $29 million; the net average value of the trading account assets and liabilities, according to the company's 1999 annual report, was about $40 billion.

VaR's great ViRtue lies in the fact that it enables comparisons of risk among portfolios and trading strategies. Therefore, the institution can allocate capital in the most efficient manner—not just to the most profitable businesses, but to the most profitable on a risk-adjusted basis. For example, it might seem obvious that if Business A generates net profits of $100 million per year and Business B generates only $75 million, any extra investment should be made in Business A. Because VaR allows a comparison of the relative riskiness of both, it is entirely possible that Business B could turn out to be more profitable on a risk-adjusted basis, thereby making it less risky and the smarter investment.

Measures of profitability that take into account the risk level of the capital used to produce the profit are generally called either return on risk-adjusted capital (RORAC) or risk-adjusted return on capital (RAROC). These have become increasingly important for managing financial institutions. Nevertheless, the PricewaterhouseCoopers banking and insurance industry survey found a fairly large Information Gap on this measure, a result of a large Reporting Gap that, in turn, resulted from an underlying Quality Gap.

Because financial institutions are not required to report RORAC or RAROC numbers, it's not surprising to find a substantial Information Gap. In the United States, however, financial institutions must disclose their accounting policies for derivatives and certain quantitative and qualitative information about market risk exposures that arise from some market-risk–sensitive instruments.

They can choose one of three disclosure alternatives—tabular presentation, sensitivity analysis, or VaR—to report and disclose their quantitative information in the notes to their financial statements and the MD&A of their annual reports. Note that these disclosures do not have to be audited; they are checked for consistency with the audited sections of the annual report.

Firms must also disclose information about back-testing, how VaR models are checked for appropriateness. This information enables analysts and investors to assess in some way the suitability of each firm's VaR model for the portfolios it holds and the markets in which it trades. It also assists in the comparison of VaR numbers across firms, although such comparisons are not as simple as they would be if all firms used standard methodologies. But in comparison to credit risk and operational risk, measuring and managing market risk has become reasonably standardized.

Credit Risk

As with market risk, credit risk was once viewed from a pure exposure perspective; that is, only the current outstanding amount of the loan or debt was considered. Take, for example, a company that owed money to a financial institution because of a derivative transaction, a contract whose value is "derived" from the price of some other asset. When viewed purely from an exposure perspective, only that day's value would be considered as the credit risk exposure, despite its dynamic nature. Every day the credit risk of this exposure could change because the value of the derivative constantly changes with changes in the underlying asset.

From an internal perspective, current leading practice in credit risk management methodology has made considerable forward progress. As with market risk, measures of credit risk now take account of the riskiness, rather than just the size of the asset. Here riskiness is determined by the credit quality of the company itself as well as the inherent riskiness of the particular product.

This is sometimes referred to as *asset quality*, and the banking and insurance industry survey identified a reasonably large Information Gap here, especially for banks. This gap occurs in part because disclosure requirements about credit risk are less quantitative and tend to focus on outright exposures rather than on a risk-based calculation.

This Information Gap, therefore, does not result from an underlying Quality Gap. Both banking and insurance company executives believe they have good internal information systems for asset quality. They also think they actively report this information. The market clearly disagrees, which is reflected in a positive Perception Gap, most noticeably for banks.

Operational Risk

The newest area of focus in the financial services industry is operational risk. But institutions have trouble quantifying operational risk because its definition, difficult to pin down in the first place, is so broad. Furthermore, data on operational losses, essential for statistical calculations, are often impossible to obtain. Before good measures can be developed here, the industry must design and implement systems that can capture the necessary data. Doing so is well worth the cost. Operational losses can be worth tens or even hundreds of millions of dollars.

Efforts are currently under way to improve the primitive state of risk measurement and risk management in operations. OpVaR, for example, is a statistical method developed by PricewaterhouseCoopers that is based on a VaR methodology. A great deal of work remains to be done in this area, however, as this risk is still managed primarily through operating metrics—number of error trades, number of amended trades, and number of overtime hours worked, for example—instead of through statistical techniques.

Disclosures regarding operational risk lag even further behind the internal measurement and management of it. Institutions are not required to disclose any quantitative data at all. In fact, they are not required to disclose anything about operational risk except as part of an overall risk disclosure requirement, found in many regulations, that specifies the inclusion of commentary about any significant risks to the business.

Even assuming that a financial institution develops good measures of operational risk, they understandably will hesitate to disclose them. Their concern will be pointing out that the magnitude of the problem is greater than the market knows. Those who disclose this information first may run the risk of appearing foolish and might take a short-term hit on their stock price. In fact, they will actually be the smart ones. By measuring operational risk and imposing the self-discipline of reporting it to the market—along with targets for reducing it—they will manage the risk better, which will ultimately be reflected in a higher stock price.

FUTURE DIRECTIONS

The field of risk management, already large, constantly expands. Accounting and consulting firms, and companies themselves, continuously develop new frameworks for thinking about risk, new analytical tools, and new information technology systems. Today's buzzword for this is "enterprise-wide risk management." It has as its central premise that risk is a continuum that starts with the purely downside issues of crisis management and compliance, extends through business continuity protection, and ends with strategic initiatives realized.

Concurrent with this broader concept of risk has been the emergence of new corporate roles, such as the chief risk officer. To date, however, this role largely focuses on the downside and the uncertainty elements of risk. It remains fairly separate from the upside opportunities, which are the focal points of strategic planning and business development. The disconnect is even greater with the CFO who, along with the CEO, plays the key role in determining what information the company reports to the market. Closing the gap between improving risk management techniques and the still-paltry risk disclosures will happen only through a better integration of managing risk and disclosing it.

9

There Is No Alternative:
The Story of Shell

Unto the pure all things are pure.
The Epistle of Paul to Titus

Even the most committed supporter of the ValueReporting Revolution would probably say by now, "Enough already. I get your message. I'm tired of words. I want some action.

"You've told me that a revolution in corporate disclosure is necessary. Volatility and concentration in value call the accuracy of stock prices into question. Traditional performance measures don't provide enough of the right kind of information for investors to make good decisions. The Earnings Game has made the markets even more dysfunctional, and earnings numbers just don't carry the weight they once did.

"To make matters worse, you've told me we need to shore up the very foundation of corporate reporting by revisiting and rethinking accounting standards. There are all kinds of gaps between companies and investors about the type and quality of information companies report and how they do it, what's important to whom, and how adequate the information is in the first place. Then we have to start thinking about risk and how to report it in an entirely different way. When will it all end?"

Even if you're convinced that it's time to join the ValueReporting Revolution, there's something else to consider—the interests of other stakeholders (employees, communities, customers, people on a mission—in short, the rest of the world) and whether or not addressing those interests creates shareholder value. Here, words alone won't do. It's the revolutionary deeds that matter.

Whose Business Is It?

Few would deny that corporations do business to create value for their shareholders and customers too. Companies couldn't stay in business very long if they didn't. Consequently, their managers constantly make decisions aimed at increasing revenues, decreasing costs, and improving the bottom line.

Many of those decisions have impacts beyond the financial realm. In fact virtually every decision to create value for shareholders has positive or negative consequences for other stakeholders. For example, closing a large manufacturing plant in a small community might improve manufacturing efficiency, which could clearly create value for shareholders. It would also create a lot of pain for the people who lose their jobs and for the communities in which they live. A major investment in new manufacturing capacity, however, might add value for shareholders, create new jobs, and bring additional revenue into the community's economy.

These are just two contrasting examples, but they illustrate how it's virtually impossible to create value for shareholders without creating consequences, good or bad, for other stakeholders. Managers today—voluntarily or not—must increasingly address other stakeholders' concerns, through both their actions and the information they provide on the consequences of those actions.

Okay, take a deep breath. This chapter doesn't prescribe what companies must do about other stakeholder interests. It does say, however, that companies must make conscious and well-thought-out choices. They can say unequivocally that shareholders and creating value for them always take precedence over anything else. They can say that shareholders rank first among equals—protect their interests first and then pay whatever attention is left to other stakeholder concerns. Or, they can decide that in the long term, shareholder interests and creating value for them are best served by also serving the legitimate interests of other stakeholders as well—one is inextricably tied to the other.

Whatever decision managers make, they must recognize that these other stakeholders will look to the company for information, just as shareholders do. They will also look for information about the company from other sources. And those others will be anxious to provide it.

Stakeholders—environmental and social activists, for example—can also become sources of information themselves and with the enormous reach of the Internet can communicate their information far and wide instantaneously. Managers, therefore, must decide just how much information they will provide themselves, and if and how they will participate in the inevitable conversations other stakeholders will have about their companies.

SHELL MADE THE CHOICE

Concern over the interests of other stakeholders, and how they fit into creating value for shareholders, is more fully developed in Europe than in the United States. One of its leading and most prominent proponents is Royal Dutch Shell, the Anglo–Dutch oil giant. Shell's efforts to implement a management philosophy based on "sustainability," in terms of practice (actually doing it) and transparency (publicly reporting on it) can serve as a lesson for others grappling with decisions about where other stakeholder interests fit into the value creation equation.

Why Sustainability?

Before reading the story of Shell, take a few minutes to consider what the philosophy of sustainability means. At the core of the concept of sustainability—or sustainable development—lies the premise that economic growth is inextricably bound up with its social and environmental consequences. In order to create long-term economic value for society—shareholders and other stakeholders alike—sustainability says that companies must also create social and environmental value.

Those who embrace sustainability believe that economic activities that irrevocably destroy the natural environment to meet certain human needs in the present will impinge on society's ability to meet even more basic human needs in the future. They also maintain that ultimately global society finds economic activities that destroy social value (e.g., through the abuse of human rights) unacceptable.

Sustainability for them means that in order to create long-term economic value, including long-term shareholder value, companies must perform well—and create value—along three dimensions: economic, social, and environmental. Put another way, they must deliver acceptable results against "the triple bottom line." Furthermore, to demonstrate that they have created this three-dimensional value for both shareholders and other stakeholders, companies must report on their triple bottom line performance.

Shell has taken the position that there is no alternative but to weave the principles of sustainability throughout the fabric of its management, decision-making, and disclosure processes and practices. As Tom Delfgaauw, Shell's vice president of sustainable development, says, "New responsibilities bring new accountabilities. Sustainability is the substance, transparency the process."[1]

STORY AROUND THE STORY OF SHELL

The Royal Dutch Shell Group of Companies came into existence in 1907 and dominates the oil industry. In August 2000, Chairman, now Sir, Mark Moody-Stuart unveiled quarterly results that set an all-time record for the Group.

He revealed that the adjusted CCS earnings (earnings on a current costs of supplies basis excluding special items) for the second quarter had risen to nearly $3,149 million, nearly double the figure for the same period the previous year. He continued, "Over the last 18 months we have regained our position at the top of the industry table: we now share the lead with a 16 percent return on average capital employed."

So what's the problem? What are the issues? A little bit of history and some real-life context can help answer those questions.

Retreat of the State

Shell has become one of the world's richest corporations, with annual sales revenues exceeding the gross domestic product (GDP) of many nation states. It also ranks as one of the most "multi" of the multinationals, operating in more than 135 countries around the world and employing around 96,000 people. Both characteristics raise concerns for some of Shell's other stakeholders.

Beginning in the late twentieth century, the twin phenomena of privatization and globalization have resulted in what some refer to as the "retreat of the state." They see large corporations, particularly multinationals, as playing new roles in society, roles previously filled by national governments.

Many other companies besides Shell have incomes greater than the annual GDPs of nation states (see Exhibit 9.1), which only serves to illustrate dramatically the scale of the retreat of the state phenomenon.

In terms of economic power, individual governments often have less than the multinationals they host. The broader implications of such economic power have not gone unnoticed, including the influence large companies may exert on government legislation and regulation. As the World Trade Organization's headline-grabbing experience in Seattle, Washington, in December 1999 illustrates, governments and corporate lobbyists can no longer ignore the social and environmental effects of the economic decisions they take and the legislative frameworks that they put in place.

Exhibit 9.1

**Corporate Income Comparisons with
National Gross Domestic Product**

Corporation/Country	Total Sales/GDP (US$ billions)
General Motors	164
Thailand	154
Norway	153
Ford Motor	147
Mitsui & Co.	145
Saudi Arabia	140
Mitsubishi	140
Poland	136
Itochu	136
South Africa	129
Royal Dutch/Shell Group	128
Marubeni	124
Greece	123

Source: 1997 figures from the *UNDP Human Development Report 1999* (New York: Oxford University Press, 1999), p. 32.

The retreat of the state has put some companies under an intense spotlight, especially those in industries that have the most noticeable impact on the environment and on local communities—for example, the extractive industries such as mining, oil, and gas. Other industries share the spotlight, but their impact runs along the social, rather than the environmental, dimension. The clothing, toy, and footwear industries, for example, source a lot of their production to low-cost developing countries, raising issues about labor practices.

Companies in these types of industries have come under the most pressure to acknowledge the wider responsibilities inherent in the global nature of their operations. Responsibilities to ensure that they minimize their negative impact on the environment and human society and maximize their positive impact. Responsibilities to take into account not only the interests of their shareholders, but also those of a much broader group of other stakeholders affected by their operations—employees, local communities, customers, and society at large.

These other stakeholders want to know how the companies discharge their social and environmental responsibilities. But where must stakeholders go to get that information? In today's world, not far. Vast amounts of information actually come to them through the press, through public relations campaigns launched by social and environmental activists, and, of course, through the Internet. Those information delivery channels raise major issues for companies like Shell.

Awash in a Sea of Information

The almost universal access to information through the Internet gives stakeholders a whole raft of data relevant to a wide range of financial and nonfinancial performance issues. On the financial side alone, a short Internet search that we conducted as an experiment soon yielded more than 50 websites with comments on Shell's performance, and that's just the tip of the information iceberg. If you start searching from the perspective of different stakeholders, you'll find any number of websites that "talk" about Shell. Exhibit 9.2 offers just a few examples. And the voices heard at these websites sound like anything but a choir in perfect harmony: some sing praises, others hit sour notes indeed.

Many of the voices on the Web accuse companies of ignoring or not taking seriously enough their social and environmental responsibilities. Because of the Internet, such accusations can spread instantaneously across the globe through websites like those run by Corporate Watch and McSpotlight.

Exhibit 9.2

Stakeholder Websites that "Talk" about Shell

Shareholders	Partners
www.wallstreetcity.com	www.asiapacific.com.my/bpt
www.bloomberg.com	www.psac.ca/international-site
www.hoovers.com	

Customers	Society
www.energy.com	www.corporatewatch.org
www.energysmart.com.au	www.corpwatch.org
www.thecomplaintstation.com	www.greenpeace.org
	www.mcspotlight.org

Employees	
www.shellus.com/jobs	
www.wetfeet.com	

The most serious problem arises when the dissident voices drown out the one voice that definitely deserves to be heard—that of the company itself. Companies, of course, have no power to silence the cacophony. They must adopt this more pragmatic point of view: some people will always take an extremely positive position and others will do just the opposite, regardless of what the company does or says. In a way, both extremes have little relevance.

Companies can help restore relevance and reason when they actively raise their own voices—for example, through their own website and other information media like social and environmental reports. Companies lack the power to stop the music, but they can make sure that the vast majority of shareholders and other stakeholders who occupy the middle ground get to hear the full score.

The volume of the company's voice is yet another issue. The companies most under pressure to acknowledge their wider social and environmental responsibilities also feel the most pressure to report publicly on their performance in relation to stakeholder interests and concerns. In fact, many companies, most notably in Europe, have begun publishing regular reports on their environmental and sustainability performance, as Exhibit 9.3 documents.

Companies that embrace sustainability believe it gives them a way to create economic value and social and environmental value concurrently. Embracing transparency allows them to demonstrate their commitment to all.

Companies that decide not to engage or communicate with other stakeholders must recognize that their detractors probably will speak out and could have significant influence over even more stakeholders' views, perceptions, and behavior.

Where's the Value?

The answer to the question of whether or not the pursuit of sustainability delivers shareholder value has become something like the Holy Grail. The search for the definitive answer continues. Analysts and investors may find it more useful to consider instead if how a company manages its environmental and social issues correlates with the quality and experience of its management team, a measure that made Chapter 7's Top Ten list of performance measures for companies, investors, and analysts.

Those looking for indications that management's attention to sustainability correlates to value creation might refer to the Dow Jones Sus-

Exhibit 9.3

Number of Environment, Health, and Safety Reports, and Verification Statements by Country

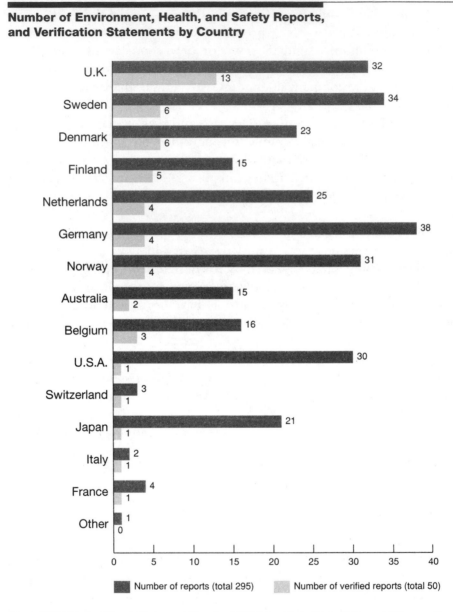

Source: *KPMG International Survey of Environmental Reporting 1999* (KPMG and the Institute for Environmental Management)

tainability Group of Indexes (DJSGI), established in 1999, which assesses corporate performance across a wide range of sustainability criteria.[2] If the DJSGI shows a positive divergence of stock prices for companies that make its list compared to companies listed on the traditional Dow Jones Group of Indexes, according to Shell's Tom Delfgaauw, "It would be naïve to suggest that this is exclusively because of sustainability, because of course it is not."

Delfgaauw explains further, "Members of the financial community are more likely to look at quality of management and sustained business success, and that will increasingly go hand in hand with a responsible involvement in such matters as climate change, human rights, engagement processes, and the like. That link eventually will cause the financial community to change their view, and will be more significant than any personal beliefs in the merits of sustainable development."

John Prestbo, president of the Dow Jones Indexes, explains his view of how the DJSGI works: "Companies pursuing growth in the triple bottom line tend to display superior stock market performance with favorable risk–return profiles. Thus sustainability becomes a proxy for enlightened and disciplined management—which just happens to be the most important factor that investors do and should consider in deciding whether to buy a stock."[3]

The very existence of the DJSGI says a lot about the growing interest of analysts and investors in such matters. The rise of the socially responsible investment (SRI) sector adds hard-currency evidence of that growing interest; more than $2 trillion invested in SRI funds in the United States and more than £70 billion in the United Kingdom. Forecasts point to massive growth in the SRI sector with the United Kingdom alone expected to top £100 billion by the end of 2000.

Want more evidence that sustainability has captured the public's and the markets' attention? In the United Kingdom, legislation has been introduced that requires trustees to make a statement about how they take environmental, social, and ethical criteria into account in their decision making about occupational pension fund investments. In a related move, the European Commission has disclosed its intention to use the financial markets to encourage companies "to assess the impact and business benefit of their social performance and to undertake voluntary social reporting."[4]

New legislation is not the whole story. Public expectations are changing as well. According to the Millennium Poll on Corporate Social Responsibility, sponsored by PricewaterhouseCoopers, 77 percent of those polled would like their pension funds to adopt an ethical policy, provided it did not harm financial returns.[5] Some of those funds are enormous; for example, the United Kingdom's Prudential and Standard Life's investment portfolio reportedly totals £189 billion—equal to the combined GDP of the 40 poorest countries in the world.[6] And activist groups know it. Amnesty International UK recently launched a campaign urging its members to contact their pension fund trustees and find out how they are responding to the new legislation.

Possibly of most interest to companies, shareholder activism in the sustainability arena has increased as well. Representatives of activist organizations sometimes buy shares in order to raise challenging questions at shareholder meetings. In May 1997, Shell faced a resolution that would force the company to appoint a director responsible for policies relating to the environment and human rights. At Rio Tinto's May 2000 annual general meeting, two union-initiated resolutions—the improvement of the company's corporate governance policies and greater compliance with international human rights standards in the workplace—received support from a significant percentage of shareholders.

SPEAKING OF SHELL

In the final decades of the twentieth century, the Royal Dutch Shell Group of Companies came to the full realization that issues like globalization, privatization, communications technology, and shareholder and other stakeholder scrutiny were effecting great and rapid changes in both society and the markets. But did that mean that Shell had to change too? Shell's answer was "yes," and it knew it had to change fast. In the mid-1990s, the company embarked on a vast corporate transformation program.

First, the company began to take a long, hard look at itself, questioning all the fundamentals: its structure, the way it conducted its business, the quality of its leadership, its relationships with people, and its vision of the future. Then in the midst of its self-reevaluation process, Shell became entangled in two very uncomfortable and highly public controversies that would have profound global implications for the company. They both hit headlines worldwide within months of each other in 1995.

The first was the case of the Brent Spar, an oil storage and loading buoy that Shell no longer used or needed and that it had planned to dispose of at sea. Shell, on the basis of two years' consulting and preparation, firmly believed that its planned method for disposal satisfied all concerns, including the environmental ones. Greenpeace thought otherwise. Protesters occupied the Spar and so successfully galvanized public opinion that senior politicians in several European countries publicly intervened. Soon, con-

sumer boycotts hit Shell's retail business and, in Germany, Shell gasoline sta-
tions came under violent attacks—50 damaged, two firebombed, and one
raked with bullets.

Soon, Shell made global headlines again, this time over human rights
in Nigeria. The Niger Delta has been described as one of the world's most
fragile ecosystems, and parts of it are densely populated, particularly the
Ogoni region. The Delta also has rich oil reserves (a capacity of around a
million barrels a day) that Shell, through a joint venture with other domestic and foreign oil companies, had tapped as a very significant revenue
source since 1958.[7]

Many stakeholders, however, maintained that developing the Ogoni oil
reserves came with much too high an environmental and social price tag.
They voiced repeated accusations of oil spills that poisoned waters, killed
fish, and destroyed vegetation and agricultural land. Gas flaring practices,
they alleged, compounded the pollution problems, contributed to global
warming, and wasted a natural resource. And, they added, apparently almost none of the economic gain found its way back to Ogoni land.

Ken Saro-Wiwa, an Ogoni, came forward to help organize and lead his
people's protests against such environmental degradation. Then came reports of the murders of hundreds of Ogoni villagers with suspicions that the
Nigerian military had punished them because their protests threatened the
oil revenues that sustained the government. In 1994, Ken Saro-Wiwa was im-
prisoned under charges of incitement to murder four Ogoni politicians.[8]
Amnesty International declared him a prisoner of conscience. Shell came
under extreme pressure to exert its influence with the Nigerian government
to secure Saro-Wiwa's release. In a letter to the Nigerian head of state, Cor
Herkströter, Shell's chairman at that time, urged clemency. All to no avail.
Ken Saro-Wiwa was executed in November 1995.

The incident is still far from forgotten. Corporate Watch named Shell
runner-up in its Earth Day 2000 Greenwash Awards for the company's
"Profits and Principles" advertising campaign. In honor of the "award,"
Corporate Watch (www.corpwatch.org) has made a website pledge to send
Shell's chairman, Mark Moody-Stuart, a free videotape of the funeral of
Ken Saro-Wiwa.

Among the evidence supporting why it believes Shell deserves the
award, Corporate Watch prints the following:[9]

> In the human rights realm, Shell's holier-than-thou "commitment"
> reeks of hypocrisy. The years of complicity with apartheid are conve-
> niently forgotten; Shell points to its support for political prisoners.

After years of complicity and sometimes active participation in the despoiling of the Nigerian environment and the suppression of basic freedoms, Shell has the gall to boast of its commitment to human rights, even pointing to Nigeria as an example, and showing a picture of a pro-Ogoni protest in London. This is the greenwash technique of blatantly co-opting your critics' message, adapted for the issue of human rights. Responsibility? Nowhere in sight. Accountability? Apparently, not one of the principles that interests Shell.

Thanks for Noticing

These controversies and their highly publicized fallout brought home to every Shell employee in exquisite detail just how vital to Shell's future the ongoing transformation had become. Without question, Shell had to commit itself to taking on new and sometimes unfamiliar roles and responsibilities, not only in its industry, but also in society at large. It sought the views of others through an extensive, worldwide program of stakeholder consultation in an attempt to understand the changing responsibilities of multinational companies.

Shell embodied these new responsibilities in its Statement of General Business Principles (www.shell.com/royal-en/content/0,5028,25481-50977,00. html), which it revised in 1997 to include support for sustainable development and human rights. Shell's recognition of new responsibilities brought with it not only an acceptance of the need for greater accountability to all stakeholders but also the imperative to continuously monitor and respond to the inevitable and unavoidable changes in its business environment and the world.

For the new Shell, there is only one way to create shareholder value in the long term—through sustainability. Chairman Mark Moody-Stuart made it crystal clear: "My colleagues and I are totally committed to a business strategy that generates profits while contributing to the well being of the planet and its people. We see no alternative."[10] Those words reflected the theme of a scenario that Shell used in its planning processes during the mid-1990s—a scenario called TINA—There Is No Alternative.

Shell began to look for ways to embed its new business principles firmly into all aspects of its operations and to convince stakeholders that the company takes its impact on society and the environment with utmost seriousness. Shell turned for help to one of its critics—SustainAbility, the prominent hybrid, nongovernmental organization consultancy headed by long-time environmental activist and guru John Elkington.

By 1998, when Shell published its first full-scale public report—*Profits and Principles: Does There Have to Be a Choice?*, which detailed the company's performance against its new business principles, John Elkington had become an ally. In the two-page spread he was given in that report, Elkington presented his personal view of what Shell was doing and his assessment of its performance to date.

"For two years after the Brent Spar and Nigerian controversies," he wrote, "my colleagues and I fended off requests from various parts of the Shell Group."[11] Because, as he said, he didn't think Shell was serious, he felt he could accomplish more from the outside, and other stakeholders would have found his involvement with Shell unacceptable. In agreeing to work with Shell alongside the consulting firm of Arthur D. Little, Elkington, in fact, put his own credibility on the line with *his* stakeholders as well. His statements of support published on Shell's website and in printed reports serve in a very real sense as a type of attestation or assurance.

Measuring Sustainability

By the time the second *Shell Report* came out in 1999, the company had made significant progress against its commitments. Shell published details of a new management system—the Sustainable Development Management Framework (SDMF)—that it had developed to create long-term shareholder value and brand strength while living up to its business principles and meeting society's expectations (see Exhibit 9.4).

Shell's SDMF is a management system that the company makes available to its managers and other practitioners to help them introduce sustainable development into the way they conduct their business. In so doing, it also captures stakeholder-relevant information on the company's performance, making reporting an integral element of the SDMF.

One central lesson Shell took to heart from its experiences with Brent Spar and in Nigeria was that the company needed a different approach to corporate decision making—a consultative, inclusive, open, and accountable approach. Following the Greenpeace protests, Shell halted its plans to sink the Brent Spar and entered into a two-year dialogue with nongovernmental organizations, opinion formers, and experts on the best disposal options available. Eventually, it decided to use the old storage buoy to build a quay extension at Mekjarvik, near Stavanger in Norway. The project was completed in July 1999.

This kind of approach to decision making is captured in the concept of stakeholder engagement. Stakeholder engagement pervades the whole of the SDMF framework, and Shell sees it as critical to the management of the

Exhibit 9.4

Sustainable Development Management Framework

Sustainable development management framework

A practical tool for embedding sustainable development into decision making

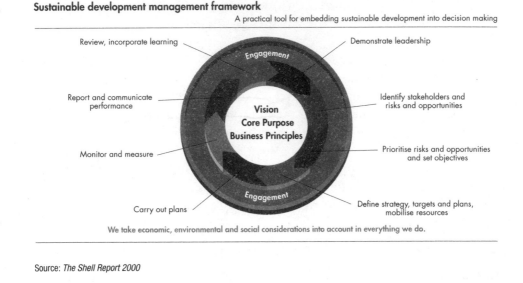

We take economic, environmental and social considerations into account in everything we do.

Source: *The Shell Report 2000*

business. As the framework emphasizes, Shell has taken the position that a responsible business must make itself accountable to stakeholders; a successful business will respond to stakeholders' concerns.

In *The Shell Report 2000*, the SDMF framework appears within a broader model (see Exhibit 9.5) that illustrates its role in creating value for shareholders and at the same time creating wealth for society. This updated model identifies four key business imperatives:

Goals

1. *Reduce costs.* Become more eco-efficient by doing more with less.
2. *Create options.* Anticipate new markets among those who want a more sustainable world.
3. *Gain customers.* Create customer loyalty and market share through products and services built on sustainability principles.
4. *Reduce risk.* Gain recognition from financial institutions of how Shell reduces risk through more responsible behavior.

While this model articulates a business case for sustainable development, the proof of the pudding lies in Shell's success in measuring and monitoring the value it creates, the sixth stage in the SDMF framework wheel.

Exhibit 9.5

Profits & Principles
The Business Case for Sustainable Development

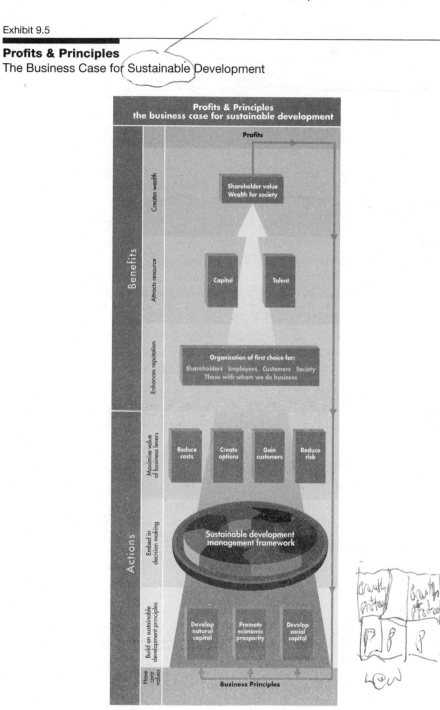

Source: *The Shell Report 2000*

Sustainable Measures

To "monitor and measure" in the context of sustainable development, Shell must develop metrics for performance across the triple bottom line. As Chapter 1 points out, when a company gets serious about identifying nonfinancial measures, the list of potentially important ones becomes very long indeed. Shell's management set out to identify those measures that really matter to their businesses and their stakeholders, and to develop those they can pay the required attention to and manage. In other words, develop a set of key performance indicators (KPIs).

Shell decided it should not develop these KPIs in isolation in the belief that stakeholder engagement has as much critical importance here as in every other facet of the SDMF. In developing the KPIs, Shell held 33 meetings with stakeholders, systematically recording, analyzing, and categorizing their input using well-defined KPI screening criteria as shown below. Shell also involved shareholders in the KPI engagement exercise, including two large institutional investors as well as a number of other distinctive stakeholder groups such as nongovernmental organizations, labor organizations, academia, and government.

Shell's KPI Screening Criteria

In developing the list of potential KPIs, Shell used the following criteria to test a measure's appropriateness for inclusion:[12]

- Shell can control or highly influence it.
- It can drive the business toward a clear target.
- It is relevant to internal and external audiences.
- It is more than a measure of compliance.
- It is related to critical activities.
- It can be benchmarked.
- It is verifiable.
- It is meaningful at the Group level.
- It builds on existing data streams.

The process resulted in the initial list of potential KPIs shown in Exhibit 9.6. Shell's plans call for introducing these KPIs over a five-year period ending in 2005. The KPIs will be used to measure and report on Shell's progress in meeting its commitments to sustainable development[13] and will form the basis for future editions of *The Shell Report*.

Exhibit 9.6

Shell's Key Performance Indicators

Economic	Social
• Economic performance ○ Return on average capital employed ○ Total shareholder return ○ Customer satisfaction ○ Innovation • Wealth creation ○ Quality of social performance	• Respect for people ○ Critical health and safety data ○ Staff feelings on how the company respects them ○ Diversity and equal opportunities ○ Human rights
Environmental	**Governance and Values**

• Management of environmental impacts
 ○ Critical environmental data
 ○ Acceptability of performance
  – Benchmarking
  – Perception
• Potential impact on climate change
 ○ Greenhouse gas emissions
	• Integrity
	 ○ Staff belief that business principles protect them and encourage them to act with integrity
	 ○ Reputation
	 ○ Degree of alignment of business processes with sustainable development principles
	• Engagement
	 ○ Stakeholder perception of quality of engagement

• KPI category   ○ Potential KPIs under development

Source: *The Shell Report 2000*

Is it surprising that so much of the information identified as being important to other stakeholders is directly important to shareholders as well? Some potential KPIs have explicitly clear links to shareholder value. "Innovation," for example, is highly likely to correlate with financial returns and bottom-line value. Shell's "customer satisfaction" KPI is a leading indicator of market share. Shell already reports on a related "brand" measure stating that in 1999 private motorists—20,000 of them in 52 countries—ranked Shell number one globally for brand preference, brand awareness, and repeat purchases.

Other KPIs may, at first glance, seem rather remote from measures that would interest the financial community. But "staff feelings on how the company respects them," for example, when unbundled into its component parts will likely include employee motivation—a measure not far removed from retention rates and productivity.

Finally, some KPIs clearly match perfectly with Shell's overall sustainable development business model, yet seem to link even less closely to shareholder value. Shell, for example, already reports on incidences of bribery in the business, an indicator linked to the KPI "staff belief that business principles protect them and encourage them to act with integrity," and on the details of its security measures at sites around the world, an indicator linked to the "human rights" KPI. Upon deeper consideration, this kind of data could suggest that Shell's activities may reduce its risk profile. Now the implications for shareholder value are clear.

Shell already reports on some of the KPIs, the "return on average capital employed" (ROACE), for example. Other KPIs, such as "quality of social performance" and "innovation," appear as little more than headings at present, and they will require much more development before they can be considered reliable, reportable metrics.

Shell declares that it will continue the dialogue with stakeholders as it further develops its KPIs. By considering them in the process, Shell acknowledges that stakeholder concerns have a legitimate role in shaping the very fabric of its corporate reporting. But the involvement of its stakeholders tells a tale beyond meeting the demands of transparency. It also says that Shell believes that creating shareholder value is intimately intertwined with meeting other stakeholders' needs.

VERIFICATION, THE HALLMARK OF CREDIBILITY

Shell sees as an important part of transparency the publication of data verified by respected independent organizations. As *The Shell Report 2000* says, "Beyond assuring accuracy and reliability, verification increases stakeholder confidence that what is being reported is a fair picture of performance."[14] In that report, KPMG and PricewaterhouseCoopers verified a range of performance data and statements about management systems and processes across the triple bottom line: economic, environmental, and social performance (see Exhibit 9.7).

The report presents the verification in an innovative style and engaging language that actually underscores the concept of transparency by making the information easily accessible to all readers. Such emphasis on transparency runs throughout the report and goes further than any other company's social, environmental, or sustainability reporting efforts to date.

Exhibit 9.7

Report from the Verifiers

To: Royal Dutch Petroleum Company &
     The "Shell" Transport and Trading Company, p.l.c.

We have been asked to verify the reliability of selected performance data and statements. We have done so and marked these sections with the different coloured symbols illustrated below within The Shell Report 2000 of the Royal Dutch/Shell Group of Companies. The preparation of The Shell Report is the responsibility of management. Our responsibility is to express an opinion on the reliability of the data and statements indicated, based on the verification work referred to below.

In our opinion:
- the data on financial performance marked with the symbol ✓ are properly derived from the audited Financial Statements of the Royal Dutch/Shell Group of Companies for each of the ten years ended 31 December 1999
- the health, safety and environmental (HSE) statements and graphs, together with the explanatory information, performance data tables and notes in the Annex (see pages 48-49), properly reflect the performance of the reporting entities for each of the HSE parameters marked with the symbol ✓
- the statements and data marked with the symbol ✓ relating to the systems and processes Shell has put in place to manage social performance are supported by appropriate underlying evidence and present a balanced view.

Basis of opinion
There are no generally accepted international standards for the reporting or verification of environmental performance data or of processes to manage social performance. We have adopted a verification approach that reflects emerging best practice, using

a framework based on the principles underpinning international standards on financial auditing and reporting. Therefore, we planned and carried out our work to obtain reasonable, rather than absolute, assurance on the reliability of the performance data and statements tested. We believe that our work provides a reasonable basis for our opinion.

Verification work performed
In planning and conducting our work, we included environmental and social experts within our team. The work carried out is described in the Report:
- Financial – page 13
- Environmental, including health and safety – page 19
- Social – page 27.

In addition, we examined the draft Report to confirm the consistency of the information reported with the findings of our work.

Considerations and limitations
It is important to read the HSE statements and graphs in the context of the explanatory information and notes in the Annex and the notes to HSE graphs and performance tables.

HSE data are subject to many more inherent limitations than financial data given both their nature and the methods used for determining, calculating or estimating such data.

We did not carry out any work on data reported in respect of future projections and targets.

It is also important to note that the financial data reported are not sufficient to ensure a thorough understanding of the financial results and the financial position of the Group.

KPMG Accountants NV
The Hague

PricewaterhouseCoopers
London

4th April 2000

Yet there are still some serious wrinkles to iron out. In a financial report, companies can reasonably assume that the sophisticated reader has a good understanding of the context in which an audit opinion is expressed and the accounting and auditing standards that underpin it. Such an assumption in the nascent world of the nonfinancial, and in particular social, audit would be far from accurate. Indeed, no generally accepted standards for reporting and verifying environmental and social information even exist.

As Shell has yet to develop all of the potential KPIs it has identified, obviously not all can be verified. Some of the most critical environmental and health and safety data, however, have been verified since 1998. And Shell sees its KPIs as the logical place to focus verification effort in the future.

Obviously, Shell recognizes the importance of verification, but it has an even more far-reaching vision. As *The Shell Report 2000* says, "Our ultimate ambition is to achieve a level of public trust and respect that will reduce the need for formal verification. This might be some years away, but we hope that widespread efforts to build better relationships between companies and civil society will lead to the emergence of trust through alliances and greater involvement."

Transparency Goes Both Ways

The approach Shell took in developing its KPIs makes a clear statement about what transparency really means to the company. To Shell, transparency is an ongoing conversation with shareholders and other stakeholders alike. Transparency means more to them than just pumping out information in the hope of influencing stakeholders; it's also fundamentally about letting the stakeholders in and engaging them. It's not just transparency in the telling, it's transparency reflected in the listening as well.

Shell turns information exchange into a true dialogue by participating in give-and-take communication directly with stakeholders, severe critics included, through a variety of media. For example, in its yearly sustainability report, Shell includes "Tell Shell" response cards inviting comments, both positive and negative, from readers. It then prints representative examples—praise and damnation—in the following year's report. Exhibit 9.8 reprints a few of these from the 2000 report to give a sense of the nature of these responses.[15]

In the year 2000 report, Shell subjected the Tell Shell process to verification, demonstrating once again the openness and transparency of its engagement with stakeholders. The scope of the Tell Shell dialogue is relatively small: Only 862 responses were received during the period March

Exhibit 9.8

Tell Shell

Selected reader comments from *The Shell Report 2000*

You told Shell	**You told Shell**
"It is great to see an oil company step up to the plate and engage in these kind of discussions and issues. Let's pray more oil companies will follow." *United States*	"I see more and more advertising by oil companies trying to give their business a green spin, and so far, only you have given me the chance to comment." *Japan*
You told Shell	**You told Shell**
"Every facet of the industry from exploration to production is at odds with environmental conservation. Is that fact lost to you people? I think not." *Australia*	"I read 'the principles are based on honesty, integrity and respect for people — our core values.' With recent downsizing I don't see much respect for Shell employees. So at page five I gave up." *Netherlands — Shell employee writing on* The Shell Report 1999

Source: *The Shell Report 2000*

---

to November 1999, but it's probably safe to say that the 862 respondents represent only a tiny proportion of those who "silently engage" with Shell.

In addition to the Tell Shell cards, the company runs discussion forums on its website that attract live and lively uncensored debate on such hot topics as human rights in Nigeria and global climate change. Exhibit 9.9 documents an example of one such discussion commentary and how Shell engaged directly and personally with the stakeholder.

Shell doesn't relegate its side of these dialogues to public relations people. Content experts and sometimes even senior leaders give full and considered responses to queries. Sometimes respondents who appear aggressive at first later register surprise at the open and personal replies they have received. Some even end up expressing support.

A Reputation Built from the Ground Up

Engaging with its stakeholders on a global scale can pay valuable reputational dividends, but overall Shell sees a shift from high-profile engagement to a more on-the-ground type of engagement with the people directly af-

Exhibit 9.9

Example of Shell's One-on-One Stakeholder Engagement
Verbatim transcription

Message posted in discussion thread

Date: March 14, 2000 08:47 AM
Author: Dan Denvir (*unity11@hotmail.com*)
Subject: Ogoni Blood

Just so you know, you are still an Amnesty International urgent action (see Just Earth, joint Amnesty/ Sierra Club project at www.aiusa.org/justearth/corporations/shell.html). Did you not supply weapons to Nigerian security forces that brutally crack down on the Ogoni people? Did you intervene in the execution of Ken Siro-Wiwa? Ken was an environmentalist protesting your pollution of the Niger Delta and the Ogoni people's homeland. His execution and your silence is unacceptable apathy equitable to manslaughter or even murder.

PS — This forum, minus real environmental and human rights efforts on your part, serves as nothing but GREENWASH.

Response from Shell expert

Date: March 31, 2000 05:06 PM
Author: Noble Pepple, Shell International Ltd
Subject: Reply to Mr Dan Denvir

Thank you for your e-mail to the Tell Shell Forum. In it, you make a number of points which I would like to respond to below.

First, let me address your statement that Shell is the subject of an "Amnesty International urgent action". This is not the case. Amnesty International has informed us that their "urgent actions" are issued only by the International Secretariat of Amnesty International based in London and that such actions are directed at individuals, not companies. No such action exists in relation to Shell.

The Web site referred to in your note belongs to the Amnesty International-USA (AI-USA), and not the International Secretariat (which is at http://www.amnesty.org). If you have not already done so, you might like to take a look at the Nigeria pages on the International Secretariat's site (at: http://www.amnesty.org/ailib/countries/indx144.htm) which provides a full and balanced picture.

I would like to turn now to the other issues you raised. We did not, and do not, "supply weapons to the security forces that brutally crack down on the Ogoni people". Since violence and armed crime in Nigeria is rife, some of the police assigned to protect Shell Nigeria's 4,000 people and property are armed. They have between them a total of 107 twenty year old hand guns. A strict control is maintained over these weapons and, apart from target practice, they have been fired once (a warning shot at an armed intruder who had invaded a Shell Nigeria guest house). The rules of engagement for the use of these weapons have been discussed extensively with Amnesty International and other Human Rights groups.

We did not stay silent on the case of Ken Saro-Wiwa and his co-accused. We spoke publicly about the rights of the accused to a fair legal process. Before the trial, Shell Nigeria said that, even though it did not agree with the allegations made against it, Ken Saro-Wiwa had a right to freely hold and air his views. After the trial verdict was announced, Shell Nigeria publicly argued against carrying out the death penalty. The former Chairman of the Shell Group, Cor Herkstroter, also sent a personal letter appealing to the Nigerian Head of State to show clemency for the accused on humanitarian grounds. Sadly this, and other appeals from concerned countries, organizations and individuals, went unheard. Despite that setback, SPDC also made its views known publicly on the detention of the Ogoni 20 — who were arrested for the same crime as Ken Saro-Wiwa — and the continued presence of the Internal Security Task Force in Ogoni land. As you may be aware, the Ogoni 20 have since been released and the Task Force withdrawn from Ogoniland.

I hope that this reply goes some way towards addressing your points. If you would like further information, I would invite you to visit Shell Nigeria's Web site at http://www.shellnigeria.com/.

Source: *The Shell Report 2000*

fected by its business decisions. In the Camisea project, for example, Shell worked to build a close dialogue with the indigenous peoples of the previously unexplored Camisea gas field in the Peruvian Amazon.

Examples of the practical outcomes of the Camisea engagement included a policy disallowing the construction of access roads into the fragile region and a community liaison program that favors community-wide investments instead of purely cash transactions with individuals to ensure a wider distribution of benefits.[16] The cost of the overall efforts—in terms of stakeholder consultation, socioenvironmental safeguards, community contracts, social capital, and sustainable development—represented only about 2 percent of the announced project start-up costs of $300 million and will likely mirror that percentage for the total development investment estimated at about $3.5 billion.

Yet these marginal investments yielded financial benefits quite disproportional to their costs, including risk reduction (socioenvironmental and country risk), goodwill, and cost avoidance in later phases.[17] In its totality, the Camisea experience exemplifies the way every operating unit in Shell is beginning to make stakeholder engagement a part of its business through the SDMF.

It's hard to find other examples of the kind of open dialogue that Shell encourages and conducts with stakeholders through its annual *Shell Reports* and on its website. It also seems perfectly reasonable for Tom Delfgaauw to see his company as one of the corporate leaders in transparency. For him, Shell has already made huge strides in the *process* world of reporting. He sees Shell's future challenges as lying mainly in making the *substance* of sustainability a reality throughout all of its businesses.

This requires a continuing cycle of engagement with stakeholders, uncompromising commitments to goals, open and honest communication about results, and reengagement for the future. For Shell, there really is no alternative. Tom Delfgaauw summed it up quite strongly: "Once you have embarked on this road, there is no turning back." So say all true revolutionaries.

Part Four

How Sweet It Is

Rather than love, than money, than fame, give me truth.
Henry David Thoreau, *Walden*

10

To the Victor Go the Spoils

Truth, like a torch, the more it's shook it shines.
William Hamilton, *Discussions on Philosophy*

Revolutionary leaders accept that others will watch them closely and talk. It isn't all that surprising then to find on the Internet a great deal of talk about such a prominent leader as Royal Dutch Shell. Leaders also accept that not everything said about them will be good. Some of it will be quite negative, sometimes even vicious. But revolutionaries don't take actions based on public opinion polls. They act because it's the right thing to do.

They act even if it means facilitating the flow of negative information about them, as Shell does on its own website. There, the company allows uncensored, online discussions, where visitors debate highly sensitive issues like pollution and human rights abuses. Even though the commentary may be quite critical of Shell, the company supports rather than squelches it. In doing so, it practices the principles of the ValueReporting Revolution, painful though it may be at times.

Does such self-inflicted pain make sense? Of course it does. Whether companies like it or not, the Internet inexorably pushes them toward greater transparency. Even if companies don't participate actively, the Internet offers up an extraordinary wealth of company information, often of the most negative sort. Nobody said the revolution would be painless.

To see for yourself just how much company information and commentary circulates in cyberspace, go to one of the advanced Internet search engines like www.google.com. Pick any well-known company's name; pair it with any disparaging adjective, verb, or phrase and conduct a search. Minimally, you should get hundreds of hits, most likely thousands. We've tried it and gotten tens of thousands. And remember, those are just hits that match one disparaging word. Much more is being said, positively and negatively, by many more people than most companies could imagine.

187

What's the point? If companies don't provide the information others seek, someone somewhere will. By providing the information itself, the company can ensure the information's accuracy and put it in an integrated, balanced context. It won't stop the negative commentary, but it will put more balance into the dialogue. Shell certainly takes this approach. It recognizes that it is impossible to control the flow of information, good or bad, regarding the company. What it has done is make sure its own voice is heard so that all of this information can be evaluated from Shell's perspective as well.

THE DISCLOSURE DICHOTOMY

One argument for better disclosure is that managers typically think they do a better job of communicating with the market than the market thinks they do. Exhibit 10.1 compares the differing perceptions on this subject among CFOs and heads of investor relations, institutional investors, and sell-side analysts in the United States.[1] When it comes to communication, perception is reality.

Exhibit 10.1

Perceptions on Corporate Disclosure in the United States

	U.S. Executives (*n*=200)	Sell-Side Analysts (*n*=31)	Institutional Investors (*n*=50)
Do not offer information beyond legal disclosure requirements	6%	0%	6%
Offer additional information to analysts considered relevant or useful	15%	45%	54%
Answer all questions put by analysts and investors, except where proprietary or sensitive information would be involved	18%	32%	26%
As above, but additionally contacts initiated with analysts and investors whenever new information becomes available	19%	10%	10%
Work actively to anticipate concerns and questions and attempt to maintain continuous dialogue with analysts and investors	41%	13%	4%
Don't know	2%	5%	0%

Granted, most managers genuinely believe they try hard to give the market the information it wants. But most analysts and investors believe managers could try harder. Better disclosure begins, therefore, with management's recognition that a disclosure problem exists in the first place, and that it's a bigger problem than most managers realize.

CFOs also believe they provide information more openly than the market thinks they do, as Exhibit 10.1 clearly shows. While 60 percent of CFOs believe they practice the two most open disclosure policies (the fourth and fifth rows in Exhibit 10.1), only 23 percent of analysts and 14 percent of investors would agree. And although U.S. executives feel that SEC regulations require greater disclosure from them than their foreign competitors' regulations require, the distribution of U.S. analysts and investors is statistically the same as that for the entire 14-country sample shown in Exhibit 10.1.

This suggests that the regulations do not address all the information needs of the market. Very similar patterns exist in surveys done of banks and insurance companies in North America, Europe, and Australia and in a survey of high-tech companies in the United States and Canada. The disclosure dichotomy is a universal one.

Furthermore, the U.S. data in the survey reconfirm a similar survey done by Eccles and Mavrinac in 1995. The earlier survey showed that calls for greater transparency from regulators and industry committees have had relatively little effect on corporate disclosure policies.[2] This says that managers have yet to fully recognize that greater transparency is in their own best interest. Fortunately, some forward-thinking managers have begun to see the light.

Analysts and investors in capital markets worldwide have seen the light already and believe that better disclosure produces some very clear benefits. The two chapters following this one discuss in greater detail what "better disclosure" really means. For now, read "better disclosure" as simply "more disclosure," which means giving the market more of the information it regards as important and less of the information it doesn't. Bear in mind, however, that merely increasing the quantity of information will not necessarily improve its quality. More on that later as well.

FIVE MAJOR BENEFITS OF BETTER DISCLOSURE

A PricewaterhouseCoopers global survey of institutional investors and sell-side analysts identified what those groups see as the five most important benefits of better disclosure: increased management credibility, more long-term investors, greater analyst following, improved access to new capital, and higher share values. Exhibit 10.2 shows the percentage of in-

Exhibit 10.2

How Investors Perceive the Benefits of Better Disclosure[a]

	Increased Management Credibility	More Long-Term Investors	Greater Analyst Following	Improved Access to New Capital	Higher Share Values
Australia	70	44	42	60	40
Denmark	90	64	12	60	48
France	92	70	94	84	80
Germany	62	47	68	66	53
Hong Kong	64	56	50	54	62
Italy	90	80	64	82	70
Japan	94	67	72	53	45
The Netherlands	70	63	63	74	64
Singapore	81	59	55	73	75
Sweden	74	64	52	66	56
Switzerland	82	63	76	68	72
Taiwan	54	56	42	50	38
United Kingdom	52	46	34	44	38
United States	80	64	34	44	58
Average	75	60	54	63	57

[a] Numbers are in percentages.

vestors perceiving these benefits by country, and Exhibit 10.3 does the same for analysts.[3]

These data are remarkable in the similarity of perceptions not only across North America, Europe, and Asia, but also between investors and analysts. Half or more of analysts and investors view these five benefits of disclosure as important regardless of the size of their countries' capital market, the accounting rules and regulations that apply, and the reporting practices of domestic companies. Virtually no significant differences exist between investors' and analysts' perceptions in any given country. Both the buy-side and the sell-side see things the same way. A closer look at each of the five perceived benefits of better disclosure sheds some light on why.

Before doing so, it's worth citing a recent academic study that provides empirical evidence that is quite consistent with these perceptual data. Healy, Hutton, and Palepu, in a study of 97 companies, found that better disclo-

Exhibit 10.3

How Analysts Perceive the Benefits of Better Disclosure[a]

	Increased Management Credibility	More Long-Term Investors	Greater Analyst Following	Improved Access to New Capital	Higher Share Values
Australia	77	64	50	53	40
Denmark	90	57	43	64	53
France	97	83	80	84	70
Germany	80	44	83	80	67
Hong Kong	87	67	56	53	60
Italy	83	83	70	80	53
Japan	92	58	77	45	36
The Netherlands	80	64	74	70	48
Singapore	91	57	72	59	65
Sweden	83	67	56	66	60
Switzerland	81	68	84	68	48
Taiwan	47	50	60	60	50
United Kingdom	70	57	23	43	43
United States	80	61	46	51	61
Average	81	63	62	63	54

[a] Numbers are in percentages.

sure resulted in higher share prices, more institutional ownership, greater analyst following, and increased stock liquidity.[4] Firms practicing greater disclosure saw an average increase in their share prices 7.1 percent higher than an industry peer group in the first year of greater disclosure and 8.4 percent the year after that.

Benefit 1: Increased Management Credibility

Exhibits 10.2 and 10.3 present a striking revelation: Increased management credibility ranks as much more important among both investors and analysts than any other benefit. Three out of four investors and four out of five analysts believe that better disclosure will lead to increased management credibility.

While it may seem rather intangible, management credibility is arguably the most important benefit of all and certainly a prerequisite for realizing all the others. When management has credibility, the market believes its claims that a particular company strategy will create value for shareholders—even when the cost of that strategy, a major acquisition or investment program, for example, requires an investment that will dilute current earnings. The market wisely recognizes that such a strategy will create value in the future.

For example, when Vodafone first offered to acquire Air Touch at $89 per share, Vodafone's stock price rose even though the company bid significantly more than the $73 per share that Bell Atlantic offered. Vodafone's stock continued to go up when the deal was concluded at $97 per share despite the company's announcement that goodwill charges would dilute earnings for years.[5]

Without a high level of management credibility, such an announcement would have evoked widespread skepticism. The market would have seen it as management simply making excuses for not delivering earnings for a particular quarter, and the company's stock would have gone down.

Why does better disclosure increase management's credibility in the eyes of the market? A management team that has confidence in both its own abilities and its strategy will not shy away from telling the market its plans for the future and how well it is doing today.

Armed with such information, the market can do its own analysis. Rather than digging for information it thinks the company is hiding or trying to second-guess a management team it doesn't trust, the market will be more inclined to share management's point of view. Credibility and transparency go hand in hand.

This proves especially true if management has made and delivered on past promises. Credibility, of course, ultimately depends on performance, but candor certainly enhances it. When objectives go unmet, or performance lags along some financial or nonfinancial dimension, management's best tack always is candor. By consistently providing information in both good times and bad, management reinforces its credibility with the marketplace. The market hates surprises, especially negative ones.

BP/Amoco offers a good example of how candor can strengthen or at least preserve the credibility that management has worked so hard to build. According to the June 5, 2000, issue of *Business Week*, in the summer of 1999 the families of six BP/Amoco scientists filed suit against the company. All six had worked in the same lab and had suddenly been stricken with the same rare form of brain cancer. By that publication date, five had already died.

How did the company respond? BP/Amoco's chairman, H. Laurence Fuller, held a press conference and described the situation in detail. According to the *Business Week* article, "By taking the moral high ground, the company deftly upstaged its foes in the court of public opinion, denying them the chance to turn it [BP/Amoco] into another corporate ogre."[6]

Failure to communicate as openly as BP/Amoco did—whether about lawsuits, earnings, or changes in strategic direction—can result in the instantaneous loss of hard-won credibility. It can result in civil lawsuits and the loss of jobs, as happened to Bergonzi and other executives at HBOC in connection with that company's accounting and reporting irregularities as described in Chapter 4. In that case, it even led to criminal lawsuits.

Between 1996 and 1998, HBOC's earnings management had turned into something quite sinister—accounting irregularities and possible illegal acts. In the aftermath of McKesson HBOC's April 1999 announcement of an earnings restatement, most analysts reduced their stock recommendations from "buy" to "hold."[7] Market analyst Raymond Hennessey in a June 21, 1999, *Dow Jones Newswire* noted, "The [McKesson HBOC] merger has been plagued by questions since its beginning, but improprieties in the way HBOC accounted for its revenue prompted a restatement of results."[8]

Brown Brothers Harriman analyst Michael Krensavage stated, "The firings [of Bergonzi and other HBOC executives] were a step that the company had to take to restore some kind of credibility." But, Krensavage warned, the firings were "also a sign that the accounting problems are most likely very, very severe."[9] In a separate interview on CNN, commenting on HBOC's accounting and reporting woes, Krensavage said, "It seems like this is a roach situation, and when you see one roach there are lots more under the cabinet."[10]

As with earnings restatements, when management delays or stops reporting information that the market sees as important, the market will assume the worst: that management has something to hide—probably because it does. And when management starts disclosing a new piece of performance information, the market will expect more of the same, unless management can make a strong and convincing argument that the additional information no longer has any impact on the company's value.

This doesn't mean that disappointing news won't have a negative effect on a company's stock price. It probably will, and it probably should if the news is sufficiently bad, and the leading indicators are negative as well. But when those indicators turn positive, the company's stock price will also be more likely to rise.

Greater transparency should also mitigate downward pressures on stock prices. When the market focuses on a single piece of performance information, such as earnings—because that's what management empha-

sizes—lower numbers or unmet expectations will have a dramatic negative effect.

For the market, that single number or piece of performance information represents everything—poor results, negative surprises, and management incompetence. The consequences can be devastating. However, when
the market has a lot of other performance information, it can interpret a
negative result in the proper, balanced context.

Some companies, of course, can sustain high stock values even though
they report little more than consistent earnings growth. These companies
play a very risky game. When earnings become the sole or primary basis for
valuing a company, the slightest hiccup can affect stock prices dramatically.
Fortunately, this is not true for those longer-term investors who don't focus
on a single measure and who are interested in a broader range of meaningful performance information. This means that management must work even
harder at providing these investors with the information they need.

Management should also work harder at explaining its strategies to the
market. Clear strategies that make sense and explain how a positive track
record will continue into the future enable investors to understand the company's potential for creating more value. The company's stock price will reflect that understanding.

In the realm of strategy, real-options thinking coupled with effective
communication can prove particularly useful. When management can articulate how the company's assets give it superior flexibility to adapt to
different circumstances, the result will be a higher stock price. The Enron
example in Chapter 3 shows how a real-options strategy can demonstrate
to the market that the company knows quite well how to manage risk and
its portfolio of businesses.[11] In Enron's case, its P/E ratio of around 65 in
August 2000 was about two to five times greater than that of its major
competitors, such as American Electric Power, Duke Energy, and the
Southern Company.

Benefit 2: More Long-Term Investors

Corporate executives would obviously prefer to have the stability that long-
term investors help ensure instead of the volatility that day traders almost in-
variably guarantee. For a stock to increase in price, of course, it must be
sold, but preferably to long-term investors who understand the company
and respect its management.

For existing investors to decide to increase their holdings, and for new
long-term investors to want to take a position, both groups need informa-

tion that will give them a higher degree of comfort in making their long-term commitments. Simply knowing next quarter's or even next year's earnings is not enough. To remain loyal or to join the faithful, investors need to know how well the company is doing on a broad range of performance measures and what it has planned for the future.

Yes, momentum investors and day traders will always be with us, but so will those who take the longer view. The proportion between the two, however, depends on the nature of the market and the information available. It is telling that within the high-tech sector, the recent darling of the day traders, 76 percent of analysts and 70 percent of investors in our high-tech survey believed that better disclosure would encourage more long-term investors compared to 60 percent of the corresponding groups in the general U.S. survey.

Strong bull markets have irresistible appeal for momentum investors who have no interest in the kind of information that ValueReporting offers. They simply bet they can get in and out of a stock before it goes down, regardless of what drives its price. But when value investors can't get the information advantages of ValueReporting, they have considerably more difficulty differentiating one company's true value from another's.

When companies truly differ in the amount of information they provide, long-term investors will find those that provide more information especially attractive. Because they know more, value investors believe they take less risk for a given level of return. And by taking long-term positions, they reduce their trading costs and the problems associated with getting out of a large position and reducing stock prices in the process.

Benefit 3: Increased Analyst Following

Throughout this book, and especially in Chapter 14, you will hear the opinion that sell-side analysts are a mixed blessing. But for smaller-cap companies and those that have just gone public, the sell-side analysts can play an important role in getting the attention of investors and providing some liquidity to the company's stock.

An investment bank that makes a market in a stock will usually provide some research coverage as well. Too often, however, an investment bank will take a company public with lots of promises of research coverage and then lose interest as bigger opportunities present themselves. This is evident from the results of the IPO survey conducted by Stapleton Communications in which respondents agreed that while an investment banking firm's research group is its most important selling point to new IPO candidates, they were least happy with the aftermarket support provided by the investment banks.[12]

When research coverage is minimal to nonexistent and liquidity is low, spreads are high. If offers are below the price at which the investors bought the stock, they have little incentive to sell it and take the loss, particularly if it represents a small portion of their portfolios.

So the stock just sits there without much interest and little prospect of going higher, whatever the company's performance. Compounding the problem in these circumstances is the fact that the company typically doesn't have a professional investor relations officer and so has little experience in getting the attention of the market.

One of the best ways to get the market's attention is to provide it with a lot of information. This gives both sell-side analysts and the investors something to analyze so they can determine if an investment opportunity exists.

Given that so much market value is concentrated in such a small number of companies, as discussed in Chapter 2, it's very likely that some real opportunities can arise. For example, remember that in 1999 the 10 largest market cap companies out of the total of about 5,100 listed on the NASDAQ accounted for nearly 56 percent of the total market cap for that exchange.[13] Medium- and small-cap companies, which have fewer analysts following them and for which relatively little information exists, will generally experience more market inefficiencies than very large-cap companies, which have a much greater following by analysts and for which a tremendous amount of information exists.

Evidence of how market cap determines analyst following comes from our high-tech survey. Eighty-nine percent of the small cap (<$500 million) companies had zero to five analysts following them. Forty-one percent of mid-cap companies ($500 million to $1.5 billion) had that same level of following, and for large-cap companies (>$1.5 billion) only 5 percent reported that level. And whereas only 1 percent of small-cap companies had 11 or more analysts following them, 20 percent of mid-cap and 79 percent of large-cap companies had that higher number of analysts following them.

This is not surprising. In the high-tech survey, 75 percent of analysts (compared to 46 percent in the general U.S. survey) and 62 percent of investors (34 percent in the U.S. survey) felt that better disclosure would result in increased analyst following.

That said, the positive impact that better disclosure has on increased analyst following is not restricted to smaller companies, especially when disclosure in general is fairly low, and when the capital markets are small relative to the size of the economy. When disclosure is relatively sparse, a company can attract analyst attention by providing more information.

Exhibit 10.4 shows, for example, that in three countries—Switzerland, the Netherlands, and Singapore—where the capital markets are well developed (as shown in the ratio of total market cap to gross domestic product) and disclosure is relatively sparse, the percentage of analysts who believe that greater disclosure leads to greater analyst following exceeds the all-country average of 62 percent. The same is true in four other countries—France, Germany, Italy, and Japan—where the capital markets are small relative to the size of the economy. Where there are fewer analysts, which is the case in smaller capital markets, one way to get their attention is to provide more information.

In contrast, in the United States and the United Kingdom, the capital markets are large relative to the size of the economy, and external reporting is relatively more open. In both of these countries, the percentage of analysts who believe that better disclosure would lead to greater analyst following is well below the average of 62 percent.

Exhibit 10.4

The Geography of Increased Analyst Following

This exhibit shows seven countries where increased analyst following proves to be an especially important benefit, and two where it doesn't.

	Capital Market Size as a Percent of Gross Domestic Product	Percentage of Analysts Who Perceive that Better Disclosure Leads to Greater Analyst Following
Switzerland	265.3	84
United Kingdom	171.0	23
The Netherlands	158.7	74
United States	148.6	46
Singapore	114.3	72
France	67.8	80
Japan	65.7	77
Germany	50.9	83
Italy	48.3	70

Source: Statistics in column 1 come from IMF International Financial Statistics, 1998.

Companies have to make it easy for analysts and investors to do their analyses. The more information the company provides and the more access the market has to management, the greater the analyst following will be. The Internet continues to lower the cost and increase the ease of providing more information. Companies have much to gain and little to lose.

Benefit 4: Improved Access to New Capital

The fourth benefit of better disclosure, improved access to new capital, relates fairly closely to the third benefit, greater analyst following, as shown in Exhibits 10.2 and 10.3. Investors who need more information—more often the case with value investors than index or momentum investors—will commit to a stock only after their information needs have been met. This includes sophisticated investors, like large-fund managers with access to many buy-side analysts, and investors like those in the United States who have become accustomed to having quite a bit of information available.

In some cases, improved access to capital can indeed lower its cost, as Christine Botosan has shown happens in companies that have low analyst following.[14] In any market, when capital providers face strong competition, the price of capital goes down as a result of a higher stock price. Improved access probably won't have a material effect on the cost of capital for the largest and most visible companies, but it can have a significant impact on the numbers for the vast majority of other companies.

The degree of importance of the cost of capital, both equity and debt, varies by industry. It has great importance in financial services, for example, because the cost of capital is such a large component of total costs. A 1999 PricewaterhouseCoopers survey of major North American, European, and Australian banks and insurance companies shows that the market recognizes both the importance of the cost of capital and how better disclosure can help lower it.

On the banking side of the survey, 69 percent of investors ranked lower cost of capital first and 64 percent of sell-side analysts ranked it second on the list of the benefits of better disclosure. This put it in a virtual dead heat with the other top benefits, like increased credibility of management and increased number of long-term investors. On the insurance side, lower cost of capital actually ranked highest among the five benefits.

Benefit 5: Higher Share Values

The first four benefits of better disclosure—increased management credibility, more long-term investors, greater analyst following, and improved access to new capital—logically contribute to a higher share price. Confirming that logic, more than half of the investors and analysts surveyed said higher share values would be a benefit of better disclosure.

Whether better disclosure actually *will* lead to a higher stock price is the $64,000 question and one that is often asked. Anyone who believes that the market has all the information it needs and uses it with total efficiency must also believe that better disclosure would have no material impact on stock price. If that were really true, what can explain why most managers think the market undervalues their companies' stocks? And they do think that, as the survey discussed in Chapter 2 and a subsequent survey of CFOs and heads of investor relations clearly show. Completed in early 1999 when the market was very strong and getting stronger, the second survey found that 61 percent of the respondents felt the market either *strongly* undervalued or *tended* to undervalue their companies. That percentage matches almost exactly the percentage of analysts and investors in the United States who think that better disclosure will lead to higher share prices.

Similarly, in the banking and insurance industry surveys, 67 percent of banking and 65 percent of insurance company executives thought their shares were undervalued. In the United States, both groups held this opinion even more strongly—fully 80 percent felt their stocks were undervalued. For high-tech companies, 75 percent agreed. These executives should take pleasure in knowing that many analysts and investors believe that better disclosure will increase their stock prices.

Fifty-three percent of bank investors (53 percent for insurance investors) and 46 percent of bank analysts (53 percent for insurance analysts) believed that better disclosure would lead to higher share prices. For high-tech companies, these figures came in at 74 percent for analysts and 56 percent for investors. The difference in perceptions between the corporate executives and the market about whether shares were properly valued reflects the reality that transparency is just one of many factors that affect share prices.

For example, the investment climate in a particular industry sector can have a significant effect. At the time of our survey—during a big high-tech boom—the banking and insurance sector had fallen out of favor with investors. As a result, banks' share prices and P/E ratios fell quite low, and far below those in the high-tech sector, even though some of them, like Bank of Montreal, were among the banking industry's better examples of disclosure.

ValueReporting is not a silver bullet for guaranteeing more value for shareholders. Many factors other than information alone determine a company's stock price. ValueReporting can guarantee, however, that a company's stock price will be closer to its intrinsic value. To believe otherwise would imply that markets are completely irrational or that stock prices are based solely on information other than a company's performance. Few managers think that.

In the final analysis, a company's performance determines its stock price. And that is the very essence of ValueReporting: reporting a company's performance as completely and accurately as possible so the capital markets can properly price its stock. Such reporting, of course, can result in a lower stock price when things aren't going as well as the market thinks.

In such circumstances, managers can use obfuscation as a defensive strategy to prop up their stock price. Hiding information, however, works only in the short term. Sooner or later, the market uncovers the truth. When it does, the consequences will be worse than if management had come clean sooner. If the market believes that management intentionally hid bad news, credibility is destroyed, and the climb to a higher stock price becomes steep indeed. More often than not, a new management team will lead that climb.

A SIXTH BENEFIT

In a 1998 discussion of the results of the global survey specific to Switzerland with Walter Kielholz, CEO of Swiss Re, he commented that if more members of his senior management team committed to targets and reported on results to the market, Swiss Re would produce a higher shareholder value. He felt that the "level of reality" of externally reported performance measures was higher than those used only internally.[15] Thus, in addition to better disclosure's five external benefits, there is an internal benefit: a better-managed company.

Now More Than Ever

Kielholz has become even more convinced of this. Swiss Re's CFO, John Fitzpatrick, shares the same view. He likens externally published targets and the promise to report actual performance against them to Cortez burning his ships when he landed in Mexico. With the ships gone, the troops under Cortez's command had no choice but to fight and win. Similarly, Fitzpatrick says, "When you go public with something, it permeates the entire organization in a way that actually makes it easier for us to accomplish our objectives. There is no way to turn back."

Kielholz adds that one of the best ways to get the message out to Swiss Re's 9,000 employees around the world is to put it in public disclosures available for the entire world to see. As noted earlier, Kielholz sees this as one of the advantages in going public with embedded value figures.

Searching for Key Measures

Kielholz, however, wants to go even further. To begin, he wants to develop some key indices and productivity measures along the dimensions of cost, people, embedded value, and loss reserves. In the case of cost, for example, he feels that with the right measures the company could drive absolute costs down by driving productivity up. Regarding the high level of knowledge and expertise of the company's people, he and Fitzpatrick acknowledge that although they talk a lot about the importance of people in creating value, they haven't done much to measure it formally. Fitzpatrick notes that because Swiss Re is "in the knowledge business" it would be extremely useful if "we could tell more about our people and how we invest in them."

Getting Your Money's Worth

Kielholz believes that once Swiss Re can develop and prove such measures, the full benefit will come from reporting them externally. As he puts it: "We will report them externally when they are stable internally. Why not help drive internal cost management and productivity by external communications?" He has set a goal of having measures for every business unit and staff function, measures for which targets and actual results can be reported to the market. According to Kielholz, "Everybody in the Corporate Center needs something they have to be held accountable for externally. When you are publicly accountable, it changes the name of the game. I want to get people to state their goals and then stand up and say what happened."

Fitzpatrick agrees that external accountability will improve internal management. "It would distribute the pressure in a constructive way," he says, to people who can take direct actions in their departments and business units. He also believes that the market would place value on this additional information. He says that the full benefit of most of the nonfinancial measures will only come once the company can attain a certain level of return on equity (ROE). Swiss Re, in his view, must first demonstrate superior financial performance (ROE) and cites evidence that financial institutions that do have high ROEs have stock prices disproportionately higher than others with average performance. According to Fitzpatrick, the analysts won't reflect the full benefit of the disclosure of nonfinancial measures in stock prices until such nonfinancial measures translate into a financial return. Or, as he put it more succinctly, "We can't expect to be paid a premium for being a knowledge company until that knowledge translates into a superior financial return."

The Present and the Future

At this higher level of financial performance, the market would want to know how capable Swiss Re would be in sustaining it. This is where measures such as productivity, knowledge, embedded value, and loss reserves become important. Performance on these measures will give the market the evidence it wants that superior financial performance will continue into the future. While these other measures cannot substitute for bottom-line performance in determining the value of the company, even a superior bottom line cannot guarantee future performance and convince the market that future returns should be reflected in the current stock price.

Some High-Tech Confirmation

With the insight gained from Swiss Re, we added the potential benefit of "greater management accountability" when we designed the high-tech survey. The results showed strong support from the market that better disclosure leads to a better-managed company. Eighty-one percent of investors and 77 percent of analysts believed that better disclosure results in greater management accountability. In fact, for both groups greater management accountability ranked as the second highest benefit, after increased management credibility. Managers who have more accountability also have more credibility.

MANAGEMENT'S VIEW

On average, executives express a less positive perception than analysts and investors of the benefits of better disclosure. Exhibit 10.5 compares the gen-

Exhibit 10.5

U.S. Perceptions of the Benefits of Better Disclosure[a]

	Increased Management Credibility General/High-Tech	More Long-Term Investors General/ High-Tech	Increased Analyst Following General/ High-Tech	Improved Access to New Capital General/ High-Tech	Higher Share Values General/ High-Tech
Executives	49/55	37/57	33/53	28/35	53/61
Investors	80/89	64/70	34/62	44/60	58/56
Analysts	80/87	61/76	46/75	51/47	61/74

[a] Numbers are in percentages.

eral perceptions of CFOs and heads of investor relations with the perceptions of investors and analysts in the United States. The global insurance survey showed the same results; the global banking survey did not.

In the high-tech survey, it was found that executives were more bullish about the benefit of better disclosure than their peers in other industries. This lends further support to our contention that in the high-tech sector the current financial reporting model suffers under special strain.

Yet, in the general U.S. survey and in the banking and insurance industry surveys, management ranked "increased share values" high among the benefits of better disclosure. Here, the executives' views pretty much matched those of the market, despite the executives' somewhat cynical attitude about what better disclosure will do for their credibility, the number of long-term investors, the number of analysts who follow their stocks, and their companies' access to new capital.

The most notable exceptions to this in the high-tech survey are "more long-term investors" (57 percent compared to 37 percent in the U.S. survey) and "increased analyst following" (53 percent compared to 33 percent). Not unexpectedly, the latter is heavily determined by the small- and medium-cap companies as only 11 percent of the large-cap executives cited it as a benefit of better disclosure.

Slightly fewer (46 percent) of the high-tech executives cited "greater management accountability" as a benefit. The fact that 77 percent of analysts and 81 percent of investors cited this as a benefit suggests that the market is much more enthusiastic than managers are about greater management accountability.

Nevertheless, even executives who believe that improved disclosure can lead to higher share prices shy away from providing more information to the market. In discussions with many executives around the world, we have found that they cite 10 common reasons for not being more transparent about their performance and plans. Although each of the 10 reasons has a certain degree of merit, more often than not they can also be seen simply as excuses for not making, as Chapter 1 characterized it, "the scary decision to disclose more."

Reason/Excuse 1: The Market Cares Only about Earnings

In our survey of U.S. analysts and investors, "earnings" tops the list of the most important performance measures. But closely on its heels are five other financial measures that analysts and investors rank very high as well: R&D investments, cash flow, costs, capital expenditures, and segment performance. Four nonfinancial measures also rank high: market growth, new product development, market share, and statements of strategic goals.

The results from the other 13 countries in that survey, as well as the results from the banking, insurance, and high-tech industry surveys showed similar, if not identical, rankings. For example, seven of the Top Ten Hit Parade of measures in the high-tech survey are nonfinancial (see Exhibit 7.2). The market clearly cares about a wide range of performance measures and wishes it could get better information on most of them.

Reason/Excuse 2: We Already Report a Lot of Information

It's not a question of how much information is being reported. It's whether the *right* information is being reported. Recognizing that companies must abide by varying reporting requirements depending on their country of origin, and that some of this information may be of marginal use to investors, they often report a significant amount of information that really isn't all that useful to the market. The solution is painfully obvious. Replace that information with other information that investors *will* find useful.

Corporate executives in the United States can legitimately claim that they face more regulatory reporting requirements than their European and Asian counterparts. But as the banking and insurance industry surveys showed, the Information Gaps in both the United States and Europe are virtually the same. U.S. bank and insurance company executives fare no better in meeting the market's information needs along such measures as customer retention, customer penetration, risk management practices, market risk exposure (especially interesting in light of FAS 133), performance by business segment, and economic profit. This is not all that surprising because accounting regulations don't even cover most of these measures. It does clearly demonstrate, however, the difference between the quantity and the relevance of the information provided.

Reason/Excuse 3: Once We Start Reporting Something, We Can't Stop

If the market finds a certain piece of performance information useful, it will certainly want more of the same. As Swiss Re's Walter Kielholz notes in Chapter 1, "Once it's out there, you can't get rid of it." Wouter de Vries, head of investor relations at Royal Dutch Shell, agrees: "There's no going back."

Management serves its own best interests when it responds to the market's desire for more information because progress on that measure will have a positive effect on the company's stock price. If, however, a particular measure becomes irrelevant, or a better one comes along, the company has no reason to continue to report on it. Management will, of course, have to explain why the company has stopped. Decisions to no longer report on a performance measure should be made very carefully as the value of information grows when it is in the context of a historical trend line and comparable to competitors.

Reason/Excuse 4: Producing and Reporting Information Cost a Lot

Thanks to the Internet, the cost of providing information to the market will continue to decrease dramatically. Generalizing from Moore's Law, the cost of providing information over the Internet goes down by about half every 18 months. Shell sees this as an opportunity to significantly reshape communications in the future. Investor relations head Wouter de Vries foresees "reporting as being increasingly tailored for every stakeholder and investor" with customized information based on the user's profile.

The real issue here is the cost of generating the information, not reporting it. Certain measures, such as customer retention or process quality, are often difficult to measure and require the development of new measurement methodologies, which can cost a lot indeed. Managers must then decide whether having this information for internal decision-making purposes justifies the cost of generating it. If managers find that it does, making the information available to the market adds very little incremental cost.

Reason/Excuse 5: No Matter How Much We Report, the Market Always Wants More

This is simply not true. The size of the Information Gap—the difference between the importance the market places on a measure and how satisfied it is with the information it gets—varies enormously. Most of the analysts and investors in our global survey said they were generally satisfied with the information they receive on the important measures of earnings and capital expenditures, as well as on the relatively unimportant measure of environmental compliance. There were a few exceptions, but mostly in countries with less strict reporting requirements.

Similar levels of satisfaction were found in the banking and insurance surveys where the Information Gap was virtually nonexistent for earnings, loan loss ratio (banks), claims ratio (insurance companies), assets under management, investment performance, core deposit growth (banks), regulatory reputation, and plans for growth. Note that not all of these measures are required by regulation and that some are rather qualitative. Satisfying the market's information needs clearly doesn't require regulations and precise numbers. In the high-tech survey, analysts reported satisfaction with the information they get on 19 of the 37 measures, and investors were satisfied on 11. Most of these measures, however, were not considered very important.

Reason/Excuse 6: Bad Numbers Will Hurt Our Stock Price

This is true. If the market believes that a financial or nonfinancial measure is important to value creation, bad numbers will hurt the company's stock price, even if earnings remain strong. However, improved performance on the measure can have a positive effect on a company's stock price, even when earnings remain weak. There is no escaping the fact: Markets reward and punish companies based on performance, whether it's earnings or any of the other important measures. That's what markets are all about.

Reason/Excuse 7: Some of These Measures Aren't Very Reliable

It's true that reporting no information is better than reporting bad information. It's also true that most companies don't have adequate internal measurement systems for some key performance dimensions, particularly the nonfinancial ones. Chapter 7 described this type of Quality Gap for the high-tech industry in detail.

With sufficient effort, however, a company can nearly always identify and track measures that have sufficient reliability. Just look at the success certain companies have had in implementing balanced scorecard systems for internal use: AT&T, Bank of America, Boots the Chemist, Ciba Geigy, Ericsson, General Motors, Johnson & Johnson, Kmart, Lufthansa, Novo Nordisk, Roche, SBC Warburg, Swiss Telecom, and United Technologies.

Reason/Excuse 8: Our Competitors Will Use This Information to Our Disadvantage

It's a possibility, but a highly exaggerated one. If a company wants information on a competitor, it has many legitimate avenues for getting it, including the Internet, a consulting firm, or hiring an executive away from a competitor.

A study done for the Australian building products company Pioneer found that at least one company in that industry reported on virtually every single performance measure. As people sometimes say, "It's a secret to everybody or it's a secret to nobody." Even if reporting to the market gave competitors information they didn't already have or couldn't get, actually using the information for competitive advantage is much easier said than done. Changing strategies and behaviors is no mean feat.

Reason/Excuse 9: Our Customers and Suppliers Could Learn How Much Money We're Making

So what? They probably have a pretty good idea already. Suppliers and customers care far less about how much money a company makes than about the economic advantages of doing business with that company. If they perceive a real benefit from the relationship, they'll stay in it. If more attractive choices come along, they'll pursue them, regardless of how much or little money the company in question makes. Customers and suppliers respond to competition in the product markets, not information in the capital markets.

Reason/Excuse 10: We'll Get Sued

In the United States especially, the risk of litigation poses a very legitimate concern. Tort lawyers have had a field day blackmailing companies who release forward-looking information, even when they do so with all the proper disclaimers. The Safe Harbor provision of litigation reform legislation passed in 1995 aimed at reducing this risk. How much positive effect it will have remains to be seen.

Experience to date suggests that a real and lasting solution remains elusive. For every day the market was open in 1998, a company was named as a defendant in a lawsuit. As one might expect, high-technology companies get sued the most frequently. Among all companies, almost 60 percent of all such suits allege accounting misdeeds and more than half allege insider sales.[16]

Commenting on such a high rate of litigation in the post–Safe Harbor legislation years, Joseph A. Grundfest, a former SEC commissioner, said, "People frequently ask why the Private Securities Litigation Reform Act of 1995 has not reduced the volume of litigation. . . . Plaintiffs claim that fraud is common in today's stock market and point to many examples of accounting restatements and trading by corporate insiders. . . . Defendants claim that honest conduct in volatile markets is often mistaken for fraud, and some courts have failed to implement the Reform Act properly because they don't subject plaintiff's complaints to sufficiently searching scrutiny."[17]

Accounting fraud and insider trading may appear a bit removed from the call for greater transparency, but the litigious environment in the United States discourages some companies from providing more information to the market. Concerns about legal liabilities under state laws and uncertainty about how the federal court will interpret the Safe Harbor provision have kept managers from taking much comfort in this legislation. As a result, many legitimate concerns still exist about providing more information, particularly forward-looking statements. It's clearly an area that regulators should examine more closely.

BETTER DISCLOSURE → BETTER MANAGEMENT

There is at least one more reason managers don't want to disclose more information on their plans and how well they are executing against them. They will be held accountable if their performance is poor. The large difference in enthusiasm between executives and the market over the benefits of greater management accountability has already been documented. But the Swiss Re example also demonstrates how senior managers can recognize the opportunity greater management accountability creates to improve management performance overall. As Exhibit 10.6 shows, better disclosure, better strategies, and better performance all reinforce each other.

Senior management and the board must ensure that this virtuous circle works as effectively as possible. It's the classic chicken-and-egg situation;

Exhibit 10.6

Virtuous Circle of Disclosure

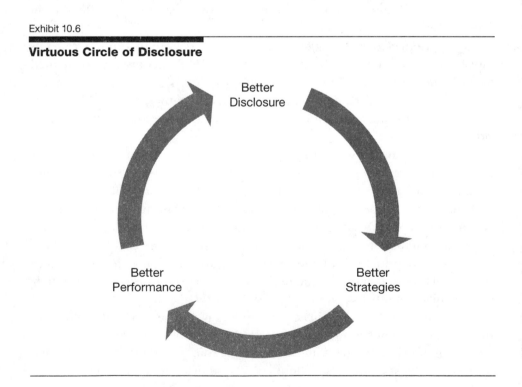

someone has to take responsibility for the dynamics. Clearly, it is in management's interest to do so.

Although companies increasingly recognize the importance of other stakeholders—such as customers, employees, and the community—for most companies, shareholders remain the first among equals. It is becoming very difficult to find companies that do not emphasize their commitment to creating value for shareholders, especially in the United States and increasingly so in Europe and even Asia. That makes today's penchant for creating partnerships and sharing more information with stakeholders, rather than shareholders, seem somewhat ironic.

Treat Them Like Partners As If You Really Mean It

If management truly views shareholders as partners, and places creating value for them near or at the top of its primary responsibilities, then it should treat them as such. Management should give shareholders information on strategic plans and performance and actively solicit their feedback on both. If shareholders don't like the strategies and register dissatisfaction with the company's performance, management should listen to their complaints and quickly learn what has caused them.

Senior executives rightly take responsibility for monitoring and evaluating the performance of the managers who report to them. They must also accept that shareholders, directly and through the board, have the same responsibility toward management. Chapter 12 takes a closer look at the board's role in achieving greater transparency.

A Little Pain . . . A Lot of Gain

Managers often have difficulty embracing the virtue of capital market discipline. It is, nonetheless, a logical consequence of creating value for shareholders when they are treated as true partners and not just cash cows. The capital they provide is as important an asset as the contributions of employees, customers, and suppliers. Consciously striving to benefit from the capital market's questions, insights, and discipline may at times cause management pain, but with that pain can come gain.

In studying Intel's disclosure practices, Miller and O'Leary[18] found that technical analysts sometimes play the monitor/evaluator role for companies. Intel provides information on new products it plans to introduce to technical analysts who sign a nondisclosure agreement. That way the technical analysts can write reports for the financial analysts before a products' introduction. This helps to minimize confusion in the capital market about complex technical developments. It can also provide Intel with some useful feedback prior to the product's introduction. If the technical analysts' reaction isn't positive, Intel can put that reaction into its decision-making hopper before proceeding with product development and launch.

As the communications manager at Intel explained, "Having somebody from outside that can call your 'baby' ugly, if in fact it is ugly, wakes you up, and you can make a decision on whether or not this thing has the opportunity to be successful in the marketplace, or how it might be successful in the marketplace."[19]

Major investors and prominent analysts can play a similar role at a more strategic level. That works well only if management carefully listens to the outsiders' questions and concerns rather than just attempting to sell them on a vision.

It is better to accept some short-term pain for greater long-term gain than to be replaced because the market finally loses patience. Management should not try to keep the market at arm's length or manage and spin it by playing The Earnings Game or releasing only as much information as minimally necessary. Instead, management should practice as much transparency as feasibly possible.

This won't happen overnight; as Chapter 1 cautioned, a revolution requires planning and preparation. But executives should begin to lay their plans now. They'll be glad they did when the revolution begins in earnest.

11

Can You See Clearly Now?

Anything more than the truth would have seemed too weak.
Robert Frost, *Mowing*

Some companies have already heeded the trumpet's call and joined the
ranks of the ValueReporting Revolution. Their senior executives have seen
clearly that better disclosure means better business—for them, their shareholders, and other stakeholders as well.

That said, even in these companies, the revolution has just begun. The
battle is clearly far from won. The task of determining what other information has true relevance to value and how best to present it is daunting. And
despite all its surrounding hype and hoopla, the Internet is still in its infancy
too. Commercial enterprises, like most of the world, have only begun to understand its capabilities and how to take fuller advantage of them.

Thanks, however, to the enlightened revolutionaries, we can include in
this chapter a few short examples of better disclosure practices that will give
clearer insight to managers in other companies, and hopefully inspire them
to action. These examples describe both the content of the information the
companies provide and how they have harnessed the power of the Internet
to make the information available on a timely basis to everyone who wants
or needs to know.

As in the early stages of any revolution, the lines of battle and theaters
of operation change quickly. As a consequence, this report from the front
will likely sound outdated even in the few weeks it will take to go into print.
True to our call to companies to embrace the Internet, we have established
a website (www.valuereporting.com) that will continuously refresh and re-
plenish the examples of better disclosure practice as companies set them.
The website will also make future reports on the revolution's progress more
timely and accessible and will include the PricewaterhouseCoopers annual
ValueReporting Forecast.

IT'S ALIVE!

To bring the concept of ValueReporting to life, the case examples in this chapter have been organized along the four dimensions of a ValueReporting Disclosure Model that captures the key elements of what a company should disclose to its shareholders and other stakeholders. While the examples are brief, you can find more detailed information and gain much greater insight simply by going to the case company's website at the address given and see for yourself how the revolution is unfolding.

A MODEL FOR BETTER DISCLOSURE

The simple ValueReporting Disclosure Model in Exhibit 11.1 serves as a starting point for companies to organize the *content* portion of their disclosure process. The model consists of four elements:

1. *Market Overview:* The company's external environment
2. *Value Strategy:* The company's competitive position and how it intends to create value in the context of its external environment
3. *Managing for Value:* The company's financial targets, how well it's meeting them, and the governance and management structures it has in place to deliver on the value strategy
4. *Value Platform:* The underlying value drivers—mostly nonfinancial— for delivering on the financial performance measures specified in Managing for Value, and how well the company manages them

Following a more complete definition of each element, a short case history uses the ValueReporting Disclosure Model to illustrate more than a century of AT&T's disclosure practices. Following that are more extended discussions of each of the four major ValueReporting Disclosure Model elements, where you will find current, but soon-to-be-historical, real-life examples of companies that have done some interesting things in their move toward better disclosure.

Incidentally, it didn't take much effort to find examples of companies that report nontraditional measures; we simply went on the Internet and there they were. Note, too, that finding "best practices" wasn't the objective of the search. The point was merely to offer evidence that, in some parts of the reporting world, the ValueReporting Revolution has already begun.

Market Overview

As the model in Exhibit 11.1 shows, effective disclosure begins with a Market Overview. This is management's take on external market forces, those

Exhibit 11.1

The ValueReporting Disclosure Model

External	Internal		
Market Overview	**Value Strategy**	**Managing for Value**	**Value Platform**

• Competitive environment
• Regulatory environment
• Macro-economic environment
	• Goals
	• Objectives
	• Governance
	• Organization
		• Financial performance
		• Financial position
		• Risk management
		• Segment performance
			• Innovation
			• Brands
			• Customers
			• Supply chain
			• People
			• Reputation
			  – Social
			  – Environmental

operating within the company's own industry and the broader forces of the overall economy. The Market Overview also includes management's views on where the market is headed. Although no one can ever predict the future, investors still want to know what a company's leadership thinks the future holds. They can then compare management's view to theirs and make up their own minds about whether the company got it right.

Value Strategy

The Value Strategy describes in as much detail as possible, without giving away the store, how a company will compete in its particular marketplace. This description should explicitly point out the company's competitive strengths and how it will exploit them. The Value Strategy also identifies the company's weaknesses, and how it will correct or compensate for them. Because strategies become real only when grounded in plans, objectives, and targets, the company should report on these as well.

Managing for Value

Shareholder value ultimately results from financial performance. Companies, therefore, should report it against targets and benchmark it against competitors and relevant peers. Managing for Value also requires the right capital structure and effective risk management. This information proves most useful when companies provide it at a segment level, compared to targets articulated in the Value Strategy, and benchmarked against peers as well. To make their own assessments of the likelihood that a company can successfully execute its strategies and plans, investors will also want information on the company's governance and management.

Value Platform

Financial performance itself ultimately depends on how well a company manages all of the tangible and intangible assets in its Value Platform. These assets are internal (people and innovation) as well as external (customers, brands, suppliers, and reputation with other stakeholders for environmental responsibility). Rather than simply reporting financial performance and assuming that it completely captures the value the company creates, managers should also provide information on the quality of the assets in its Value Platform and how it manages them to create shareholder value.

A SHORT LESSON FROM A LONG HISTORY

So far, this discussion has focused primarily on what the future holds for corporate transparency. Those who have already enlisted in the ValueReporting Revolution recognize that better disclosure is not only an inevitable force that is redefining the future, it's an historical one as well.

A brief review of more than a century of AT&T's evolving disclosure practices will show that the march toward greater transparency has pretty much been in one direction. There are very few reasons to think that the march will reverse itself. Many more reasons suggest that it will continue and accelerate.

In the belief that history can teach much to revolutionaries, here is a quick look through the lens of the ValueReporting Disclosure Model at how the disclosure practices of AT&T have changed over time. AT&T was chosen for this exercise because of its central role in the history of U.S. business and because very few companies have survived the tumult of economic events so well.

Based on a review of AT&T's annual reports at roughly 10-year intervals beginning with 1881, Exhibit 11.2 summarizes the findings and shows the company's one-way movement toward increasingly greater transparency. As the exhibit shows, AT&T's disclosure practices seem to self-organize into three reporting eras:

1. 1881–1909, a period of overall low disclosure
2. 1919–1959, a period of overall low/medium disclosure
3. 1969–1999, a period of overall medium/high disclosure

Exhibit 11.2

Evolution of Corporate Disclosure at AT&T

	Market Overview	Value Strategy	Managing for Value	Value Platform
1881	Medium	Low	Low	Low
1889	Low	Low	Low	Low
1899	Low	Low	Low	Low
1909	Medium	Low	Low	Low
1919	Low	Low	Medium	Medium
1929	Low	Low	Medium	Medium
1939	Low	Low	Medium	Medium
1949	Low	Low	Medium	Medium
1959	Low	Low	Medium	Medium
1969	Medium	Low	Medium	Medium
1979	Medium	Medium	High	High
1989	Medium	Medium	High	High
1999	High	Medium	High	High

If anything, this look at 119 years at AT&T understates the degree to which disclosure has progressed. For one thing, it does not take into account information the company reported in presentations to analysts and investors. Nor does it include information from the company's website. It simply examines one communications medium that AT&T has used for the entire period—its annual report.[1]

Even the oldest of this book's authors can't offer an eyewitness account of the very first of AT&T's reporting eras. We feel comfortable, nonetheless, in speculating that management then would have resisted greater disclosure for the same reasons many managers resist it today. Had they read an account of just how much their executive heirs would disclose at the turn of the twenty-first century, they would have assumed that Jules Verne had penned it. If they read the account as fact, they no doubt would have bemoaned the onerous reporting requirements awaiting their successors and predicted dire consequences for one and all.

Between 1881 and 1909, not surprisingly, AT&T ranked relatively low on all the ValueReporting Disclosure Model elements. No doubt it was in good company in that regard. The U.S. capital markets had just begun to

take root, companies were subject to very few external reporting regulations, and AT&T had a virtual monopoly. Management felt no significant
pressures to disclose more and saw no real benefit in doing so. The first of
AT&T's early reporting eras, however, saw some interesting disclosures in
the Market Overview elements. In 1881, for example, the company reported
on the competitive environment and its part in a very controversial patent
regulation debate. In 1909, the annual report included a lot of competitive
and regulatory information surrounding the development of the telephone
system. The defensive tone of that discussion reflects the pressure the company felt as a result of external concerns over its monopolistic position.
Then as now, when management has a good reason to report more information, it will.

The second reporting era, 1909 to 1959, witnessed a notable increase
in disclosure in the Managing for Value and the Value Platform elements. In
Managing for Value, the level of detail of financial information, such as for
business segments and subsidiaries, increased significantly. Reporting on
risk varied throughout this period, fairly detailed in some years, hardly mentioned in others.

The company made significant strides, however, in Value Platform reporting, providing information on operating performance, research and development, employees, branding strategy, and the quality of service to
customers. Testament to the truth that there are few things new under the
sun, the 1939 annual report discussed the "continued importance of intangible but very real elements such as courtesy, the spirit of helpfulness, the consideration of the needs of the individual subscriber, and the use of initiative."
Management, however, said very little about the competitive environment,
strategies for competing (probably because AT&T had no competitors), or
company goals and objectives.

When AT&T lost its monopoly on January 1, 1984, the day Judge Harold
Green's order to break the company up went into effect, management could
no longer afford the luxury of not discussing the competitive environment or
not explaining its strategy to investors. That's when disclosure on Market
Overview and Value Strategy started to show significant improvement.

In the third reporting era, the annual reports began to discuss in considerable detail both the competitive and regulatory environments, eventually including analyses of both. By 1999, this section offered a great deal of
fairly technical information.

In terms of Value Strategy, the most significant improvements came in
the form of explicit statements of goals and the progress the company had
made in achieving them. Similar to discussions of risk in the first era, discus-

sions about governance in the third era varied—there was considerable discussion in some years and low or no mention at all in others.

This third era also saw significant improvements in reporting on Managing for Value and the Value Platform with much more detailed financial information and more analysis. Although an abundance of information was reported, it was highly technical in content and not very accessible to less sophisticated investors. These latter-era annual reports also paid a great deal of attention to risk management. In terms of the Value Platform, AT&T continued to provide more and better information about employees, customers, brands, and issues regarding its reputation with other stakeholders.

Looking back, this 119-year history of external reporting by AT&T demonstrates a consistent and dramatic movement toward greater transparency. It's also very much in alignment with the principles of Value-Reporting.

MARKET OVERVIEW

All well-managed companies formulate their strategies in the context of their own explicit views of the markets in which they compete. They take into account the company's competitors and competitive position, assumptions about macroeconomic and industry growth, views on the regulatory environment, and perceptions about current and future technologies.

Because so very little of this kind of information has proprietary value, managers should not hesitate to report it, accompanied of course by the proper disclaimers regarding "forward-looking information." Investors find this kind of information enormously useful. It enables them to form their own opinions about whether management has a realistic view of the competitive environment, for example, or if management feels overly optimistic about the industry's future and the company's place in it.

A few examples of companies reporting useful Market Overview information include:

- Volvo (www.volvo.com), in its 1999 annual report, gives market share data by product line and by country; it also provides data on the expected growth of ground transport, an indicator of market growth.
- Noranda (www.noranda.com), the international metals and mining company, shows the impact on after-tax earnings of a 10 percent change in the price of zinc, copper, nickel, aluminum, silver, and lead—essentially part of an overall "business model" for the company, a concept discussed in Chapter 1.

VALUE STRATEGY

Most investors have a great deal of interest in management's strategy for creating shareholder value. (Momentum investors, who simply play movements in stock prices, do not share the same level of interest.) Managers who make explicit commitments in terms of Value Strategy and then deliver on them, as reported in Managing for Value, can gain and sustain a great deal of credibility. And as just discussed in the previous chapter, increased management credibility is the highest-ranked benefit of better disclosure.

Companies should provide strategy descriptions at the corporate level and for major business units. Frequently, however, they provide only a glossy description of the former and very little of the latter. Diversified firms also often miss another element in the Value Strategy—explicit explanations of the synergies that they say arise from the whole of the enterprise being greater than the sum of its parts.

The Bank of Montreal (www.bmo.com) serves as a good example of how a company can describe corporate strategy and its specific targets. In its 1999 annual report, the bank describes its overall corporate strategy as well as specific strategies for its major business units. The report emphasizes the bank's commitment to creating shareholder value through a value-based management framework for measuring net economic profit. As shown in Exhibit 11.3, the Bank of Montreal sets very explicit targets for performance on this and other key financial measures.

A complete Value Strategy description also includes information on how the company intends to implement the strategy, such as through its organization and governance structures and processes. Few companies do a good job of providing data on organization and governance. Typically, they provide fairly sterile organization charts, lists of key executives and directors with their titles and brief backgrounds, and vague statements about the company's commitment to good management.

Royal Dutch Shell (www.shell.com) serves as a notable exception to the generally poor state of corporate disclosure on organization and governance. As described more fully in Chapter 9, the company's website and its annual social responsibility report provide detailed explanations of how it intends to achieve its commitment to sustainable development through a "road map" (Exhibit 11.4), which describes the standards, systems, targets, continuous improvement processes, verification processes, reporting standards, and methods for creating internal and external engagement. An essential adjunct to the road map is a set of key performance indicators that are being developed with stakeholders and the help of other organizations.

Exhibit 11.3

Financial Performance Objectives

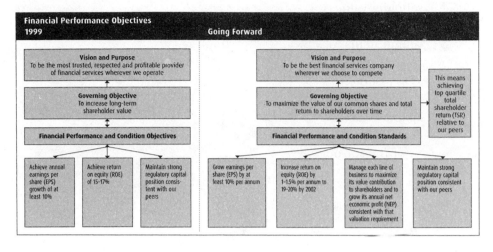

MANAGING FOR VALUE

Managing for Value calls on companies to report information on the financial measures they believe correlate most closely with shareholder value—particularly with respect to competitors. For example, a company might compare its total shareholder return (TSR)—stock appreciation plus dividends—to the same measure within a peer group.

The financial measures in Managing for Value include both income statement measures of financial performance and balance sheet measures of financial position. Historically, the former focused on earnings, but increasingly companies have started to report on other bottom-line measures such as cash flow and economic profit (profit less a cost of capital). For companies that have operations in a number of different business segments, investors want to see financial information by those segments as well. Finally, investors want to know about the risks taken to create value and how the company manages those risks, a topic discussed in much greater detail in Chapter 8.

A few good examples of companies providing the kind of information the market is looking for in Managing for Value are:

Exhibit 11.4

Sustainable Development Road Map

Sustainable development road map

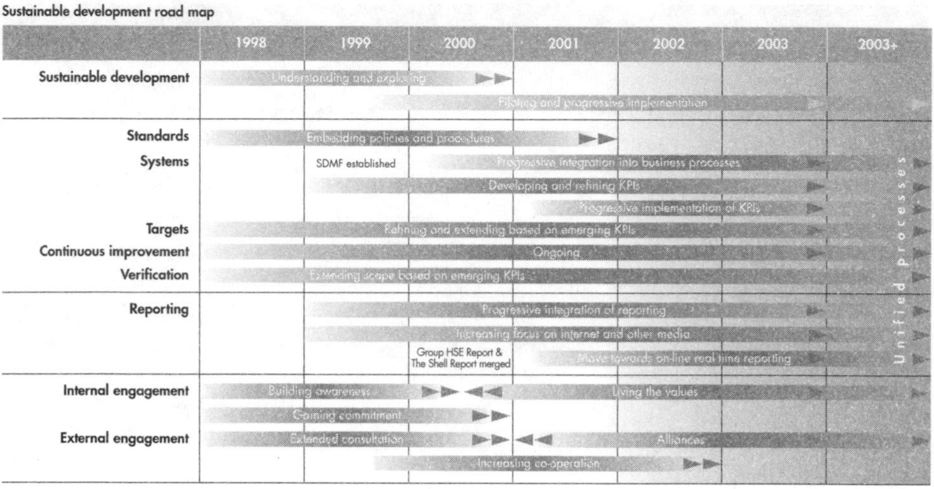

Source: *The Shell Report 2000*

○ *Economic Value Added® (EVA®):* Manitowoc (www.manitowoc.com), a U.S. manufacturer of food-service equipment, cranes, and marine-related services, does a good job of telling shareholders what it thinks creates value and then reporting on it. The company provides EVA targets as part of its overall strategy and discloses the seven-year trend in its performance on this measure. Company management has also identified a link between EVA and market capitalization showing that its market value has increased in line with the increase in the company's EVA. Manitowoc's 1999 annual report said, "EVA touches nearly every facet of our company. As we continue to apply and educate our employees on the power of EVA, we'll create even more value for our shareholders in the future."

○ *Total shareholder return (TSR):* The Bank of Montreal (www.mbo.com) reports its TSR targets and actual performance benchmarked against both a Canadian and a North American peer group. The bank also benchmarks itself against these groups on a number of other measures and reports quite frankly about where it does a better job and where it doesn't.

- ·*Segment performance:* Siemens (www.siemens.de) reports detailed segment analysis of the weighted average cost of capital, along with segment EVA results. Siemens provides a clear and succinct description about EVA and how it is calculated. To assist in independent calculations, management also reports the weighted cost of capital for a total of 16 operating groups. It then reports EVA at three levels: operations, finance, and real estate.

VALUE PLATFORM

On the whole, when managers don't report on the first three elements of the ValueReporting Disclosure Model—Market Overview, Value Strategy, and Managing for Value—it is for the simple reason that they choose not to. Even though they generally have most of the relevant information available and use it extensively for internal decision making, they assume that the risks and costs of disclosing it will exceed the benefits. As their views change—and they will, either by choice or by necessity—managers should have little technical difficulty reporting substantially more information on these three elements of the model.

This is less true for the information on the elements of the Value Platform that relate to assets the company uses to create value for shareholders. Those assets, typically nonfinancial in nature, include innovation, intellectual capital, customers, brands, the supply chain, people, and reputation.

The measurement methodologies for these assets are much less well developed than those for traditional financial measures. The growing popularity of balanced scorecards, as discussed in Chapter 1, shows that companies continue to make substantial efforts to develop valid ways to measure nonfinancial value drivers and intangible assets. "Customers" is one of the most well-developed measurement categories in the Value Platform because of the emergence over the past several years of concepts and information technologies for better customer relationship management, but even here it is in a relatively primitive state.

Once a measure in the Value Platform has reached a reasonable degree of reliability, management can begin to report it externally. This has already begun to happen, and in a few cases, these measures have been attested to in some fashion. The measures in the platform include:

- *Innovation.* Axcan Pharma (www.axcan.com), a Canadian-based pharmaceutical company, for example, says in its 1999 annual report found on its website, "Our aim for the next five years is to have one product or new indication from our research program approved each year in the United States." The company also gives an estimated time frame for government approval of seven new products and the potential revenues it expects from them.

○ *Intellectual capital.* The Danish company Coloplast began reporting information on intellectual capital in its 1997/98 annual report, following a Business Excellence model the company had worked with since 1995. The figures reported in the 1998/99 annual report include:

  ○ Number of patent applications
  ○ Patent rights held
  ○ Share of new products in total turnover
  ○ Complaints
  ○ Overall customer satisfaction

  The firm's auditor, PricewaterhouseCoopers, provides an Auditor's Opinion, although it is not as extensive as that of an audit, "since generally accepted principles for the statement and presentation of intellectual capital statements . . . have not yet been established." The opinion concludes with the recommendation for "further development of supporting, recording, and reporting procedures to ensure completeness and accuracy."

  Carsten Lonfeldt, Coloplast's chief financial officer (CFO), recognizes the importance of doing this. He notes, "It continues to be a process of development and we have more changes and improvements we wish to make to the statements produced to date."

○ *Customers.* Westpac (www.westpac.com.au), an Australian bank, reports (1) its number of priority customers, (2) the percentage of customers buying one, two, three, and four products, and (3) that the 40 percent of Australian customers who currently buy only one product could add an additional A$500 million (Australian dollars) in revenue if they bought just one more.

  A company called i2 Technologies (www.i2.com), which helps companies design and implement e-business strategies, publishes an annual Customer Value Report prepared and verified by an independent group called Miller-Williams. This customer audit calculates the value i2 creates through reduced costs, delayed or avoided expenditures, increased customer responsiveness, and increased revenue growth. The company's customers themselves contribute to these calculations by ascribing the percentage of performance improvements attributable to i2. "As of 1999, the cumulative value generated from i2's work for customers was estimated at $7.64 billion US."[2] i2's goal is to create $50 billion of cumulative customer value by 2005.

○ *Supply chain.* SAS (www.scandinavian.net), the Swedish airline, reports a great deal of supply chain data, including information on 25 traffic and production measures (e.g., number of passengers carried, total load factors, average passenger trip length, punctuality, and regularity) for the past 10 years. They compare one of these measures, the break-even load factor, to data from the Association of European Airlines and the International Air Transport Association as well as to that of the major U.S. airlines. SAS also publishes quality goals for:

   ○ Accidents or serious incidents (zero)

   ○ Cancelled flights

   ○ Flights delayed more than 15 minutes

   ○ Flights delayed more than 2 minutes

   ○ Percentage of lost customer reservation calls due to excessive wait times

   The company notes, quite frankly, that although in 1999 "SAS was one of the absolute top performers in terms of quality compared with other European airlines," it "failed to meet its own goals for a number of reasons." While SAS adds that some of the reasons for this failure were beyond the company's control, it also makes clear that some were not, and that performance fell far short of the company's own goals in certain cases. For example, SAS set a goal for a maximum of 5 percent lost calls, yet in 1999 that number came in at 22 percent, only a bit better than the 23 percent in 1998.

○ *People.* BT (www.bt.com), the British telecommunications giant, in a separate Environmental Report, compares the company's performance along seven dimensions of employee satisfaction against a benchmark of data collected by an independent firm on 88,000 employees in the United Kingdom. The company has also begun to benchmark its "people" performance against other global telecommunications companies. One of the measures where BT has a lower favorable response (39 percent) than the U.K. benchmark (43 percent) is "leadership" and it candidly acknowledges and discusses this fact.

○ *Reputation.* Royal Dutch Shell, as discussed in Chapter 9, is a leading example of a company that recognizes how the perceptions that stakeholders have of the way the company manages its environmental and social responsibilities affect its reputation. More and more companies are beginning to do so as well.

HIGH TECH . . . HIGH TENSION . . . HIGH TIME

Unless you've lived in a cave since the late 1990s, you couldn't have missed the phenomenon of the Internet as it burst onto the scene as the platform of choice for the dissemination, even democratization, of information. Many companies have already jumped onto the platform; others have just begun to see that it's there.

Whether companies find themselves on, near, or far away from the Internet, e-business will forever change the way they collect, consume, produce, and disseminate relevant information about their performance. Like any change agent, the Internet creates a basic tension between the comfort of the familiar and the thrill and/or the threat of the unknown.

It's much more than the technology's unfamiliarity that creates the tension. The very nature of the Internet itself makes companies very tense. The speed at which companies can produce and send information, and the breadth and distance it can travel instantaneously, all imply that companies will have to face enormous changes in what they report and how. And then there's the tension created by chat rooms and Usenet/newsgroups with their snipes and jabs at companies, not to mention the Web crawlers, spiders, and even more exotic denizens that inhabit the Internet jungle, scurrying about to find bits of information and analyze it for all sorts of purposes,

---

Why Seek When You Can Find?

"Search" in the realm of the Internet has traditionally been highly labor intensive for users. No longer. Increasingly, search features are being incorporated into the fabric of user applications, turning them into more of a "find" than a "search" function. These "find" agents simply and easily deliver to the user the results of a series of queries (created through behind-the-scenes activities like spiders, categorization, and filters, to name a few) that reflect the optimal content for the user's particular interests or needs.

Essential to this ability are tools that combine the best features of contextual search engines like www.yahoo.com with content search engines like www.northernlight.com that can index the vast depth of Web content. For more on content and context, see Chapter 15.

honorable or not. (See the sidebar "Why Seek When You Can Find?" for more on the Internet's nonhuman users.)

THE BATTLEGROUND AND THE WEAPON

Most people think about the Internet as an electronic infrastructure for sending, receiving, and locating information. From a ValueReporting perspective, the Internet is the battlefield where the revolution will ultimately play out. And it's more. It's also a strategic weapon for revolutionizing corporate disclosure.

In the heat of battle, however, companies must always remember that they don't have unilateral control of the weapon. As easily as a company can deploy the firepower for its own advantage, others can train the weapon on the company itself.

Perhaps such cautionary words come too soon—or too late. Most companies today, unaware that they have a weapon of Star Wars magnitude, have been using the Internet more like a peashooter.

This is not all bad—sharpshooters would probably recommend using a low-caliber weapon when first learning to shoot straight anyway. As companies have started to learn more about the Internet arsenal, many, if not most, of them have begun using it to communicate and gather information for the right reasons—it's cheaper, faster, easier, and of course, much hipper. They also use it to varying levels of sophistication, for example:

- To post HTML, Excel, and PDF file formats so human beings can read things like press releases, product brochures, technical manuals, executive speeches, and seemingly endless lists of company contact information
- To link users to other information and websites, hopefully filled with relevant content—for example, analysts' reports, industry updates, trade association news, and press releases
- To communicate with employees—current, past, and future
- To communicate with vendors and suppliers
- To broadcast live (more often canned) speeches, meetings, and press conferences in real time for "public" consumption

Companies deserve credit for at least seeing the Internet for its obvious inherent advantages—speedier, easier, less costly, ubiquitous. For the most part, however, companies have stuck to an electronic version of the "Paper Paradigm." They use the Internet as the world's largest copy machine. They have a mental model of the Internet based on a communications medium the Chinese invented well over a millennium ago. Like the paper documents they've used for years, the content that companies post or send on the Web has usually been designed for the human eye to read.

Granted, such uses are faint but encouraging signals of a reporting revolution to come, but they still look and feel more like evolution—just a faster, easier way to use existing reporting formats, content, and protocols. True, companies have hardly begun to leverage the Internet's capabilities and engage stakeholders in meaningful dialogue, but right now, with very little extra effort, they could take much greater advantage of the Internet through any or all of the following:

- Accessible archives of corporate knowledge
- Real-time reporting
- Drill-down capabilities
- Analytical and search agents
- Interactive communication
- Personalized reporting, virtual portfolios, dynamic reporting
- Authorship authentication and validation

Accessible Archives of Corporate Knowledge

Traditionally, in most corporations much of the collective memory simply faded away. If records were kept or the collective wisdom of a firm documented, the information therein proved extremely difficult to catalog and even more difficult to retrieve and use. Corporate memory came with a very high price tag.

The Internet now offers access to untold volumes of corporate memory and current best practices, much of it already recorded and organized. The total cost of corporate memory, therefore, has become relatively low, while the possibility and capability to access it and use it has risen enormously, both inside and outside the firm.

Any company today that is serious about "knowledge management"—and most say they are—needs to learn how to refine its managerial skills using Internet capabilities. Although memory alone does not constitute knowledge, without memory, knowledge must always be created from scratch.

Real-Time Reporting

Real-time reporting can really mean only one thing: making information available as soon as it comes into existence. It can happen. Using sophisticated internal systems, executives can monitor corporate performance across all relevant value drivers on a real-time basis. Reporting in real time, therefore, requires nothing more than making this information available to all who have a legitimate need to know, both internally and externally. Cisco's Virtual Close, widely regarded as the leading best practice, offers an excellent example of just how "real" real-time reporting can be.[3]

Real-time reporting does not, however, solve all the problems. In the business information marketplace, the most accurate and timely information has the most value. Late, inaccurate, or false information has much lower or even negative value. Once companies report poor quality or just plain bad information to the public, they find taking it back and repairing damage done extraordinarily difficult, if not impossible. Real-time ValueReporting means getting the information right the first time and attesting to its veracity on time.

Drill-Down Capabilities

In the Paper Paradigm, most quantitative and qualitative information, even when reported electronically, comes in a linear, hierarchical format. Some of these "documents," of course, allow users to click a hypertext link and find even more—guess what—documents! What users can't do is drill down to a deeper level of detail for any given performance measure, financial or otherwise. This seems somehow ironic as published performance figures derive directly from the granular detail the company already has.

What users want is the ability to look behind and beneath the summary figures so that they can understand where the numbers came from. Essentially, they want the reports that management gets.

Through drill-down capabilities, companies could easily provide such detail today, with built-in levels of access geared to the individual's information needs. For example, employees, shareholders, creditors, and board members would look at the content and level of detail of a piece of information from very different perspectives based on their information needs. To the relief of those who steadfastly oppose revealing more than they must, the existing reporting regulations offer comfort, temporary though it may be.

Analytical and Search Agents

Real-time information, available in great detail, represents only the beginning of what many users really want. They want the ability to analyze the information on their own, for example, along product, segment, or geographical lines. Analytical agents—nonhuman in form—can automate the "find" features of today's "search" engines by crawling through a wide variety of sites to deliver information specifically relevant to a particular user's analytical needs.

Again a bit of irony. Most corporate websites have been designed for aesthetic appeal, rather than for meaningful use by these analytical agents and search engines. Lacking the human appreciation for beauty, they have only utilitarian purposes. The irony is that their purposes have a decidedly more direct effect on a company's share price than a design award for best website of the year ever could.

Analytical and search agents, like humans, have frailties. They need structured content written in a language and grammar they can read, understand, and use. Structured content requires clear definitions and specific rules governing informational relationships that all users, human and not, can access. You'll find more about that in Chapter 15.

Interactive Communication

Many companies post audio or video files of executive speeches, shareholder briefings, and press conferences on their websites so users can download and play them back. Imagine the impact if users could initiate interactive dialogue—in the United States within the guidelines of Regulation FD, of course—with the most relevant contact at the company to address a particular question, issue, or concern. The operative word here is *dialogue*—back and forth, give and take, you and me, yin and yang. When dialogue occurs, the users get their learning needs met, and the companies learn more about what users need. If they believe in ValueReporting, they will seriously consider meeting the need.

Personalized Reporting, Virtual Portfolios, Dynamic Reporting, and More

In the Paper Paradigm, the corporate reporting imperative is mass production. The economics of traditional public disclosure impose a one-size-fits-all approach. The Internet, however, makes complete customization of corporate disclosure economically feasible. The combination of structured information and the abilities of analytical and search agents to find and interpret it enables every user to have a personalized "book" on a company's performance.

Furthermore, these books can be like constantly running soap operas, with new events happening continuously. Even better, users can take the director's chair and speculate about potential scenes for tomorrow's episode. And that's not an episode from *Search for Tomorrow,* it's straight out of *The Days of Our Lives,* as anyone can see at Microsoft's website. There, users can construct "what-if" scenarios on a forecast template by specifying certain assumptions about rate of revenue growth, cost of sales, research and development, sales and marketing, and many more dynamic elements of corporate performance.

Authorship Authentication and Validation

Who's talking to whom and how do you know that who you're talking to is actually who they tell you that they are? The Internet makes that sound less like an old comedy routine and much more like a very serious problem with potentially disastrous results. Validating the source and authenticity of Internet information has become a major issue for companies worldwide.

Remember the case of the bogus press release that caused one company's stock to lose 60 percent of its value in less than half a day?[4] What kind of world is it when a single piece of unsubstantiated, highly damaging information can have such an adverse effect on a company's value? When you can't really know if the Web address you keyed in has actually led you to the site you wanted? When there's no guaranteed correlation between a company's name and its URL?

It's an electronic world, that's what, and those risks just described can be managed, lowered, and even eliminated. Not tomorrow. Right now. The responsibility to do so falls squarely on companies: to ensure that users of their information can authenticate quickly and easily that any and all information that purportedly comes from the company actually does. However, one can legitimately ask if some form of third-party assurance might be useful here.

THE DOUBLE-EDGED E-SWORD

It's up to individual companies to decide whether to embrace the Internet and use its capabilities to the fullest. Rest assured, or more likely rest uneasily, that all over the world other people have done so and are doing so at this very minute. In some of these cases, no doubt, they're looking for ways to use the Internet either to obtain useful, but otherwise unavailable, information on the company or to influence investor or stakeholder opinions about its performance.

Royal Dutch Shell has already accepted that the Internet creates and

enables an ongoing worldwide conversation about its performance, financial and otherwise. Shell now takes the position that it should participate actively in the conversation as well. By sitting at the table, it can work to make
sure that the quality or at least the accuracy of the dialogue will improve.

Beam Me Up

Corporate executives can decide to board the starship Internet and start
beaming their information to earth, or they can sit stoically in their caves, in
effect chiseling disclosures on tablets of stone. If they allow others to structure their information and develop the strategies for analyzing it, the company's voice in the conversation about itself will be faint, if it's heard at all.

To lead or at least influence the ongoing conversations about their
companies, executives must pay as much attention to how they and others
use the Internet as they pay to the information content itself. They must
make sure that this strategic weapon, the Internet, isn't used only against
them, but that they seize and master it for their own purposes. They must
take to heart that just as e-business requires a transformation of their planning, management, and operational processes, it also transforms their information supply chain as well.

BOUNDLESS, NOT LAWLESS

The Internet may create boundless opportunities for companies to improve
their corporate disclosure practices and reap the rewards. It does *not*, however, eliminate one boundary: legal liability for disclosing information that
misleads investors. Some argue, quite convincingly, that reporting on the Internet actually raises the stakes of the legal liability crapshoot.

Prentice, Richardson, and Scholz examined corporate website disclosures from the perspective of Section 10(b) and accompanying Rule 10b-5
of the Securities Exchange Act of 1934.[5] They commented, "These rules impose obligations of accuracy and completeness, dictate content and timing
of disclosure, and otherwise shape both formal and informal corporate disclosure of information."[6]

The researchers studied 259 companies rated by the Association for
Investment Management and Research (AIMR), which they supple-
mented with 231 high-tech companies. (This, of course, was a U.S.-centric
study, but it serves to make the point.) Among the total sample, they
found that 82 percent had websites. They summarized their conclusions
in terms of low-risk disclosures and high-risk disclosures after noting that
"A continual tension exists between the information advantages of post-

ing financial and other data on corporate websites and concerns about pesky plaintiffs' lawyers."

Low-risk disclosures include such things as safe harbor disclaimers contained in paper documents but not posted on the website, innocently posting inaccurate historical information, and providing new material that might be interpreted as "hyping" the company prior to a securities offering. The first could be managed by paying more attention to detail. The second could be managed by regular updates and separation of information into current and archival sections. And the third can be managed by having a separate website on which the prospectus is placed with no hyperlinks to other materials.

The more problematic of the high-risk disclosures that Prentice, Richardson, and Scholz identified on the websites studied include excerpts from annual reports, analysts' reports or links to analysts' reports, speeches by executives, and discussions of the advantages of buying the company's stock. Ironically enough, these high-risk disclosures exemplify some of the more enlightened ways that companies can leverage a greater share of the Internet's full capabilities.

The researchers don't offer any ready remedies but their sympathy clearly lies with plaintiffs: "To avoid becoming a test case, companies must be careful. After all, the investors who visit company sites to obtain convenient financial information may become the plaintiffs who return to find evidence."[7]

The information highway has its full measure of legal liability potholes and warning signs. Its pace of change far outstrips the ability of any legal system to interpret existing regulations or to formulate new ones for how companies should communicate through the Web.

We do not intend to counter the sound advice legal counsel may offer. We do, however, offer one bit of our own counsel to any executive standing at the edge of the Internet platform and trying to decide whether to climb on board. Do not use legitimate legal concerns simply as an excuse to hide behind your lawyers' skirts. Caution is not a virtue when it's merely an excuse for inaction. Change always involves risk. The upside opportunity in taking advantage of the Internet to protect and build shareholder value far exceeds the downside of the legal risks. The greatest risk of all is to do nothing at all.

Company Efforts

Despite the legal concerns, there are still some interesting examples of how companies extend their use of the Internet beyond posting elec-

tronic versions of paper documents. The International Accounting Standards Committee (IASC), working groups for both the Financial Accounting Standards Board (FASB) and the Canadian Institute of Chartered
Accountants, and numerous academic studies have all recently addressed
the subject.

Because the way companies actually use the Internet to distribute and
report value-relevant information is evolving even more rapidly than the content of this information, we again refer the reader to the PricewaterhouseC-
oopers ValueReporting website (www.valuereporting.com) for more current
information.[8]

One report, published in the February 2000 issue of *CFO Magazine*,[9] offers some practical insight into how companies use the Web to varying degrees of success. Stephen Barr, the author, reports on 50 corporate websites
in terms of the following characteristics, along with the websites of two companies regarded as doing a particularly good job:

- Easy access to data (www.boeing.com and www.merck.com)
- A clear and unique message (www.dhc.com and www.eds.com)
- Multimedia disclosures (www.hostmarriott.com and www.microsoft. com)
- "Push" technology (www.immunex.com and www.lycos.com)
- Standard investor data (www.omnicom.com and www.homedepot. com)
- Robust data and analytics (www.cisco.com and www.federalexpress. com)
- Direct investor contacts (www.aetna.com and www.trw.com)

Generally, however, the magazine's study found that most companies do a
poor job in one or more of these categories and "only two sites, Dayton
Hudson Corp. (www.dhc.com) and Motorola, Inc. (www.motorola.com),
came anywhere close to excelling in all seven categories."[10] (Note that in
2000, Dayton Hudson Corporation became Target Corporation.)

An IASC report, "Business Reporting on the Internet," also cites some
interesting examples of companies that take more advantage than most of
the Internet's capabilities. Ironically, you can link electronically to a press
release about the report at www.iasc.org.uk/frame/cen3_26.htm, but to get
the report itself, you must request a hard copy. Go figure. Another report,
"Electronic Distribution of Business Reporting Information," which resulted
from a study sponsored by the FASB, also provides information on how com-

panies are moving beyond the Paper Paradigm in Internet reporting. The objectives of the study were to survey the state of reporting business information over the Internet and to identify notable practices. Fortunately, this report is available on the Internet (at www.rutgers.edu/Accounting/raw/fasb/brrp.pdf).[11]

Here are a few brief examples from the IASC report:

o RWE AG (www.rweenergie.de/index_eng.htm), a German energy and energy-related services company, offers extensive and effective links among financial statements, annual reports, and many other sources of information.

o Intel (www.intel.com) provides extensive 10-year financials in spreadsheet form that users can easily download and analyze offline. Intel also clearly demarcates when the viewer has left the annual report as a way to distinguish information that has been audited from that which has not.

o Microsoft (www.microsoft.com) provides financial statements prepared according to U.S., U.K., Australian, Canadian, French, German, and Japanese Generally Accepted Accounting Principles (GAAP) in the appropriate language and with links between the reports for different reporting regimes. It goes one step further than Intel by providing a number of advanced analytical tools that enable visitors to do such things as represent data in three-dimensional formats and do projections under different sets of assumptions.

UP CLOSE AND PERSONAL

Legal implications notwithstanding, more information delivered through the Internet is better than less—provided that the user can clearly see its levels of quality and reliability. As the story of how companies use more of the Internet's capabilities more often continues to play out, it will no doubt be punctuated by some headline-grabbing lawsuits. Progress is never smooth, and reconciling the interests of multiple groups is never easy.

Even if all concerns about legal liability disappeared and companies effortlessly adapted to making full use of the Internet's capabilities for providing detailed real-time information to all stakeholders—in a multimedia format with accompanying analytical tools and hyperlinks—the market's information needs would still not be completely satisfied. The Internet, after all, serves as but one, although increasingly one of the most dominant, distribution channels.

An equally important distribution channel is the market's real-time interaction with key company executives. Of course, the Internet can abet this, as shown by the growing popularity of quarterly conference calls on the Web to all investors and pressures to give individual investors electronic access to Web-based IPO road shows.

Even such enhanced electronic access to higher-level information can never replace the experience of getting the information in person, whether in a group or an individual setting. In fact, Eccles and Nohria have argued that the greater the possibilities for electronic communication, the greater the necessity for more interpersonal communication.[12] It's a matter of heightening the overall level of communication rather than replacing one medium with another.

Seeing live executives "up close and personal" respond to tough questions in the "realest" real-time of all, still offers the most effective way to form an opinion about the executives' capabilities, the strength of their convictions, and their integrity. The combination of firsthand experience and perceptions with documented information on the executive's background and track record is how the market makes its assessment of the "quality of management." It's an important way for managers to build credibility as well as for others to hold them accountable.

Here too a tension exists between effective information disclosure and legal liability. Driven by concerns about selective disclosure, many lawyers have cautioned that companies should severely restrict the number of company representatives who communicate directly with analysts and investors, and that they should carefully control how these representatives communicate. To the extent that executives follow this well-intentioned legal advice, they will no doubt reduce their potential legal liabilities. In doing so, however, they trade an enormous opportunity to increase their credibility in exchange for their lawyers' peace of mind.

Our advice is exactly opposite the lawyers'. The CEO, CFO, and head of investor relations should make a concerted effort to involve as many as possible of the senior management team in dealing with analysts and investors. This includes all executives in charge of major products and geographical units, as well as the key functional staff heads. Of course, they should train managers how to do it well!—which includes knowing the relevant securities laws relating to disclosure—and coordinate their activities.

These costs and legal liabilities of expanded and improved executive communication are small relative to the benefits that can be obtained if the process is properly managed. *Properly managed* means managing to provide as much interaction with as many executives as possible.

If a common strategy exists, if all executives know their own role in it, and if the management team is strong, the market will see this for itself. It will perceive a high level of management quality and credibility, and that will translate into an acceptance of management's plans and projections for creating value for shareholders. But if the market perceives the quality of the management team and its credibility as low, it will discount management's plans and projections and the stock price as well.

Better disclosure by itself is not enough. In the end, as we've said many times before, performance matters. But it is through better disclosure that a company's performance—and its stock price—can be fully appreciated.

Part Five

Part of the Solution or Part of the Problem?

The beginning of wisdom is to call things by their right names.
Chinese Proverb

12

Get on Board

We are not afraid to follow truth wherever it may lead.
Thomas Jefferson, Letter to William Roscoe

Who should take responsibility for making the dramatic changes in external reporting that this book calls for and that everyone who uses the information—the market and other stakeholders—seems to want? Certainly, top executives must take the primary responsibility. They must insist that senior business unit managers clearly articulate their business models and define the measures that will be used to evaluate performance.

Furthermore, the business unit managers should use these measures to manage their businesses. Corporate executives should assess business unit performance against them. The board of directors, which represents the interests of shareholders, should ensure that investors get the information on these measures they need. But to do this, the board first must make sure it has the information it needs.

If the board doesn't get that information, it must demand it. Those who sit on the boards of publicly traded companies and who agree that external reporting should be broadened and improved, must ultimately make it happen. It's an integral part of their responsibility to shareholders. Odd though this may seem, the distinguished men and women who serve in this important capacity have no choice but to be on the vanguard of the revolution if they are to serve well.

In some cases, those who serve on audit committees will play a key role in ensuring that the board gets as much relevant financial and nonfinancial information about tangible and intangible assets as possible, including information about the relationship between risks taken and return realized.

Whoever takes responsibility for ensuring that such information gets reported to the board—whether the audit committee or the board as a whole—must do the task well. For that very reason, we will make a specific ValueReporting proposal for boards of directors a bit later in this chapter.

TO HAVE BUT NOT TO HOLD INFORMATION

Just as ensuring that directors and shareholders have the information that they need to evaluate management's performance is a hallmark of good governance, reporting the information improves both management and governance. As Louis Lowenstein, a leading expert on corporate governance, put it in discussing the role of financial accounting in the U.S. capital markets:

> It [financial accounting] is also an important corporate governance tool. It provides the brightest light and the most objective, detailed, and textured portrait of managerial performance. Without it, neither the financial press nor the shareholders nor markets could scrutinize that performance, except by inference from sketchy data or by reliance on inside information of uncertain quality and consistency.[1]

Arthur Levitt, chairman of the Securities and Exchange Commission, voiced a similar opinion: "As more countries move to an equity culture, high-quality financial information becomes the currency that drives the marketplace" and "nothing honors that currency more than a strong and effective corporate governance mandate."[2]

While we agree with Levitt and Lowenstein's observation about the importance of financial accounting to good governance, we also think the model needs updating. The current one no longer meets the information needs of shareholders, nor does it enable directors to completely fulfill their responsibilities. Good governance both requires and comes from ValueReporting, as described in Chapter 8. Boards of directors, therefore, should not only embrace its concepts, they should make them reality.

GOOD GOVERNANCE IN GENERAL

The last two decades of the twentieth century witnessed a growing interest in corporate governance, beginning first in the United States, the United Kingdom, and Australia, and then more recently in continental Europe and Asia. This growth in interest stems primarily from the concerns of large institutional investors on a wide range of issues: persistent underperformance of some companies, certain celebrated and spectacular failures, widespread

corporate restructuring, the movement toward privatization, th.
raise capital in local and foreign markets, the interests of other stakeho...
(customers, employees, and communities, to name a few), and, of course,
pressures from virtually all corners for greater transparency.

Some notable outcomes of this heightened interest include: the Cadbury Committee's 1992 Report on the Financial Aspects of Corporation
Governance in the United Kingdom, the U.S. Blue Ribbon Committee
(BRC) on Improving the Effectiveness of Corporate Audit Committees
sponsored by the New York Stock Exchange (NYSE) and the National Association of Securities Dealers (NASD), and the Ad Hoc Task Force on
Corporate Governance established by the Organization for Economic Co-
operation and Development (OECD) with the mandate to "develop a set
of non-binding principles that embody the views of member countries on
this issue."[3]

In 1999, the OECD's Task Force released a very general set of corporate governance guidelines based on input from the organization's 29 member countries.[4] It identified five main principles, the fourth of which directly
addresses external reporting. The principles are:

1. The rights of shareholders
2. The equitable treatment of shareholders
3. The role of shareholders
4. Disclosure and transparency
5. The responsibilities of the board

The report also defines seven categories of information that are material and should be reported, but notes that these categories do not necessarily comprise an exhaustive list:

1. Financial and operating results of the company
2. Company objectives
3. Major share ownership and voting rights
4. Members of the board and key executives, and their remuneration
5. Material foreseeable risk factors
6. Material issues regarding employees and other stakeholders
7. Governance structures and policies

These seven categories of information address many of the same dimensions of external reporting that we believe are important, including

financial performance, risk, objectives, and other stakeholders' desires and information needs. If ValueReporting is adopted as the standard for external reporting, however, greater emphasis should be placed on the importance of information about intangible assets and nonfinancial performance drivers. A broader definition of risk should be developed and adopted as well.

In their book, *Corporate Governance and the Board—What Works Best*, Richard Steinberg and Catherine Bromilow emphasize the importance of performance measurement to good governance. They state very explicitly that the board should come to agreement with management "on the financial and nonfinancial information that will serve as fundamental performance measurements, and concur on targets and behaviors."[5] Steinberg and Bromilow also emphasize that these performance measures, especially those that are leading indicators, should be reviewed on a timely basis in case corrective actions are necessary.

Finally, as noted previously, *how*—not just *what*—information is reported also has significance. The Ad-Hoc Task Force report makes this distinction as well: "The Internet and other information technologies also provide the opportunity for improving information dissemination."[6] Once more, an OECD publication treats this issue in more detail, suggesting that new information technologies "promise to change the relationship between companies and regulators" and that the Internet "may also profoundly change the relationship between shareholders, the company, intermediaries and the public."[7] We tackle this issue in much greater detail ourselves in the next chapter.

STRENGTHENING THE AUDIT COMMITTEE

While the OECD Task Force was reasonably explicit about the principles of good governance, it said very little about how to put the principles into practice. In contrast to the OECD, the Blue Ribbon Committee focused specifically on "producing a blueprint for meaningful change."[8]

Its sponsors, the NYSE and the NASD, asked for "recommendations on strengthening the role of audit committees in overseeing the corporate financial reporting process."[9] According to the BRC's report, "Disclosure and transparency have become the first hallmark of good governance looked to by investors."[10]

The report concluded that a strong case could be made for improved financial reporting. At a minimum, these improvements would address some

The Ten Recommendations of the Blue Ribbon Committee on Improving the Effectiveness of Corporate Audit Committees

1. That the NYSE and the NASD adopt a new definition of independence, to be applied to members of audit committees.

2. That the NYSE and the NASD require that listed companies have audit committees comprised solely of independent directors.

3. That the NYSE and the NASD require that listed companies have audit committees comprised of at least three members, all of whom are or become "financially literate" and at least one of whom has financial expertise.

4. That the NYSE and the NASD require the audit committee of each listed company to (i) adopt a formal written charter that is approved by the full board on the scope of the audit committee's responsibilities and how it carries out those responsibilities, and (ii) that the charter's adequacy be reviewed and assessed on an annual basis.

5. That the SEC require companies to disclose whether they have adopted such a charter and, if so, whether the audit committee has fulfilled its responsibilities during the prior year in compliance with the charter; this charter should be published at least every three years.

6. That the NYSE and the NASD require that the audit committee charter of every listed company specify that the outside auditor reports directly to the board and the audit committee, which have the ultimate authority over selecting, evaluating, and replacing the outside auditor, if necessary.

7. That the NYSE and the NASD require that the audit committee charter for all listed companies include the requirement that the audit committee receive and discuss with the outside auditor a listing of all relationships between the auditor and the company (consistent with Independence Standards Board Standard 1), and take any actions needed to ensure the outside auditor's independence.

8. That Generally Accepted Auditing Standards (GAAS) require the outside auditor to discuss with the audit committee the quality, and not just the acceptability, of the company's accounting principles.

9. That the SEC require that all reporting companies include a letter from the audit committee in the annual report to shareholders and Form 10-K Annual Report.

10. That the SEC require that a reporting company's outside auditor conduct a SAS 71 Interim Financial Review prior to the filing of the company's Form 10-Q and that SAS 71 be amended to require the outside auditor to discuss with the audit committee or its chair any significant matters prior to the filing.

of the problems already discussed in this book, such as excessive earnings management and outright fraud. It would also produce some upside benefits as well. The Committee cited as the two most important benefits a more efficient allocation of capital and a lowering of its cost.

Offering guidance on how to realize these benefits, the Committee made 10 very specific recommendations to the NYSE, NASD, SEC, and the auditing profession (see sidebar). The basic thrust of these recommendations was to strengthen the independence of the audit committee, make the audit committee more effective, and address the mechanisms for improved accountability among the key players. In December 1999, the SEC, NYSE, NASD, and the American Stock Exchange adopted new rules based largely on these recommendations. The American Institute of Certified Public Accountants' Auditing Standards Board also adopted related rules for outside auditors.

Although we hope the new rules, which reflect the BRC recommendations, will have a significant impact on the effectiveness of the audit committee's oversight responsibilities, they don't address the reporting issues raised in this book and recognized by the OECD from a broader governance perspective. And they stop at the responsibility of the audit committee, largely ignoring the overriding responsibility that the board of directors has to oversee information and communication.

A Broader View for the Board

Why can't boards merely maintain the status quo and stay satisfied with the current reporting model and the role the audit committee plays in overseeing financial reporting? Because the financial information that companies must report represents a shrinking percentage of the information that management uses to run the business and the market considers important, the board must concern itself with a much broader set of information. And, the audit committee might be the natural group to take responsibility by ensuring that a broader set information exists in the first place, that it is reliable, and that it is available on a timely basis. Accepting this responsibility, however, would add a new dimension to the committee's role.

If the audit committee accepts the responsibility to oversee "information" and not just "financial information," however, it becomes repositioned as a group that not only protects the company from the downside, but also supports management's pursuit of the upside. This gives the audit committee the responsibility for taking a broader view of risk as well, as Chapter 8 discusses. In its broadened role, the committee must ensure that information about the company's risk management practices explicitly articulate the risks being taken in the pursuit of value, what the expected value is, and how the downside of the risks will be managed.

A VALUEREPORTING PROPOSAL FOR THE BOARD

We propose that the board of directors or audit committee, if it decides to expand its scope of responsibility, take a proactive role to:

- Require the company to identify the key financial and nonfinancial information that it regards as important in creating and measuring value
- Ensure that management provides this information to the board on a timely basis
- Report key information externally to stakeholders
- Ensure the company puts in place systems for managing risk that include information about the expected relationship between risk and return
- Report on these systems and the information they generate to the board
- Report on these systems and the information externally to stakeholders
- Gain management's assurance that it regularly assesses the effectiveness of all nonregulated performance measures, systems for managing risk, and the information on risk generated by these systems

By expanding the focus and the need for assurance from nonfinancial reporting to value-based reporting, this recommendation also potentially changes the role that outside auditors should play in improving corporate governance. Similar to the audit committee's potentially expanded responsibilities, the outside auditor's expanded role is simply a matter of aligning its current responsibilities with the broader range of information that has relevance to the capital markets today. Chapter 13 explores this in much greater detail.

WILL IT MAKE A DIFFERENCE?

The research to date on the relationship between good governance and performance turns out to be ambiguous. In a study commissioned by The Conference Board, for example, D. Jeanne Patterson, professor of finance and public policy at Indiana University, reviewed 14 studies on the relationship between governance and performance. She concluded that, taken together, these studies "have achieved only scattered success at establishing a link between corporate governance and corporate performance," primarily because of measurement problems with both governance and performance.[11]

Yet a June 2000 worldwide investor opinion study conducted by McKinsey & Company found that four out of five U.S. investors would pay more for stock in a company that had good governance than they would for a comparable company that had poor governance. The worldwide average for investors in the survey was only slightly less. How much more would those investors pay? In the United States, they said they would pay about 18 percent more; on average worldwide, they would pay 22 percent more.[12]

The McKinsey study defined good governance according to six criteria:

1. A clear majority of outsiders on the board
2. Truly independent directors with no management ties
3. Directors who have significant stock holdings
4. Directors who are formally evaluated
5. Directors who receive a large proportion of their compensation in stock/options
6. Boards that are very responsive to investor requests for information on governance issues[13]

These criteria reflect the nature of all such studies. They focus on the structure of the board and actions by outside activist investors such as CalPERS (California Public Employees' Retirement System) or so-called relationship investors. None have focused on what information the board uses to make major decisions, such as information about mergers and acquisitions, or how boards measure and monitor management's performance.

We offer a hypothesis that can be empirically tested: Companies whose boards insist that management use ValueReporting for both internal and external purposes, including reports to the board itself, will perform better over the long term than companies whose boards do not.

The basis of this hypothesis is straightforward. Because ValueReporting provides useful information to management for decision-making purposes, it can also provide useful information to investors. And, as we've demonstrated over and over again, well-informed investors make better investment decisions and value companies at their proper stock prices.

Boards and management, however, must balance the virtue of sharing
critical information with shareholders with the risk that it could benefit
competitors and, as a result, diminish the company's value. And the proof of
our hypothesis assumes, of course, that boards make sure that they get the
right information themselves and that the company makes it available to investors, both individual and institutional.

The U.K. Committee on Corporate Governance (generally referred to
as the Hampel Report, after its chairman, Ronnie Hampel) made this point
very explicitly. It noted in its final report that the effectiveness of a board "is
dependent to a substantial extent on the form, timing, and quality of the information which it receives."[14] Ultimately, the board itself has the responsibility for making sure it gets the right information. This implies a certain
level of good governance in the first place.

A survey of CEOs and board members in Canada found that boards
that adopt effective governance practices receive more of the information
they need, particularly nonfinancial information, to assess how well the
company is doing in accomplishing its strategic priorities.[15] In turn, these
measures and the information they provide improve corporate governance.
Good governance and the right performance information reinforce each
other in a positive way.

A REAL AND TRUE PARTNERSHIP

What are we really asking for here? Simply that if management believes in
creating value for its shareholders, it should treat them as partners just as it
does its customers and employees. This means soliciting their feedback on
strategies, plans, and performance. It means listening to their concerns and
the suggestions they offer.

The Cadbury Committee in the United Kingdom noted that if "long-
term relationships are to be developed, it is important that companies
should communicate their strategies to their major shareholders and that
their shareholders should understand them."[16] It also said that this communication should flow both ways: "It is equally important that shareholders should play their part in the communications process by
informing companies if there are aspects of the business which give them
cause for concern."[17]

Of course, there's the lingering concern that companies give institutional investors material information not made available to individual investors. Cadbury noted this concern; its importance has grown since then.
We address this issue in more detail in Chapter 15.

Management already gets feedback from the market in many ways. Large institutional investors, in particular, don't hesitate to make their views known, especially when they own large portions of the company's stock. Building on the recommendations of the Cadbury Committee, a joint City/Industry working group in the United Kingdom developed the idea of creating a contract between companies and institutions. They included the recommendation that investors become more open about giving feedback to management on strategies and performance.[18]

Too often, unfortunately, management regards such unsolicited views as uninformed, too short-term, or simply wrong. Plain and simple, senior management pays more attention to feedback from customers and employees than it does to its shareholders. This is reflected in management's ongoing efforts to manage shareholders, not only in terms of their earnings expectations, but also in what information it offers them about future plans and current performance.

If senior executives want to start treating shareholders as true partners, they must give them the information they need and want. The board must close the loop and make sure this happens. If the market dislikes a strategic initiative or a proposed acquisition, or thinks that a particular business unit should be divested, it probably has good reason. Management needs to either accept the market's judgment or offer up enough information to change investors' minds.

13

Standard Setters

Every man is fully satisfied that there is such a thing as truth, or he would not ask any question.

Charles Sanders Peirce, *Collected Papers (1931–1958)*

Every revolution needs a standard bearer to guide the troops into battle. It's a vital, exciting role to play, but certainly filled with risks. Highly visible to the enemy, standard bearers often take hits, and some even perish.

On the ValueReporting Revolution battlefield, one of the most dangerous enemies is confusion. Confusion reigns when information abounds but cannot be interpreted, or when it lacks validity, consistent meaning, or comparability across information sources.

In this revolution, information confusion will be eliminated when the standard bearers become standard setters. When the validity of information becomes certain. When its meaning stays the same over time, and when it can be compared with information from others.

Sad to say, the role of standard setter also comes with risk. Even sadder, the most dangerous enemy on the information battlefield may be the troops themselves.

TURNING THE BATTLEFIELD INTO COMMON GROUND

Allies and adversaries in the ValueReporting Revolution must call a cease-fire and seek common ground. They will reach it only when information confusion goes away and companies can accurately measure their nonfinancial performance and then report the relevant, meaningful results across companies and over time.

The value of common ground to investors is obvious. For corporate executives, the value comes from their enhanced ability to manage more effectively and to benchmark their company's performance against competitors', just as they do with financial measures.

Finding common ground usually means reconciling controversies. In this case, the controversy arises from the implication that new and more standards must emerge, whether by self-regulation, external imposition, or some combination of the two. You can already anticipate the reluctance of corporate executives to accept this notion: "The last thing I need is more reporting regulations. It all sounds like a full employment act for accounting firms."

Granted, regulation adds cost for companies, but some form of regulatory oversight is unavoidable. Comparability requires standards, and standards require a certain degree of regulation. The best sort is self-regulation grounded in companies working with others to develop the standards they will use.

Whether this will indeed lead to full employment for accounting firms remains to be seen. In the spirit of transparency and putting cards squarely on the table, we think accounting firms *can* play a very useful role in the self-regulation movement. If they do, the markets will be the better for it.

For the major accounting firms to play an important role in developing nonfinancial measurement standards, however, they must make some dramatic internal changes, in both form and function, in attitude and purpose. Whether they will remains an open question.

WHY THE WORLD NEEDS STANDARDS

Chapter 6 discussed the importance of accounting standards developed by the accounting profession in collaboration with national regulatory agencies. It also noted the problems that ensue when the number of standards continuously proliferates, and the complexity of the rules follows suit.

Audited financial figures have their virtues. For one, they are more or less comparable across companies. You can compare revenues in one firm to revenues in another, sometimes with minor adjustments because different companies may count revenues in slightly different ways. You can compare earnings in one firm to earnings in another—sort of—for the reasons discussed in Chapter 5. Even though you can't mindlessly and mechanically compare financial measures across firms in an industry, most investors can make sufficiently meaningful comparisons for their purposes, sometimes exercising judgment to bring measures more directly in line with each other.

A second virtue of financial figures is that they're based on reasonably consistent measurement methodologies. The combination of cross-sectional and longitudinal comparability, to use a bit of technical jargon, means that a great deal of meaningful analysis can be done. This enables investors to make judgments about the intrinsic and relative attractiveness of investing in a particular company or its competitors.

To make the measures for intangible assets and nonfinancial value drivers as meaningful as financial measures, standards will have to be created for them as well. Then investors can at least begin to make apples-to-apples comparisons between companies along such key measures as market share, customer retention, speed-to-market, employee turnover, and intellectual capital. And companies can compare their performance against competitors'. Both groups can then develop deeper insights into the relationships among the many different performance measures using the concept of the "business model," discussed in Chapter 1. As with financial measures, the users of the information will have to use judgment and make some adjustments here as well.

Once outside the relatively orderly realm of financial measurement, the terrain starts to look uneven, perhaps even treacherous. For a number of the nonfinancial measures, it looks eerily similar to that of the early twentieth century when each accounting firm had its own set of standards, which it applied to its client work.

In the best of today's world, individual companies have developed reliable and valid measurement methodologies for value-relevant, nonfinancial performance measures that have predictive value. In the worst of circumstances, the company hasn't even figured out its most important value drivers. In terms of accounting firms, or any other independent organization for that matter, few have developed their own set of standards for key measures, even within a specific industry.

Many people believe this must happen. Professor John Hunt of the London Business School, for example, argues that the importance of human assets in the dot-com sector (particularly since they often have very little else!) makes "reliable measures of those human assets" essential.[1]

Hunt acknowledges that "There will always be disputes about the choice of criteria for valuing these intangible assets," but he regards them more as "minor questions" and says, "In 10 years' time, valuing human assets will be normal." And in a wake-up call to the accounting profession, he concludes, "It is of marginal interest whether accountants will play a role."

ONE BIG INITIATIVE

One of the most ambitious efforts to develop a set of nonfinancial standards is the Global Reporting Initiative (GRI). It is a long-term, multistakeholder, international undertaking focused on developing and disseminating globally applicable *Sustainability Reporting Guidelines*. Companies can then use the *Guidelines* voluntarily to report on economic, environmental, and social measures—the triple bottom line. In June 2000, the GRI published a new set of guidelines that include recommendations on which indicators companies should report on their triple bottom lines.[2]

Progressive Progress

The GRI has worked hard to achieve consensus among companies that report triple-bottom-line information and stakeholders who use it. They've made more headway on some indicators than others. The greatest degree of consensus surrounds the environmental indicators—not surprising, as the environment is the most widely understood and well-established triple-bottom-line dimension. The environmental categories to be reported against include: energy, materials, water, emissions, effluents and waste, transport, land use and biodiversity, compliance, and environmental issues relating to suppliers and to products and services. For each of these categories, definitions do exist on what should be measured although they are not universally agreed, and there is significant agreement on the methodologies that could be used to report these measures.

The GRI has made slower progress on developing the economic and social indicators. It has, however, published its recommended economic and social indicators, as shown in Exhibit 13.1. The GRI has published these indicators with a request for feedback as an initial step in developing the same degree of consensus for them as exists for the environmental indicators.

As was true for the performance measures in the shareholder-focused surveys described in previous chapters, these new performance indicators include both financial and nonfinancial measures. Some relate to tangible assets, others to intangible assets. Some focus on the short term, while others have a more long-term orientation.

Exhibit 13.1 also shows that there's a great deal of overlap between the GRI's measures and some of the measures that our industry surveys identified as very important to the respondents. Quality of management, employee retention rates, customer satisfaction levels, and training/education of the workforce are all examples of this overlap, which supports the conclu-

Exhibit 13.1

Economic and Social Indicators Proposed
by the Global Reporting Initiative

Economic Dimension

Category	Indicators
Profit	− Net profit/earnings/income − Earnings before interest and tax − Gross margin − Return on average capital employed − Dividends
Intangible assets	− Ratio of market capitalisation to book value
Investments	− Human capital − Research and development − Other capital investments − Debt/equity ratio
Wages and benefits	− Total wage expense, by country − Total benefits expense, by country
Labour productivity	− Labour productivity levels and changes, by job category
Taxes	− Taxes paid to all taxing authorities
Community development	− Jobs, by type and country, absolute and net change − Philanthropy/charitable donations
Suppliers	− Performance of suppliers relative to economic components of programmes and procedures for supply chain and outsourcing − Number and type of incidences of non-compliance with prevailing national or international standards − Nature and location of outsourced operations − Value of goods and services that are outsourced − Performance of organisation in honouring contracts with suppliers, including meeting payment schedules
Products and services	− Major economic issues and impacts associated with the use of principal products and services, including disposal, where applicable

(continued on following page)

Exhibit 13.1 *(continued)*

Economic and Social Indicators Proposed by the Global Reporting Initiative

Social Dimension

Category	Indicators
Workplace	
• Quality of management	– Employee retention rates – Ratio of jobs offered to jobs accepted – Evidence of employee orientation to organisation vision – Evidence of employee engagement in shaping management decision making – Ranking of the organisation as an employer in internal and external surveys – Job satisfaction levels
• Health and safety	– Reportable cases – Standard injury, lost day, and absentee rates – Investment per worker in illness and injury prevention
• Wages and benefits	– Ratio of lowest wage to national minimum – Ratio of lowest wage to cost of living – Health and pension benefits provided to employees
• Non-discrimination	– Percentage of women in senior executive and senior and middle management ranks – Discrimination-related litigation — frequency and type – Mentoring programmes for minorities
• Training/education	– Ratio of training budget to annual operating costs – Programmes to foster worker participation in decision making – Changes in average years of education of workforce
• Child labour	– Verified incidences of non-compliance with child labour laws – Third-party recognition/awards for child labour practices
• Forced labour	– Number of recorded grievances by employees – Incidences identified through organisation's auditing of suppliers
• Freedom of association	– Staff forums and grievance procedures in place – Number and type of legal actions concerning anti-union practices – Organisational responses to organising non-union facilities or subsidiaries

(continued on following page)

Exhibit 13.1 *(continued)*

Economic and Social Indicators Proposed by the Global Reporting Initiative

Social Dimension *(continued)*

Category	Indicators
Human Rights	
• General	– Demonstrated application of human rights screens in investment – Evidence of systematic monitoring of organisational practices – Number and type of alleged violations, and organisational position and response
• Indigenous rights	– Evidence of indigenous representation in decision making in geographic areas containing indigenous peoples – Number and cause of protests
• Security	– Examples of incorporating security and human rights into country risk assessment and facility planning – Remuneration/rehabilitation of victims of security force action
Suppliers	– Performance of suppliers relative to social components of programmes and procedures relating to supply chain and outsourcing – Number and type of incidences of non-compliance with prevailing national or international standards – Frequency of monitoring of contractors regarding labour conditions
Products and services	– Major social issues and impacts associated with the use of principal products and services – Customer satisfaction levels

Source Data: http://www.globalreporting.org/Guidelines/June2000/June2000GuidelinesDownload.htm

sion that meeting the needs of other stakeholders can contribute substantially to meeting the needs of shareholders as well.

Who's at Work Here?

In developing triple-bottom-line standards, GRI works with 21 companies that serve as pilot sites to help develop reporting guidelines along with the necessary definitions and measurement methodologies. Shell has been an active participant in this group, and there is a reasonable degree of overlap among the GRI indicators and Shell's planned key performance indicators, discussed in Chapter 9.

Other pilot companies include two more petrochemicals companies,

SASOL and Sunoco, along with TXU Europe, British Airways, Van City, Novo Nordisk, Bristol-Myers Squibb, General Motors, Ford, and Baxter International. In 1999, Bristol-Myers Squibb was the first to publish a report following the *Guidelines*.

Where Are the Accounting Firms?

In the world of the triple bottom line, accounting firms don't occupy a privileged position. They play little or no role at all in developing the measurement and auditing standards. Shell explicitly called attention to this in *The Shell Report 2000*: "Conventional verification methods alone do not provide the assurance needed." How, for example, would one of the Big Five accounting firms audit the human rights performance of Shell in Nigeria? Even though both KPMG and PricewaterhouseCoopers worked closely with Shell on its transparency initiative, how well could either assess the company's security arrangements, for example, or the quality of its stakeholder engagement with the indigenous peoples living close to a gas field in a Peruvian rainforest?

And then there are the measures and the standards. In the area of indicators of social, environmental, and ethical performance, the GRI is working in cooperation with a not-for-profit group called AccountAbility to develop guidelines for auditing that will support AccountAbility's emerging process standard on social and ethical accounting, auditing, and reporting (SEAAR).

An entire profession of quality auditors, health and safety verifiers, environmental specialists, and hybrid NGO (nongovernmental organization) consulting firms has emerged, and they compete among themselves as well as with accounting firms for work in these areas. Companies such as SGS, Arthur D. Little, and ERM have already established respected reputations as a result of their knowledge of the issues and their experience in this arena. Many of the NGOs have actually campaigned against accounting firms playing a significant role.

That said, these new audit professionals have their own independence issues. In providing consulting services, they may risk losing credibility with their stakeholder groups if they provide assurance to a company's environmental, health, and safety reports as well. In the multistakeholder world, nothing is simple. Roles remain very much in flux, and even their very definitions lack universal agreement.

DEVELOPING STANDARDS

No one ever said the revolution would be painless. Executives have legitimate concerns about increasingly onerous reporting regulations. Those concerns arise more from the prospect of detailed, rules-based regulations than they do from a set of broadly accepted standards for a wider range of performance measures. Once managers have accepted the inevitability and benefits of greater transparency, they will probably happily trade off lots of rules for a few measures in exchange for the same number of rules for a lot of measures. And as the examples above show, if standards *should* exist, market forces will push for this to happen.

So how should these standards be developed? In the spirit of the earlier examples, standards would best be developed through a market-driven process that tracks along the following steps:

- A few leading companies in each industry would agree that developing standards is the right thing for them to do; without their participation a market-driven approach simply won't take flight.
- They would identify the measures that have large Information Gaps, as PricewaterhouseCoopers did through its industry-specific surveys in the high-tech, banking, and insurance sectors.
- A consortium of companies and other members of the information supply chain would work with information users (e.g., analysts, investors, NGOs) and third-party experts (e.g., accounting firms, research organizations, database companies, academics, consultants, measurement boutiques) to identify how companies in a given industry currently measure, or at least try to measure, the identified value drivers.
- The consortium would develop recommendations reflecting the best, currently available methodology for measuring a particular value driver in order to close the Quality Gap as much as possible.
- Companies represented in the consortium would adopt this standard and use it in their external reporting practices, thereby reducing the Reporting Gap.
- Representatives of the users of the information that companies report would press other companies to provide corresponding information.
- Consortium members would review the standards as often as necessary—timed to the pace of the industry—to assess their relevance, reliability, validity, and predictive value based on real-world experience using them.
- The consortium would make adjustments as necessary, striking the right balance between validity and historical comparability.

Market Driven Standards Is Not an Oxymoron

Why do we need a market-driven solution? For a couple of reasons. First, without the voluntary participation of companies, no standards will emerge unless the regulators intervene directly. This seems unlikely in the short term as regulatory bodies worldwide already have their hands full with a backlog of purely historical financial accounting matters.

Getting corporate managers to participate actively in the process, however, will require convincing them that developing standards will serve their best interests: that it will enable them to better manage their companies, that it will allow them to better serve the interests of their stakeholders, and that it will reduce the probability that regulators will impose arbitrary and detailed measurement standards.

In addition, managers should realize that an external regulatory solution would more likely lead to a rules-based approach, whereas a market-driven, self-regulatory solution will more likely lead to a principles-based approach. Chapter 6 described the advantages of the latter for financial measures; the same logic applies for all other measures as well.

The second reason for a market-driven approach to setting standards is that it involves the capital markets and other stakeholders. It explicitly recognizes that shareholders and other stakeholders are the ultimate users of externally reported information. It makes eminent sense, therefore, to get their input. They "work with the numbers" and they know what they want to do with them, both in assessing performance on a particular value driver and in examining its relationship to others.

Because these users have become accustomed to scouring for information wherever they can find it, they should at least have familiarity with the measures and methodologies that others—consulting firms, third-party database companies, and such—have developed. Some of these may well form the foundation for developing generally accepted standards for nonfinancial measures.

What About the Real Regulators?

Assume that standards are developed. What will the external regulators do about them? In all candor, regulators will probably prick up their ears and eventually get involved. When and how are the questions.

As standards become more refined and widely accepted, most companies will recognize that they put themselves at a competitive disadvantage if they don't adopt them. That underscores the need to ensure that *every* company reports these measures using *common standards* developed by an industry consortium. Enter the regulators and their regulations.

It is hoped, of course, that the result will be regulation "lite." This will more likely happen if the industry-based standard-setting consortia exercise their best judgment and take seriously their responsibilities for developing good standards and reliable measurement methodologies, and then adhere to them rigorously.

HOW STANDARD CAN STANDARDS BE?

We've made a strong case for standards developed by company-led, industry-based consortia. We do not, however, explicitly argue for universal standards that would apply across all industries. This strategy clearly differs from the GRI's approach. While certain measures on the GRI list may apply across all industries, some of the environmental ones, for example, most probably won't. In the short term—and real progress must happen soon—the best strategy is an industry-by-industry one. Time will then tell which measurement standards will apply across industries.

But what exactly is an industry anymore anyhow? This question will probably go begging for a while. A market-driven approach requires, as it should, that market forces define what constitutes a specific industry. For example, the boundaries between banking and insurance continue to blur as financial services firms diversify into related businesses. Those participants should decide whether they should form separate banking and insurance consortia, or if a combined one would be more effective.

That said, three points should be made:

1. Market forces must establish reasonable definitions for relevant industries. These definitions would best be couched in terms of those companies that compete for the same customers.

2. Some conglomerates compete in many industries. What happens to them? There's a simple, although perhaps unpalatable, answer. Each industry business segment would report as if it were a separate, publicly traded company, which the market wants anyway.

3. As new industries emerge, new consortia must form. Rather than force-fit new companies into existing industries, better to simply recognize when a new industry definition has emerged. This won't happen overnight. In the interim, new companies will be classified in an existing industry, perhaps several, creating problems for both the new companies and the industries where they're temporarily parked.

Because there's no reason to carve in stone either industry definitions or industry membership, new classifications and reclassifications should be made as necessary. Flexibility and standards can peacefully coexist, especially in a market-driven, self-regulated approach.

Does this mean that we will never have universal standards for measuring intangibles and nonfinancial value drivers that apply across all industries? Never is a very long time, but it is highly doubtful that all industries could ever agree on common valid measures for such value drivers as intellectual capital or customer penetration. If this is true, then universal standards that cover all nonfinancial measures will never emerge.

Probably the most that can be hoped for in terms of a completely general measurement framework is a global set of common accounting standards, as discussed in Chapter 6. This doesn't mean that *some* universal measurement standards won't emerge that apply to all industries, just that this doesn't need to be an immediate goal for real progress to happen.

Simply having industry-based measurement standards would represent an enormous step forward. For example, insurance companies in Europe, the United States, and Asia would all report embedded value in the same way. Similarly, software companies throughout the world would all report speed-to-market in the same way.

Settling for industry-based standards alone does not create as big a limitation as a first glance might suggest. In developing their investment strategies, investors first determine the risk profile for their portfolios, and then determine which industry mix fits that profile. Only then do they pick individual stocks within an industry. Industry standards that enable investors to compare the performance of all companies within an industry across all relevant performance measures will suffice.

AN INTERNET EXAMPLE

The Internet provides an example of how standards *will* emerge if the market demands them. In our example—Internet traffic—the standards for the measure apply across a range of industries but still remain quite compatible with the suggested industry-based approach. Industry consortia members will simply benefit from work that others have done to develop standards for some of the key measures of interest to them.

Internet traffic, a nonfinancial measure, has fairly recently emerged as an important measure in determining value, as Chapter 6 discussed. In late summer 2000, an article in, appropriately enough, *The Standard*, which bills itself as "intelligence for the Internet economy," announced the creation of a new website called Audit Central.

This website provides investors and media buyers comparable information on Web traffic data that has been "audited" by the three site-traffic auditors that collaborated in creating the site: ABC Interactive, BPA International, and Engage I/PRO. Note that none of these companies is an accounting firm. Also note that companies are voluntarily allowing Audit Central to post the results of their online audits on the site. They, no doubt, see the capital and advertising revenue benefits that can accrue from demonstrating a high level of high-quality Internet traffic on their websites.

But before these results could be posted, several content and process issues that might typically arise in any effort to set measurement standards had to be addressed.

- The measures to be audited had to be identified. They included: number of pageviews, average number of pages viewed per surfer visit, which pages are viewed most often, what top-level domains request the information, the number of unique visitors to the site, how often visitors return, and how long they spend at the site.

- These measures included both quantitative and qualitative information.

- The three firms behind Audit Central regarded their methodology, based on server log file data, as superior to the other major alternatives used by competing firms such as Media Metrix and Nielsen NetRatings, which are panel-based measurements.

- Some technical problems needed to be solved to adopt the server log file data methodology.

Audit Central represents a market-driven standards and reporting solution to a market demand. It involves the willing cooperation of "audit clients" in the measurement methodologies used and how to make the results publicly available. Companies performing well on these measures will get better terms from media buyers and investors. They will also be able to compare their performance to competitors for internal management purposes, such as performance measurement, strategic planning, and even compensation.

Having standards is clearly a good thing. But their mere existence doesn't mean that the right decisions were made in creating them. Not being Internet experts, we have no idea whether "server log file data" are superior to "panel-based measurements." What we do know is that once standards are set they are hard to change, which makes the decision about which methodology to use extremely important. This directly supports the recommendation for a consortium approach that relies on market forces, but ensures that all relevant voices are heard.

CAN WE COUNT ON ACCOUNTING FIRMS?

Developing new standards poses an enormous challenge for all concerned. It is no more daunting, however, than the one the accounting profession faced 100 years ago when it came together to create common standards for financial measurement and reporting within each country. And remember from Chapter 6 that when the SEC was pressing for those standards, many in the profession felt that they could not be developed. True, many more of the new nonfinancial measures lack the preexisting overarching framework that traditional financial measures had. Double-entry bookkeeping, for example, dates back five centuries and has its basis in an underlying set of cash transactions.

At the same time, businesses have made enormous advances in management concepts, tools and techniques, and in information technology, especially enterprise resource planning systems and the Internet. Without a doubt, the collective business community has the knowledge, or can develop it, to set meaningful industry-based measurement standards. Solid frameworks for other types of measures, such as customers or human resources, will emerge through the collaboration of academics and executives.

It is less certain that the accounting profession can accomplish this task as successfully as it accomplished the task of developing financial standards, measurement methodologies, and reporting as it did a century ago. The world has changed much since then. When national accounting standards first came into being, management consulting firms, sell-side analysts, and computer and software companies did not exist. At that time, accounting firms stood solidly atop the financial information food chain. One of the most important services they offered their clients was advice on providing shareholders more and higher-quality information on the company's financial performance. In so doing, the accounting firms played a very proactive role. They took the high road and occupied the moral high ground.

Things Change

Today, the influence that audit firms have on corporate management has declined, due in part to a combination of market and regulatory forces. On the market side, other service providers, including the consulting divisions of the major accounting firms themselves, now help managers measure many of their important performance factors, and then help them use these measures to manage their businesses more effectively. Consulting firms and investment banks now have high-level access to CEOs and CFOs and can offer advice on how to create value, often using a broad range of management relevant measures. In some cases, accounting firms attest to these measures; in many, they do not.

Hardware and software companies also have legitimately established themselves as experts in applying advanced technology to performance measurement. Even the best ones, however, have a way to go in helping managers figure out just what to measure and how the measures relate to one another in creating value.

Accounting firms have felt for some time the impact of this increased reliance on information technology for measuring performance. To better serve their clients' needs, most, if not all, of the larger firms have built large information technology (IT) consulting practices of their own. On the audit side, the focus has clearly shifted away from just verifying the numbers produced by measurement processes and more toward confirming the reliability of the processes themselves.[3] This results in a very different kind of audit with the accounting firm looking over the shoulder of management to ensure the accuracy of the reported numbers on a real-time basis.

Back to Basics

Even as accounting firms grapple with adapting traditional audit processes to increasingly automated measurement processes, regulators have put increasing pressure on them to ensure their independence. The regulators, quite understandably, have concerns that if accounting firms get too close to management in advising on strategies and on mergers and acquisitions, as well as in implementing large and expensive IT systems, they will compromise their fundamental responsibility—to ensure that shareholders get relevant and reliable performance information.

Regulators also have concerns that if accounting firms focus too much of their own resources on these newer service lines—in terms of service development investments, advertising, marketing, and recruiting—they will pay insufficient attention to making sure that the audit practice delivers what clients need and shareholders expect—relevant and reliable performance information.

No doubt, this broader range of fast-growing services, typically fairly well divorced from the audit practice (which has essentially served as a "marketing function" for them), has enabled the major accounting firms to grow substantially in a relatively short time. During that same time, a networked economy has emerged that increasingly requires consulting firms to enter into joint ventures and alliances with other players—something that accounting firms find difficult to do because of the audit independence rules. Consequently, several of the major accounting firms are divesting their consulting businesses. At the time of this writing, Ernst & Young already had; PricewaterhouseCoopers had announced its intention to do so.

While such actions will substantially reduce the perception of conflicts of interest, they will challenge these firms to find ways to provide the services their clients and their shareholders need. Similarly, regulators like the SEC must recognize that if the core audit product becomes a purely compliance function—and all that accounting firms are asked or allowed to do—the information needs of investors will be poorly served.

Life Is What You Make It

The combination of market forces and regulatory pressures has only exacerbated the more fundamental reason for the declining access and influence of accounting firms. Many observers believe that they have allowed themselves to be reduced to the role of opining that their clients have adhered to the letter of the law. These critics further argue that accounting firms have given up on the spirit of the law in urging and assisting executives to identify and report the information that truly matters to shareholders and other stakeholders, and being willing to put their seal of approval on this information.

One explanation for this is that regulations have multiplied. For the audit practice, the trees have almost totally obscured the forest. Also, in today's litigious society—especially in the United States—firms want to avoid exposing themselves to unnecessary legal liabilities. Auditing firms also find themselves in a somewhat awkward and ironic situation. Although the users of the audited figures are investors, it is the audit firm's clients—the very companies owned by the investors—that pay the bills. It has always been thus, and there's no readily apparent or practical alternative to this economic arrangement.

Whatever the explanation, the blunt fact remains: The relative influence auditors have on management practice has become dramatically less than it was a century or even 50 or 25 years ago. This does not mean that firms do not take their professional responsibilities as auditors seriously.

They do. Many studies confirm it, as does the recent report by The Panel on Audit Effectiveness (the Panel) sponsored by the Public Oversight Board,[4] under the chairmanship of Shaun F. O'Malley (the O'Malley Report).[5] Although both companies and shareholders still consider the audit important, its relative importance has declined in proportion to the decline in relevance and importance of historical financial figures. The growth business for accounting firms has become the broad range of consulting and IT services that enable managers to identify and capture all the other measures with more importance to creating value—whether companies report it or not.

What Life Could Be

If accounting firms are to play a meaningful role in the ValueReporting Revolution, they must make changes much greater than those that appear in the O'Malley Report's recommendations, useful though they are. Rather than asking what the profession could do, the Panel focused on what it does—provide assurance on increasingly complicated and decreasingly relevant financial performance measures.

Our disagreement is not with what the Panel identified as a significant problem when it said, "The high market valuations of equity securities have created pressures on corporate management to achieve earnings or other performance targets, especially in response to the expectations of securities analysts."[6] In fact, an entire chapter of this book focuses on The Earnings Game and the attendant problems of earnings management, the quality of earnings, earnings restatement, and outright fraud in reported earnings. On this issue, the Panel deserves due credit.

Our concern is that the Panel focused more on one of the consequences of The Earnings Game—that the pressures felt by managers get passed along to their auditors, potentially compromising the audit process—rather than on the underlying causes. The Panel got it right in recommending tightening audits, setting the right "tone at the top" of audit firms, enforcing uniform audit standards around the world, and getting the "best people" into the profession. The Panel failed, however, to say much at all about two particularly important underlying causes of why accounting firms might feel these pressures:

1. Too much focus on the single measure of earnings to the exclusion of other, often more important, value drivers
2. The sell-side pressures on companies to manage and deliver on expectations about earnings

On the first point, the Panel recognized that "investors can quickly access information and consequently have expanded their demands for both financial and non-financial information."[7] As standards emerge for these measures, their relative importance will increase even more, diminishing excessive and irrational market reactions to small deviations from expectations in reported earnings. Accounting firms can play a very useful role, but only if they want to. As for the second point, Chapter 14 will examine the role of sell-side analysts in detail.

TAKING BACK THE HIGH GROUND

What can accounting firms do to serve their clients, shareholders, and other stakeholders as completely as possible? What should they do to get back to their former role of urging clients to do the right thing, rather than just the required thing?

They can and should work with their clients to:

o Identify all the key components and value drivers
o Become experts on the business processes and related controls surrounding the measurement of value drivers and financial and operating risks
o Specify the relationships among value drivers (the "business model")
o Develop methodologies for measuring value drivers
o Participate in or even organize the industry consortia that will turn the methodologies into industry standards
o Encourage their clients to report information on the measures in as timely and detailed a fashion as possible

Accounting firms cannot do this if their role is limited to simply performing statutory audits. Instead, they must have a much broader advisory role that involves developing business models, creating measurement methodologies, and applying these methodologies in processes, many of which require a high level of IT skills. In a real-time world with many performance measures, the distinctions between monitoring and controlling and between auditing and advising largely disappear.

Performance Monitoring ↔ Performance Improvement

Some who have concerns about auditor independence will argue that this new role might compromise the audit product. They will say that audit firms can't serve two masters—that the auditor can't advise management and at the same time render an objective opinion for shareholders about the performance management reports.

The O'Malley Report discusses this very contemporary and controversial subject and notes that it has been around for a long time.[8] Reflecting the issue's high level of controversy, the Panel did not issue any firm recommendations. It simply, and justly, reviewed the arguments on both sides of the debate.

Our position on this issue won't surprise anyone. If the markets demand relevant and timely information, the best way for accounting firms to ensure its reliability is to involve themselves in defining and generating it. This recognizes that the distinction between monitoring performance and providing advice to improve performance is ill defined and arbitrary.

The very process of auditing performance—based on benchmarks, models, and a deep understanding of the company's business and its management—yields insights about how to improve that performance. Should the audit firm really keep these insights to itself to the detriment of better performance for shareholders? We think not.

In a real-time, multiple-performance-measurement world, accounting firms must develop an even deeper understanding of their client company's business and how it's managed. IT systems, which spit out numbers, do not put them in an overall context that presents a true and fair view of business performance. To do this requires knowledge of the business, its managers, and how the information is produced and used. Such knowledge cannot help but have as much relevance to improving performance as to reporting on it. Why shouldn't it be put to its fullest use?

CAN THEY DO IT?

The SEC and other regulatory and professional bodies certainly don't urge the accounting profession to take an active role in developing measurement and auditing standards for a broad range of other measures. They don't explicitly forbid them to, either. Accounting firms certainly seem to have an opportunity to take back the moral high ground. But will they seize it?

That depends on two things. First, they must have the will. Accounting firms should reestablish the role they played many years ago when they led rather than followed their clients in establishing measures and reporting practices.

Like doing quality audits, taking back the lead will depend on the "tone at the top." The leaders of the Big Five accounting firms must decide whether they want to play this role. Doing so defines true independence, because it comes from a deep conviction within the profession itself to give its best advice and exercise its best judgment for the benefit of its clients, their shareholders, and all other stakeholders.

Second, the will must be matched with capability. The accounting firms must have people who have the skills to do it. The Panel hit the nail squarely on the head with its concerns that the profession today doesn't attract enough of the best and the brightest. The highly qualified prospects have enormously attractive opportunities in strategy consulting, investment banking, money management, industry, and even in the partially melted-down "dot-com" world. To attract the highest-quality people, the accounting profession must offer them exciting careers in which they can develop personally and professionally and, incidentally, earn at least a comfortable living wage.

Money Matters

Let's be frank. Money *is* important. To recruit and retain the best professionals, accounting firms must offer a certain level of compensation—at the entry level, at levels along the way to partner, and at the partner level.

Accounting professionals shouldn't necessarily gain the wealth of successful dot-com entrepreneurs. In general, most of these professionals make far less than highly successful entrepreneurs or very senior executives. Most are comfortable with their choices because they find inherent meaning in the work they do. But the profession simply can't ignore the labor markets completely. It must ensure that it provides enough value to its clients to ensure it can provide enough value to its members.

Skills That Matter

The compensation that professionals receive depends on the contributions they make. To contribute at a higher level requires higher-level capabilities. But what capabilities must accounting professionals develop to take on the new role we have described and advocated? They fall into seven broad categories:

1. Knowledge of existing accounting and auditing standards
2. Deep understanding of risks and controls
3. Mastery of broad-based measurement and attestation processes
4. Thorough knowledge of industries and how value is created within them

5. Complete grasp of strategy and its implementation
6. Continuous updating of IT expertise and skills
7. Absolute objectivity

The first capability needs no further explanation. The second is not a new area for auditors, but clients will increasingly need their in-depth understanding of financial and operating risks and how to measure them, combined with expertise in designing and implementing controls. The third capability derives directly from the need for new measures and the necessity to develop standards for them. The skills developed in accounting and auditing are certainly transferable to other types of measures. After all, what core competency do accountants possess if not measurement?

The measurement skills that accountants now have, of course, relate to a well-defined accounting model based on rules, guidelines, and experience gained over many years. In developing new measures, accountants must exercise intelligence, business judgment, and creativity. They can't simply borrow techniques from financial measurement and assume that they apply to measuring customers, human resources, innovation, and all the other nonfinancial value drivers. These new content areas for measurement will require knowledge of the content itself. For example, individuals active in triple-bottom-line efforts will need knowledge about human development, socioeconomics, and stakeholder engagement.

To extend their core skills in financial measurement, accountants must also develop deep industry knowledge. This implies specialization by industry, at least for a while. After all, one cannot learn overnight about the value drivers of an industry, their importance, and how their relationships vary according to strategy. While some measures, such as employee turnover, are relatively well-defined across industries—even though the very definition of an employee can vary—other measures, such as customer penetration, are much more industry specific.

When accountants simply ensure that a well-defined set of accounting rules, no matter how complex, has been applied in any given company, they do not need to specialize by industry any more than other professionals do. For lawyers, for example, functional expertise has more importance than industry knowledge.

This changes, however, when accountants begin to help businesses understand their value drivers, how to measure them, and how to make sure that investors get the information they need. To do this, accountants must have a level of industry knowledge comparable to those they advise. Strategy consultants and investment bankers have clearly applied this model. It will work well for accountants, too.

Accountants then need to understand the strategy management has chosen for creating value for shareholders. Although certain measures, especially financial ones, have relevance for all strategies, the relative importance of others, or even what they are, depends a great deal on the strategy. If accountants do not understand a company's strategy, they cannot truly say that the reported information represents a fair view of how well the company performs.

Similarly, accountants must understand how strategies are implemented in terms of organizational structures, management control systems, human resource policies, culture, and the leadership skills and personalities of individual executives. As the production of information becomes more deeply embedded in IT systems, and as auditing becomes a virtually continuous process, the ability to assess how these systems were developed, how they are being managed, and the people using them will take on paramount importance. The more information becomes automated and ingrained in the basic operations of the business, the more important personal judgment becomes about the softer side of management.

Understanding the soft side goes hand in hand with sophisticated IT skills. Accountants must not separate the financial accounting and measurement part of the audit from the IT systems that produce the measures. Attesting to the numbers that systems produce will require an understanding of the systems themselves. Conversely, simply understanding how a system works will be insufficient to render an opinion about whether the information generated is relevant, reliable, and valid, and that it has predictive value.

Every accountant will need much more than a casual knowledge of information technology. Gaining this knowledge now begins at an early age, continues through college and graduate school, and must become a career-long pursuit. Staying abreast of new information technologies presents a constant challenge to audit professionals. Even today, most accountants, like most executives, have only a modest understanding, at best, of the Internet and few of the special skills required to use it effectively. Similarly, accountants must develop a deeper knowledge of how systems are used to manage risk, both the upside and the downside.

Essential as all these new skills are, they should not obviate the fact that the very foundation of the accountant's contribution to society is objectivity, both real and perceived. It's as fundamental today as it was 100 years ago. Executives, shareholders, and other stakeholders need to know that the opinions rendered by accountants are truly independent of the desires and wishes of any group. There can be no compromise on objectivity. Lost even once, it can never be retrieved. While objectivity must be perceived to be real, this perception comes only from the fact that indeed it is real.

Revolutionary Behavior

Retaking the high ground won't be easy. For years, accountants have had a "stick to the audit" mentality, which has meant not challenging their clients except on accounting and reporting standards. They must transform this attitude into a strong stance with clients about the benefits of doing more than regulations require and the necessity to meet the information needs of shareholders.

One reason that strategy consulting firms and investment banks have so much access to management stems from the strong positions they take and the compelling arguments they make. Whether it's sound advice or bad, managers appreciate the stimulation, when done well, and enjoy the freedom to accept or reject it. Most important, they must take ultimate responsibility for their company's strategic direction and M&A deals. Accounting firms should do the same in their arena—identify the information investors and other stakeholders need and make sure their clients report it in a quality and timely way.

Cassandra Prophecies

What are the alternatives? Very few, and not very attractive.

Cassandra Prophecy 1
Unless accounting professionals resume taking responsibility for ensuring that their clients provide the information their shareholders and other stakeholders need, they will become increasingly less relevant. Shareholders and other stakeholders will satisfy their need for information, one way or another. Wouldn't they be better served if the information they got met the high standards that the accounting profession could ensure, if only it would do what it should?

Cassandra Prophecy 2
Turnover within the Big Five will increase. Recruiting new people will become even more difficult. Who wants to be part of a declining industry? The leadership of the major accounting firms will face a cruel dilemma: Reduce revenues and risks by retaining only the highest-quality clients, or maintain

revenues but take on more risk with the threat of litigation and liabilities that could put them out of business.

Cassandra Prophecy 3

Regulators will see this problem and become even more concerned than they are today. Powerless to reverse the flow of market forces, they will exercise the only option they have left. In one fashion or another, the major accounting firms will become "nationalized" as part of a government bureaucracy. So much for a worldwide approach to auditing standards. So much for global accounting standards. And so much for investors getting all of the relevant and reliable information they need on a timely basis.

PRACTICE WHAT YOU'VE PREACHED

Imagine a world in which the accounting firms get their collective acts together and take full advantage of the enormous opportunity that has presented itself. One big challenge for them would still remain: increasing their own transparency. When asked whether accountancy firms should become more transparent themselves, Royal Dutch Shell's Tom Delfgaauw, an expert on transparency in a firm that practices it as well as any, said, "The answer to the question is a bit like the answer someone once gave in response to a question about what he thought of Western civilization, 'Seems like a good idea!' "

Now with one last bit of admittedly painful candor: Accounting firms don't perform very well when it comes to transparency. While not surprising in an industry that has long been accustomed to the closed cultures that pervade private partnerships, history can't serve as an excuse to not move into the future. Accounting firms should become more transparent themselves. Why should their clients do it if the accounting firms won't? "Do as I say, not as I do" doesn't work very well, even with children anymore.

Fortunately, some progress has already been made. KPMG UK announced in its 1999 annual report its commitment to integrate social, ethical, and environmental performance management into decision making for the firm. The firm plans to institute policies, strategies, and programs informed by an understanding of social, ethical, and environmental impacts as much as by economic factors.

Furthermore, it intends to publish, during 2000, a report on its commitment to clients, communities, and the environment, as well as on its commitment to share and develop knowledge. KPMG says, "We acknowledge that . . . we must develop trust and understanding with our stakeholders through dialogue, transparency, and a demonstration of accountability. This is fundamental to turning knowledge into value."[9]

PricewaterhouseCoopers, meanwhile, launched a new U.K. website in April 2000, designed to engage stakeholders in an ongoing dialogue about where the firm's social responsibilities lie and how well it is addressing them. At least part of the impetus to move toward more open and transparent engagement with stakeholders comes from the fact that the firm now works with companies like Shell on social and environmental reporting and other sustainability-related projects. Accounting firms can learn from their clients, just as their clients can learn from them. For accounting firms, as for Shell, there is no alternative to transparency.

14

Should You See an Analyst?

Am I a god? I see so clearly.

Johann Wolfgang von Goethe, *Faust*

Imagine, for a moment, a world in which companies provided audited information on every key performance measure using a common set of standards. Would that signal that the ValueReporting Revolution had been won? Of course not. Information alone doesn't determine how accurately the market sets stock prices. Accurate valuations also depend on how the market analyzes and uses the information it gets.

Many years ago, what little information companies published they provided directly to their investors. Investors, in turn, analyzed the information in whatever way they chose, using the limited tools they had, and came to their own investment decisions. The world has grown more complicated. Investors still get information directly, and more of it more quickly, than they did in the past. But between the companies and their ultimate investors, whether individual or institutional, are sell-side analysts. Their job is to take the information provided by companies, analyze it, and then make recommendations to their clients.

These analysts often get more information—and sooner—than all except the very largest investors. This puts them in a strategically central position. Unlike directors on boards, analysts have a choice about whether to join the revolution or to fight against it. For analysts, this choice is not easy because their current position is a privileged one.

Yet a strong argument can be made that it is in their self-interest to become some of the revolution's most ardent advocates. Given the complexities of most industries today, how quickly they change, and the time constraints on investors, one can easily see how full-time, dedicated experts who know an industry inside and out could provide a very valuable service. These expert, professional analysts could:

- Challenge management on its performance and its plans
- Dig beneath potentially incomplete, misleading, and self-serving information provided by companies
- Compare the performance of competing companies against each other
- Study external forces and trends that do, or could, affect an industry and the companies in it

Given the explosion of information available on the Internet, the professional analyst's value to investors should become more rather than less important in the future. Neal Lipschutz, a senior editor at Dow Jones News Service, describes an opportunity they can seize if they will: "Recently democratized markets and the glut of corporate information and news available to institutional and individual investors increases, rather than decreases, the need for cogent analyses about the prospects for individual stocks."[1] For the opportunity that Lipschutz describes to ever materialize, however, those who say they offer cogent analysis today—the sell-side analysts who work for investment and merchant banks—must change in some fundamental ways.

The model for providing in-depth and objective research has failed investors to the same degree that the corporate reporting model has. The ValueReporting Revolution cannot succeed simply by having companies provide more information. How analysts use and spin the information must change before investors can be truly and fully informed.

The flaws here gape as large and as significant as do those in today's external reporting practices. Unless this structural feature of the capital markets gets fixed, the full benefits of better disclosure will never be realized. This chapter investigates the nature and depth of the structural problem. Chapter 15 explores what should be done so that the revolution can be truly and completely won.

INSIDE THE EXCITING WORLD OF SELL-SIDE ANALYSTS

Listen to this jaundiced, but not unrepresentative, view of sell-side analysts posted by an individual investor on a website the Securities and Exchange Commission (SEC) created to solicit comments on Regulation Fair Disclosure. The disillusioned soul writes:

I see the role of analysts and business reporters as follows:

1. Scare the public into selling, thus driving the equity price lower.
2. Once the equity price is down, then the "manipulators" buy.
3. After a little time passes, let out a little bit of good news about the equity.
4. Wait for the public to buy, after a short upward price movement.
5. Let out more bad reports about equity or again scare the public to sell, sometimes called the final shakeout.
6. Equity prices drops [*sic*] again as public gets scared and sells way too soon.
7. "Manipulators," "insiders," "strong hands" really buy now.
8. Usually a long quiet period follows this "final shakeout."
9. Suddenly, for no apparent reason the equity's price start [*sic*] to rise, sometimes dramatically.
10. Public see [*sic*] equity rise, get excited, buy at too high a price level.
11. "Manipulators" sell at new high prices, equity drops like a rock, with the public holding the bag.[2]

Conspiracy theories aside, the role of sell-side analysts has changed dramatically over the last 50 years and, from an investor's perspective, not for the better. This role must go through a metamorphosis again before analysts can provide true value to investors by analyzing the increasing amount of information the revolution urges companies to provide. If analysts and their employers don't change, market forces and regulatory actions will make sure that this analysis comes from somewhere else.

A Little Bit of History

One hundred years ago, when companies first started making information available to their investors, sell-side analysts did not exist. But investment banks did, and they helped companies raise money by issuing stocks and bonds.

The sell-side analysts were conceived and born many years later, starting their lives first in independent research boutiques. They had as their customers institutional money managers who paid them for their research through "soft dollars" in the form of trading commissions generated through buying and selling stocks at their customers' bidding.

The large investment banks recognized the value of such research and started doing it themselves. They also bought out many of the independent research houses. Today, very few are left standing. The vast majority of the research now provided to investors comes from analysts employed by the full-service investment banks. By one count, about 9,000 analysts toil thusly.[3]

The investment banks were able to acquire the independent research houses, at least in part, because trading commissions had steadily gone down, first through deregulation and later as a result of electronic technology. Consequently, the cost of the research function has been increasingly borne by the investment banking function—the part of the firm that advises companies on mergers and acquisitions (M&A) and underwrites initial public offerings (IPOs), secondary equity issues, and bonds. The margins on M&A and IPOs are very high, and in the 1990s both were boom businesses, funneling hundreds of millions of dollars into an increasingly expensive research function with increasingly highly paid analysts.

Who's the Client, Anyway?

Such changing economics have had enormous and far-reaching consequences. Analysts today find themselves caught in a rather awkward position. Their "clients" are now as much the companies about which they supposedly write objective and unbiased research as they are the investors who use the research to make investment decisions.

Their investment banking brethren expect the analysts to help cover their often extraordinary salaries by helping to recruit IPO and M&A business for the bank. Samuel Hayes, professor emeritus of investment banking at the Harvard Business School, says, "Research analysts have become integral members of the investment banking units. Their compensation is tied importantly to the fee revenue that they generate for the investment banking unit and they are expected to be supportive of any companies that are brought in as investment-banking clients."[4]

Walter Kielholz, CEO of Swiss Re, a major global reinsurance company, confirmed this view when he observed that "When you talk to these analysts off the record, they acknowledge that they are under tremendous pressure to generate investment banking business." Jeffrey Hooke, a former investment banker himself and now a business school professor and author of a book on security analysis, put it even more succinctly and pointedly: "Providing unbiased research to investors ranks low on their priority list."[5]

Thomas K. Brown, a former top-ranked regional banking analyst for many years, expressed this sentiment even more colorfully: "There's no conflict. That's been settled. The investment bankers won."[6]

A Star Is Born

High-profile sell-side analysts, well known in their industries and by investors, have become enormous assets to their firms. But considering that more than 9,000 of them in the United States alone compete for a starring role, the task of becoming and staying highly visible is not easy.

Stardom is not just a metaphor here. Some analysts appear frequently on news programs and try to attract media attention in any number of ways. *The Standard* noted that Merrill Lynch Internet analyst Henry Blodget got more media mentions in the past year (1,072 mentions by their count) than Meg Whitman, the CEO of eBay. The closely followed Whitman was followed closely in the media visibility marathon by Morgan Stanley Dean Witter analyst Mary Meeker (598 mentions), who ranked ahead of the CEOs of CMGI (David Weatherall with 536 mentions) and Yahoo! (Tim Koogle, with 388 mentions).[7]

"When it comes to celebrity analysts, few can move stocks like Mary G. Meeker," says *BusinessWeek Online*. Such high-profile status helped her earn a third-place ranking in *Fortune* magazine's 1999 list of the most powerful women in business in America.[8]

Not everyone believes that becoming a media darling is entirely consistent with doing high-quality research. A cover story in *Business Week* titled "Wall Street's Hype Machine" declared, "The bull market has caused a revolution in the role of the analyst, who is fast becoming less of a researcher than a celebrity pitchman" by feeding "on another aspect of the hype machine—the cable-television outlets and the exploding number of personal-finance Web sites."[9]

Here's one example of what *Business Week* refers to, this reported in *The Wall Street Journal*'s "Heard on the Street" column.[10] After only a few years in his job, a former installer of telephones and fixer of computers turned research analyst issued a report that the auction site QXL.com's shares would soar to $333 in two years. The stock's price doubled in a single day! The article called this just the most recent example of "the new research game on Wall Street" where "an unknown analyst initiates coverage of an Internet stock with an eye-popping price target" by which the "analyst gains fame and potential fortune."

Fame and fortune, however, don't always come true for investors who buy such highly touted shares. Too often, their headlines read "crash and burn." And, just for the record, the investment bank where this particular analyst worked had also underwritten part of QXL.com's October 1999 IPO. A company spokesman denied any relationship between these two facts.

"Our equity research is unimpeachable, beyond reproach," he said.[11] By September 25, 2000, the stock had declined to less than $4.

Can We Talk?

When developing their high profiles, analysts can get enormous help by having especially good access to company executives. Being human themselves after all, executives may tend to favor analysts who say positive things about them over those who don't.

Arthur Levitt, chairman of the SEC, in a February 27, 1998, speech pointedly titled "A Question of Integrity," voiced his concern about companies that "selectively disclose information to certain influential analysts in order to curry favor with them and reap a tangible benefit, such as a positive press spin."[12] In a subsequent speech, he elaborated on his concern: "An all too candid memo from a leading Wall Street firm's corporate finance department couldn't have framed the conflict more plainly: '. . . We do not make negative or controversial comments about our clients as a matter of sound business practice. The philosophy and practical result needs to be 'no negative comments about our clients.'"[13]

The mutual dependence between companies and analysts—positive press in exchange for access—cements the investment bank–client relationship with the analyst squeezing on the Super Glue. Investors who get the analysts' priority attention and their inside tips before the rest of the investing world can certainly benefit from being called to the table first. Everybody else eats stale leftovers.

Investors Have Their Say

The information-starved masses—the growing number of individuals who invest directly and are not getting quality and timely information—might recall all too clearly the famous line often attributed to Marie Antoinette: "Let them eat cake." They feel that better access, not greater savvy, gives sell-side analysts their *raison d'être* today. If everybody had equal access, individual investors, in their own words as posted at the SEC's website, "might be able to use the information and bypass the 'professionals' altogether,"[14] resulting in "the selfish fear that with the public's ongoing trend of self sufficiency, analysts see their positions becoming extinct as time goes on."[15]

Institutional investors, who generate lots of trading commissions for the firms that offer them research, have also become more skeptical about the value the sell-side analysts add. The PricewaterhouseCoopers global survey of institutional investors found that only 8 percent strongly agreed that the recommendations of sell-side analysts influenced their investment deci-sions. The U.S. investors in this survey had an even more negative view. Not a single respondent strongly agreed. This negative opinion also held true in the high-tech survey. Thirty percent disagreed and 44 percent strongly dis-agreed (combined, that is nearly three-quarters of the total sample) that they relied on sell-side analysts in making their investment decisions.

To compensate for this, investors have upgraded their own "buy-side" research capabilities by hiring analysts to work directly for them. Very large money managers, who can spread the costs of hundreds of analysts across portfolios worth hundreds of billions of dollars, find the economics of this especially attractive. Fidelity, for example, is said to have more than 200 ana-lysts on its staff, rivaling the number of such Wall Street giants as Merrill Lynch with its 250.[16]

WHAT ANALYSTS REALLY DO

So why aren't sell-side analysts extinct already? The very good ones add value for their large institutional money management clients in two ways: in-formation and knowledge.

Information value-added comes from access to research before others get it and then passing it along to their clients. The sooner they can get the in-formation, the sooner they can pass it along. The more exclusive the list of recipients and the more it affects short-term stock prices, the more valuable it becomes. The big investors can get relevant data on their own, of course, by literally scouring the world, but increasingly it comes from having privi-leged access to companies.

Wherever it comes from, such information has a short shelf life be-cause sooner rather than later relevant information finds its way into the public domain. In a high-stakes, volatile market, simply having information a few days or even hours ahead of everyone else can result in a big-time, short-term advantage.

Providing information value-added through an especially close rela-tionship with a company can make the analysts heavily dependent on the company's willingness to spoon-feed them information. Such dependency can translate into complacency. It also tends to make analysts loath to say anything negative about the company for fear of closing down their source of value to their investment management clients. All of this taken together results in lower-quality research.

Richard Jenrette, one of the founders of the first independent re-search boutique Donaldson, Lufkin & Jenrette (DLJ), which long ago became a full-service investment bank, decried the declining quality of sell-side research in a speech to corporate investor relations executives. Analysts, he said, "have stopped using their brains and their analytical abilities" and instead rely on investor relations departments "to do their homework for them, through guidance," with the result that "Wall Street research has become incredibly superficial and short-term."[17]

The Wall Street Journal expressed the same view in a December 17, 1999, editorial. It recognized that some analysts do very good work "though increasingly these are fund managers and gadflies who work somewhere besides the blue-chip banks." But the editorial goes on to say, "Other analysts are simply overpaid suits and skirts who recompile the numbers companies dish out and scratch a few words restating the obvious."[18]

Academic research statistically supports these opinions. Amir, Lev, and Sougiannis examined the overall contribution of financial analysts' forecasts to investors' decisions.[19] They concluded that for the entire sample, "the contribution of analysts to investors' decisions is modest, at best" beyond the information already available in financial statements, and that contribution decreases with firm size and systematic risk.[20] They also suggest that analysts learn as much from investors as investors learn from them, saying, analysts "also observe stock price behavior and *learn* from investors' decisions."

The contribution of analysts is higher for companies losing money, for high-tech industries (especially compared to firms in regulated industries), and for companies with large R&D expenditures. In all of these situations, the information value of financial statements ranks low, giving analysts more of an opportunity to add value.

The researchers note that analysts prefer expensing R&D expenditures and other intangibles and that "disclosing more information about the value of intangible assets in the financial statements may reduce the value of analysts' earnings forecasts and increase the value of financial statements."[21] They conclude, "Analysts' arguments about accounting for intangibles may be just an attempt to protect their own product—forecasts of earnings."[22] In other words, although greater transparency about intangible assets may bode well for investors, a common theme throughout this book, it won't necessarily do so for analysts. Better information from companies to investors will make the analysts' intermediary role less necessary.

The Value of Information

Nevertheless, one can still find analysts who do the kind of digging and scratching that Jenrette thinks they should, although they often do it for the short-term goal of figuring out next quarter's earnings. Kevin Mc-Carthy, an analyst at DLJ predicted on June 7, 1999, that IBM's fourth-quarter earnings would be $1.10 per share compared to a First Call consensus estimate by 22 analysts of $1.33 per share.[23] IBM's fourth-quarter earnings came in at $1.12.[24]

How did he do that? The old-fashioned way. He learned it. McCarthy did some research of his own. In the process, he learned some things that even IBM didn't know. With the help of a dozen colleagues at DLJ, McCarthy called the chief information officers at 1,700 companies to find out their spending plans. He got only 100 responses, and 78 said they would continue spending regardless of Y2K concerns. The remaining 22, however, planned cutbacks averaging 44 percent. Extrapolating from this sample—not without its own risk given the small sample size—McCarthy estimated that overall corporate spending on computer hardware would decline by about 2 percent in 1999, with most of the decline concentrated in the fourth quarter. Based on this, he made corresponding adjustments in the fourth-quarter earnings of a number of computer companies, including IBM.

The Value of Knowledge

Analysts could also focus their research on the more fundamental issues that determine how much shareholder value a company will create over the long term. This kind of research results in *knowledge value-added*, which has a longer shelf life and diminishes less in value when shared with others compared to information value-added.

Knowledge value-added gives investors insights on a company in the context of its competitors, new technologies, and other forces shaping the industry. A study by Deloitte/Holt Value Associates found that 74 percent of the portfolio managers and buy-side analysts surveyed regarded the sell-side as helpful or very helpful in terms of their knowledge of companies, and 63 percent felt the same way about updates and timeliness of company news.[25]

Investors factor this knowledge into their own analyses and arrive at their own investment decisions. John Kattar, senior vice president and director of U.S. equities at The Boston Company Asset Management, explained it this way:

> Sell-side analysts are extremely knowledgeable people. They know more about an industry than you'll ever hope to, but they can't freely express their opinions. Traditionally, the model has been for them to

make recommendations. That's not why I use sell-side firms. What I'm paying for is access to analysts so I can talk to them about what I want to talk about. These conversations are more important than the paper they produce.

Kattar also noted that, useful though such input from analysts is, he and his portfolio managers and buy-side analysts have many other sources of information they tap into for making investment decisions. These include both formal sources and casual opportunities for gaining more information:

- Analysts working for other investment banks
- Analysts covering different but related industries
- Trade publications
- Trade shows
- Market intelligence
- Bulletin boards ("where you can find people who work at the company that give you the buzz on things like morale," Kattar notes)
- People you meet on airplanes

Ted Truscott, managing director and co-director of equities at Scudder Kemper Investments, also thinks that sell-side analysts can add value, although he was more dubious about just how much:

Some of our people aggressively use analysts for data points, but not their recommendations. There is no independent opinion on Wall Street. It's all shrouded in hints and offhand comments. So some of our people don't use them at all.

ANALYZING THE ANALYSTS

Compelling though Kattar's and Truscott's observations and examples are, two views alone cannot be treated as conclusive. A little independent analysis of our own is called for here to substantiate the conclusion that as much needs to be done to change information analysis as to change the information that is reported itself.

Our analysis of analysts comes from reviewing some statistics and studies about analysts' recommendations, both in general and in the special case of IPOs. We then examine the problems created by analysts who make buy recommendations for certain stocks at precisely the same time their firm's

private equity arm is busy selling that stock. Finally, we show how deeply conflicted analysts can become when they get actively involved in M&A deals.

Hey Buddy, Wanna Buy a Stock?

An assumption implicit in any recommendation to buy or sell a stock is that
the market is at least somewhat inefficient. If it were completely efficient, no
stock would be "undervalued" or "overvalued." Every stock would be properly valued, and investors would simply choose among them to earn a return
commensurate with the risk they take.

Based solely on an analysis of some recent sell-side analysts' recommendations, it would appear that most stocks today are either properly valued or undervalued, despite the tremendous increase in equity values over
the past decade—the correction in the high-tech sector earlier in 2000
notwithstanding.

First Call examined 27,000 recommendations by analysts and did the
following breakout of these recommendations:

○ Strong buy: 33.5 percent
○ Buy: 36.0 percent
○ Hold, neutral: 29.1 percent
○ Sell: 0.6 percent
○ Strong sell: 0.2 percent[26]

Such statistics inspired Mr. Levitt's melodious remark: "Is it any wonder that today, a 'sell' recommendation from an analyst is as common as a
Barbra Streisand concert."[27] (Ms. Streisand's reluctance to perform live
has been widely noted.) It's like we live in a corporate suburb of Garrison
Keillor's Lake Wobegon where all companies are good looking and above
average.

Or consider that one well-known Internet analyst at a so-called "bulge
bracket firm" (one of the leading investment banks) said in December 1999
that 90 percent of Internet stocks were overvalued, but had never placed a
sell recommendation on one. At that time, the analyst had issued buy recommendations on all 15 Internet stocks covered except for one, which was
restricted because of a pending merger.[28]

Even more remarkably, another sell-side analyst was quoted in *The Wall
Street Journal* as saying, "Let's call a spade a spade. Nobody on the sell side
puts negative ratings on stocks. Very few people have anything less than a
positive rating."[29]

The incredibly positive skew in analysts' recommendations is a fairly recent phenomenon. In mid-1983, they made sell and buy recommendations in almost equal proportion—24.5 percent and 26.8 percent, respectively.[30]

What has happened since then to create such imbalance? Have analysts gotten that much smarter compared to the market? Do they know something the market doesn't, in spite of the proliferation of information on the Internet? The empirical evidence certainly suggests they neither have nor do. In November 1999, the same month that First Call did its analysis of analysts' recommendations, the weekly average percentage of NASDAQ stocks that went up in price was 50 percent compared to 42 percent that went down.

The cognoscenti among investors, of course, know quite well that the analysts' recommendation jargon has undergone the moral equivalent of "grade inflation" seen in many schools. They know that "hold" really means "sell" and that only a "strong buy" really means "buy."

Such linguistic subtleties become even more difficult to interpret by anyone who has tried to read the stock-grading systems used by some major investment banks. Consider such ratings as "buy/buy (1-1)" and "neutral/buy (3-1)" used at a bulge bracket firm. An August 8, 2000, article in *The Wall Street Journal* tried to help crack the code, pointing out that these ratings translate roughly into "strong buy" and "hold," respectively. The article notes that "the actual rating nomenclature, which often combines words and numbers, can be confusing." Investors, therefore, "have to parse analysts' ratings carefully."[31] A "whisper number" is to a "consensus estimate" as a "hold" is to "sell" and a "strong buy" is to "buy." In this Tower of Babel, "sell" can only mean "You're an idiot for owning that stock."

Another trick of the trade is to simply stop covering a company rather than issuing a sell recommendation on it. This apparently happened with San Diego–based FPA Medical Management.[32] As the company pursued a string of acquisitions and paid substantial investment banking fees in the process, analysts praised the company effusively. When FPA filed for bankruptcy, however, hardly an analyst could be found to explain why, let alone one who had warned of this possibility.

Rigorous academic studies support the *prima facie* evidence that the skew in analysts' recommendations reflects a marked lack of objectivity. The most charitable view is that analysts simply have an understandable optimistic bias because they have chosen to follow companies in an industry they find interesting and exciting.

Easterwood and Nutt found evidence of the analysts' resulting rose-colored view in a study that showed "that analysts underreact to negative information, but overreact to positive information." Siva Nathan's study of 250 companies presents even more disturbing findings. He found that when the firm had an investment banking relationship with a company, the analyst's earnings were 6 percent higher and a buy recommendation was 25 percent more likely than when the firm had no such relationship.[33]

I'd Love to Take You Out in Public

The potential for upward bias becomes especially great in analysts' recommendations about companies that an investment bank has recently taken public in an IPO. The bank wants the stock to go up so that the investors who bought it will be happy. Former investment banker Jeffrey Hooke says, "Following the placement of the offering, favorable research reports support the share price, publicize the issuer's business, and foster trading interest in the stock."[34] The underwriter also wants the executives in the company, who typically still own a substantial amount of the company, to see their net worth go up and rejoice as well. This will predispose them to use the investment bank for any secondary offering, M&A advice, or other service.

The market doesn't always support the positive evaluations by analysts working in the underwriting firm. A recent study by Michaely and Womack found that the stock price of companies that got a buy recommendation from an analyst with the same firm that underwrote the IPO had gone down 5.4 percent one year later compared to having gone up 12.3 percent for buy recommendations from analysts whose firms were *not* involved in the underwriting.[35]

Similarly, stocks recommended by nonunderwriters did better than those recommended by underwriters two months after the IPO. Whatever information advantage a firm may have from doing the underwriting pales in comparison to the bias in their view.

Michaely and Womack posit three hypotheses for this bias, the first two reflecting a cognitive bias and the third, obviously the most cynical of the three, a conflict of interest:

1. Because the firm has underwritten the company, it has developed a positive view, and this is reflected in excess but honest optimism about its prospects.
2. Companies pick the more optimistic investment banks as their underwriters.
3. The analyst is knowingly overly optimistic about an investment-banking client.

Michaely and Womack evaluated each of these hypotheses through a survey of 26 sell-side and buy-side professionals. Every single one of the buy-side respondents thought the conflict-of-interest hypothesis best explained these results. More tellingly, 77 percent of the sell-side professionals did so as well. The researchers concluded that there is "a conflict of interest between analysts' fiduciary responsibility to investing clients (to make accurate recommendations) and their incentive to market stocks underwritten by their firms."[36]

Arthur Levitt voiced his concern about this in an October 1999 speech to the Economic Club of New York. "Analysts are fixtures on business pitches and investor road shows—doing their bit to market their own firm's underwriting talents and to sell a company's prospects."[37]

Companies know this and look for investment banks that have analysts who will cast them in a favorable light. A previously cited editorial in *The Wall Street Journal* noted that when Web companies "openly admit" they gave their IPO business to an investment bank with a well-known analyst in hope of "a favorable tout," it's not unreasonable "to wonder whom the analysts are really working for."[38]

Skepticism—and evidence for it—continues to mount about the objectivity of analysts when it comes to investment banking clients. One well-known Internet analyst issued a report grouping 32 e-commerce companies into three tiers based on their probability of survival. Seven of the eight in his top tier happened to be clients of the firm, including one company whose stock at that point had declined approximately 94 percent from its IPO price. Only one of the firm's clients ranked in tier two, and none appeared in tier three.[39]

The analyst insisted that his research had not been influenced by investment-banking ties.[40] And, in all fairness, some investors agreed with him. The analyst said the factors he used in his analysis went beyond a simple cash burn-rate analysis and included online merchandising capabilities, customer service, marketing, and management—mirroring exactly the kinds of things ValueReporting recommends be disclosed. They also represent the kinds of nonfinancial performance drivers identified as highly important in our high-tech survey.

The possibility also exists that through careful prescreening, the investment bank had picked Internet companies that were much more likely to be winners than losers. And perhaps the bank's credibility had partially enabled these companies to raise the large amount of capital needed in such high cash burn-rate companies.

This more charitable interpretation comes under fire because even when analysts shift their recommendations in a negative direction, they sometimes do so only when the horse has left the burning barn quite some time ago. For example, another leading Internet analyst downgraded 11 of the 29 Internet stocks he follows "after the issues have long since plunged in price since their 52-week highs," some by "as much as 90 percent."[41] In reporting on this, *The Wall Street Journal* justifiably asked, "Given that the stock prices have already fallen sharply, isn't it a bit late to be downgrading his recommendations to investors?"[42]

This analyst's view that these recommendations shouldn't be taken as short-term forecasts deserves some sympathy; many, as our surveys point out, are already troubled by excessive short-term-ism in today's markets. Yet, it is still a little troubling when one of the best and the brightest of the lot fails to downgrade Internet stocks until long after their prices have plunged, and even the most novice of individual investors knows it. No one expects analysts to play soothsayer with crystal ball in hand, but no one thinks they should write ancient history either—in Internet time ancient history could be as short as six months.

The positive skew on recommendations, and the tardiness with which recommendations change in a negative direction, comes from the very real pressure analysts feel to "play ball" with the firm's investment banking clients. A study by Womack, Krigman, and Shaw found that 88 percent of the senior executives in their study who had replaced their original underwriter for another firm did so to get better research coverage. In a review of this paper, *The Wall Street Journal* noted that "The findings bolster the view that analysts often win fans among corporate issuers by touting their stocks." If they don't tout the stocks, their firm may lose the issuers as clients, and the analyst may lose access to senior management.[43]

Analysts alone are obviously not the full measure of the problem. It is a structural problem deeply embedded in the complex relationships between investment banks and their corporate clients. Analysts fail to produce objective research, in part, because companies don't want them to. Executives have many ways of sending this signal, including withholding access and investment banking fees. They, too, feel trapped in The Earnings Game of managing and beating quarterly expectations that result in positive stories about their long-term prospects.

Information versus Allocation

Investors long ago lost their naïveté about the pressures analysts feel from their corporate clients. They can judge for themselves whether an analyst has been bullish simply because the company is a client—assuming investors have this information. They can then make their own judgments about whether a stock has gone beyond its true value.

Being able to derive value from this, however, depends on having as much access to the stock as to the information for evaluating its price. What good does it do to know that a stock has become too expensive when you won't have the opportunity to buy it at a lower price?

Yet many individuals and smaller institutional money managers find themselves in just that situation with respect to the really hot IPOs. Institutional investors get the lion's share of allocations in an IPO, with the very largest ones being treated like kings of the jungle. Being a king feels especially good when an issue is oversubscribed by a factor of 10, as can easily happen with a sizzling new one.

If demand runs so high, why not increase the allocations or raise the issuing price of the stock? Here, the investment banks have proven themselves the masters of managing supply and demand. Even though the issuing company may leave a lot of money on the table, it can get a lot of positive buzz when its stock price rockets skyward—at least for a while—and the equity the founders still have in the company shoots up along with it.

A number of studies have shown that this so-called underpricing of IPOs is a deliberate decision.[44] Rather than selling a small number of shares for a high price, or selling a larger number of shares for a lower price, a smaller number of shares are sold for a lower price. This results in a rapid increase in price as a larger number of investors try to get their hands on the stock. When the value of the stock has an immediate run-up in price and the kings of the jungle "flip it" out, they benefit from a one-day pop.

While this doesn't do much for one's long-term track record, a few every quarter can certainly help money managers deal with the short-term performance pressures they themselves are under as many have their performance reviewed every quarter. This is one of the ways investment banks compensate their large institutional money management clients for the lack of objective recommendations and the compromises inherent in having analysts serving corporate clients as well. According to Steven Galbraith, an analyst at Sanford C. Bernstein,[45] one of the few major research houses that doesn't have an investment-banking business, "We suspect deal allocations may have supplanted research in importance as part of the institutional commission structure."[46]

One-day gains on extra-hot IPOs can be impressive indeed. VA Linux saw its shares go up 698 percent on the first day of trading. The Internet community site company theglobe.com went public at $9.00 per share and experienced a first *trade* at $90 per share. On average, the shares of Internet IPOs went up 38 percent on the first day of trading.[47]

Yet today, individual investors get only between 10 and 20 percent of an IPO[48] even though they represent about 60 percent of the NASDAQ's trading volume.[49] For many of them, their first opportunity to buy the stock comes after it has already substantially appreciated, and the institutional investor is ready to sell. Unless one has a very long-term orientation, it's hard to make money buying on the flip.

A recent study found that "extra-hot IPOs" (those with first-day returns in excess of 60 percent) offer the worst future performance.[50] Consider that as of April 26, 2000, the average IPO since the beginning of 1999 had fallen 4.3 percent from its *first day closing price*. Yet, based on the *offering price*, the average IPO had an impressive return of 72.3 percent.[51]

Clearly, those who got in on the ground floor did very well. Those who didn't unhappily rode the elevator to the basement, not the penthouse, perhaps flipping out themselves along the way. Pity the poor individual investor who buys an extra-hot IPO at the end of the first trading day long after the large institutional investors have taken their profit. In the stock market jungle, the food chain is clearly defined.

You Buy, I'll Sell

There's one more twist on the IPO story that further compromises the ability of analysts to do really objective research—at least in appearance if not in fact. Many investment banks have their own venture capital (VC) arms. They make private equity investments in start-up companies and often take these companies public. In 1999, investment banks invested in 305 venture-backed companies, a dramatic increase from their 104 in 1998.[52]

So far, these VC investments have proven very lucrative. In 1999, private equity gains of two major investment banks represented 15 to 20 percent of net income, up from 4 percent in 1998.[53]

On an individual deal basis, VC gains can dwarf underwriting fees. Vignette Corp., an Austin, Texas, company that makes Internet customer-tracking software, paid $6 million in underwriting fees to a syndicate of 13 investment banks that took it public. But three of the banks that invested in the company, including the two lead underwriters on the deal, earned profits of nearly $135 million.[54]

What can investors make of strong buy recommendations from analysts when the private equity parts of their own firms are selling out their positions? It may very well be that the analyst, under no pressure from anyone, truly believes that the company offers a good long-term investment. The VC arm has simply taken well-earned profits on high-risk capital invested a year or more earlier. Perhaps this rings true even if the analyst and executives at the investment bank invested pre-IPO, either directly or through an employee VC fund. Yet, a July 24, 2000, article in *The Wall Street Journal* suggested that "as investing in privately held companies on the verge of going public becomes a new profit center on Wall Street, it also is creating potential conflicts of interest for the banks."[55]

One may experience a little nervousness about these recommendations for the same reason one becomes suspicious about buy recommendations for investment-banking clients. Private equity gains that can dwarf investment-banking fees by a factor of 10 or 100 might tempt even the most righteous. While the investment banks admit the appearance of a conflict of interest, they also insist that none really exists and, besides, they have become accustomed to managing such conflicts.[56]

Others remain skeptical. Ted R. Dintersmith, a principal at Charles River Ventures, a Waltham, Massachusetts, firm that invests in start-up companies, says that Wall Street firms that invest in private companies and then take them public have created a "new investment banking model." He also thinks it "crosses the line" when "you see analysts at investment banking firms issuing aggressive buys at high prices and see the same investment banks aggressively selling. Something about that seems inappropriate."[57]

Let's Make a Deal

The dual, and dueling, role of analysts as part of the investment bank's marketing team for IPOs and as advisor to investors on stocks raises thorny issues. But that pales in comparison to the dual role of analysts as part of the M&A team and as advisors to investors on whether an M&A deal enhances a company's stock price.

How objective can analysts be if they advocate for a deal by talking up the buyer's stock price to make cutting the deal easier or talking up the seller's stock price to prevent a deal or get a better price? Not very much, if you listen to one finance executive who requested anonymity when he observed that he gets more calls directly from the buy-side because today "they're having difficulty determining whether a recommendation is the result of a deal or bona fide research." Not being so bashful, Art Zimmer, a portfolio manager at Denver's Oppenheimer Funds and a former sell-sider, agrees, "All of us feel differently today about most analyst recommendations."[58]

In one celebrated case reported by *Business Week*, critics called to task a prominent telecommunications analyst: "Instead of simply offering up objective opinions about the companies he covers, he is helping those companies make crucial decisions."[59] His critics maintained that his actions amounted to effectively turning the role of the analyst inside out. Describing his close relationships with some well-known telecom CEOs with an appetite for acquisitions, the *Business Week* article noted that "When an analyst is that entwined with a company—at times even helping it to craft its strategy—questions are raised about whether it's possible to offer objective analysis."[60]

This analyst didn't deny his role in "sculpting the industry" based on getting "information from institutions and CEOs." He actually saw this as a "virtuous circle."[61]

Again, in fairness, the institutions were well aware of this, and many applauded him for it, both literally and figuratively, as the article describes. Over the long term, the analyst may very well create a lot of value for shareholders. But this sounds like being more of an excellent investment banker/strategy consultant than it sounds like being an independent research analyst. Both jobs have merit; rolling them into one without creating conflicts proves very difficult.

As with IPOs, companies see opportunities to use the expanded role of the research analyst for their own purpose. Research analysts didn't create their conflicted role all alone. The companies that want analysts to represent their interests rather than investors' have had a heavy hand in creating it, too. Thinking back on The Earnings Game described in Chapter 4, the executive/analyst relationship certainly seems to display aspects of both love and hate.

On the love side, executives try to use analysts to gauge the market's reaction to a deal, usually a big acquisition, but they can do it for divestitures as well. By going public with possible deals, sometimes at the instigation and support of management, the analyst can actually test the waters to see how the market would react to a deal.

Executives can go further than this and use the analyst to actually tee up deals by "suggesting" something that the analyst can "suggest" to another company who can then "suggest back" the response. Useful though this may be, it's awfully tough to referee a game in which one is a key player.

TRY A LITTLE TRANSPARENCY

The multiple roles played by investment banks that create the potential conflicts over truly objective analyses have become deeply ingrained in current practice. The conflicts result from the changing economics of the investment banking business and the ways executives seek to subvert the original calling of analysts.

A lot of money in trading commissions and investment banking fees is at stake here and the banks can be expected to defend the status quo. One aspect of this status quo is that analysts who work for investment banks do a very large percentage of the sell-side research produced today.

Although Arthur Levitt has expressed concern about this, many feel that he will not likely do anything about it through regulation because he can't. As reported by the Dow Jones News Service, "The U.S. Supreme Court ruled in the 1983 *Dirks vs. SEC* case[62] [*sic*] involving disclosure that analysts play an important role in informing the markets of developments, so the commission probably won't tread too heavily on that relationship."[63]

One way of not treading on the relationship, but of changing its very nature, is to change the context in which it exists. To that end, some have even gone so far as to suggest that investment banks should be required to spin off their research operations.

Writing for *TheStreet.com*, Adam Lashinsky suggested, "If SEC Chairman Arthur Levitt really wants to level the playing field for the public instead of offering politically popular sound bites, he'd figure out a way to de-couple investment banking from research. Then analysts would be working all of the time for their brokerage clients, institutional and otherwise."[64]

The wisdom and long-term effectiveness of such a meat-ax approach seems questionable, although other industries have applied it. Even if such a structural solution were offered, implementing it would be difficult. A more measured response, and one certainly in the spirit of this book, is transparency. If the analysts practiced it with the same resolve that we have urged executives to adopt, much of the criticism might be dispelled.

It is not hard to specify the content of such a transparency model. Investment banks should provide full information about the nature of their relationships with the companies their analysts write about. By publicly answering the following few simple questions, they could easily put this model into practice:

- Did a fund and/or individual employees in your firm make a venture capital investment in this company?
- If so, for how much, when, and for what percentage of the company's equity?
- What returns (or losses) have been earned on that investment to date?
- What underwriting, M&A, and other services has your firm performed for this client? When and for how much?

o Is your firm represented on the board of directors or involved in the
   governance or management of the company in any way?

With tongue somewhat in cheek, Lois Yurow, a plain-English consultant, suggests the following language for an investment bank's disclosure
statement: "What we need to tell you is that our famous analyst, Joe Blow,
who just said you should buy ABC company—we underwrote the last five
deals and the company is one of our best clients and if he said anything bad
we'd fire him."[65] Don't expect to ever hear language spoken quite that
plainly. But doesn't it capture the spirit of transparency most eloquently?

Speak to Me

If investors could get such information, in plain words or not, they could decide for themselves how much, if any, to discount the recommendations of a
particular analyst. In reality, investors can already get a good deal, although
certainly not all, of this information from public sources, if they take the
time and acquire the tools to assemble it.

Something that is readily available—and free of charge—at least gets
to the consequences of the relationships in question, if not the relationships
themselves. BulldogResearch.com (www.bulldogresearch.com), a company
started by two former brokers at Lehman Brothers for high-net-worth individuals, uses an objective and sophisticated quantitative analysis to evaluate
and rank some 3,000 research analysts at more than 350 firms. The site
ranks them in terms of the accuracy of their earnings predictions (quarterly
and for the last three years) and the performance of a hypothetical portfolio based on their recommendations.[66] It also identifies the top analysts for
each company and for each industry sector.[67]

This ranking of analysts by their performance directly addresses the issue of whether investment-banking relationships lead to conflicts. If an analyst changes a stock's positive ranking to neutral, hold, market perform, or
sell, BulldogResearch.com removes it from the hypothetical portfolio. As
Heidi Brown, writing in *Forbes*, says, "Although this might sound a bit aggressive, the terms 'neutral,' 'hold,' and 'market perform' are euphemisms that
often mean that analysts no longer like the stock."[68]

BulldogResearach.com offers yet another example of how market
forces themselves will ensure that the market's information needs get met.
Read on for more on this and how two other powerful forces create even
more pressures for greater transparency.

Part Six

Nothing Can Stop Us Now

The truth is found when men are free to pursue it.
Franklin D. Roosevelt
Address at Temple University, Philadelphia

15

Send Lawyers, Guns, and Money

The great consolation in life is to say what one thinks.
Voltaire, Letter, 1765

A fine mess indeed. Here's why—and where—we stand on the eve of a revolution. The lack of a broad set of performance information has contributed to inaccurate stock prices and extreme volatility. Analysts and investors don't get the information they need from companies and rely instead on rumor, innuendo, and gossip.

Companies don't provide timely information—often because their internal information systems can't or just don't produce sufficiently reliable data—even though they agree with the market on the key value drivers in any given industry. Companies also barely touch the tip of the iceberg in providing the information investors want on the risks they take to create value. Few really seriously pay attention to the needs of other stakeholder groups, and for most of them, transparency is a slogan, not an action plan.

To top it all off, the sell-side analysts, who have the skills and time to make sense of the information, if they could get it, are horribly conflicted about which client they really serve.

Given all that, does the ValueReporting Revolution really stand a chance? After all, revolutions don't always succeed. Wanting success and actually achieving it are two very different things.

Despite this brief moment of despair, the conditions seem most felicitous for winning the revolution. Lawyers, guns, and money—that's what the revolution needs, and all three are there for the asking. Regulation. Technology. Enterprise. Combined, these three forces give hope that the markets will one day get the information they need, perhaps even sooner than they think.

It will begin with a little regulatory push. In the United States, the SEC's recently passed Regulation Fair Disclosure (Regulation FD) now requires companies to make material information available to everyone at the same time. The SEC's intent is to create a more level playing field between analysts and investors of all stripes.

Fortunately, the Internet will greatly assist managers in meeting both the letter and the spirit of Regulation FD. Posting information on websites costs relatively little and effectively makes the information available to people all over the world. This alone, however, will not satisfy Regulation FD requirements; the SEC assumes that not everyone has equal access to the Internet. That won't last long.

In the United States, according to a report by David Lake in *The Standard*, the Internet now reaches as many as 134 million people. That's about half the population, compared to the one in ten the Internet reached in 1996. Lake also cites estimates that by 2003, that reach will extend to almost 70 percent of the total U.S. population.[1] Just around the corner waits a set of technical specifications that will make the power of the Internet even greater for users and preparers (companies) alike. It's called Extensible Business Reporting Language (XBRL), but don't let the name throw you off. You'll be speaking it like a native in no time.

The combination of Regulation FD and the Internet enabled by XBRL will create great opportunities for enterprising firms and individuals. Investors, both individual and institutional, will have more information, more quickly than ever. Empowered by technology, they will swiftly sort and analyze it to make smarter and timelier investment decisions.

Sell-side analysts, accounting firms, and software companies can all reap the rewards, too. As a result of Regulation FD and XBRL, they can help investors get wealthier and create value for themselves in the process. Most likely, other new players will also join in and offer up new business models. Some of them may even lead the pack, if not the revolution itself.

SEND IN THE LAWYERS

Here's the regulatory push. On August 10, 2000, the SEC approved a new rule that would, in the words of its chairman, Arthur Levitt, "end the practice of selective disclosure, whereby officials of public companies provide important information to Wall Street insiders prior to making the information available to the general public."[2]

They called it Regulation FD, as in fair disclosure. In his opening statement at the open meeting in which the SEC took its vote, Levitt observed, "High-quality and timely information is the lifeblood of strong, vibrant markets" and "at the very core of investor confidence." He also, once again, decried the recent trend: "As analysts become more and more dependent on the 'inside word,' the pressure to report favorably on a company has grown even greater as analysts seek to protect and guarantee future access to selectively disclosed information." Recognizing that it takes two to tango, Levitt reiterated his concern about executives who "treat material information as a commodity—a way to gain and maintain favor with particular analysts."[3]

The SEC's vote was not a unanimous one—three in favor, one against—a rare occurrence among SEC commissioners. But such an unusual lack of unanimity barely hinted at the controversy surrounding this decision. Even though the chairman made a number of compromises that watered down the original proposal—for example, excluding conversations with customers, suppliers, rating agencies, and the media—the commissioners could not reach total consensus.

A few other mollifications made their way in. Regulation FD applies only to senior executives in the company. Express provisions limit the legal liabilities of companies if executives inadvertently violate the regulation. Foreign companies were excluded completely.

The Firestorm Begins

During the comment period for Regulation FD, which began December 20, 1999, the Commission received 6,000 comments, many on its website, and the vast majority from individual investors. They almost uniformly supported Regulation FD.

The following comment reflects a commonly held view among the growing army of individuals who invest directly, often via the Internet, to take advantage of significantly lower trading costs:

> It alarms me that a debate exits [sic] over public dissemination of sophisticated financial information for traded companies. That the SEC would consider analysts more worthy by not requiring companies to fully disclosure [sic] financial information simultaneously to individual investors is an affront to one of the most highly educated, egalitarian and entrepreneurial populations of the world.[4]

Most securities industry professionals opposed the proposal, one of the most vociferous voices being the Securities Industry Association (SIA). Its Ad Hoc Working Group on Proposed Regulation FD and Legal and Compliance Division filed one of the longest comment letters (nearly 50 pages!). The letter expressed the SIA's support for "the maximum flow of information to issuers, whether directly or through securities analysts and the media." It also noted that the "Internet has given rise to both a widespread demand for more information, and an ability on the part of the issuer to respond to that demand."[5]

The SIA and other opponents of Regulation FD raised a number of legitimate concerns:

o The complexities of enforcing it—what information is really material?

o Potential legal liabilities for companies if executives inadvertently disclose material information on a selective basis

o The likelihood that boatloads of lawyers would get even more involved in the disclosure process in order to limit this liability

o The likely chilling effect this would have on disclosure

"Well-meant, but likely to have the opposite effect of actually decreasing rather than increasing information available to investors," was the essence of the message from the opponents of Regulation FD. The SIA and many of the brokerage firms that weighed in on the issue suggested that encouraging companies to follow "best practices" in corporate disclosure, rather than more strictly regulating it, would have more effect on improving information flow to analysts and investors of all types.

The SIA's letter expressed concern about how the proposed regulation would limit analysts' ability to "pursue an independent line of inquiry and ferret out negative information that management would rather not disclose or would prefer to disclose at a time of its choosing and with its own spin."[6] Such work, the letter suggested, "results in more continuous disclosure, fewer surprises and less volatility." But, it went on, "Analysts cannot do their work nearly as well as they do now if they are forced to do their work, at least when it comes to interaction with issuers, collectively—in a pack," along with everyone else.

The letter also said, "Leveling the playing field for analysts, as among themselves and vis-à-vis the general public, will undermine the great advantages of the current system." This would be unfortunate, it suggested, because "It hardly needs saying that analysts perform a necessary and very valuable function in the U.S. capital market."

Individual investors who read this letter reacted as strongly to it as they did to proposed Regulation FD—although in the opposite direction. One wrote:

I feel that the Ad Hoc Working Group on Proposed Regulation FD and the Legal and Compliance Division of the Securities Industry Association is way out of line in its filing dated April 6th of this year. The whole thing smells of analysts fearful of losing their "old boy" network. . . . Finally, I question the claim that "it hardly needs saying that analysts perform a necessary and valuable function in the U.S. capital markets." I think that if it is true, it certainly does need some saying, because you'll be hard pressed to convince me otherwise. What exactly do they do that is so beneficial?[7]

The Sky Is Falling! The Sky Is Falling!

Reactions to the adoption of Regulation FD were swift and predictable. Many individual investors and those who advocate their interests were delighted. Steve Chanecka, the founder and chairman of Informed Investors, Inc. and InformedInvestor.com, both devoted to ensuring that individuals have access to executives and information, applauded the ruling.[8] So did Nilus Mattive at individualinvestor.com: "I'm happy to report," Mattive wrote, "that Arthur Levitt and the SEC recently passed a ruling that benefits individual investors by discouraging the practice of selective disclosure."[9]

Others, while pleased, didn't think Regulation FD went nearly far enough. One said, "This proposal is a half measure at best," and another remarked, "What's been interesting is how violently the coddled securities industry has responded to this attack."[10]

Most groups representing securities industry professionals and corporations predicted problems, if not disaster:

- *"It levels the playing field, but it takes the playing field down about five notches."* Gary Lapidus, automotive analyst at Goldman, Sachs.[11]
- *"People say they want a more level playing field. I'm just afraid that it will be empty, that the sum of information they receive will be substantially diminished."* Stuart Kaswell, senior vice president and general counsel of the Securities Industry Association.[12]
- *"Although well intentioned, this action will have the opposite effect of what it is intended to do. Corporations will almost certainly curtail the information flow to the market to avoid having to decide 'on the spot' whether certain information will be deemed to be material after the fact by the SEC."* Michael S. Caccese, senior vice president and general counsel of the Association for Investment Management and Research.[13]

Apparently confirming such concerns, stories soon appeared citing examples of companies that had started to provide less information to analysts and institutional investors than they had in the past.[14] For some, this was "I told you so." For others, it offered evidence that Regulation FD was already working, even though it wouldn't go into effect for another few months.

According to Mark Coker, president of BestCalls.com, an organization that broadcasts company conference calls on the Internet at no cost to company shareholders, "If the new rule has a chilling effect on selective disclosure, that's great."[15]

What It Really Means

At this writing, it's been only a month since Regulation FD gained approval. Time will tell its ultimate consequences. That said, we'll go out on a limb a bit and make some modest predictions, on which we'll offer an opinion as well.

By itself, Regulation FD will not create the Elysian, level playing field so many individual investors want. Even if companies wholeheartedly embrace Regulation FD, both in practice and in the spirit of its intent, the amount of information investors can gather, how quickly they can collect it, and the speed and depth at which they can analyze it will vary in proportion to the resources available to them. Some leveling will no doubt occur, but the field will remain far from leveled enough for a fair tennis match to begin.

Nor will this leveling hamstring the analysts who look to add knowledge value instead of information value. Analysts will adapt soon enough to the modest restrictions placed on the access to companies they have for so long enjoyed. Some will look for ways around the new rules. Others will accept them and look for other ways to add value—for example, by doing more analysis.

Visionary analysts may even see the opportunity they have to escape some of the pressures that companies put on them to offer favorable views and that large institutional clients exert to give them early scoops. Companies will have less ability to favor analysts favorable to them, and clients will have fewer expectations about getting the scoops.

This leaves more time for analysts to do what analysts do best—analyze. Need we offer our opinion on that? It's a good thing, and so is Regulation FD. With respect to the SIA, we think that real analysis focuses on far more than ferreting out negative information that companies are reluctant to provide.

Recognizing that companies have only now begun to figure out how to play by the new rules, we also think Regulation FD creates a real opportunity for them as well. Companies can use it to start changing some other rules—the rules of The Earnings Game. No longer will they need to curry the favor of analysts through privileged access in their attempts to manage expectations about quarterly earnings and gain favorable reports in order to keep their stock price as high as possible.

Instead, executives should embrace the ValueReporting Revolution. In doing so, they will also embrace the spirit and not just the letter of Regulation FD. This means that executives should:

- Make all material information available as quickly as possible to everyone at the same time, both to comply with the regulation and because it's the right thing to do
- Make sure they have the tools available to do that, including using all relevant communications channels and actually harnessing the power of the Internet
- Develop sound measurement methodologies for the key nonfinancial value drivers and intangible assets that the market finds important
- Make the resulting quality information available in an organized and structured communications process

Seen in this light, Regulation FD actually offers executives the opportunity to better serve their shareholders' information needs. ValueReporting gives them the information content. Regulation FD offers a useful guideline for how to communicate it.

In return for embracing ValueReporting and Regulation FD, executives should expect the market—the whole market—to set stock prices based on performance. Over time and in the end, only performance matters. Companies should embrace that belief every day and in every way they communicate to shareholders and all other stakeholders. It's the right thing to do.

BRING GUNS

Revolutions shift the balance of power. Winning them requires taking advantage of the best and most relevant technologies. In the ValueReporting Revolution, the well-known Internet and the nearly unknown XBRL offer the most power and relevance of all.

The SIA, in its April 6, 2000, letter to the SEC, which so many individual investors enjoyed reading and commenting on, pointed out that "The Commission itself deserves credit for improvement in the flow of information."[16] It cited a recent survey conducted by the National Investor Relations Institute (NIRI) that by the year 2000, 90 percent of companies planned to conduct conference calls and 90 percent of them planned to provide access to individuals. It argued that more companies were following the clear trend toward providing information to more people, and that "perhaps the most important reason is technology." True enough, but companies have only begun to tap the power of technology to communicate *with* rather than simply *to* the market.

George Gilder, technology commentator and author of the *Gilder Technology Report*, says that in order to fully "realize the benefits of the World Wide Web on those information markets that focus on stocks, the current rules on the disclosure of material information should be rescinded."[17] He also says, "Inside information—the flow of intimate detail about the progress of technologies and product tests and research and development and daily sales data—is in fact the only force that makes any long-term difference in stock performance." Using "the promise of the Internet" for "the instant spread of information" that comes from "deep inside companies" can do this.

This would result in "a steady outpouring of knowledge—some of it hype, some confusing, most of it ambiguous like business life itself." In Gilder's brave new "technological utopia," the irrationality and volatility in today's markets that result from well-meaning but misguided efforts to create a level playing field would be replaced by "the intelligent investment of capital."

Chapter 11 supports Gilder's opinion that the vast potential of the Internet remains largely untapped. It is also useful to look at the market through a pure technological lens, as he does.

Do It on the Internet

Irate at being denied access to a conference call held by Legato Systems, a software company that backs up and recovers computer data, Mark Coker started BestCalls.com in March 1999. His website tracks such conference calls and lobbies companies for more open disclosure. Other websites, such as Vcall, Broadcast.com,[18] PR Newswire, and the Corporate Communications Broadcast Network, help companies conduct Internet broadcasts, or Webcasts, of conference calls.

The growing number of high-speed modems combined with streaming video plug-ins has dramatically reduced the cost to companies of such "cybercasts" from $3,500 or more per event to around $700, which includes 90 days of archiving and increased availability of the content to the investing public.[19] One provider, Vcall, reports hosting calls with as many as 15,000 participants.[20] Some of the prominent companies that provide real-time access to sessions with analysts include Cisco Systems, Microsoft, and Intel. Declining costs mean that soon all companies will be able to afford to Webcast, creating a major opportunity for the vast majority of less visible companies to get more market attention.

With the passage of Regulation FD, virtually every public company will inevitably adopt this practice. Companies that fail to do so will put themselves at a competitive disadvantage as rivals go live on the Internet. They will also miss the opportunity to provide timely, accurate, and relevant information to investors. Coker of BestCalls.com identifies this as the third step in the "three stages of enlightenment" that companies go through in the process of deciding to go live with their calls:

- *Stage 1:* Paralysis from fear of what might happen by letting people listen
- *Stage 2:* Opening up calls out of fear of private or SEC lawsuits on selective disclosure
- *Stage 3:* Realizing that opening up calls gives them the opportunity to market their company to long-term investors and to deal with rumormongering and speculation in Internet chat rooms[21]

As companies adapt to and adopt this technology, they will enjoy a more stable investor base because fewer investors will make decisions based largely on chat room conversations and rumors. But rumors will never go away completely. In fact, some capital market virtual communities may actually encourage more rumors. Laudable though improved access is, BestCalls.com offers only one example of the many ways companies could tap the Internet to more fully and quickly inform investors.

Many companies have already made the initial foray into Internet reporting, but nearly all of their efforts thus far have been only electronic extensions of the Paper Paradigm described in Chapter 11. They simply post electronic versions of paper documents on their websites using Adobe® Acrobat® and Hypertext Markup Language (HTML) files. The most common examples include their annual reports, 10-K filings, and presentations given to analysts and investors.

These electronic proxies for paper create burdens for investors who want to analyze the information they contain. The interested investors must manually reenter the individual data into whatever software program they're using. If they want to perform an analysis across a number of companies, they must go through the same laborious process at all the other companies' websites.

In fairness, a number of sites actually assist the user with some level of financial analysis, including EDGAR Online (www.edgar-online.com), Microsoft's Research Wizard (www.moneycentral.msn.com/investor/research/wizards/SRW.asp), and http://cbs.marketwatch.com. Useful as these sites are, they typically offer financial information purchased from aggregators and distributors that have "normalized" the data. They must normalize to make a basic level of comparative analysis possible, but doing so results in some apples-to-oranges comparisons, or at least Red Delicious to McIntosh.

Moving Right Along

Companies have moved rapidly to leverage at least a bit of the Internet's power to speed up and expand their basic disclosure practices. Painful as the move has been for some companies, they've really only taken baby steps. As mentioned earlier, in the majority of these steps, they've simply converted current practices based on the Paper Paradigm onto the Internet platform. Transferring information and disclosure practices from paper to the Internet is like using an Exocet missile to kill a mosquito. It doesn't even come close to maximizing the Internet's potential for rapidly disseminating relevant information to investors and other stakeholder groups.

Although executives today could seize the initiative and go much further much faster than others have gone before, they need something else before they can unleash the full power of the Internet for their reporting purposes.

What they're missing is an enabling technology called Extensible Markup Language (XML). The Internet, as companies know it today, is itself constrained by current practice in how information is formatted and coded. It's the Paper Paradigm again, using the Internet's current primary language, HTML.

Using HTML intertwines the content and formatting of information contained in a single document. That works (barely), but in real-world terms, it is the equivalent of every automobile manufacturer having its own proprietary brand of gasoline formulated for only its cars. Drivers would have to search for a specialized gas station every time they needed a fill-up. Soon, they would become frustrated and would start demanding the convenience of a universal brand of gasoline. In the emerging e-business world, this universal gasoline is called the Extensible Markup Language or XML.[22] In its application in the supply chain for corporate reporting, it goes by XBRL.

If you have a highly refined palate that can appreciate technology alphabet soup, read on. If not, read the sidebar "An XBRL Primer" now.

E-Business Comes to Corporate Reporting

It is often hard to separate XML hype from its reality. Some have proclaimed XML a technological innovation on par with the Internet itself, the lightbulb, and no less than the standard rail gauge that ensured the success of transcontinental railroads. In the brief time since the World Wide Web Consortium (www.w3.org) recommended XML's adoption in February 1998, every major software developer has promised to support it.

Although still in its infancy, XML has ignited into a "brushfire" technology. Every ERP (enterprise resource planning) vendor has already integrated XML into its software environment. Several hundred supply chain consortia across a wide range of industries and infrastructure channels are working to create their own adaptations of XML, to truly make it the language of e-business (for progress updates on XML efforts, go to www.xml.org).

Much sooner than later, every company will have to do business the XML way, or it won't do business at all. The same thing will happen with XBRL. Companies that can't report in XBRL won't do business with the capital markets.

Imagine that world: all companies using XBRL to communicate with shareholders and other stakeholders. What would it look like? Predicting the future consequences of XBRL can be no more certain than with Regulation FD. But having already gone out on a limb with the lawyers on Regulation FD, we might as well put on our guns with some speculation about the general characteristics of the future business world. Three stand out as particularly important in terms of XBRL:

1. The need for greater and greater speed
2. The desire to perform more and more analysis
3. The increasing importance of alliances, joint ventures, and other such "soft contracting" relationships

An XBRL Primer

To understand XBRL, you must first understand that it is just a specific application of XML developed for use in the corporate reporting supply chain.[a] XML stands for Extensible Markup Language (XML), the next big step in Internet technology after Hypertext Markup Language (HTML).[b]

HTML makes access to information easier by providing blueprints and formats for display. HTML, however, has a serious weakness. It doesn't address the *context* of the information within the document. It describes the *information* within the document in a way that reflects the Paper Paradigm.

For example, if you look at a piece of paper that has "Purchase Order" printed at the top and lots of numbers printed below, you can interpret those numbers in context. You can pretty easily find out how many items of a certain product a particular customer has ordered for a certain price, plus the discount they get for early payment. If, however, you saw those same numbers on an otherwise blank piece of paper, you wouldn't have any idea what they meant because you wouldn't have the context.

XML electronically provides context for every single number or piece of information, thereby enabling any user (even nonhuman, electronic ones) to know what it represents and, therefore, in many cases how to use it. XML serves as sort of a bar code for information on the Internet.

XML and HTML both use "tags," instructions contained within angle brackets ("<" and ">"), to annotate the content of the files. The big difference between XML and HTML is that with HTML, the tags are limited to instructions for software (usually of the Web-browsing variety) on how to present the information content in a particular format. It says things like "bold this," "italicize that," "put that in a table."

XML comes tagged with definitions that describe the individual pieces of data at a much more detailed, "molecular" level regardless of the format in which they are presented. These tags introduce each item and tell its story; for example, a number from a purchase order might say, "Hi there, I'm the 'units' number for an order of PCs at $1,000 apiece, and my number is 500."

Because XML allows business partners of all kinds to exchange information for virtually any type of transaction over the Web, it is rapidly becoming the *lingua franca* of e-business. Regardless of whose information system produces the data, companies can conduct business over the Internet easily and seamlessly. In essence, XML allows the integration of applications across the entire supply chain.

XML can also have as much relevance to a company's relationship with its shareholders as it does to its relationships with suppliers and customers. A consortium (www.xbrl.org) founded and sponsored by the American Institute of Certified Public Accountants (AICPA, www.aicpa.org) has begun developing a special XML dialect called "Extensible Business Reporting Language" (XBRL) that includes tags for business reporting data. Members of this consortium include com-

(Continued)

panies, accounting firms, the accounting profession itself, institutional investors, investment-banking firms, software vendors, and application service providers (ASPs) from around the world.

Current efforts to develop XBRL have focused on definitions relating to the existing accounting standards used in various countries, U.S. GAAP and IAS, for example. Plans call for extending that focus into other areas including regulatory reports, tax returns, credit reports and applications, journal entries, and business events.

Guess what? XBRL could also serve as the Internet platform for the nonfinancial value drivers discussed throughout this book, even for qualitative information. But only when standards are developed for these nonfinancial measures, similar to those for financial measures, can the full benefits of XBRL be realized in the ValueReporting environment.

---

a. Mike Willis, "Corporate Communications for the 21st Century," white paper (New York: PricewaterhouseCoopers, October 2000).
b. Ibid.

The Need for Speed

Virtually everyone must learn to live in Internet time. XBRL will help the corporate reporting world do that. A lot of people talk about "real-time reporting," but there's a big difference between real-time information and real-time use of it. A number of companies, Cisco Systems for example, can provide real-time reporting through its "virtual close," which makes management information available on a continuous (or pretty close to continuous) basis. Even if users today could get information on a real-time basis, they would still have to take it in the format they get it and then transform it into the format in which they plan to use it. They typically do this through an error-prone manual process.

This process takes time—real time—and creates lag time between reporting the information and using it. Users sometimes simply run out of time. The great virtue of XBRL is that it vastly reduces the time-consuming and clumsy transformation process. With XBRL, information users (human or electronic) can analyze information as soon as they get it, whoever they are, wherever they are—just as management does when internal information systems function properly. That's real speed.

Not quite sure about those little parenthetical hints about human and nonhuman information users? In the Internet world, all inhabitants are not necessarily human. Creatures, often referred to as "smart agents," toil there too and can use information for their own purposes. Some obvious examples include automated credit approval and dynamic loan pricing based on contractual indicators, rebalancing of stock portfolios, treasury risk management, and automated inquiries from analysts and investors for specific information. Remember the bar scene from one of the *Star Wars* movies? In the Internet version, think twice before you make eye contact with one of these nonhuman e-entities.

Back to Analysis

Once people (and e-entities) really have their hands on information, they want to analyze it. They turn into one of those multipurpose kitchen gadgets sold on late-night infomercials. They want to slice information and dice it and combine it with other information and slice and dice it some more. When they get their information in XBRL form, at the data element level, they can analyze to their hearts' content.

Software developers already know this and have begun creating tools to enable investors to chop away. You can already easily see how future software products will enable users to do a hyper-multidimensional spreadsheet analysis at whatever level of detail they desire using years of a company's financial performance, and then compare it to peers.

This is only the beginning. Since we're already in the realm of imagination, imagine that the standards discussed in Chapter 13 also exist—at least for many industries on key nonfinancial value drivers. Those standards could be XBRL-icized, just like the financial ones. Managers, analysts, individual investors, institutional investors, and e-entities could propose and test business models (remember Chapter 1?) of all the relationships between the key value drivers in an industry or even a company. They would finally know, for example, whether the relationship between customer retention and stock price has significance, whether it's linear, and (testing your mathematical memory here) the slope of the line.

Why stop there? This analysis can be souped up (to continue the kitchen analogy), by using expert systems, smart agents that perform data searches, neural nets, relational databases, and graphical user interfaces—technologies that already exist and are rapidly improving every day. Users could pull in information of any kind (quantitative, qualitative, audio, and video), analyze it in all kinds of ways, and present the results in a multimedia format on a multitude of information delivery devices. Just around the corner, the Jetsons will look like the Flintstones.

Consider a scenario that could easily happen and most probably will. Today, modeling and analytical work typically use data loaded into software programs installed on personal computers (PCs). With so much else already moving to the Web, why not move this work there too? Envision industry-oriented websites or sites dedicated to a particular analytical approach. You could further imagine that some sites would take an approach similar to what Napster did with music CDs, and start sharing financial and business modeling and analysis tools with everyone. Talk about democratization.

Members of user communities would go to these websites where all the analytical tools and focused data access would reside. Users could then do their Veg-O-Matic thing on the Internet. These sites would also have links and connectivity to any other sites that have relevant data, giving the users the Web at their fingertips, being careful, of course, not to chop them. Some of these sites might be free. Others would charge a royalty, and the most popular sites would make the most money—the subject of the last section of this chapter.

Entangling Alliances

In a world filled with strategic alliances, joint ventures, outsourcing of core functions, ASPs, and e-business integrated supply chains, there's the fundamental question about what entity—the company or the company and any combination of its business partners for example—is relevant to shareholders or other stakeholders. With XBRL, users could look at the performance of the entity defined in many different ways.

For example, a user might want to know the aggregate profit of all of a company's strategic alliances and whether the individual companies that perform better have higher employee satisfaction scores and brand recognition. Today such an analysis could hardly happen, even for financial results. (Chapter 6 discusses why.) With enhanced standards and XBRL, users could analyze just about anything they want with very little huff or puff.

Will This *Really* Happen?

Probably. As a direct result of their memberships in XBRL, a number of leading companies already report, or at least have committed to reporting, their financial results in XBRL. Some come from the high-tech sector—Microsoft, IBM, Oracle, Peoplesoft, Sage, and Hyperion, for example. Others include financial institutions like J.P. Morgan, Morgan Stanley Dean Witter, and Fidelity Investment Funds.

Not all of them reside in the United States—for example, Germany's SAP, the United Kingdom's Reuters, and Japan's NEC. A number of the members of the XBRL consortium believe that by 2005 a majority of the Global *Fortune* 1,000 will have begun reporting on their websites using XBRL files for the benefit of their shareholders—as well as themselves.

No predictions here about exactly when this will happen, but happen it will. Companies that don't make themselves a part of the happening will become companies that might happen to just go away. Use the XBRL gun before someone uses it on you.

SEND MONEY

Software developers and ASPs have already invested in developing products that will enable users to take full advantage of XBRL-based reporting. They clearly anticipate that there's money in it for them.

They aren't the only ones. Others can also satisfy investors' needs for analysis of and analytical tools for the flood of information that ValueReporting, Regulation FD, and XBRL will make available. To the extent that sell-side analysts fail to satisfy investors with their analyses, investors have two choices. They can analyze themselves, or they can buy analysis from others. Both are happening. Both create opportunities for new products and services. Free enterprise will thrive during and after the ValueReporting Revolution.

Do It Yourself

For many years, institutional investors have hired in-house "buy-side analysts" to produce research exclusively for their own use. Many of these analysts have migrated from sell-side firms for the opportunity to do truly independent research, albeit usually for less money.

Scudder Kemper, for example, has 55 research analysts for its $100 billion portfolio. The very largest funds have three or four times as many, rivaling the largest investment banks in number of analysts and breadth of industries covered. To the extent that the money management industry consolidates, the economics of "making" rather than "buying" research will become increasingly attractive.

This has profound implications for the market. Understanding how well a company performs on measures that truly create long-term value would appeal more to most investors than anticipating next quarter's earnings. Doing the fundamental analysis that will inform investors in the manner they wish to become accustomed requires the kind of information that ValueReporting provides. The very real "demand pull" from the large institutional investors will become greater as their clout increases because they can take larger and larger positions as a result of their increasing scale—more fuel for the revolutionary fire.

Find Another Supplier

No law says that only investment banks can provide research on companies, although they have vast resources and the talent to do it well. Other organizations also have capabilities they can use to produce research of great value to investors—for example, strategy consulting firms like Bain, Boston Consulting Group, McKinsey, and Monitor. Large institutional investors occasionally use such firms to address specific questions.

The research they can provide offers two distinct advantages:

1. It is completely customized and addresses exactly the precise questions the investor wants answered.
2. Once investors buy it, they own it; it's completely proprietary.

These advantages mean that investors can get objective input directly relevant to their own particular investment strategy. Rather than taking a general research report issued to the world and then picking the brain of the analyst who wrote it, investors can specify exactly what type of analysis they want in the first place.

Second, this research yields insights that can generate superior investment returns, which won't be traded down as others jump in. Rather than relying on the first call from an analyst with a tip about this quarter's earnings, investors get insights that are relevant to long-term value creation.

Another source of analysis includes independent research firms that specialize in certain industries—Forrester, Gartner, Giga Information Group, and META Group, for example. John Kattar, senior vice president and director of U.S. equities at The Boston Company Asset Management, mentioned all of these firms as "pretty high value-added for what I look for and good at identifying the long-term trends in technology."

Unlike the strategy firms, who primarily do client-specific projects, these independent research firms sell their research to a broad group of clients. Although it is not proprietary, such research provides insights into long-term value drivers—the measures our high-tech survey identified as important (see www.valuereporting.com for more on that). Investors can then combine insights gained from that research with their own opinions and valuation analysis to make their investment decisions.

Buying research offers a variable cost advantage. If investors find the research worthwhile, they will continue to buy it. If they don't, they'll simply stop.

The traditional "soft dollar" pricing structure in the investment management industry has somewhat constrained investors from buying independent research. "Soft dollar" means research is purchased through trading commissions that are allocated on an annual basis. Even with this constraint, investors have found ways to get what they want by directing brokerage firms to write hard-dollar checks for independent research. The largest money managers, especially, have the clout to get them to do it.

Again, no predictions about whether and how much soft-dollar trading commissions paid to brokerage firms for sell-side analysis will shift to hard-dollar payments for research from in-house buy-side analysts or other independent providers. But if that will add more value than the sell-side research does, economic forces will prevail as they always do. Pricing structures will adapt, and money will flow to where the most value resides.

Organizations that see an opportunity here will find ways to serve the needs of institutional investors. New organizations with new business models for supplying independent analysis may also emerge. The users of research spend billions of dollars on the sell-side approach and billions more beyond that. The market is big and growing. This growth rate will accelerate as the revolution takes hold and the market gains access to more information that it must analyze to understand. Investors spend wisely when they buy a high-quality research product that helps yield superior returns.

Individual Investors, Join In

Very few individuals have the required resources to hire their own analysts or to buy research from others. This doesn't mean they have to stay out in the cold. The percentage of equity assets owned by individuals who invest directly has grown rapidly in the United States, and as an equity culture spreads, the same will happen in other countries. In the aggregate, individuals will invest hundreds of billions or trillions in equities.

Different business models and different distribution channels will probably emerge to meet their needs. Independent research firms, news organizations, third-party database companies, software companies, and ASPs could all fit the bill by supplying information, analysis, and analytical tools that individuals will pay good money for to help them get a better return on their investments.

This has already happened. iExchange.com, which bills itself as "an innovative source of investment ideas and insights,"[23] invites individuals, whether professional analysts or avid amateurs, to register on iExchange.com's website and post their stock picks. iExchange ranks the stocks according to such measures as average rate of return, directional accuracy, and predictive accuracy. Investors who want deeper insights can then purchase more detailed reports for a modest fee, which gives high-performing analysts an opportunity to get paid for their advice.

Interestingly, Ernst & Young certifies "that iExchange establishes and maintains effective controls over its Scoring and Payment Systems."[24] So here's an Internet-based, market-driven solution to providing investment advice, one that involves certification by a Big Five accounting firm. "Bring accountants, guns, and money," we might say, although no one has written that song yet!

Under Pressure

None of this suggests counting out the investment banks just yet. We would be the last to do so, especially since one of the authors wrote a highly complimentary book about them more than 10 years ago.[25] Despite the criticisms of some of their practices, investment banks have demonstrated the flexibility, adaptability, and willingness to take risks over the past 30 years. They have proven themselves remarkably resilient when markets change, finding new opportunities and creating new products as old ones have diminished and margins have come down. Accounting firms have much to learn from them.

The investment banks will, no doubt, have the opportunity to prove their resiliency once more by addressing the questions about the value of the research they produce. A 10-year bull market in trading, high-technology IPOs, and mergers and acquisitions has funded burgeoning research budgets. This has resulted in built-in structural conflicts, but at least the wolf has been kept from the door.

Bull markets don't last forever, however, and new competitors have sprung up to attack the lucrative businesses the investment banks have today. Electronic communication networks (ECNs) like Archipelago, Datek, and Instinet continue to push down the already greatly diminished trading margins for institutional investors. Companies like E*Trade and Charles Schwab put pressure on commissions for retail trades, which can now go as low as $9.95 or as much as 90 percent lower than commissions once were. At least one company even offers trading at no charge. Most of the large investment banks have chosen to establish their own Internet channels, reducing the average commission per trade in the process.

New investment banks, like W.R. Hambrecht & Co. and Wit Sound-View Group, both of which focus on the Internet and technology sectors, have put pressure on IPO margins by offering online Dutch auctions. Hambrecht & Co., for example, says that it's "leveraging technology to bring transparency to capital formation and securities exchange processes."[26] This approach means higher prices for the issuers and simultaneously opens up the process to individual investors, who can then buy at the opening and receive research support after the issue.

These underwriting services come at a lower cost than traditionally charged. A description of Hambrecht & Co. at www.hoovers.com, a website specializing in providing information about sources of information to investors, says that it "charges less than the 7 percent levied by investment banks."[27]

What will the investment banks do if the combination of a bear market and new competitors takes away a lot of the profits they use today to pay for their expensive research functions? As pointed out by Ted Truscott, managing director and co-director of equities at Scudder Kemper Investments, "Margins in financial services will fall, just nobody knows when and by how much," but when they do, "What will happen to the expensive research function?"

Truscott suggests one possibility. The investment banks may unbundle research from sales and trading. "Wall Street will render the existing sales and trading model extinct because research is so deeply compromised," he says. Unbundling could bode well for Wall Street even if the soft-dollar commission structure stays in place.

Truscott imagines a scenario in which "Wall Street unbundled and let me decide to pay five cents a share if I use the research and one cent a share if I don't." In this situation, firms would have a real incentive to find ways to provide high-quality research that investors perceived as truly objective and independent. Truscott thought this could easily happen because "a case can be made for any of the top four firms to have great research."

Out of the Woods?

Not surprisingly, the investment banks have already begun to respond to the challenge. On September 12, 2000, seven of the world's largest (The Goldman Sachs Group, Merrill Lynch, Morgan Stanley Dean Witter, Salomon Smith Barney, Credit Suisse First Boston, Deutsche Bank Alex. Brown, and UBS Warburg) announced the creation of TheMarkets.com. A press release described the creation as "an information-rich portal for institutional investors that offers commingled equity research, new issue information, news, and market data, as well as easy direct-access to the proprietary Web-sites of the participants."[28]

This site will also provide "comprehensive personalization tools" that "will permit portfolio managers, analysts, and other clients to organize, prioritize, and filter the vast amount of information that comes their way daily."[29] And all of this in real time, of course.

What's especially interesting about TheMarkets.com is that it will allow institutional investors to very easily compare the recommendations of analysts for any given company and to sort out for themselves whether biases exist, although this was certainly not the collaborating founders' primary intention.

It is also interesting to note how much this site charges the institutional clients of the investment banks that formed it. It's free to them, under the theory that they already pay for the research through trading commissions. Yet, in the spirit of looking forward, one can't help but wonder if this doesn't simply foreshadow the consolidation of the research function in one place, solving both the cost and the objectivity problems at the same time. Imagine the value of a shared pool of The Street's best analysts, beholden to no particular investment bank, and therefore removed from a company's pressures to say less or different than what the analyst really means. Now that's a revolution in itself!

Whatever happens here, the investment banks will be as aware of market forces as anybody else will. You can bet they will look hard for ways to respond.

Let the revolution begin!

Epilogue

A Call to Arms

These proceedings may at first appear strange and difficult; but, like all other steps which we have already passed over, will in a little time become familiar and agreeable; and, until an independence is declared, the Continent will feel itself like a man who continues putting off some unpleasant business from day to day, yet knows it must be done, hates to set about it, wishes it over, and is continually haunted with the thoughts of its necessity.
Thomas Paine, Common Sense
February 14, 1776

The end of a book. The beginning of a revolution. Now you must decide. When and how will you take your place in the ValueReporting Revolution?

o *Regulators.* You hold high office in the current regime. Lend your wisdom and good counsel. But let the people lead the revolution.

o *Analysts.* You do the research that can enlighten investors. How can you lose in a revolution that gives you more to do your job better? Come with us.

o *Technologists.* You're a revolution unto yourselves. Thanks for inviting us to yours. Tell us once more, how do you spell XBRL?

o *Accountants and accounting firms.* You were the heroes of an earlier revolution. Look back at your medals with pride. Turn around. There are many more still to be won.

o *Individual investors.* Get your guns. Grab the cake and eat it too. You have everything to gain and nothing—literally nothing—to lose.

o *Institutional investors.* You are the customer. You already have the ammunition. Put it to good use. Demand the information you need and deserve.

o *All other stakeholders.* Continue to trust your hearts and your minds. But keep your eyes and ears open. You will like what you see and hear.

- *Boards of directors.* The revolution needs strong leadership. It should and must come from you. You really have no choice but to lead.
- *Corporate executives.* Enlist today. Prove your worth. Get full credit for the value you create. Deep in your heart, you know it is right.
- *Everyone.* Log on to the revolution at www.valuereporting.com

Notes

PROLOGUE   A MANIFESTO FOR THE SECOND REVOLUTION

1. Robert G. Eccles, "The Performance Measurement Manifesto," *Harvard Business Review* 69 (January–February 1991): 131–137.
2. Ibid.

CHAPTER 1   COMMON SENSE

1. Robert G. Eccles, "The Performance Measurement Manifesto," *Harvard Business Review* 69 (January–February 1991): 131–137.
2. Robert S. Kaplan and David P. Norton, "The Balanced Scorecard—Measures That Drive Performance," *Harvard Business Review* 70 (January–February 1992): 71–79.
3. Lawrence S. Maisel, "Performance Measurement: The Balanced Scorecard Approach," *Journal of Cost Management* (Summer 1992): 47–52.
4. See, for example, Robert G. Eccles and Philip J. Pyburn, "Creating a Comprehensive System to Measure Performance," *Management Accounting* 74 (October 1992): 41–44; Robert S. Kaplan and David P. Norton, "Putting the Balanced Scorecard to Work," *Harvard Business Review* 71 (September–October 1993): 134–42; Robert S. Kaplan and David P. Norton, *The Balanced Scorecard* (Boston: Harvard Business School Press, 1996); Robert S. Kaplan and David P. Norton, "Using the Balanced Scorecard as a Strategic Management System," *Harvard Business Review* 74 (January–February 1996): 75–85; and, most recently, Nils-Goran Olve, Jan Roy, and Magnus Wetter, *Performance Drivers: A Practical Guide to Using the Balanced Scorecard* (New York: John Wiley & Sons, 1999).
5. Kaplan and Norton, *The Balanced Scorecard.*
6. Olve, Roy, and Wetter, *Performance Drivers: A Practical Guide to Using the Balanced Scorecard.*
7. Mark A. Mowrey, "Thank You, Please Come Again," *The Industry Standard* 3 (March 27, 2000): 196–97. See also: www.thestandard.com/article/article_print/1,1153,13016,00.html
8. Christopher D. Ittner and David E. Larcker, "Are Non-Financial Measures Leading Indicators of Financial Performance? An Analysis of Customer Satisfaction," *Journal of Accounting Research: Studies on Enhancing the Financial Reporting Model,* 36 supplement (1998): 1–35.

9. Rory Morgan, "A Consumer-Oriented Framework of Brand Equity and Loyalty," *The International Journal of Market Research* 42 (Winter 1999): 65; and Robert Bittlestone, Metapraxis Ltd., "Linking Consumer Behaviour to Shareholder Value."

10. Peter Miller and Ted O'Leary, "ValueReporting and the Information Ecosystem," a study funded by PricewaterhouseCoopers.

11. Ibid.

12. Anthony J. Rucci, Steven P. Kirn, and Richard T. Quinn, "The Employee-Customer-Profit Chain at Sears," *Harvard Business Review* 76 (January–February 1998): 82–97.

13. Ibid., 86, 88.

14. Ibid., 89.

15. Ibid., 91.

16. This comment and subsequent comments by both Walter Kielholz and John Fitzpatrick were made in interviews conducted by Robert G. Eccles in August and November 2000.

CHAPTER 2   WHERE HAS ALL THE VALUE GONE?

1. Paul Krugman, "Roller-Coaster Markets," *The New York Times*, April 5, 2000, A23.

2. Gregory Zuckerman and E.S. Browning, "Stocks Fall Off a Cliff—and Climb Back: NASDAQ, Dow Drop Over 500, Reverse Course," *The Wall Street Journal*, April 5, 2000, C1.

3. "Mercurial Markets," *The New York Times* (editorial), April 5, 2000, 22.

4. Andrew Hill, "A White-Knuckle Ride: Extreme Volatility May Be Due to the Nervousness of Investment Institutions Rather Than Small Shareholders," *Financial Times*, April 6, 2000, 23. See also www.globalarchive.ft.com/search-components/index.jsp

5. Andrew Hill and Gerard Baker, "A Test of Nerves," *Financial Times*, April 17, 2000, 18.

6. E.S. Browning, "After Market's Wild Quarter, Future Is Just a Guess," *The Wall Street Journal*, April 3, 2000, C1.

7. Pui-Wing Tam, Bridget O'Brian, and Aaron Lucchetti, "The Diary of a Mad Quarter: Tech-Stock Performance Took Funds for a Ride; Here's an Insider's Look," *The Wall Street Journal*, April 10, 2000, R1, R19–20.

8. Zuckerman and Browning, "Stocks Fall Off a Cliff."

9. Deborah Stern, "US Tech Stocks Takes a Caning," *ABIX—Australasian Business Intelligence: The Age 5*, April 6, 2000, 5.

10. John Yang, "Gates in the Poor House?" *The E-Meter*, April 17, 2000, 76.

11. Value based on shares outstanding as of 7/6/00 from www.exchange-data.com and historical prices from http://finance.yahoo.com

12. Scott Thurm and E.S. Browning, "Cisco Sees Market Cap Rise to No. 1—Old Leader Microsoft Drops 6.8%, Dragging Major Indexes Down," *The Wall Street Journal*, March 28, 2000, C1.

13. Paul Bagnell, "Tech Stocks Worth Their Lofty Valuations—Merrill: Faster Earnings Growth," *The Financial Post*, March 14, 2000, D1.

14. E.S. Browning, "Tech Lovers Begin to Fret About 'V' Word," *The Wall Street Journal*, March 23, 2000, C1.

15. Ibid.

16. Peter M. Donovan, "Where Do We Go From Here?" (Address to The New York Society of Security Analysts, December 16, 1999).

17. Global Financial Data, www.globalfindata.com

18. International Federation of Stock Exchanges, www.fibv.com/stats/Ta17.xls

19. Robert McGough, "P/Es Now Top Fabled 'Nifty Fifty' Era," *The Wall Street Journal*, February 24, 2000, C1.

20. Ibid.

21. Ibid.

22. "Perspectives on Investor Relations in the United States: The 1999 *Investor Relations Magazine* Survey for Determining Excellence in Investor Relations," *Investor Relations Magazine*, March 1999.

CHAPTER 3   ANALYZE THIS

1. Charles M.C. Lee, James Myers, and Bhaskaran Swaminathan, "What Is the Intrinsic Value of the Dow?" *The Journal of Finance* 54 (October 1, 1999): 1693–741.

2. Jeremy J. Siegel, *Stocks for the Long Run: The Definitive Guide to Financial Market Returns and Long-Term Investment Strategies* (New York: McGraw-Hill, 1998), 283.

3. Andrew Smithers and Stephen Wright, *Valuing Wall Street: Protecting Wealth in Turbulent Markets* (New York: McGraw Hill, 2000), 24.

4. Robert J. Shiller, *Irrational Exuberance* (Princeton, NJ: Princeton University Press, 2000), xii–xiii.

5. Investment Company Institute, www.ici.org/facts_figures/trends_0600.html

6. Shiller, *Irrational Exuberance*, xiii.

7. Smithers and Wright, *Valuing Wall Street*, 9.

8. Ibid., 13.

9. Ibid., 25.

10. Ibid., 6.

11. Ibid., 202.

12. Ibid.

13. Ibid., 229.

14. Smithers and Wright show why P/E ratios, dividend yields, and bond/equity yield ratios do a poor job of providing insights on market values by subjecting each of them to four key tests for any indicator of value. In contrast, they argue that the q ratio *does* meet all four of these tests but say that it is little used for two reasons, both of which are inimical to the interests of stockbrokers.

15. Michael Edesess, "Overvalued? Stocks' Price Is Finally Right," *The Wall Street Journal*, January 15, 1999, 10.

16. Ibid.

17. James K. Glassman and Kevin A. Hassett, *Dow 36,000* (New York: Times Books, 1999), 3.

18. Baruch Lev and Paul Zarowin, *The Boundaries of Financial Reporting and How to Extend Them* (Paris, France: Organization for Economic Co-operation and Development, 1998), 17.

19. John R.M. Hand, "Profits, Losses and the Non-Linear Pricing of Internet Stocks" (Chapel Hill, NC: Kenan-Flagler Business School, University of North Carolina, June 20, 2000).

20. Elizabeth Demers and Baruch Lev, "A Rude Awakening: Internet Value-Drivers in 2000," working paper (Rochester, NY: Simon School of Business, University of Rochester, 2000), 21.

21. Brett Trueman, M.H. Franco Wong, and Xiao-Jun Zhang, "The Eyeballs Have It: Searching for the Value in Internet Stocks" (Berkeley, CA: Haas School of Business, University of California, Berkeley, January 2000).

22. M.J. Whitman, www.mjwhitman.com/1q99.htm

23. Lev and Zarowin, *The Boundaries of Financial Reporting and How to Extend Them.*

24. Steven M.H. Wallman, "The Future of Accounting and Financial Reporting Part II: The Colorized Approach," remarks before the American Institute of Certified Public Accountants' Twenty-Third National Conference on Current SEC Developments (Washington, DC, February 15, 1996). See also www.sec.gov/news/speeches/spch079.txt

25. David Aboody and Baruch Lev, "The Value-Relevance of Intangibles: The Case of Software Capitalization," presented at the American Accounting Association 1998 Annual Meeting (New Orleans, August 19, 1998).

26. S.L. Mintz, "Seeing Is Believing: A Better Approach to Estimating Knowledge Capital," *CFO Magazine* 15 (February 1999): 28–37.

27. S.L. Mintz, "The Second Annual Knowledge Capital Scoreboard: A Knowing Glance," *CFO Magazine* 16 (February 2000): 52–62.

28. These figures are based on earnings for 1998 and market values as of September 30, 1999. Mintz, "The Second Annual Knowledge Capital Scoreboard: A Knowing Glance," 52–62.

29. Michael Murphy, *Every Investor's Guide to High-Tech Stocks & Mutual Funds*, 3rd ed. (New York: Broadway Books, 2000), 153.

30. Greg Ip, "Thursday's Markets: NASDAQ Pumps Up to 5000—Tech-Stock Rally Spurs Milestone in Hyper Time," *The Wall Street Journal*, March 10, 2000, C1.

31. Susan Pulliam, "Analysts Stretch Their Yardsticks to Justify P/Es of Cisco, Others," *The Wall Street Journal*, April 12, 2000, C1.

32. Ibid.

33. Alan M. Webber, "New Math for a New Economy," *Fast Company*, January/February 2000, 214. See also *www.fastcompany.com/online/31/lev.html*

34. Aaron Lucchetti, "Internet-Firm Valuations Prove a Challenge Amid Fluctuations," *The Wall Street Journal*, November 30, 1998, C1.

35. Pulliam, "Analysts Stretch Their Yardsticks," C1.

36. Edward Kerschner, Thomas Doerflinger, and Michael Geraghty, "New Economy: Yes, New Metrics: No," *PaineWebber Market Commentary*, March 12, 2000, 1.

37. Jeremy Siegel, "Manager's Journal: Are Internet Stocks Overvalued? Are They Ever," *The Wall Street Journal*, April 19, 1999, A22.

38. Demers and Lev, "A Rude Awakening."
39. Ibid., 2.
40. "Unique visitor: The number of different people or computers to visit a Web site. A truer measure of readership than pageviews, the term unique users distinguishes between one person visiting a site five times, and five people visiting a site once." "Pageview: A standard measurement of Web traffic. A Web page might contain a headline, some body text, and a Java applet—elements that a client computer must request and download individually. Each request is one hit; the combination of hits and downloads that make up a screen is one pageview. Of course, spelling it right doesn't guarantee that a user actually read the viewed page." Constance Hale and Jessie Scanlon, "Wired Style—Principles of English Usage in the Digital Age" (New York: Broadway Books, 1999), 135, 165.
41. Trueman, Wong, and Zhang, "The Eyeballs Have It," 2.
42. Christopher D. Ittner and David E. Larcker, "Are Nonfinancial Measures Leading Indicators of Financial Performance? An Analysis of Customer Satisfaction," *Journal of Accounting Research: Studies on Enhancing the Financial Reporting Model* 36, supplement (1998): 1–35.
43. Susan Pulliam, "Analysts Stretch Their Yardsticks," C1.
44. Ibid.
45. Michael J. Mauboussin, "Get Real: Using Real Options in Security Analysis" (New York: Credit Suisse First Boston, June 23, 1999), 3.
46. Ibid., 15.
47. Ibid., 10.
48. Peter Coy, "Exploiting Uncertainty: The 'Real Options' Revolutions in Decision-Making," *Business Week*, June 7, 1999, 118.
49. Robert McGough, "If Concept Stocks Are Stuff Dreams Are Made on, Does a Rude Awakening Loom," *The Wall Street Journal*, February 17, 2000, 16.
50. Market Data, National Association of Securities Dealers, www.marketdata. nasdaq.com/asp/Sec9Nq.asp

CHAPTER 4   THE EARNINGS GAME

1. Excluding acquisition-related charges and a gain from the exchange of some equity investments, http://docs.yahoo.com/docs/pr/1q00pr.html
2. Multex.com, Inc., "ACE Consensus Estimates: Yahoo! Inc.," (New York: Multex.com, Inc., 4 March 2000). See also http://multex.multexinvestor.com/data/mxcache/1412654.PDF
3. Ibid.
4. Kara Swisher, "Yahoo! Net Slightly Tops Forecast on Growth in Revenue, Audience," *The Wall Street Journal*, April 6, 2000, A3.
5. Ibid.
6. However, Penman, and Zhang show that "conservative" accounting policies are used to produce temporary earnings that are not sustainable and that the market does not fully recognize their temporary nature in setting stock prices. Stephen H. Penman and Xiao-Jun Zhang, "Accounting Conservatism:

The Quality of Earnings and Stock Returns," working paper, Graduate School of Business, Columbia University, New York, and Haas School of Business, University of California, Berkeley, December 1999, 1–22.

7. Rivel Research Group, "A Study of Corporate Disclosure Practices," Second Measurement, May 1998. A study conducted for National Investor Relations Institute. The total number of responses to this question was not reported. The percentages shown on page 17, Chart 4, are by market cap: 8 percent for large (over $1.5 billion), 7 percent for medium ($500 million to $1.5 billion), and 11 percent for small (under $500 million).

8. Carl Quintanilla, "For Its Profit Streak, Emerson's Reward Is a Laggard Share Price," *The Wall Street Journal*, May 11, 1999, A1.

9. Wall Street Research Net, www.wsrn.com

10. Gretchen Morgenson, "The Earnings Waltz: Is the Music Stopping?" *The New York Times*, October 24, 1999, 1, C1.

11. Arthur Levitt, chairman, Securities and Exchange Commission, "The 'Numbers Game'," NYU Center for Law and Business, New York, NY, September 28, 1998. See also www.sec.gov/news/speeches

12. Arthur Levitt Chairman, Securities and Exchange Commission, "Quality Information: The Lifeblood of our Markets," Economic Club of New York, October 18, 1999. See also www.sec.gov/news/speeches/spch304.htm

13. National Investor Relations Institute, op. cit., 17, Chart 3.

14. Ibid., 16, Charts 1 and 2.

15. Stephen Barr, "Back to the Future: What the SEC Should Really Do About Earnings Management," *CFO Magazine* (September 1999): 42–52.

16. David Burgstahler and Michael Eames, "Management of Earnings and Analyst Forecasts," working paper, draft 5, University of Washington, Seattle, and Santa Clara University, Santa Clara, CA, September 22, 1999, 1–19.

17. Ibid., 5–6.

18. Marc H. Gerstein, "Paradise Lost," *Market Guide*, www.marketguide.com/mgi/research/mar2000/ar_cybercorner_03152000_tx.asp?nss=www&rt=research/mar2000&rn=ar_cybercorner_03152000_tx

19. Earnings per share estimates and actual results, as reported by First Call and Dow Jones & Company, after adjusting for stock splits, the effects of certain business combinations reported as "poolings of interest," and "one-time" charges.

20. Tom Walker, "How Georgia Stocks Fared," *The Atlanta Journal, The Atlanta Consultation*, April 3, 1998, C;04;04.

21. "Health-Care Software Concern HBO's Earnings Top Estimates," Dow Jones Online News, April 14, 1998.

22. "HBO & Co. Earns 'Strong Buy' Rating, EDI Health Care Firm Doubles Value," EDI news, March 30, 1998, www.ptg.jdnr.com/ccroot/asp/publib/story_clean_copy.asp?rndnum=567481

23. "Earnings Expectations," *Capital Markets Insight*, Issue 4, Special Edition (January 2000): 2.

24. Ibid.

25. William Kinney, David Burgstahler, and Roger Martin, "The Materiality of Earnings Surprise," working paper, University of Texas at Austin, Austin, University of Washington, Seattle, and Kelly School of Business, Indiana University, Bloomington, July 8, 1999, 2–3.
26. Robert McGough, "Sunny Profits: Why Firms Are Delivering," *The Wall Street Journal*, April 20, 2000, C1.
27. Ibid.
28. Burgstahler and Eames, "Management of Earnings," 2.
29. Ron Kasznik, "On the Association Between Voluntary Disclosure and Earnings Management," *Journal of Accounting Research* 37 (Spring 1999): 57–82.
30. Ibid.
31. Paul M. Healy and James M. Wahlen, "A Review of the Earnings Management Literature and Its Implications for Standard Setting," *Accounting Horizons* 13 (December 1999): 365–83.
32. Ibid.
33. SEC Staff Accounting Bulletin: No. 99—Materiality, August 12, 1999.
34. Robert McGough, "CEO Prefers to Take Rough With Smooth Regarding Earnings," *The Wall Street Journal Europe*, April 16–17, 1999, 5B.
35. Ibid.
36. "SEC Charges Former Executives in Massive Financial Reporting Fraud at McKesson HBOC," press release, United States Securities and Exchange Commission. San Francisco District Office, September 28, 2000.
37. Securities and Exchange Commission v. Jay Gilbertson, Albert Bergonzi and Dominick DeRosa, ND Ca 912712000 (2000). *See also* United States of America v. Albert J. Bergonzi and Jay P. Gilbertson, Grand Jury Indictment, ND Ca 912812000 (2000).
38. Ibid.
39. Kitty Pilgrim, Alan Dodds Frank, and Tony Guida, "P&G Earnings Analysis," Cable News Network Financial Network (CNNfn): Market Coverage, March 7, 2000, Daniel Peris interview.
40. Kinney, Burgstahler, and Martin, "The Materiality of Earnings Surprise."
41. Ibid., 24–25.
42. Bhaskaran Swaminathan and Charles M.C. Lee, "Do Stock Prices Overreact to Earnings News?," working paper, Johnson Graduate School of Management, Cornell University, Ithaca, NY, January 4, 2000.
43. Barr, "Back to the Future."
44. Rivel Research Group, "A Study of Corporate Disclosure Practices," 18, Chart 5.
45. Barr, "Back to the Future."
46. Mark Bagnoli, Messod D. Beneish, and Susan G. Watts, "Whisper Forecasts of Quarterly Earnings per Share," *Journal of Accounting and Economics* 28 (November 1999): 27–50.
47. Tom Byrnes, "BID & ASK: How Whisper Numbers Mess With the Individual Investor," August 20, 1999, www.blackstocks.com/ed/qs/whispernums.htm
48. Ibid.
49. Bloomberg, www.bloomberg.com/personal/ft2_new99.html

50. WhisperNumbers.com, www.whispernumbers.com/about.cfm
51. EarningsWhispers.com, www.earningswhispers.com
52. Jack Reerink, "Pssst. Want to Manipulate a Whisper Number?" Reuters, April 23, 2000, www.uk.news.yahoo.com/000423/91/a4jhq.html
53. WhisperNumber.com, www.whispernumber.com/whisperstatistics.cfm
54. Bagnoli, Beneish, Watts, "Whisper Forecasts of Quarterly Earnings per Share."
55. David Streitfeld, "Microsoft Manages to Surprise; By Playing Down Earnings, Company Beats Expectations," *The Washington Post*, October 19, 1999, E1.
56. Marcia Vickers, "Should You Listen to 'Whisper Numbers'? These Web Sites Can Help Investors—But Be Careful," *Business Week* (September 27, 1999): 150 E8.

CHAPTER 5   FALSE PROPHET OF EARNINGS

1. Reed K. Storey, "The Framework of Financial Accounting Concepts and Standards," *Accountants' Handbook*, 9th ed., D.R. Carmichael, Steven B. Lilien, and Martin Mellman (Eds.) (New York: John Wiley & Sons, 1999), 1:1–5.
2. Cary John Previts and Barbara Dubis Merino, *A History of Accountancy in the United States: The Cultural Significance of Accounting* (Columbus, OH: Ohio State University Press, 1998), 274.
3. Ibid., 271.
4. Ibid., 278.
5. In terms of global audit, tax, and financial advisory service–related fees, 1998–1999. Source: International Accounting Bulletin, August 1999. Note that Deloitte & Touche and KPMG appear to be at approximately the same level.
6. Previts and Merino, *A History of Accountancy in the United States*, 278.
7. Elizabeth MacDonald, "First Call Will Add Cash EPS Estimates for 20 Web Firms, Responding to Street," *The Wall Street Journal*, April 4, 1999, A4.
8. Laura Johannes, "No Accounting for the Net? Profit Issue Sparks Conflict," *The Wall Street Journal*, May 1, 2000, C1.
9. Ibid.
10. United States, United Kingdom, Germany, France, Italy, The Netherlands, Switzerland, Sweden, Denmark, Australia, Japan, Hong Kong, Singapore, and Taiwan. These data were collected in 1997 and 1998.
11. These percentages are based on the number of respondents who believed that the market is too short-term oriented.
12. Paul M. Healy and James M. Wahlen, "A Review of the Earnings Management Literature and Its Implications for Standard Setting," *Accounting Horizons* 13 (December 1999): 8.
13. Baruch Lev and Paul Zarowin,"The Boundaries of Financial Reporting and How to Extend Them" (Paris, France: Organization for Economic Co-Operation and Development, 1998), 18.
14. Healy and Wahlen, "A Review of the Earnings Management Literature," 15.
15. Lev and Zarowin, "The Boundaries of Financial Reporting," 8.

16. Elizabeth McDonald, "Analysts Increasingly Favor Using Cash Flow Over Reported Earnings in Stock Valuations," *The Wall Street Journal*, April 1, 1999, C2.

17. Ibid.

18. G. Bennett Stewart, III, *The Quest for Value: A Guide for Senior Managers* (New York: HarperBusiness, 1999), 2.

19. Ibid.

20. Arthur Levitt, "The 'Numbers Game'" (remarks at New York University Center for Law and Economics, New York, September 28, 1998. Also see www.sec.gov/news/speeches/spch220.txt

21. Ibid.

22. Warren Buffett, letter to shareholders in "Berkshire Hathaway, Inc." (annual report) (Omaha, NE: Berkshire Hathaway, Inc., 1998), 15. See also www.berkshirehathaway.com/letters/1998pdf.pdf   or www.berkshirehathaway.com/letters/1998htm.html

23. Carol J. Loomis, "Lies, Damned Lies and Managed Earnings," *Fortune*, August 2, 1999, 74.

24. Nanette Byrnes and Richard A. Melc with Debra Sparks, "Earnings Hocus-Pocus: How Companies Come Up with the Numbers They Want," *Business Week*, October 5, 1998, 134–142.

25. Stephen Barr, "Back to the Future," *CFO Magazine* 15 (September 1, 1999): 42–52.

26. Ibid.

27. Arthur Levitt, "The 'Numbers Game.'"

CHAPTER 6   INSIDE THE EXCITING WORLD OF ACCOUNTING STANDARDS

1. David Lake, "One-Stop Shop for Net-Traffic Numbers," *The Standard* 16, August 2000, at www.thestandard.com/article/display/0,1151,17713,00.html

2. AICPA Special Committee on Financial Reporting, *Improving Business Reporting—A Customer Focus: Meeting the Information Needs of Investors and Creditors* (Jersey City, NJ: AICPA Special Committee on Financial Reporting, 1994). See also www.rutgers.edu/Accounting/raw/aicpa/business/main.htm

3. AICPA Special Committee on Financial Reporting, "Business Reporting in an Era of Change," Chap. 1 in *Improving Business Reporting—A Customer Focus: Meeting the Information Needs of Investors and Creditors* (Jersey City, NJ: AICPA Special Committee on Financial Reporting, 1994). See also www.rutgers.edu/Accounting/raw/aicpa/business/main.htm

4. Ibid. See also Steven M.H. Wallman, "The Future of Accounting and Financial Reporting Part II: The Colorized Approach," *Accounting Horizons* 10 (June 1996): 138–48.

5. Steven M.H. Wallman, "The Future of Accounting and Disclosure in an Evolving World: The Need for Dramatic Change,"*Accounting Horizons* 9 (September 1995): 86.

6. Randy Myers, "Indecent Disclosure," *CFO Magazine* 13 (January 1997): 20–28. See also www.cfonet.com/html/Articles/CFO/1997/97JAinde.html

7. Ibid.

8. Ibid.

9. "The CPA Journal Symposium on Recommendations for Improving Business Reporting," *The CPA Journal* at www.nysscpa.org/cpajournal/old/16349261.htm

10. Company Law Review Steering Committee, "Modern Company Law for a Competitive Economy: Developing the Framework" (March 2000): paragraph 5.74.

11. John Waterhouse and Ann Svendsen, *Strategic Performance Monitoring and Measurement: Using Non-Financial Measures to Improve Corporate Governance* (Toronto, Ontario: The Canadian Institute of Chartered Accountants, September 1998), v.

12. Sven-Age Westphalen, "Reporting on Human Capital: Objectives and Trends" (presented at the International Symposium "Measuring and Reporting Intellectual Capital: Experience, Issues and Prospects," Technical Meeting, Amsterdam, June 9–10, 1999), 5.

13. James R. Adler, "Leases," Chap. 18 in *Accountants' Handbook: Financial Accounting and General Topics*, 9th ed., R. Carmichael, Steven B. Lilien, and Martin Mellman (Eds.) (New York: John Wiley & Sons, 1999), 5–6.

14. John R. Harbison and Peter Pekar, Jr., *Strategic Alliances: A Practical Guide to Repeatable Success* (San Francisco: Jossey-Bass, 1998), 1.

15. Ibid.

16. Ibid., 1–2.

17. William J. Radig and Brian Loudermilk, "Leading the Way to Uniform Accounting Principles," *Review of Business* 19 (March 22, 1998): 22–26.

18. Fields Wicker-Miurin as quoted in Terzah Ewing and Silvia Ascarelli, "One World, How Many Stock Exchanges?—Global Barriers Are Falling as Markets Rush to Meld," *The Wall Street Journal*, May 15, 2000, C1.

19. Radig and Loudermilk, "Leading the Way to Uniform Accounting Principles."

20. As of August 2000, the market values (month end)($000) were: NASDAQ: 6,026,815,530, NYSE: 12,900,000,000, and AMEX: 134,148,811; www.marketdata.nasdaq.com/asp/Sec1Summary.asp

21. "Selling the Nasdaq," *The Wall Street Journal* (editorial), March 16, 1998, A22.

22. New York Stock Exchange website at www.nyse.com

23. Stephen A. Zeff, "The IASC's Core Standards: What Will the SEC Do?" *The Journal of Financial Statement Analysis* (October 1, 1998): 72.

CHAPTER 7   OUT, OUT DAMNED GAP!

1. Robert G. Eccles and Sarah C. Mavrinac, "Improving the Corporate Disclosure Process," *Sloan Management Review* 36 (Summer 1995): 11–25.

2. PricewaterhouseCoopers Global Survey refers to aggregate results from 14 independent country surveys conducted by PricewaterhouseCoopers. The countries included: the United States, the United Kingdom, France, Germany, Italy, Switzerland, the Netherlands, Sweden, Denmark, Australia, Japan, Hong Kong, Singapore, and Taiwan. The data were collected in 1997 and 1998.

3. A measure was deemed "extremely important" if 80 percent or more of investors and analysts regarded it as "particularly important in making investment decisions." The country-results of the survey are available at www. valuereporting.com.

4. The survey sample included 160 high-tech companies, 51 sell-side analysts, 28 institutional investors, and 134 venture capital firms.

5. The high-tech survey sample included 56 percent CFOs, 31 percent heads of investor relations, and 12 percent other executives such as CEO or president. One percent of the respondents did not specify their title or role in their organizations.

6. Substantial variation exists in the importance of the measures in the low-importance category, depending on how high-tech the company is. For example, Internet companies say traffic growth and traffic are more important, while semiconductor companies place more importance on reject rates and inventory write-downs.

7. Respondents were asked to rate the extent to which their internal systems produced sufficiently reliable information on a scale where 1 = Extremely Reliable and 5 = Not At All Reliable. A measure was considered high quality for scores of 1.00 to 1.99, medium quality for scores of 2.00 to 2.99, and low quality for scores of 3.00 to 3.99. There were no scores above 3.99.

8. Respondents were asked to rate how actively they communicated information to analysts on a scale where 1 = Very Actively and 5 = Not At All Actively. A measure was considered to be high in how actively it was reported if it was between 1.00 and 1.99, medium if it was between 2.00 and 2.99, and low if it was between 3.00 and 3.99. Nine measures received scores of 4.00 or greater.

9. Respondents were asked to rate the data they were getting from companies on a scale where 1 = Very Adequate and 5 = Not At All Adequate. A measure was considered to be high in adequacy if it was between 1.00 and 1.99, medium if it was between 2.00 and 2.99, and low if it was between 3.00 and 3.99. There were no scores above 3.99 for either analysts or investors.

CHAPTER 8   RISKY BUSINESS

1. J. Richard Dietrich, Steven J. Kachelmeier, Don N. Kleinmuntz, and Thomas J. Linsmeier, "Market Efficiency, Bounded Rationality and Supplemental Business Reporting Disclosures," *Journal of Accounting Research* (forthcoming).

2. Ibid., 25.

3. Ibid., 25.

4. Ibid., 1.

5. Baruch Lev and Paul Zarowin, "The Market Valuation of R&D Expenditures," ACC-99-6 in a joint series of working papers, Vincent C. Ross Institute of Accounting Research and The Department of Accounting, Leonard N. Stern School of Business, New York, 1998.

6. Zhen Deng, Baruch Lev, and Francis Narin, "Science and Technology as Predictors of Stock Performance," *Financial Analysts Journal* 55 (May/June 1999): 20–32.

7. Lee Puschaver and Robert G. Eccles, "In Pursuit of the Upside: The New Opportunity in Risk Management," *PW Review* (December 1996): 1–16.

8. Shapira reports that when managers were asked, "Do you think of risk in terms of a distribution of all possible outcomes? Just the negative ones? Just the positive ones?" 80 percent of respondents said they considered the negative outcomes only. Zur Shapira, "Risk in Managerial Decision Making," unpublished, Hebrew University, Jerusalem, Israel, 1986.

9. As of August 17, 2000. Wall Street Research Net, www.wsrn.com

10. Historical prices on Bloomberg (www.bloomberg.com) as of October 11, 1999. Shares outstanding from companies' 10Ks as of December 31, 1999.

11. Lisa Bannon, "eToys' Strategy to Stay in the Game—E-Tailer Plans Web-Site Ads, Private-Label Products, Yearlong Sales Season Items," *The Wall Street Journal,* April 25, 2000, B1.

12. Chet Dembeck, "eToys Should Find a Partner," *E-Commerce Times,* January 31, 2000, www.ecommercetimes.com/news/viewpoint2000/view-000131-1.shtml

13. Terzah Ewing, "IPOs More Boldly Disclose Risk Factors," *The Wall Street Journal,* April 30, 2000, C1.

14. See Robert G. Eccles and John K. Fletcher, "Value and Reporting in the Banking Industry" (New York: PricewaterhouseCoopers, 1999); and Robert G. Eccles and Michael P. Nelligan, "Value and Reporting in the Insurance Industry" (New York: PricewaterhouseCoopers, 1999).

CHAPTER 9 THERE IS NO ALTERNATIVE: THE STORY OF SHELL

1. Thomas Delfgaauw, interviewed by Jennifer Woodward and David Wright, August 2000, Shell Centre, London, England. All subsequent statements attributed to Mr. Delfgaauw in this chapter are also from this interview. Mr. Delfgaauw participated actively in developing much of the content for this chapter. His openness and willingness to assist demonstrate another facet of the company's commitment to transparency. His valuable contribution is gratefully acknowledged.

2. See Dow Jones Sustainability Group Index, www.sustainability-index.com

3. John Prestbo (Dow Jones Indexes president), "Explaining the Dow Jones Sustainability Group Index," remarks at the World Business Council for Sustainable Development (WBCSD), Liaison Delegates Meeting, Montreux, Switzerland, March 29, 2000. See www.wbcsd.ch/Speech/s83.htm

4. Announced by a European Commission representative at the European Business Network for Social Cohesion, Workshop 1, Social Reporting, Transparency, and Accountability, Brussels, May 12, 2000.

5. The Millennium Poll, conducted by Environics International Ltd., with the collaboration of The Prince of Wales Business Leaders Forum in London and The Conference Board in New York, September 1999. Corporate sponsors included PricewaterhouseCoopers, BP Amoco, and Bell. Further information available at www.environics.net/eil/

6. Rob Lake, "Social Accountability: the Challenge for Investors," paper presented at the Traidcraft Exchange, PIRC Annual Corporate Governance Conference, London, March 29, 2000.

7. John Madeley, *Big Business, Poor Peoples: The Impact of Transitional Corporations on the World's Poor* (London: Zed Books, September 1999), 122.

8. Ibid, p.123.

9. Royal Dutch Shell, www.corpwatch.org/trac/climate/gwshell.html

10. Royal Dutch Shell, www.shell.com/royal-en/content/0,5028,31770-56749,00.html

11. Royal Dutch Shell, www.shell.com/download/2872/pages/soc_view.html

12. This list represents a slight rephrasing of the original language. Those interested can find the original list as published in *The Shell Report 2000* at www.shell.com/royal-en/content/0,5028,31770-56749,00.html

13. *The Shell Report 2000*, p. 32.

14. *The Shell Report 2000*, p. 4.

15. Extracts from *The Shell Report 2000*, pp. 19, 26.

16. Peter May with Alan Dabbs, Patricia Fernandez-Dávila, Valéria Vinha, and Nathan Zaidenweber, "Corporate Roles and Rewards in Promoting Sustainable Development: Lessons Learned from Camisea," p. vii, Resources Group, University of California, Berkeley, 1999.

17. Ibid, p. ix.

CHAPTER 10   TO THE VICTOR GO THE SPOILS

1. PricewaterhouseCoopers Global Survey refers to aggregate results from 14 independent country surveys conducted by PricewaterhouseCoopers. The countries included the United States, the United Kingdom, France, Germany, Italy, Switzerland, the Netherlands, Sweden, Denmark, Australia, Japan, Hong Kong, Singapore, and Taiwan. The data were collected in 1997 and 1998. Respondents were asked to indicate on a five-point scale where 5 = A Great Deal and 1 = Not At All whether they thought a particular benefit would result from improved disclosure. The percentages in Exhibit 10.1 are for responses of 4 or 5.

2. Robert G. Eccles and Sarah C. Mavrinac, "Improving the Corporate Disclosure Process," *Sloan Management Review* 36 (Summer 1995): 11–25.

3. PricewaterhouseCoopers Global Survey refers to aggregate results from 14 independent country surveys conducted by PricewaterhouseCoopers. The countries included the United States, the United Kingdom, France, Germany, Italy, Switzerland, the Netherlands, Sweden, Denmark, Australia, Japan, Hong Kong, Singapore, and Taiwan. The data were collected in 1997 and 1998. Respondents were asked to indicate on a five-point scale where 5 = A Great Deal and 1 = Not At All whether they thought a particular benefit would result from improved disclosure. The percentages in Exhibits 10.2 and 10.3 are for responses of 4 or 5.

4. Paul M. Healy, Amy P. Hutton, and Krishna G. Palepu, "Stock Performance and Intermediation Changes Surrounding Sustained Increases in Disclosure," *Contemporary Accounting Research* 16(3) (Fall 1999): 485–520.

5. Robert G. Eccles, Kersten L. Lanes, and Thomas C. Wilson, "Are You Paying Too Much for That Acquisition?" *Harvard Business Review* 77 (July–August 1999): 136–46.

6. Michael Arndt, "Commentary: It Pays to Tell the Truth," *Business Week Online*, June 5, 2000.

7. "McKesson HBOC/Moody's −2: Citing Delay in 10-K Filing," *Capital Markets Report*, Dow Jones & Company, June 28 1999. In April 1999, McKesson HBOC announced that it was restating revenues and earnings at the newly acquired HBO & Co. due to a determination that some sales had been improperly recognized.

8. Raymond Hennessey, "Despite Firings, Doubts Linger about McKesson's Future," *Dow Jones Newswire*, Dow Jones & Company, June 21, 1999.

9. Ibid.

10. "Brown Bros. Analyst: Worst May Not Be Over for McKesson," *Dow Jones Newswire*, July 15, 1999.

11. Peter Coy, "Exploiting Uncertainty: The 'Real-Options' Revolution in Decision-Making" *Business Week*, June 7, 1999, www.businessweek.com/1999/99_23/b3632141.html

12. AnswerSleuth, www.answersleuth.com/words/u/underwriter.shtml

13. International Federation of Stock Exchanges, www.fibv.com/stats/Ta17.xls

14. Christine A. Botosan, "Disclosure Level and the Cost of Equity Capital," *The Accounting Review* 72 (July 1997): 346.

15. Walter Kielholz, conversation with Robert G. Eccles, on or about November 5, 1998. Subsequent comments by both Kielholz and John Fitzpatrick were made in an interview with Robert G. Eccles, New York, August 7, 2000.

16. PR Newswire, "Securities Fraud Litigation Sets Record in 1998—Companies Sued at a Rate Close to One-a-Day," press release (Stanford, CA: PR Newswire), January 27, 1999, www.securities.stanford.edu/news/990125/pressrel.html

17. Ibid.

18. Peter Miller and Ted O'Leary, "ValueReporting and the Information Ecosystem," a study funded by PricewaterhouseCoopers.

19. Ibid.

CHAPTER 11   CAN YOU SEE CLEARLY NOW?

1 See www.att.com for examples of AT&T's recent disclosure practices including environmental, health, and safety reports.

2. Miller-Williams Inc., "i2 Customer Value Report 1999," Miller-Williams Inc. and i2 Technologies, Inc., October 1999, 3. See also www.i2.com/lostsheep.cfm?PageLocation=http%3A//www.i2.com/company/press

3. H. Darr Beiser, "Cisco Chief Pushes 'Virtual Close,'" *USA Today Tech Report*, October 12, 1999. See also www.usatoday.com/life/cyber/tech/ctg405.htm

4. For more on the case of the fraudulent press release that caused so much tur-

moil for Emulex, see *The Wall Street Journal Interactive Edition*, August 28, 29, and 31, 2000 and September 1, 2000, http://public.wsj.com/home.html

5. Robert A. Prentice, Vernon J. Richardson, and Susan Scholz, "Corporate Web Site Disclosure and Rule 10b-5: An Empirical Evaluation," *American Business Law Journal*, July 1, 1999, 531.

6. Ibid.

7. Ibid.

8. While PricewaterhouseCoopers updates the ValueReporting website on a continual basis, the material contained thereon is intended for informational purposes only. Visitors to the site must not rely on the website as a complete and accurate guide to the current use of the Internet to distribute and report value-relevant information. For more complete information, please contact a PricewaterhouseCoopers ValueReporting professional.

9. Stephen Barr, "How the Web Was Won: *CFO* Looks at 50 Corporate Web Sites to Assess How Well They Keep Investors Informed," *CFO Magazine*, February 2000, www.cfo.com/html/articles/CFO/2000/00FEhowt.html

10. Ibid.

11. *Business Reporting Research Project: Electronic Distribution of Business Reporting Information*, Steering Committee Report Series (Financial Accounting Standards Board, 2000).

12. Robert G. Eccles and Nitin Nohria, "Face-to-Face: Making Network Organizations Work," *Networks and Organizations: Structure, Form, and Action*, edited by Nita Nohria and Robert G. Eccles (Boston: Harvard Business School Press, 1992), 288–308.

CHAPTER 12   GET ON BOARD

1. Louis Lowenstein, "Financial Transparency and Corporate Governance: You Manage What You Measure," *Columbia Law Review* 96 (June 1996): 1335–62.

2. Arthur Levitt, "Corporate Governance in a Global Arena," remarks at the American Council on Germany, New York, October 7, 1999.

3. Organization for Economic Co-operation and Development, "OECD Principles of Corporate Governance" (Paris, France: Organization for Economic Co-operation and Development, Ad-Hoc Task Force on Corporate Governance, Directorate for Financial, Fiscal and Enterprise Affairs, April 19, 1999), 2.

4. The Organization for Economic Co-operation and Development's member countries are Australia, Austria, Belgium, Canada, Czech Republic, Denmark, Finland, France, Germany, Greece, Hungary, Iceland, Ireland, Italy, Japan, Korea, Luxembourg, Mexico, the Netherlands, New Zealand, Norway, Poland, Portugal, Spain, Sweden, Switzerland, Turkey, United Kingdom, and United States.

5. Richard M. Steinberg and Catherine L. Bromilow, *Corporate Governance and the Board—What Works Best* (New York: PricewaterhouseCoopers, sponsored by The Institute of Internal Auditors Research Foundation, 2000), 34.

6. Organization for Economic Co-operation and Development, "OECD Principles of Corporate Governance," 13.

7. Organization for Economic Co-operation and Development, "Background and Issues Paper for the OECD Symposium on the Role of Disclosure in Strengthening Corporate Governance" (Paris, France: Organization for Economic Co-operation and Development, February 12–13, 1998), 8.

8. U.S. Securities and Exchange Commission, "SEC, NYSE and NASD Announce Blue Ribbon Panel to Improve Corporate Audit Committees: John Whitehead and Ira Millstein to Co-Chair Panel," news release (New York: U.S. Securities and Exchange Commission, September 28, 1998), 1.

9. Ibid.

10. John Whitehead and Ira Millstein, "Report and Recommendations of the Blue Ribbon Committee on Improving the Effectiveness of Corporate Audit Committees," report (New York: U.S. Blue Ribbon Committee on Improving the Effectiveness of Corporate Audit Committees, sponsored by the New York Stock Exchange and the National Association of Securities Dealers, 1999), 7.

11. D. Jeanne Patterson, "The Link between Corporate Governance and Performance" (report no. 1215-98-RR) (New York: The Conference Board, 1998), 8.

12. McKinsey & Company, "McKinsey & Company Investor Opinion Survey on Corporate Governance" (London: McKinsey & Company, June 2000), 16.

13. Ibid., 8.

14. The Committee on Corporate Governance and Gee Publishing Ltd. "Committee on Corporate Governance Final Report," report (London: Gee Publishing Ltd., 1998), 23.

15. John Waterhouse and Ann Svendsen, "Strategic Performance Monitoring and Management: Using Non-Financial Measures to Improve Corporate Governance" (Toronto, Ontario: The Canadian Institute of Chartered Accountants, 1998).

16. The Committee on Corporate Governance and Gee Publishing Ltd., "Report of the Committee on the Financial Aspects of Corporate Governance" (London: Gee Publishing Ltd., 1992), 51.

17. Ibid., 51–52.

18. "Committee on Corporate Governance Final Report," 43.

CHAPTER 13   STANDARD SETTERS

1. John W. Hunt, "Accountants Fail to Get the Measure of the Person," *Financial Times*, August 30, 2000, 10.

2. "Sustainability Reporting Guidelines on Economic, Environmental, and Social Performance," *Global Reporting Initiative*, June 2000. See also www.globalreporting. org

3. Jonathan Hayward, "Continuous Auditing and the Future of Assurance," working paper (New York: PricewaterhouseCoopers, October 1999).

4. In October 1998 Arthur Levitt, chairman of the Securities and Exchange Commission, requested that the Public Oversight Board (POB) appoint a Panel on Audit Effectiveness (the Panel). The POB is an independent, private sector body

that monitors and reports on the self-regulatory programs and activities of the SEC Practice Section (SECPS) of the Division for CPA Firms of the American Institute of Certified Public Accountants (AICPA). The Panel "was charged with the responsibility to review and evaluate how independent audits of the financial statements of public corporations are performed and assess whether recent trends in audit practices serve the public interest." Shaun F. O'Malley, "The Panel on Audit Effectiveness: Report and Recommendations" (Stamford, CT: The Public Oversight Board, August 2000).

5. Shaun F. O'Malley, "The Panel on Audit Effectiveness: Report and Recommendations." After many interviews and Quasi Peer Reviews (QPRs), in-depth reviews of the quality of 126 audits of SEC registrants in 28 offices of the eight largest audit firms found that audit firms are doing a very commendable job. Nevertheless, it did issue some recommendations for how to improve the quality and integrity of audits including: (1) tightening up audits in order to better detect fraud and earnings management when it constitutes fraud; (2) making sure that the "tone at the top" of audit firms emphasizes the importance of the audit product, rather than simply treating it as "a commodity" alongside high-margin consulting services; (3) improved governance of the audit profession by unifying these activities under a strengthened, independent POB; (4) implementing worldwide audit methodologies to ensure a uniform quality audit product across all countries; and (5) making the profession more attractive to the best people who, with better training, will be willing to stand up to their clients and say, "No, that's not right!"

6. Ibid.
7. Ibid., Chap. 8.
8. Ibid., Chap. 5.
9. KPMG UK, "Values and Opportunities @ KPMG.com," annual report (London: KPMG, 1999), 19.

CHAPTER 14 SHOULD YOU SEE AN ANALYST?

1. Neal Lipschutz, "Point of View: Pity the Poor Wall Street Analyst," *Dow Jones Newswire*, December 17, 1999.
2. David Bechtel, April 20, 2000 (9:24 P.M.) e-mail to RULE-COMMENTS at 03SEC. See www.sec.gov/rules/proposed/s73199/0420b01s.htm
3. Jeffrey C. Hooke, *Security Analysis on Wall Street: A Comprehensive Guide to Today's Valuation Methods* (New York: John Wiley & Sons, Inc., 1998), 19.
4. Susan Pulliam, "Goldman's E-Commerce List Reduces Non-Client to Low Tier," *The Wall Street Journal*, June 20, 2000, C1.
5. Hooke, *Security Analysis on Wall Street*, 22.
6. Jeffrey M. Landerman, "Wall Street's Spin Game: Stock Analysts Often Have a Hidden Agenda," *Business Week*, October 5, 1998, 152.
7. Eileen Buckley, "Holding Analysts Accountable," *The Industry Standard*, June 5, 2000, 86–87. Also see www.thestandard.com/article/display/0,1151,15700,00.html

8. Marcia Vickers and Gary Weiss, "Wall Street's Hype Machine: It Could Spell Trouble for Investors," *BusinessWeek Online*, April 3, 2000. Also see www.businessweek.com/2000/00_14/b3675001.htm

9. Ibid.

10. Gregory Zuckerman and Jesse Eisinger, "New Economy, New Analysts, New Math? Forecast Raises QXL.com," *The Wall Street Journal*, April 7, 2000, C1.

11. Ibid.

12. Arthur Levitt, "A Question of Integrity: Promoting Investor Confidence by Fighting Insider Trading," remarks to SEC Speaks Conference, February 27, 1998. See also www.sec.gov/news/speeches/spch202.txt

13. Arthur Levitt, "Quality Information: The Lifeblood of Our Markets," remarks to The Economic Club of New York, October 18, 1999. Also see www.sec.gov/news/speeches/spch304.htm

14. Eddie Arrington, April 20, 2000 (6:38 P.M.) e-mail to RULE-COMMENTS at O3SEC. See www.sec.gov/rules/proposed/s73199/0420b01w.htm

15. Gray Williams, April 20, 2000 (11:07 P.M.) e-mail to RULE-COMMENTS at O3SEC. See www.sec.gov/rules/proposed/s73199/0420b01s.htm

16. Hooke, *Security Analysis on Wall Street*, 19–20.

17. Lynn Cowan, "Flirting with 40: DLJ Founders Ponder Analysts, Internet," *Dow Jones Newswire*, December 9, 1999.

18. "Analyze This," *The Wall Street Journal* (editorial), December 17, 1999, A14.

19. Eli Amir, Baruch Lev, and Theodore Sougiannis, "What Value Analysts?" (Tel Aviv, Israel: Recanati Graduate School of Management, Tel Aviv University, November 1, 1999).

20. Ibid., 11.

21. Ibid., 1.

22. Ibid., 19.

23. Robert McGough, "One Analyst Anticipated IBM News," *The Wall Street Journal*, October 22, 1999, C1.

24. Yahoo! Finance, http://finance.yahoo.com

25. Deloitte/Holt Value Associates LLC, "First Annual Deloitte/Holt Value Associates Portfolio Manager Survey," (Chicago: Deloitte/Holt Value Associates LLC, September 1997).

26. James B. Kelleher, "Are Wall Street Analysts Reliable?" *The Salt Lake Tribune*, December 29, 1999, D5.

27. Arthur Levitt, "Quality Information: The Lifeblood of Our Markets."

28. Marcia Vickers and Gary Weiss, "Wall Street's Hype Machine: It Could Spell Trouble for Investors," *Business Week*, April 3, 2000, 112.

29. Randall Smith, Deborah Solomon, and Suzanne McGee, "Grubman's Missed Call on AT&T Stock Could Affect Influential Analyst's Stature," *The Wall Street Journal*, October 4, 2000, C1.

30. Landerman, "Wall Street's Spin Game," 150.

31. Robert McGough, "Merrill's Web Guru Changes His Mantra," *The Wall Street Journal*, August 8, 2000, C1.

32. James B. Kelleher, "Analysts' Corporate Ties, Power to Move Markets a Dangerous Combination," *The Orange County Register*, December 16, 1999.

33. John C. Easterwood and Stacey R. Nutt, "Inefficiency in Analysts' Earnings Forecasts: Systematic Misreaction or Systematic Optimism?" *The Journal of Finance* 54 (October 1999): 1777–97.

34. Hooke, *Security Analysis on Wall Street*, 21.

35. Roni Michaely and Kent L. Womack, "Conflict of Interest and the Credibility of Underwriter Analyst Recommendations," *The Review of Financial Studies* 12 (special issue) (1999): 653–86.

36. Ibid., 683.

37. Arthur Levitt, "Quality Information: The Lifeblood of Our Markets." Also see www.sec.gov/news/speeches/spch304.htm

38. "Analyze This," *The Wall Street Journal* (editorial).

39. Pulliam, "Goldman's E-Commerce List Reduces Non-Client to Low Tier," C1.

40. Ibid.

41. McGough, "Merrill's Web Guru Changes His Mantra," C1.

42. Ibid.

43. Michael Siconolfi, "U.S. Small-Stock Focus, Many Firms Dump IPO Underwriters for Star Research," *The Wall Street Journal Europe*, December 28, 1998, C1.

44. See, for example, Laurie Krigman, Wayne H. Shaw, and Kent L. Womack, "The Persistence of IPO Mispricing and the Predictive Power of Flipping," *The Journal of Finance* 54 (June 3, 1999): 1015–44.

45. On July 20, 2000, Sanford C. Bernstein announced that it had agreed to combine with Alliance Capital Management, a top-tier investment management company.

46. Pulliam, "Goldman's E-Commerce List Reduces Non-Client to Low Tier."

47. Greg Ip, "There's No Mania Like Internet Mania—Historically, This May Take the Cake," *The Wall Street Journal*, December 30, 1999, C1.

48. Terzah Ewing and Joshua Harris Prager, "Many Are Finding IPOs Still Out of Reach," *The Wall Street Journal*, February 28, 2000, C2.

49. Terzah Ewing, "Individual Investors Take Lead in Bull Market Now," *The Wall Street Journal*, March 27, 2000, C4.

50. Krigman, Shaw, and Womack, "The Persistence of IPO Mispricing and the Predictive Power of Flipping."

51. Terzah Ewing, "Burnt Offerings? Debuts Are Fizzling After Pop," *The Wall Street Journal*, April 26, 2000, C1.

52. Mark Maremont, "Raising the Stakes—As Wall Street Seeks Pre-IPO Investments, Conflict May Rise—Are Analysts Compromised When They Say 'Buy' When the Bankers Sell?" *The Wall Street Journal*, July 24, 2000, A1.

53. Ibid.

54. Ibid.

55. Ibid.

56. Ibid.

57. Ibid.

58. Stephen Barr, "What Chinese Wall?" *CFO Magazine* 16 (March 2000): 63–64.

59. Peter Elstrom, "The Power Broker," *Business Week*, May 15, 2000, 70–82.
60. Ibid., 72.
61. Ibid.
62. See *Dirks v. SEC*, 463 US 646 (1983).
63. Lynn Cowan and Phyllis Plitch, "Coming SEC Selective Disclosure Rule May Not Be Cure-All," Dow Jones News Service, October 18, 1999.
64. Adam Lashinsky, "The SEC Disclosure Rule Goes Only Halfway, But That Hasn't Stopped the Bellyaching," TheStreet.com—Silicon Valley: Sharing the Club Pool, Yahoo! Finance, August 14, 2000 at http://biz.yahoo.com/ts/000814/valley_000814.html
65. Phyllis Plitch, "After SEC Disclosure Scolding, It's Wall Street's Move," *Dow Jones Newswire*, November 10, 1999.
66. Heidi Brown, "Analysts Analyzed," Forbes.com, September 21, 2000, at www.forbes.com/forbesglobal/00/0612/0312097a.htm
67. BulldogResearch.com, www.bulldogresearch.com "Frequently Asked Questions," last revised June 26, 2000.
68. Brown, "Analysts Analyzed."

CHAPTER 15   SEND LAWYERS, GUNS, AND MONEY

1. David Lake, "Access Up, Divide Shrinks," *The Industry Standard* 3 (June 26, 2000): 186–89. See also www.thestandard.com/research/metrics/display/0,2799,16072.00.html
2. Securities and Exchange Commission, "Commission Votes to End Selective Disclosure: Chairman Arthur Levitt Hails Leveling of Information Playing Field," press release (Washington, DC: August 10, 2000).
3. Arthur Levitt, "SEC News Supplement: Opening Statement of Chairman Arthur Levitt Open Meeting on Regulation Fair Disclosure," remarks at Open Meeting on Regulation Fair Disclosure, Washington, DC, August 10, 2000).
4. Victoria Love at Internet, April 20, 2000, 10:23 P.M. at www.sec.gov/rules/proposed/s73199/0420b01s.htm
5. The Ad Hoc Working Group on Proposed Regulation FD and the Legal and Compliance Division of the Securities Industry Association to Jonathan G. Katz, Secretary, Securities and Exchange Commission Re: Proposed Regulation FD—File No. S7-31-99,Washington, DC, April 6, 2000. See also www.sia.com/2000_comment_letters/html/sec_regulation_fd_4-6.html
6. Ibid.
7. Steve Kang at Internet, April 20, 2000, 11:36 P.M. at www.sec.gov/rules/proposed/s73199/0420b01s.htm
8. "Informed Investors, Inc. Applauds SEC 'Regulation FD' as Good News for Individual Investors and Good Business for Companies," *PR Newswire*, August 10, 2000.
9. Nilus Mattive, "Nilus' Trading Post: Individual Investors Rule!" August 17, 2000, www.individualinvestor.com/boards/article.asp?ID=23122

10. Adam Lashinsky, "Sharing the Club Pool: The SEC Disclosure Rule Goes Only Halfway, but That Hasn't Stopped the Bellyaching," August 14, 2000, http://biz.yahoo.com/ts/000814/valley_000814.html

11. Noelle Knox, "SEC Rule Puts Small Investors in the Info Loop," editorial, *USA Today*, August 11, 2000, 1B.

12. David Henry, "Eye on the Street: Small Investors to Get Equal Access to Company Information," *USA Today*, August 10, 2000, 1B.

13. "Leading Investment Professional Association AIMR 'Profoundly Disappointed' at Reg FD Passage by SEC; Regulation Will Have Opposite of Intended Effect, Curtailing Market Communication," *Business Wire*, August 11, 2000.

14. Jeff D. Opdyke, Aaron Luchetti, and Christopher Oster, "Mum's the Word in Wake of SEC Rule," *The Wall Street Journal*, August 16, 2000, C1, C8.

15. Michael Schroeder and Randall Smith, "Disclosure Rule Cleared by the SEC: Wall Street Firms Say Fairness Issue Skirted," *The Wall Street Journal*, August 11, 2000, C1, C16.

16. The Ad Hoc Working Group to Jonathan G. Katz, www.sia.com/2000_comment_letters/html/sec_regulation_fd_4-6.html

17. George Gilder, "The Outsider Trading Scandal," *The Wall Street Journal*, April 19, 2000, A30.

18. Broadcast.com was acquired by Yahoo! in 1999.

19. "Companies Increasingly Cybercast Investor Relations Event," *PR Newswire*, September 16, 1999.

20. Lynn Cowan, "More Firms Allow Investors to Listen to Conference Calls Via Web," *Dow Jones Business News*, May 21, 1999.

21. David Henry, "SEC Encourages Open Conference Calls on Net," *USA Today*, December 16, 1999, 3B.

22. XML is a trademark of MIT and a product of the World Wide Web Consortium.

23. Printout from iExchange.com's website, www.iexchange.com

24. Ibid.

25. Robert G. Eccles and Dwight B. Crane, *Doing Deals: Investment Banks at Work* (Boston: Harvard Business School Press, 1988).

26. W.R. Hambrecht & Co., www.wrhambrecht.com/wrhco/

27. Hoovers Online Business Network's website, www.hoovers.com/co/capsule/0/0, 2163,59160,00.html

28. "TheMarkets.com: Seven Leading Investment Banks to Build Global Financial Information Portal," press release, CNN Disclosure through Dow Jones Interactive, September 12, 2000.

29. Ibid.

Index